Entrepreneurial Genius

Entrepreneurial Genius

The Power of Passion

GENE N. LANDRUM, Ph.D.

Brendan Kelly Publishing Inc.
7091 Villa Lantana Way
Naples, FL 34108
and
2122 Highview Drive
Burlington, Ontario
Canada L7R 3X4

ISBN 1-895997-23-2

Cover design: Pronk&Associates

Photo Credits

Henry Ford: U357649ACME © Bettmann/CORBIS/MAGMA
Coco Chanel: BE060065 © Bettmann/CORBIS/MAGMA
Jean Paul Getty: HU056253 © Hulton-Deutsch Collection/CORBIS/MAGMA
Buckminster Fuller: U1293652INP © Bettmann/CORBIS/MAGMA
Sam Walton: 7198 © Mike Stewart/Corbis Sygma/MAGMA
Hugh Hefner: BE053637 © Bettmann/CORBIS/MAGMA
Ross Perot: 0000283707-001 © Markowitz Jeffrey/Corbis Sygma/MAGMA
Martha Stewart: 177993 © Steve Azzara/Corbis Sygma/MAGMA
Donald Trump: SS001813 © Robert Maass/CORBIS/MAGMA
Richard Branson: ET001049 © John Garrett/CORBIS/MAGMA
Jeff Bezos: NF115081A © Najlah Feanny/CORBIS SABA/MAGMA
Michael Dell: UT0076046 ©Reuters NewMedia Inc./CORBIS/MAGMA
Dymaxion House and Dymaxion Car–Courtesy, The Estate of Buckminster Fuller
EPCOT Geosphere and Gardens © Nik Wheeler/CORBIS/MAGMA
The Fuller Projection Map design is a trademark of the Buckminster Fuller Institute ©1938, 1967 & 1992. All rights reserved.

To the world's
entrepreneurs and visionaries
who see risk as an opportunity,
not a threat,
that leads almost inevitably to
fame and fortune.

Some men see things as they are and ask why.
Others dream things that never were and ask why not.
                                    –George Bernard Shaw

Contents

Contents

Acknowledgments

Many people have contributed to this book, including friends, students and family. Perhaps the greatest impetus has come from my association with entrepreneurial wunderkinds Nolan Bushnell, Joe Keenan, Zoltan Kiss and Charles Muench. Working with such gifted colleagues in Silicon Valley, Princeton, NJ and Naples, Florida, I acquired valuable insights into the vagaries and enlightened perspectives of the entrepreneurial mind. A special thanks is owing to Playboy Bunny Patty Stogner, who offered valuable insights into the nature and character of Hugh Hefner from her years working at the Playboy Mansion and the Chicago Playboy Club.

Editing is a long and enduring process. Entrepreneurs like myself are hard pressed to deal with the tedious work and patience it demands. This book would have been far less readable and organized without the diligent editing by Brendan and Teresa Kelly whose sagacity and insight made it more than it would have been without their tender and loving care. Their efforts have made the work far more viable as a tool for the aspiring entrepreneur and small business owner, and as a college textbook for entrepreneurial and small business classes.

A special acknowledgment is owing to Rosemary Tanner who prepared the final edit of the manuscript. Her professional expertise has purged the manuscript of the inconsistencies, ambiguities, and inadvertent oversights that appeared in earlier drafts. Her suggestions pertaining to issues of content and cosmetics have further enhanced the final form of this book.

I also wish to express my gratitude to the many readers who perused the early drafts and made recommendations that enhanced significantly the quality of the final manuscript. Listed alphabetically by surname, they include, Len Collins, Robert Gatley, Aaron Kelly, H. Michael Kelly, Don Schafer, Steve Smith, Robert Williams and John Wood.

PREFACE

This book has evolved from my life's work–dealing with the entrepreneurial process, teaching its theory and helping others launch novel products. In the early 1970s, I introduced the first handheld calculators to sell for less than $10 and the first featuring transcendental functions to sell under $100. I was appalled by the resistance I encountered in bringing this technology into our schools. Many teachers didn't see the advantage of allowing students to use the machines to perform low-level computations so these young minds could engage in higher-level problem solving. Two decades of research in mathematics education subsequently demonstrated the cognitive advantages of this technology, and has led, ironically, to the mandatory use of calculators in classrooms throughout America.

In 1977, when I was building the prototype for the Chuck E. Cheese chain and installed a ball-crawl apparatus within the restaurant, conventional restaurateurs were aghast. Many said the idea was absurd, because allocating space to a children's playground in a restaurant was not cost effective. Others said the noise would interfere with the casual conversation that people expect in a restaurant environment. Then I found some cities across America banning the restaurant chain for fear the games and rides would create an arcade-style facility that would become a hangout for drug addicts and other unsavory characters. Such are the challenges of proposing new ideas in a world mired in current practice.

THE EVOLUTION AND ACCEPTANCE OF NEW IDEAS

An entrepreneur who breaks new ground will find the experience stimulating but frustrating, exciting but maddening, and heady but debilitating. About 150 years ago, German philosopher Arthur Schopenhauer described three stages through which a new idea passes between its inception and its subsequent acceptance. In the first stage, it is ridiculed by all but 1 percent of the population. As it passes into the second stage, it secures the support of about 2 percent, but most of the remaining 98 percent are violently opposed to it. In the third and final stage, there is general acceptance of the new idea and it is no longer new.

The entrepreneur must be prepared for stages one and two and, in the words of Sam Walton "be prepared to swim upstream." For the entrepreneur, opportunity exists only during the first two stages. Once an idea is accepted, the opportunity is over. Therefore, adventurers with a novel idea must be prepared for ridicule from the establishment–even from family and friends. Such are the vagaries of trying to alter existing paradigms.

THIS BOOK: WHAT IT IS AND WHAT IT IS NOT

This work is not a compendium of biographies. It is rather a composite psychobiography that analyzes the motivations and personality traits that characterize the entrepreneurial genius. It is not about entrepreneurial successes, but about how people with limitations and eccentricities were able to get to the very top. What were the strategic thinking processes that led relatively average people like Ford, Chanel, Walton, Bezos and Dell to achieve such astounding success? This book is about how they did it and what key inner drives and passions propelled them to the elite class of the powerful, rich and famous.

If you are an aspiring entrepreneur, it is far more important for you to know the motivations and processes of entrepreneurial geniuses than the details of what they have achieved. The goal of this book is to analyze the processes, inspect the environmental influences, and examine the lives, loves and lusts that played such a critical part in their trek to the top. We will look incisively at the importance of early upbringing, position in the family constellation, and the genesis of those qualities and traits that made them special.

WHAT IS AN ENTREPRENEURIAL GENIUS?

The phrase "entrepreneurial genius" in this book is used to describe someone whose vision has transcended traditional thought, leading to an innovation or creation that has brought significant benefits to society. All 12 of the great entrepreneurs profiled in this book were geniuses in that sense. Some may have high IQs, but generally their genius resided in other qualities that played a stronger role in their success. In *Intelligence Framed* (1998), Harvard researcher Howard Gardner wrote:

> *The right set of genes hardly suffices to yield a creator. Highly creative people are more likely to stand out in terms of personality rather than sheer intellectual power. They differ from their peers in ambition, self-confidence, and passion about their work.*

LANDRUM'S LAWS OF ENTREPRENEURIAL GENIUS

From each of the lives of the 12 eminent geniuses profiled in this book, I have gleaned a prescient principle that captures the dominant theme in that person's climb to success. Together, these 12 principles are presented as *Landrum's Laws of Entrepreneurial Genius* (see Chapter 14). Each law is featured in the chapter that profiles the entrepreneurial genius who modeled its application most conspicuously.

The research for this book involved a variety of sources including authorized and unauthorized biographies, autobiographies, periodicals, Internet retrievals and other sources such as A&E Biography. Triangulation, i.e., the use of several different sources on particular issues, was used to factor out inaccuracies in information from autobiographical sources that might contain inherent bias. What remains is the distillation of volumes of information and data into a book that presents the major psychological factors underpinning entrepreneurial success.

By sharing these findings, I hope to reveal the extent to which your success lies within your own locus of control. If this work helps you overcome the self-imposed limitations standing between your entrepreneurial dreams and their realization, then I will have been successful in my quest.

Introduction

Knowledge is limited. Imagination encircles the world
–Albert Einstein

ENTREPRENEURS MUST VISIT THE EMERALD CITY

The Emerald City, that place where the Wizard of Oz dispenses qualities like courage, self-esteem and intelligence, is where we find our internal strength. Though the Wizard awards the physical symbols of these attributes, the genuine articles can be neither given nor granted–they must be earned and won. The great achievements of scientists, artists and entrepreneurs begin with a vision or a dream that first takes root in the imagination and then ignites the passion that fuels the journey. In his book *Prometheus Rising* (1997), Anton Wilson observes:

> *The future exists first in the imagination, then in the will, and only then in reality.*

The visionary transcends his innate talent and surpasses many who possess superior knowledge because he first takes a flight of fantasy before conceiving a plan. Fantasy is an integral factor in all success. It permits us to live outside convention and gives free rein to the childhood imagination within us that is so crucial to the creative process. Such flights of fantasy are possible only after we release ourselves from the constraints of traditional belief and make a brief visit to the world of what might be. The chapters that follow present the personality traits and behaviors that rocketed a dozen entrepreneurial geniuses to the top of the business world. Their stories provide us with insights that empower us as individuals to overcome our self-imposed limitations and reach our goals.

LEADERS AND FOLLOWERS

A popular description of the human race divides people into three categories: those who make things happen, those who watch things happen, and those who wonder what happened. The third group is sometimes described collectively as the "lost souls." These people are always in a reaction mode, trapped in tradition and terrified to depart from accepted practice. The lost souls are vulnerable to the dogma of shamans, politicians, cultists or religious despots because they trade their individuality for the promise of security. They are the world's disciples.

The members of the "watch-things-happen group" are sometimes given the moniker "care-takers" because they take care of the status quo by paying homage to accepted wisdom about what is possible and what is appropriate. By following fashion in manners, dress, deportment and beliefs, they avoid or reduce the risk of ostracism, failure and/or public humiliation. The discomfort that care-takers feel when confronted with ambiguity or anything threatening their system of beliefs prompts them to resist change–especially radical change. These qualities contribute to a stability in society that ensures that change will evolve at a pace that does not require major adaptation. For this reason, the care-takers are the backbone of a society, the defenders of its customs and the citizens who define *normalcy*.

The "make-things-happen group" consists of a motley collection of diverse and distinct personalities who travel in highly eccentric orbits around normalcy; yet, in spite of these differences, they exhibit characteristics that are common to all members of their group. These special personality traits–shared by virtually all the great achievers–are the focus of this book. As Shaw observed in *Man and Superman* (1903):

> *The reasonable man adapts himself to the world; the unreasonable one persists in trying to adapt the world to himself. Therefore, all progress depends on the unreasonable man.*

In the chapters that follow, we shall visit the lives and the personality traits of some of these "unreasonable" men and women and reflect briefly on their psychological origins. From these reflections, we shall derive some general principles that are delineated in Chapter 13. However, before we proceed, we must pause to consider why the entrepreneurial personality has become a central focus in the twenty-first century.

THE ERA OF THE ENTREPRENEUR

The *new* economy of the information age is now moving at warp speed. It is not a hospitable place for the weak, the faint of heart, or those seeking security. Such a world rewards entrepreneurs willing to bet their reputations and futures on their dreams.

In his landmark book *Telecosm* , George Gilder predicted the future as the preserve of the entrepreneur (Gilder, p. 258):

> *As networks become dumber, they attract more and more smart entrepreneurs.*

Later he predicted:

> *Entrepreneurial energy will be more morally edifying in the world of the Telecosm than leisure diversions that many consider to be the end and meaning of life.*

Recent evidence suggests that white-collar downsizing has led to an entrepreneurial life for many, especially for those over age forty. During the 1990–1991 recession, 25 percent of those who lost their jobs turned to an entrepreneurial life, according to a study conducted by Babson College. During this period it is estimated that 246,000 people started new ventures. In 2001, Rochester Institute of Technology professor Robert Barbato told *USA Today* (Dec. 18), "We're in the midst of an entrepreneurial revolution," on account of the extensive layoffs resulting from the dot-com debacle and the 2001 recession. Since small business enterprises create about 75 percent of all new jobs, entrepreneurs will play a crucial role in leading society out of business downturns. Jeffry Timmons of Babson College says, "Entrepreneurs are the single most important part of the recovery process."

This book is dedicated to those aspiring entrepreneurs who are ready to pursue their dreams with unabated passion and tenacity. The journey will be fraught with challenges, sacrifices and struggle, but it will yield even greater rewards than the imagined destination.

Henry Ford

To Learn How to Succeed, Fail

b. Dearborn, MI July 30, 1863
d. Fair Lane, MI April 7, 1947

"Whether you think you can or think you can't, you're right!"

SELF-DESCRIPTION
"I refuse to recognize that there are impossibilities."

MOTTOS
"All history is bunk."
"We learn more from our failures than from our successes."
"There are no big problems, only a lot of little problems"
"An expert is someone who knows all the reasons a new idea won't work."

INNOVATION	Vertical cylinders, 1905; moving assembly line, 1913; $5-per-day wage, 1914; V-8 engine, 1932; built the largest manufacturing plant in the world at River Rouge
UNIQUE QUALITIES	Visionary perfectionist with a passion for simplification
OBJECTIVE	"As long as I live I want to pay the highest wages in the automobile industry."
NET WORTH	A billionaire within ten years of starting
HONORS	Ford for President movement; nearly won a senate seat
BIRTH ORDER	First born of eight; Irish agrarian roots
EDUCATION	Quit school at age 15; apprenticed in mechanics
PERSONALITY	Intuitive visionary and "control freak"
HOBBIES	Auto racing during early years; bird appreciation
POLITICS	Democratic with a right-wing orientation; the only American named in Hitler's *Mein Kampf*; according to Lee Iacocca, "Ford is the father of 20th-century American industry and the American middle class."
RELIGION	Puritanical upbringing; lifelong Episcopalian
FAMILY	Wife: Clara; Children: one son, Edsel

1

Henry Ford

To Learn How to Succeed, Fail

Failure is the opportunity to build again, more intelligently

Overview

At the dawn of the 20th century, America was essentially a society of two classes–rich and poor. The rich were a small minority who enjoyed the privileges of wealth usually gained through entrepreneurship or inherited through good fortune. However, the vast majority of Americans belonged to the working class and were employed in a wide variety of occupations ranging from farming, fishing and mining to factory work and itinerant labor. Members of this diverse working class shared the common struggle for survival that left little time or money for leisure or luxuries. In the decades that followed, one man–a school dropout named Henry Ford–laid the foundations for the creation of a middle class in America. Lee Iacocca, former CEO of Chrysler Corporation, would remark almost a century later (*Time,* 2001), "If it had not been for Henry Ford, America wouldn't have a middle class today."

Inspired by the ideology of Ralph Waldo Emerson, Henry Ford was driven to "democratize the automobile" by making it financially accessible to the common man. His *people's car* (the Model T), designed for the working man, represented a lofty goal at a time when most experts believed the automobile industry was a "classes-not-masses" market. The affluent could afford to buy them, service them, and use them, while members of the working class were tied to nine-hour work days six days a week and had little discretionary income.

Uncommon in Ford's day, the integration of an ideology into a business plan met with resistance on several fronts. The *Wall Street Journal* and the *New York Times* initially criticized Henry for his low wages and assembly lines, and later for his low prices. His shareholders, who were also at odds with his ideology, launched a series of lawsuits to block the implementation of his vision. In challenging the separation of ideological and business principles, Ford paved the way for today's entrepreneurs Larry Ellison and Bill Gates, who have also rooted their personal philosophies in their Oracle and Microsoft ventures respectively.

To make cars affordable, Ford realized that he had to reduce costs by increasing the efficiency of production. To achieve this, he instituted the moving assembly line, whereby workers installed car parts on the chassis as it moved past at a fixed rate. This moving assembly line revolutionized production methods and ushered in a new era of mass production. Although it increased the efficiency of production significantly, it forced workers to quicken their pace of work in a fashion satirized in the Charlie Chaplin movie, *Hard Times*. Eventually the workers became disenchanted with the new working conditions and labor turnover began to escalate.

Having come from working class beginnings, Henry Ford identified with his employees and set the hourly wages higher than those typically paid for unskilled work. He also reduced the number of hours of labor below the standard work week, providing each worker with more time off for rest or leisure. When he reduced the price of his cars below their cost, his Chief Financial Officer quit and filed a lawsuit, announcing to the press that Henry had gone mad. The suit alleged that Ford's moves were self-serving and contrary to the best interests of the shareholders. But Ford was striving toward higher ideals and longer-term goals. He was prepared to lose in the short run for long-term gain. He felt that by reducing the prices of his cars so that everyone could afford them, and simultaneously raising the worker wage, he would be seeding his own market.

Gradually, the efficacy of Ford's innovations became apparent. Their success was manifest in the growth of the Ford Motor Company from a firm with a nominal capitalization of $100,000 in 1903 to a behemoth with a surplus of $700 million in 1927. In the two decades between 1908 and 1927, exactly 15,458,781 Model T cars rolled off Ford's assembly lines. The Model T had established itself as the car for the masses. In the process, Ford established himself as the father of modern mass production and a founder of the auto manufacturing industry. More importantly, Ford's "democratization" of the automobile had profound long-term implications for the social fabric of America through the creation of a middle class.

The Formative Years

EARLY UPBRINGING AND ITS IMPACT

On July 30, 1863, America was in the throes of the Civil War. The tide had turned in favor of the Union army at the Battle of Gettysburg just a few weeks before, and the strength of the industrial North was beginning to assert itself. It was into this world, a few hundred miles away from the conflict, that Henry Ford was born. He was the eldest of eight children of Irish parents, William Ford and Mary Litigo. His mother, the major influence of his life, died in childbirth when Henry was twelve. Devastated, Henry was forced to develop self-reliance and find his way in the world with limited guidance. He later wrote of his mother, "She taught me patience and self-discipline." Reflecting on her admonitions issued in his formative years, Ford recalled (*Ford: The Times*, pp. 49–50):

> ...*[Mother] was always reminding us that life cannot be all fun. [She said], "You must earn the right to play...the best fun follows a duty done."*

In a later tribute to her, Ford named his grand estate Fair Lane in honor of her homeland in Cork, Ireland.

Farming was his father's life's work and Henry was expected to follow suit. However, Henry's natural inclinations lay in another direction that would eventually make him an entrepreneurial icon.

Within months of his mother's death, Henry was transformed by two major occurrences. After Henry's father gave him a watch for his birthday, he tore the watch apart and rebuilt it over and over. Ever after he was obsessed with mechanical things. On another occasion, he was riding with his father on the family wagon when a (steam-driven) horseless carriage thrashing machine drove past them. Henry was awe-struck by the sight of a self-propelled vehicle and he jumped off the wagon in total wonderment. Forty-seven years later he would say, "I remember that engine as though I had seen it only yesterday."

Ford attended a one-room school in Dearborn, Michigan until age fifteen and then he dropped out to become an apprentice for a mechanic. As an inquisitive teenager, he built his first steam engine and actually started a watch manufacturing business. He further developed his skills as an apprentice at James Flower & Company and the Dry Dock Engine Works in Detroit. He would always have a disdain for higher education and throughout his career as CEO of Ford Motor Company, he was reluctant to hire college-educated individuals. On one occasion, when asked about his hiring strategies, he responded, "We hire a man, not his history. It is all one to me if a man comes from Sing-Sing prison or Harvard."

When Henry Ford was approaching 22 years of age, he attended a party where he met a beautiful eighteen-year-old woman, Clara Jane Bryant. Clara, the eldest of ten children, was also raised on a farm. They courted and, on her twenty-second birthday, they were married. Henry and Clara began married life on their farm in Dearborn. In 1891, when Henry was hired by the Edison Illuminating Company, they moved to Detroit. By the time Henry reached the age of 30, he had risen through the ranks to the position of chief engineer at a salary of $100 per month. Henry and Clara's only child, Edsel, was born on November 6, 1893.

An Epiphany

Henry's climb to greatness was launched one day in early 1896, when he read an article in *The American Machinist* on building engines. It so intrigued him that he decided to build his own engine and house it in a "horseless carriage." He spent countless hours in the evenings after work building in his shed that was attached to the house. His friends wondered when he slept and some conjectured that his unrelenting obsession would result in a nervous breakdown. However, on June 4, 1896, around 3:00 a.m., he completed his masterpiece. This new vehicle–he called it a *quadricycle*–was a four-wheeled bicycle with a motor. However, there was one problem–the quadricycle was too big to pass through the front door. Not to be denied the joy of launching the quadricycle, Henry took an axe and smashed the door frame to smithereens, leaving fragments of bricks and mortar in his wake.

The quadricycle proved to be a success. It proved to Henry that he could design a gas-driven vehicle that would run with a significant level of reliability. He was now driven more than ever to improve its design and function. This experience transformed Henry's mindset from employee to entrepreneur and he would never turn back. He was almost 33 at the time.

The Climb to the Top

LEARNING THROUGH FAILURE

Throughout his mid-thirties, Henry Ford fluctuated between making a living and making things. The former was never as high on his list of priorities as the latter. Consequently, Ford would experience two outright failures before reaching the age of forty.

Impressed with the performance and reliability of the quadricycle, family friend and Mayor of Detroit, William Maybury financed Henry's work on a successor. Henry used this money and $200 from the sale of his quadricycle to create a gas-driven horseless carriage that had more style and greater functionality. In 1898, R. W. Hanington, a preeminent engineer who was touring the country to assess the state of the art of automobile developments, examined Ford's successor to the quadricycle and reported (Lacey, pp. 46-7):

> *The design of the motor is excellent...similar to that of the Springfield Duryea's wagon. The sparker is better however...*
> *The cooling tanks show ingenuity and thought...The Duryea wagons have no device for cooling...The carburetor is good. The measuring device is complete and ingenious...*
> *The whole design strikes me as being very complete, and worked out in every detail...the carriage should equal any that has been built in this country.*

When Henry Ford took William Murphy, another of Detroit's influential Irish investors on a test ride in his new vehicle, Murphy became excited and exclaimed, "Well, now we will organize a company."

In 1899, the Detroit Automobile Company, the first automobile firm in the city, was incorporated by a dozen investors, including his previous benefactor William Maybury. They gave Henry Ford a small amount of stock and appointed him superintendent to oversee the building of ten production cars. At that time, Henry was still employed by the Edison Illuminating Company which offered him the position of General Superintendent on the condition that he abandon his work on the gas engine. Ford was faced with a choice between retaining a responsible and secure job as an employee, or risking all and following his passion. In the true spirit of the entrepreneur, Henry Ford chose the latter. This was his crossing of the Rubicon.

On September 6, 1901, President McKinley was shot. In the period of mourning that followed, Henry became unusually reflective and he discussed with his friend, Oliver Barthel issues of life, death and existence. Barthel shared with Henry a copy of Orlando Jay Smith's philosophical essays titled *A Short View of Great Questions.* This book was an inspiration to Henry, moving him to tap into his heroic potential. He later explained that he regarded the reading of that book as the turning point in his life, for it introduced him to the concept of reincarnation and the idea that the experiences and knowledge we gain in this life can be carried forward and built upon in the next (Lacey, p. 61):

> *It was as if I had found a universal plan...Time was no longer limited. I was no longer a slave to the hands of the clock. There was time enough to plan and to create.*

He decided that he wanted to build a car for the masses. However, Ford never got started on the construction of the ten production cars for the Detroit Automobile Company, because he spent all of his time designing a new racing car. Ford's biographers are not agreed on why Henry lost his commitment to producing the cars that he had agreed to build. Henry, himself, claimed that he wanted to perfect the car rather than merely fix on a particular prototype and reproduce it for short term profits. However, biographer Lacey suggests that Ford's reluctance might have derived from a lack of manufacturing know-how (Lacey, p. 52):

> *[In the early years of automobile development], an efficient and economic manufacturing process was the key to whether money was made, or lost...Henry had not yet come to terms with the new dimension he was working in.*

Henry reasoned that if he could win a national race, investors would back him on developing the car that he envisioned. Gradually, the investors, realizing that Henry was more interested in producing a racer than a production car, became disenchanted and, within two years, filed for bankruptcy.

The American speed champion at that time was car builder Alexander Winton. But, when Ford beat him in the October 1901 road race in Gross Pointe, Michigan, investors (including some of the previous participants in the ill-fated Detroit Automobile Company) began to line up at his door, giving credence to the adage that perception is reality when it comes to raising venture capital. Just seven weeks after Ford's victory at Grosse

Point, the Henry Ford Company was established. Henry was employed as Chief Engineer and was given a $10,000 interest in the firm.

However, within four months, Henry was fired by the board of directors for working on the car he wanted to build instead of the car he was contracted to build. Henry and the Henry Ford Company parted company, and Henry walked away with only $900 for his efforts. The stockholders recruited Henry Leland, changed the company name to Cadillac, and began building motorcars. Cadillac would eventually become the flagship company for a conglomerate known as General Motors. Unperturbed, the indomitable Ford began working on another racing car with investor and racer Tom Cooper. Two decades later, Henry attributed his obsession with building a racing car to the supernatural forces of destiny (Lacey, p. 64):

> *I was always pushed by invisible forces within and without me...I was forty when I went into business, forty when I began to evolve the Ford plant. But all the time I was getting ready.*

In the first decade of the twentieth century, automobile manufacturing was a cottage industry, much like the computer industry near the end of that century. At the beginning there were over 500 companies that manufactured automobiles and by 1917, only 23 remained. The companies that would survive would be those that could manufacture and deliver a quality product.

Once again, Henry dedicated himself to working around the clock on the sleekest and fastest car in the world–the 999 racer. It was so fast that Tom Cooper was afraid to get behind the wheel. Ford recruited daredevil Barney Oldfield to race the 999 against the national champion. Simplicity won the race for Ford, for he had refused to include any parts on his car that served esthetics rather than function. The competitors' cars were adorned with more elaborate but less functional parts that broke down under stress, so the 999 racer won the race on reliability rather than speed. However, by October 1902, his 999 Racer had set the American speed record at less than one minute and six seconds per mile (almost 60 mph) over a five-mile course.

The success of Henry's 999 Racer prompted an investor, Alex Malcomson, to come forward with venture capital for a new firm to be named Ford & Malcomson. Malcomson was to be President and Ford the Chief Engineer. Ford contributed his patents and Malcomson the money. On capitalization, the firm became known as the Ford Motor Company.

Investors included the Dodge brothers who were principal suppliers of engine parts. It was during this period that Ford, in his role as engineer, contributed what has been acknowledged as an "innovations coup": he turned the cylinders on his Model A to a vertical rather than horizontal orientation. The first Ford car was delivered in January 1904. In the same year, Barney Oldfield drove Ford's experimental car to a new world speed record, and Henry knew he was on his way.

GOING IT ALONE

By now Henry was forty. His relationship with Malcomson, shaky from the start, disintegrated when the two disagreed on whether to build cars for the elite or the masses. Henry set up a competing firm called Ford Manufacturing Company to squeeze out Malcomson. His strategy worked. On December 6, 1905, Malcomson resigned and Henry Ford at 42 became the master of his own destiny. Never again would he work for anyone else.

Ford had a prescient vision of what the world needed. He listened to his instincts and they served him well. All mass consumer products, no matter how expensive, begin as specialty products and evolve into commodity products. Metaphorically speaking, it is important to pick the low fruit before picking the high fruit, since the latter is more costly and tougher to reach. The mass market represented the accessible fruit. Henry understood this intuitively. His Model T, engineered in 1907 and launched in 1908, had 10,000 sales by 1909. Within ten years it would be the dominant automobile in the world, as Henry had predicted in 1905.

Henry Ford knew that mass production offered remarkable advantages in terms of simplicity and cost savings. To this end he built the most automated plant in the world at Highland Park, Michigan, in 1909. It dwarfed all others of the era: it turned out 18,864 cars in 1910, 34,528 cars in 1911, and 78,440 cars in 1912. By 1913 he had introduced the first moving assembly line, reducing chassis production time from 5 hours and 50 minutes to just over an hour and a half.

During this period, Ford introduced a marketing innovation: establishing automobile dealerships in various cities to sell and service his cars. He virtually created the franchised dealership concept. Long before Ray Kroc began setting up McDonald franchises, Henry Ford was setting up franchised dealers to sell and repair his Tin Lizzies. By 1912 he had 7000 dealers in the U.S. Ford was also an early proponent of opening gas stations on major thoroughfares for his growing brood of cars for the masses. Later he would vertically integrate the company by acquiring his own coal and limestone mines, railroads, and other components to supply the world's largest manufacturing plant that he was planning to build.

CREATING A CAR FOR THE MASSES

The final phase in Ford's rise to success began in 1913 when he discovered the writings of Ralph Waldo Emerson and William Burroughs. Both authors triggered in him some latent inner spirituality that bordered on mysticism. At the time, the Model T was widely acclaimed as the "people's car"; however, it sold for $500, and the typical factory worker earning $2.34 per day couldn't afford to buy one. Furthermore, Ford had just introduced the revolutionary moving assembly line and his employees, disgruntled over the hectic pace of the new mass production process, were leaving Ford faster than he could replace them. An inspiration from Emerson's *Self Reliance* moved Henry to take a larger step in life–to build a car that even his production workers could afford. The memorable lines, "To be great is to be misunderstood," inspired him to pursue his dream undaunted by adversaries. He suddenly envisioned his destiny as playing the heroic role in making Emerson's *Compensation* a reality in the burgeoning world of cars. As early as 1905, Ford had told the media that his cars would be priced so low that anyone could own one. He was quoted in the *Detroit Journal* as promising, "Ten thousand cars a month at $400 apiece." Not all believed him but they listened. In 1913, Ford turned his promise into a reality.

Emerson had written, "Pay the price for honest labor since there can be no cheating. The thief steals from himself." Such thinking was foreign to the industrial enterprise of the early 20th century that regarded labor as a mere cog in the wheel of productivity. Emerson's words motivated Henry to take on his directors and challenge conventional strategies. "Give and you will get" eventually gained credibility as a viable strategy in manufacturing.

Within months, Ford would make the decisions that would change the world. His inspiration–partly economic and partly humanitarian–was underpinned with the Christian ethic. It appealed to Ford's need for ethical and economic efficiency. Within a year of his inspiration Ford had implemented the $5-a-day wage, dropped the work day from nine hours to eight, and had dropped the price of his Model T from $400 to $340. This led to one of the most fascinating stories in the annals of economic history.

Ford's competitors did not understand how a reasonable man could drop the price of a car when the factory was already at full production. However, by reducing the length of the work day, Ford was able to run two shifts. Reducing it further enabled him to create three shifts. Between 1908 and 1916 Henry Ford dropped his prices by 58 percent, even in the face of stockholder suits. His market share increased, his costs dropped precipitously, and within a few years he was building half the automobiles in the world.

Ford's first overseas sales branch opened in France in 1908, followed in 1911 with a manufacturing plant in the United Kingdom. The world demand for the Model T was so strong that by 1918, Ford was impelled to build the world's largest manufacturing plant at River Rouge.

THE DECLINING YEARS

In 1919, when Henry Ford was 56, his son Edsel who was 26 became the president of the Ford Motor Company. Although Henry was no longer the president, he remained in control and undermined Edsel's leadership through the sheer force of his personality. By 1927, it was clear that the best years of the remarkably successful Model T were behind them. The Model T had sold over 15 million units, but the market was shifting away from Ford to General Motors. To recapture a dwindling market, the Ford Motor Company shifted gears from production of the Model T to production of a retooled Model A.

Henry Ford's last significant contribution was the introduction of the V-8 engine in 1932. This innovation made the newly designed Model A an extremely successful product with total sales exceeding 4 million units. However, Ford's profitability gradually declined in the decade that followed. As Tedlow observes (*Giants of Enterprise*, p. 170):

> *From 1927 to 1937 inclusive, the Ford Motor Company lost almost $95 million, while General Motors was making $1.9 billion. The company was slowly and unknowingly drifting into insolvency.*

As the founder of the Ford Motor Company entered his sixty-fifth year he was seen to be in physical and mental decline. His declining mental faculties were manifest in his gradual transition from entrepreneurial innovator to authoritarian company owner. He attempted to suppress a union movement in his company by hiring thugs to physically intimidate those who solicited membership. Henry also became vocal in expressing anti-Semitic opinions and in praising the efficiency of the Nazis in rebuilding Germany. Unlimited power and wealth seemed to have taken a toll on the insights and values that had catapulted Henry to the top.

In 1938 at the age of 75, Henry Ford suffered a mild stroke. A second, more severe stroke that led to subsequent hallucinations befell him in 1941. Then in 1943, his son Edsel, at the age of forty-nine, died suddenly of what was called "a complication of ailments: stomach cancer, undulating fever, and a broken heart." Henry re-assumed the presidency at the age of 80. The Ford Motor Company languished like a rudderless ship for over two years until Henry Ford II, Edsel's eldest son, became president and CEO at the age of 25. After relinquishing control of the company he had founded, Henry Ford stepped down and went into seclusion. Two years later, on April 7, 1947, Henry died of a cerebral hemorrhage at the age of 83.

Ford's Decade-by-Decade Climb

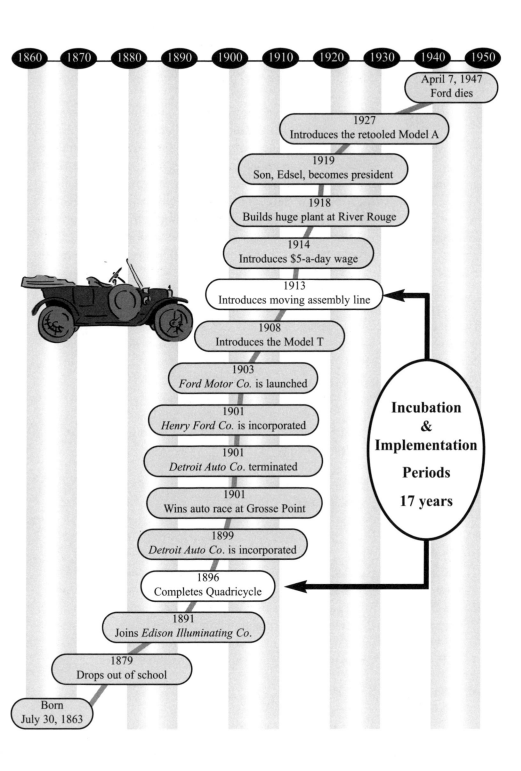

1860 1870 1880 1890 1900 1910 1920 1930 1940 1950

April 7, 1947
Ford dies

1927
Introduces the retooled Model A

1919
Son, Edsel, becomes president

1918
Builds huge plant at River Rouge

1914
Introduces $5-a-day wage

1913
Introduces moving assembly line

1908
Introduces the Model T

1903
Ford Motor Co. is launched

1901
Henry Ford Co. is incorporated

1901
Detroit Auto Co. terminated

1901
Wins auto race at Grosse Point

1899
Detroit Auto Co. is incorporated

1896
Completes Quadricycle

1891
Joins *Edison Illuminating Co.*

1879
Drops out of school

Born
July 30, 1863

Incubation
&
Implementation

Periods

17 years

A Personality Profile

COMMUNICATION STYLE: INTRANSIGENT

Ford was not only different, he was *really* different. Although a soft-spoken charismatic type, he was strongly opinionated to the point of arrogance. Some of his associates regarded him as highly combative and tenacious. Consistent with these traits is his classification as a strong Type A personality–one of those individuals who identifies self-worth with achievement. A risk-taking renegade, Ford was comfortable with ambiguity and was polyphasic in that he proceeded on many different fronts simultaneously.

An early investor characterized Ford as having "some kind of magnet." He could draw people to him and he used this power when it served his purpose. Though he was a technologist, he had a flair for effective communications. Ford's sense of the dramatic was also vital in establishing a public persona. Like his friend Thomas Edison, he used publicity rather than advertising to promote his products. After his 1914 $5-a-day wage coup, he achieved a special access to the press that he often used to disseminate his personal gospel. In 1918 he bought his own newspaper, the *Dearborn Independent.*

It didn't take long for Henry to discover the ephemeral nature of public opinion and the perils of media exposure. The ever-loquacious Ford alienated many groups with his anti-Semitic and chauvinistic stances. In 1920, his *Dearborn Independent* featured an article titled *The International Jew: The World's Problem* followed by a series of articles on the subject. The *Chicago Tribune* labeled Ford "an anarchist." Others suggested he was a Nazi sympathizer, calling into question his claim to be an ardent pacifist. The capitalist in Ford hated Communism. He saw Hitler as a potential antidote to the spread of communism in Europe. This led, a short time later, to Hitler's inclusion of a favorable reference to Ford in his *Mein Kampf*–the only American mentioned in that work.

In 1923 Henry told the *Ladies Home Journal* (Lacey, p. 135):

> *I consider women to be only a temporary factor in industry. Their real job in life is to get married, have a home, and raise a family.*

Even in the early 1920's, such attitudes were highly offensive to many. According to Harry Bennett (his long-time right-hand man) and other associates, Henry was seen as a high-libido, hard-driven aggressive male. Ford's image as an opinionated tyrant was reinforced by his purchase of the *Dearborn Independent*. He used that acquisition as a vehicle to impart his views to the masses. He felt he knew the path to success and wanted to tell the world. However the newspaper caper cost him $5 million over the seven years he owned it. More significantly, it made him millions of enemies and probably cost him prestigious political appointments.

INTUITIONAL STYLE: A PROMETHEAN

Ford dared do what he felt was right, even when told he was crazy. His messianic zeal and philosophic feel for world order caused him to see his moves as fitting into a larger picture. This allowed him to take the blue-collar workers' dilemma into account when making decisions and to ignore conventional wisdom as he did so. Henry was a man who saw the forest but was also adept at not losing touch with the trees. On the Myers-Briggs personality type he was an intuitive-thinker, making him what psychologists use as a metaphor–a Promethean. Prometheans tend to chase opportunities and possibilities at the expense of minutia. That was Henry.

Never impressed by quantitative displays of either revenues or profits, Ford prided himself on his visual and spatial skills rather than numerical skills. Budgets were not important for him nor were detailed drawings. Biographer Lacey described his engineering approach (Lacey, p. 96):

> *Never very happy with blueprints, he found it much easier to work three-dimensionally.*

CREATIVITY: INNOVATIVE RESPONSES TO CRISES

Henry Ford's creativity seemed to shine brightest in the face of adversity. At one point, his innovative moving assembly line set demands that stressed the factory workers, prompting them to quit. The turnover rate at the factory at Highland Park had reached an astronomical 380% by the end of 1913, making it difficult to run. This crisis helped him get management to agree initially to some radical changes. In his inimitable fashion, he turned this success into a publicity coup by doubling the wage of his production workers and shortening the working day. Within one month, the mass exodus of workers abated and long lines of men applying for jobs formed outside the plant. Subsequently, sales quadrupled, costs dropped precipitously, and before his competitors could figure out what happened, he was captain of the auto industry. Virtually overnight, Ford was transformed into a national hero and many of his former detractors became disciples.

In 1916, however, management panicked, fearing that Henry had lost his mind. Minority shareholders John and Horace Dodge filed a lawsuit against Ford to force him to distribute more of the profits of the Ford Motor Company as dividends. Even the *Wall Street Journal* had not grasped the implications of Ford's innovations. It opined:

> *Ford has committed an economic crime that will soon return to plague him and the industry he represents as well as organized society.*

But the uneducated farm boy knew more than the pundits on this issue. He would write (Gilder, 1983 p. 159):

> *Our policy is to reduce the price, extend the operations, and improve the article. You will notice that the reduction of price is first. We have never considered any costs as fixed. Therefore, we believe more sales will result, then we go ahead and try to make the prices. We do not bother about the costs. The new prices force the costs down.*

Eventually proved right, this prescient insight altered manufacturing and pricing forever. In spite of this, Ford lost the suit filed by the Dodge brothers and was compelled to increase the dividends to the shareholders. What Ford's dissenters had failed to realize was that the wage increase was actually small in relation to the productivity improvements in what he called "taking the work to the men instead of the man to the work." Without the moving assembly line and the three shifts per day that Ford introduced, it would have cost $20 per day to generate the productivity equivalent to what Ford was now getting for $5. The creation of three eight-hour shifts re-defined the American work day and reduced the work week to 40 hours. This made the workers happy for it enabled them to spend more time with their families.

PROPENSITY FOR RISK

Most of Ford's conquests came at some great risk. Even after he was financially secure, he continued to make huge investments. He bought railroads, ore plants and an airline. He financed a revolutionary new airplane and a rubber plantation. Never quite satisfied if he wasn't on the leading edge of change, Henry was a fearless competitor and seldom backed down, even when his adversaries carried a bigger stick. His contemporaries had labeled him "Ford the Fighter" in his early years, and age didn't mellow him much.

INTENSITY: DRIVEN BY A PASSION FOR PERFECTION

The intensity that was evident in Henry's perpetual sense of urgency was driven by his passion for perfection. His agonizing, painstaking dedication to making Tin Lizzie the best car that could be built reflected his unrelenting quest for quality. "Average" and "mediocre" were not in Ford's vocabulary.

Time was always of the essence for Henry. A man on a mission, speed was part of his fuel. He had moonlighted during his early years as an employee by working on his own creations and was accustomed to working two shifts each day. He was a workaholic's workaholic. When he got excited about an idea like the Model T, he would work day and night and often went days without going to bed. Ford's time clock was on double time and his associates knew it. Like his close friend Thomas Edison, Henry Ford became a model for the maxim, "If at first you don't succeed, try, try, again"–even if you have to cheat sleep.

SELF-IMAGE: A MESSIANIC COMPLEX

One of the secrets of Ford's success was an assumption of omniscience. Like most great entrepreneurs, Ford believed he was special and right. Even when he was wrong he was hard pressed to back down, writing in his memoirs, "I was always pushed by invisible forces within me and without." When he demanded that his son Edsel fire an employee he didn't like, Edsel responded, "If he goes, I go." Henry told him, "Then get him out of my sight," forcing Edsel, the President of Ford Motors in his late thirties, to transfer the valuable executive to the West Coast. This feeling of rightness came from an unfounded optimism that had forgotten his many failures as a young man.

CRITICAL THINKING STYLE: LEARN FROM MISTAKES

Henry Ford used failure to motivate his own learning. He had failed as a farmer. He met with failure again in his first two automobile ventures. He was fired from his own firm, Henry Ford Company, when he attempted to build the "people's car." Anyone with less tenacity would have quit and taken a job to support his wife and young son. But Henry viewed each setback as a learning experience, regarding each adversity as one more mistake to avoid next time.

When the automobile industry was in its infancy at the turn of the century, over 500 firms attempted to capture the auto market. By 1910 there were 300 new car models. Ninety-five percent failed. That is the nature of any new market arena. (A similar phenomenon was seen at the turn of the next century with the commercialization of the Internet followed shortly after by the demise of the early dot.com companies.)

Like many great entrepreneurs, Ford was an iconoclast of the first order. Convention and tradition were never in vogue at Ford Motors. What psychologists now describe as being "broken to be reborn" was true of Henry Ford. Often challenged in his trek to the top, he met the challenges by breaking all the rules of marketing, pricing, labor rates and capacity scheduling to create a new business paradigm.

INITIATIVE: AN UNRELENTING QUEST FOR CONTROL

Ford could be described colloquially as a "control freak." He was intolerant of mediocrity and impatient with those who didn't see the world as he did. This brought him many adversaries in the industry. His view of the Company was the only view tolerated and took precedence over Edsel's–even after the latter had become President of Ford Motors. Some biographers believe that Henry Ford was partially responsible for the premature death of Edsel.

When faced with unionization, the fiercely independent Ford told his employees:

> *Organization serves evil purposes, but independence best serves good purposes.*

While this statement is self-serving, Ford believed it passionately since it was he, and not some union, who had doubled the workingman's wages. Now, he felt that his employees were colluding to gain control of his company.

Henry's insatiable need for control was further manifested when he quit the Company in 1919 and moved to California, turning over the reins to Edsel. He was so disturbed over the legal battle for his right to build a car and sell it on his own terms that he was willing to abandon the business rather than surrender his ideals. He even purchased land in California on the ruse that he was starting a new auto company to compete with Ford. He told the California press that he was there to build the most innovative breakthrough car. He wanted to instill fear into his adversaries to encourage them to sell out. They didn't waver and won their lawsuit against him. Furious in defeat, he subsequently bought them out for $105.8 million and was once again in control.

ECCENTRICITIES AND PERSONALITY PARADOXES

High testosterone is related to manic-depression, and Ford displayed many of the symptoms of a bipolar personality. When he was up, he was manic; when he was down, he crashed. Ford was an anomaly. The machismo of his outward persona belied his basic caring nature. He was a contrast in styles that could change quickly. Oliver Barthel, an early investor in the Ford Motor Company, wrote:

> *Mr. Ford seemed to have a dual nature. One side of his nature I liked very much and I felt I wanted to be a friend of his. The other side I just couldn't stand. It bothered me greatly.*

The Reverend Samuel Marquis was Henry's long-time minister. He and Ford were close when Henry was building the River Rouge plant just prior to America's entry into World War I. Marquis wrote of the "astonishing transformation" that took place within Ford from one day to the next. He wrote (Lacey, p. 189):

> *Henry could be happy as a child, and filled with the child spirit of play, with a soul of a genius, a dreamer, an idealist ... a soul that is affable, gentle, kindly, and generous to a fault. But the very next day Henry Ford could be exactly the opposite. His body became drooped and shrunken.*

Such observations provide additional support for the assertion that Ford was bipolar. If he indeed suffered from a bipolar disorder, it would explain the ambivalence of his personality. He was shy but arrogant. He was an introvert who dominated every conversation, and a control freak who ran for the Senate.

The paradox of Ford is that he was described as a haughty snob who produced an affordable car for the masses with whom he never deigned to associate. Yet he paid them high wages and in so doing, helped create the American middle class. He expressed his unrelenting dedication to his dream on the eve of the launch of the Model T:

> *I will build a car for the great multitude ... so low in price that no man making a good salary will be unable to own one.*

Ford was a simple man with a complex nature. He never liked nor associated with the wealthy. The only people for whom he had an affinity were other entrepreneurs, such as his best friends Thomas Edison and Harvey Firestone. His rural roots led him to defend the common man, but he fought ferociously to keep them in their place. Though he believed the customer was king, he asserted, "they can have a car in any color as long as it is black." He was so pompous that no one dared address him as anything but "Mr. Ford."

Pacifism led to his sponsorship of the European Peace Ship in 1915 that was intended to end World War I. However, he supported the war effort in World War II by building the Willow Plant that produced B-24 bombers. That giant facility produced one plane per hour, for a total of 86,865 aircraft between May 1942 and the end of World War II.

Henry was an interesting dichotomy, especially in his dealings with his only son Edsel. He doted on him and wanted him to grow, but stifled his development through his authoritarian ways. At age eight, Edsel was given a car that he drove to school. Since there were no laws against minors driving, Henry was not in breach of any law. Of course, he may have ignored any such regulation anyway, since he was always more prone to make laws than follow them. When Edsel turned twenty-one he was given $1 million.

Money was not of paramount importance to Henry Ford, although he did value the power it gave him. He wrote:

> *If money is your only hope for independence, you will never have it. The only real security that a person can have in this world is a reserve of knowledge, experience, and ability.*

Money was never a key element in his decisions. He wrote, "A business that makes nothing but money is a poor kind of business." This ideology led to many conflicts with his backers and fellow executives. After many years of working with his CFO, James Couzens, the two split over his decision to lower the price of the Model T so all men could own one. Ford would later write:

> *There are two fools in this world. One is the millionaire who thinks that by hoarding money he can somehow accumulate real power, and the other is the penniless reformer who thinks that if he can take the money from one class and give it to another, all the world's ills will be cured.*

Couzens often found unanswered correspondence and bills and checks for large amounts stuffed away in Ford's desk. His wife Clara once found a check for $75,000 tucked away in a suit pocket. Henry was too busy chasing life's possibilities to deal with minutia. Biographer Lacey (1986) wrote, "Money never mattered much to Henry." Ford wrote in his notes, "Money is the root of all evil." For him, money caused executives to lose focus on the truly important facets of the job.

Though he preached the importance of strong ethics in all business transactions, Henry was quite devious in how he dealt with his own stockholders. He preached the importance of family life and the wayward ways of being single, yet he shared a long-time love affair with his personal secretary Evangeline Dahlinger.

The ultimate paradox in the life of Henry Ford was his last ride to the cemetery in a Packard. Ford never made a vehicle elegant enough for use as a hearse, so he had to take his last ride in a carriage built by his competitors.

Honors & Achievements

MAGNITUDE OF SUCCESS

Few men have started so late in life and achieved so much as Henry Ford. At age forty, Henry was still in search of his niche in life. He had already invented many machines but none had been successful. Though many would have abandoned the quest and pursued a different career path, Henry persisted. His first car at Ford Motor Company, the Model A, did not fit the need, so it was scrapped for the Model T within two years. This revolutionary car made all other cars obsolete. Within five years of its introduction, the Model T had sold 500,000 cars and by 1914 was selling 250,000 each year. By 1927, it had reached the status of a classic and was the pre-eminent automobile in the world. Ford's intransigent focus on quality at a low price eventually brought him the success that had evaded his early efforts, and by age 50 he headed the most successful car company in the world. By age 60, he was a titan and a billionaire tycoon.

 By the 1920s, half the cars on the road were Fords. The Ford Motor Company had become vertically integrated to the point that Henry controlled all the elements of auto manufacturing. He owned rubber plantations in Brazil, a fleet of ships and a railroad to import and export his products, 16 coal mines, and thousands of acres of timberland and iron-ore mines in Michigan and Minnesota. When he made it to the top, he was so revered by the working class that they petitioned him to run for President of the United States. Henry's unconventionality and his need for control were unsuited to the role of President, so he abandoned all political aspirations.

Within ten years of implementing his radical ideas, Ford had increased his market share to over 60% while General Motors watched their market share plummet from 23% to 8%. An indication of the success of the Ford venture was the stock purchase by James Couzens' sister. A school-teacher, she lent her brother $100 in 1906 so he could invest in the newly organized Ford Motor Company. When Henry Ford bought out the minority shareholders in 1919, she received $262,036.67 for her original $100 investment.

HONORS

Ford has been lauded for having introduced such innovative ideas as the moving assembly line, interchangeable parts, the economic learning curve theory, high wage rates to increase productivity, and aggressive retail pricing strategies. If imitation is the sincerest flattery, then indeed Ford has received the highest order of praise, for his ideas now permeate manufacturing around the world. Almost a century after Ford's introduction of his revolutionary marketing strategies, a contemporary college textbook asserts:

> *Learning curve theory dictates that costs drop with each doubling of accumulated volume from a static run-rate. That is axiomatic for all mass-market consumer product businesses and Henry Ford showed us how such maneuvering can work.*

Ford's strong conviction that paying his workers enough money so they could afford one of his cars was vindicated by his market domination. Even more significant than the economic implications were the social implications of his new practices. By increasing the income and the leisure time available to his workers, Ford contributed to the creation of a class of people between those who were rich and those who were poor. This was a new middle class that had more discretionary income for a higher quality of life and more discretionary time to pursue education and leisure.

Ford's Model T did change the world. It made it easier for farmers to get to the city and for city dwellers to find solace in the country. It influenced American highway development more than any other single factor. The "people's car" spawned the "Volkswagen" in Germany and a myriad of copy cats in other nations.

One magazine called Ford the "greatest entrepreneur of the 20th century." Another poll listed him along with Jesus and Napoleon as the greatest man in history. In 1918, Ford was nominated for the Senate seat from Michigan and narrowly lost the election on account of his lack of interest in campaigning. Of all the honors and accolades bestowed upon Henry Ford, perhaps the single greatest tribute to his accomplishments was the turnout of 100,000 people who came to pay their last respects at his funeral in 1947.

Lessons Learned from Henry Ford

PRICE-ELASTICITY AND LEARNING CURVE THEORY

Ford has been touted as a manufacturing and engineering genius. But the truth is that he was a marketing genius. The flow chart shown below displays the industrial model that Ford conceived empirically.

Ford's Industrial Model for Production

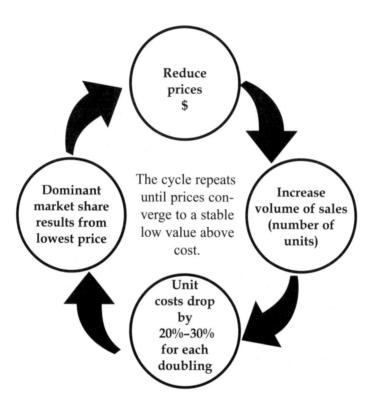

Henry Ford's industrial model for production became the blueprint for the mass production of consumer goods. Increased efficiency in the production of goods leads inevitably to lower costs, which in turn increase the volume of sales. With the increased volume, it becomes necessary to increase production by expanding production facilities. Large volume production leads inexorably to lower production costs and the cycle repeats.

History has validated Ford's insights and shown us that most costs in a business are relative rather than fixed. For example, if a machine that costs one million dollars is required to produce one million widgets it adds a dollar to the cost of each widget. However, if sales double, it is used to produce two million widgets, adding only 50 cents to the cost of each widget. Therefore, it is the cost per widget that is important in computing profits and so increasing the volume of sales is an effective way of reducing the cost per widget. Selling more cars reduces the cost of producing each car. Ford understood this idea at an intuitive level and that was a key factor in his becoming such a great entrepreneur.

These ideas about pricing are now embedded in a sub-discipline of economics called *price-elasticity theory*. An axiom of this discipline asserts that if you lower the price of an item, you will sell more –especially if you have a mass consumer product. Furthermore, if that price drop as a percentage is less than the percentage increase in sales, then your profit will increase. Why does this work? An empirical rule of thumb in price-elasticity theory asserts that doubling volume reduces costs (per item) by approximately 30%. In the words of economist writer George Gilder in *The Spirit of Enterprise* (1984, p. 158):

> *The learning curve ordains that in any business, in any era, in any capitalist competition, unit costs tend to decline in predictable proportion to accumulated experience–between 20 and 30 percent with every doubling of accumulated volume.*

Henry Ford was never exposed to any formal representation of this rule, but he understood the concept intuitively and his strong convictions enabled him to persist in the face of strong opposition. Such steadfastness is typical of the entrepreneurial genius.

MANAGERIAL PRINCIPLES

Ford left us a legacy of entrepreneurial management principles such as never invest in mediocrity, and never let security get in the way of opportunity. This entrepreneurial genius was willing to sacrifice in the short term to win in the long.

Decades later, it was the Japanese who would become the most ardent implementer of Henry Ford's managerial principles. The Japanese manufacturing coup between 1965 and 1985, which vanquished the American consumer electronics industry, was merely a replication of what Henry had done in automobiles in the early part of the century. The Japanese formulated long-term goals aimed at domination of the consumer electronics industry. The result was America's loss of such industries as radios, stereos, calculators, TVs, VCRs and all microprocessor-driven consumer products. Like Ford, the Japanese were willing to trade off short-term profits for long-term market share. While America was focused on the space program and landing on the moon, the Japanese were landing in American living rooms.

FAILURE AS A SPRINGBOARD TO SUCCESS

Many of the world's greatest thinkers have recognized that in the analysis of our mistakes reside the most powerful opportunities for learning. In the words of philosopher Francis Bacon, "Truth comes out of error more easily than out of confusion." Centuries later, Soichiro Honda observed:

Many people dream of and hope for success. To me, success can be achieved only through repeated failure and introspection. In fact, success represents 1% of your work, which results from the 99% that is called failure.

This expresses a relationship between success and failure exemplified by Henry Ford's rise to greatness. Henry's life shows us how failure can lead to success. Failure for Ford was but a temporary distraction on the trek to the top. Had Henry not failed in his early attempts to build a car manufacturing company, the Tin Lizzie would never have been built. Had he capitulated to the will of others, he would have built cars for princes, not for the people. Had he listened to experts, he would have taken the more conservative approach to pricing and building cars. Henry said it best: "We learn more from our failures than from our successes." With him it was axiomatic.

Henry Ford and the other entrepreneurial geniuses whom you will encounter in successive chapters had the audacity to break things that weren't already broken. His temerity won him the millennium title "America's first great entrepreneurial genius." At a time when over 500 firms were competing for the burgeoning automobile business, the middle-aged Ford succeeded when most others failed–not because he followed the rules, but because he broke them. Ford was always willing to fail to succeed, and that runs counter to the standard approach in business.

Gabrielle (Coco) Chanel

Synthesize to Success by Attacking Weakness

b. Saumur, France   August 19, 1883
d. Paris, France   January 10, 1971

"Nobody can live with low horizons."

SELF-DESCRIPTION
"Arrogance is in everything I do. It is in my gestures, the harshness of my voice, in the glance of my gaze –in my whole person."

MOTTO
"There is a time for work, and a time for love. That leaves no other time."

INNOVATION	Created House of Chanel, Flapper Look, Chanel No. 5; an aristocrat wrote, "Women no longer exist; all that's left are the boys created by Chanel."
UNIQUE QUALITY	Made androgyny upscale. Poet Jean Cocteau wrote, "Her sexual appetites are virile. She sets out to conquer like a man." Pragmatic practicality was her forte.
OBJECTIVE	"I'd rather be respected than respectable."
NET WORTH	In 2000, the House of Chanel was a $1-billion-per-year business. Her estate was estimated at $4.5 billion.
HONORS	"Coco was to couture what Picasso was to painting." –Cocteau
BIRTH ORDER	Second born in a dysfunctional family; deserted and orphaned by age 12
EDUCATION	Six years at Aubazine orphanage
PERSONALITY	Introverted renegade with an obsession for style and chic
HOBBIES	Men, horses, seduction, roulette and the theater
POLITICS	Apolitical, but hated communism
RELIGION	Pragmatic Roman Catholic with a mystical nature
FAMILY	She had no husband or children–a seductress who conquered dukes, artists and political leaders like few women in history.

2

Gabrielle (Coco) Chanel

Synthesize to Success by Attacking Weakness

"In order to be irreplaceable one must always be different."

Overview

In the blockbuster hit movie *Titanic* (1997), actress Gloria Stuart in the role of an aged Rose De Witt Bukater drops a priceless heart-shaped blue diamond necklace into the ocean to reject its donor and declare her love for her heartthrob, Jack Dawson. This scene was art imitating the life of Coco Chanel, the greatest female entrepreneur of the 20th century.

When the wealthiest man in England, the Duke of Westminster, was courting Ms. Chanel, he took her on his opulent yacht, *The Flying Cloud,* for a Mediterranean cruise. As the yacht pulled into port, Coco observed a beautiful young female companion emerging from the duke's cabin. Coco was furious at the duke's betrayal. Attempting to placate Coco, the duke presented her with a priceless pearl necklace. In a gesture of haughty defiance, Coco Chanel held the necklace overboard and let it slip slowly into the ocean. "Coco Chanel," she asserted, "cannot be bought." This story told by friend Serge Lifar captures the free spirit and arrogance that characterized the queen of couture.

Coco Chanel was one of a kind. She wrote, "I was the one who changed, it wasn't fashion. I was the one in fashion." And in a moment of introspection she confided, "In order to be irreplaceable one must always be different." The mistress of haute couture was, indeed, different! She was an interesting blend of sensuous female and aggressive male. An inner seething rage against convention made her defy traditional modes of dress and conduct. In her sense of style and presentation, Coco was a true visionary. In the area of women's fashions, she was revolutionary.

Gabrielle Bonheur Chanel was born in a small village in southern France on August 19, 1883. Deserted and orphaned by age 12, she was placed in the care of nuns at the Aubazine orphanage in France. There she learned to read, write and sew. At age 21, she met a man, Etienne Balsan, who became her lover and benefactor. Etienne began calling her "little coco" and the name took. Balsan was smitten with the pretty country urchin with no formal breeding. He was enchanted enough to invite her to become a member of his estate at Royallieu.

At Royallieu, Chanel became a sponge, soaking up the cultural aspects of life she never knew in the small orphanage. The woman who would become a femme fatale and be adored by some of the most learned and aristocratic Europeans was, in those early years, a mere waif looking for a ticket to a legitimate life. In spite of such an unlikely beginning, Coco would ultimately be credited with simplifying women's fashions, raising hemlines, making costume jewelry acceptable, introducing short hair as more chic than functional, and elevating the color black from mourning to modishness. She told the media (Sleeper, 2001):

> *People laughed at the way I dressed, but that was the secret of my success. I didn't look like anyone...I borrowed ideas from a mechanic's blouse, a ditch digger's scarf, and the white collar and cuffs of a waitress.*

Shortly after opening her first millinery shop in 1911, she purchased a Rolls-Royce, complete with chauffeur and footman. Though she could not afford this luxury, it fit her need to appear worthy of the business from the Parisian aristocrats–the women she needed, but hated. The Rolls-Royce was her magic carpet to the world of the elite. When she stepped out of it, she acted the role of a reigning queen . When she walked into a room, conversation stopped. When she spoke, people listened.

Once she developed momentum, nothing could stop her. She created the "flapper" look that defined the 1920s, costume jewelry for those who could not afford a king's ransom for real diamonds, and Chanel No. 5 perfume that emanated from her highly refined sense of smell. The *Times* of London wrote, "If ever there was a marketing queen before her time, it was Gabrielle Chanel." Indicative of her belief in shooting for the stars was her aphorism, "Nobody can live with low horizons, a narrow outlook will choke you." After reaching the pinnacle of her celebrity, Coco continued to live in a lavish suite in the fashionable Ritz Hotel where she hosted salons for the rich and famous.

Obsessed with her work, she continuously rejected suitors and played the field, while the House of Chanel grew into a billion-dollar enterprise. Arguably, Coco was the first female entrepreneurial genius and possibly the greatest ever. She created an empire that was estimated to be worth $4.5 billion on her death in 1971, when she was 88 years of age!

The Formative Years

EARLY EXPERIENCES

Coco was christened Gabrielle Bonheur after the nun who delivered her. The pretty brunette child came into the world with little and left a lot behind. Without a dowry, a French girl had virtually no chance of reaching Coco's ultimate destination. Her father, Albert Chanel, was a womanizing itinerant trader. Her mother, Jeanne Devolle, was a farm girl who had already given birth to an illegitimate child named Julie. Her parents would bring six children into the world, but the strain of repeated childbirth cost Jeanne her life at age 32. Not wanting to be saddled with a family, Albert mysteriously disappeared and the six children were dispensed to various homes, with Gabrielle ending up in the Aubazine orphanage.

At Aubazine, Gabrielle learned to read, write and sew. The lonely girl escaped into novels while the nuns acted as a backdrop for romantic fantasies from Decourcelle and Colette novels. Gabrielle identified with Claudine, the bright and audacious heroine of the Colette books. In Colette's stories, the talented but unworldly country girl, Claudine, finds her way to Paris and makes it big in the swirl of Parisian life. Escape into a self-deluding world of fantasy enabled Coco to bear her dismal surroundings and keep her dreams alive. Years later, when Coco met her favorite author, Collette, the two discovered they had a common past and became good friends.

The Climb to the Top

GAINING A GLIMPSE OF THE ARISTOCRACY

On leaving the orphanage, Gabrielle and her younger sister Antoinette found work in a local Vichy boutique. There she learned the art of hat design. In 1904, when Gabrielle was 21 years of age, some officers of the Tenth Light Horse Brigade stopped by their shop while on leave and asked the two out for a date. Gabrielle's date was the debonair Étienne Balsan, a 26-year-old from a good family who groomed horses for polo players. That first date ended at a cabaret. After much wine and song,

Gabrielle was asked to sing a song about a poor dog titled *My Poor Coco*. Although inebriated, she was sensational and received a rousing ovation. The name "Coco" would become permanently etched into her psyche–a success imprint of a poor woman on her way up the social ladder.

Her affair with Balsan resulted in her employment that enlightened her to life at the top. It was at Étienne's apartment, around 1909, that Gabrielle first began making hats for his long line of sophisticated mistresses. Under his tutelage she learned about horses and the wiles of females on the hunt for wealthy men. Polo and art were the venues for meeting women who would be a potential market for her clothes. It was in this environment that Coco learned to marry male functionality with female seductiveness–what she would later describe as "defiant femininity." For the fox hunt, Coco showed up elegantly attired in an outfit that stood out in stark contrast to the frilly femininity of the era. She evoked the image of an elegant femme fatale. During the six years she worked out of Étienne's apartment, Coco dressed in her "counter-culture" fashion and was able to establish some respectability, in spite of her obvious departures from the norm.

In 1910, the androgynous household helper and mistress of Étienne met world-famous British polo player Arthur Capel (who went by the nickname "Boy") while on a fox hunt in the Pyrenees, and they fell in love. Although he became the love of her life, Capel was a darling of the social set and irresistible to most women. When Boy Capel was about to arrive in Paris, his friend, Étienne, was leaving for Brazil. As such men are wont to do, Étienne offered his apartment in Paris to Boy with Coco as a live-in companion. Boy accepted and so did the smitten Coco.

GAINING ACCESS TO THE ARISTOCRACY

At this time, Coco was accepted in social circles as the temporary escort of Boy Capel. As a new arrival, she was *persona non grata* with Capel's fans–the effete snobs who invited him to their parlor parties. It wouldn't be long, she promised, before "I will have those bluebloods groveling at my feet" (Madsen, p. 109). Capel had class, style and money. His name opened vaults, but the doors to the drawing rooms remained closed to her. This bred a hatred of the landed gentry that Coco never transcended. To them she was a lowly mistress, even as she gained acceptance as their couturier. The ultimate irony is that Coco would one day personify all that she had detested when she was a young upstart. She would learn to be as haughty as the worst of them.

Étienne introduced Coco to a world of stately elegance, while Capel introduced her to the world of urban society. Boy was personal friends with French Prime Minister Georges Clemenceau and Great Britain's Prime Minister David Lloyd George. As a successful sportsman and international celebrity, Boy was invited to society balls and he brought Coco along. It was in this atmosphere that the inquisitive and observant Coco learned the wiles and the ways of the aristocracy.

THE BIRTH OF AN ENTERPRISE

In 1910 at age 27, Coco established her career as a hat maker for Capel's wealthy Parisian friends. She began sewing for the elite and modeling her creations. Still in the infancy of her craft, Coco would buy simple hats in a department store and alter them in a style that would later become her signature. Soon the word spread that she could make women look distinctive as well as stylish. Coco knew how to create the look of feminine elegance, and women flocked to her designs.

When Capel returned to his English estate, Coco busied herself making hats and building a clientele base. By 1911, the business had grown too large to be run from a private apartment. Capel loaned her some money to open a millinery shop on Rue Cambon in Paris. Coco invited her sister, Antoinette, to assist her in meeting the growing demand for her work. With a commercial location, Coco's business continued to flourish. Not one to rest on her laurels, Coco opened a second shop in 1913, while on holiday with Capel in Deauville on the English Channel. She had realized that catering to the shopping needs of women on holidays from England offered an excellent business opportunity. This second shop, bearing the storefront name Gabrielle Chanel, was a spectacular success.

ESCAPING WORLD WAR I

In 1915, Boy and Coco traveled to Biarritz in the south of France for a romantic holiday. The First World War was raging in Europe, and Biarritz, located near the border of neutral Spain, had become the playground of the rich and famous who wanted to escape the ominous clouds of conflict. Recognizing the potential for another successful coup like the shop in Deauville, Coco and Boy rented the Villa Larralde across from the casino. There, on July 15, they opened Biarritz's first fashion house, the House of Chanel. More grandiose than any of her other shops, the House of Chanel made a large variety of garments including trend-setting dresses that fetched the equivalent of $2000 in today's currency.

By 1916, when Coco was 33 years old, the combined staff of the Chanel stores in Paris, Deauville, and Biarritz exceeded three hundred workers.

One day in 1919, while on his way to visit Coco, Boy Capel was tragically killed in a car accident. Devastated, Coco vowed that she would immortalize her lover and benefactor. "I'm going to put the whole world in mourning for Boy Capel," she wrote. She told the press, "I lost everything. He was my brother, my father, my whole family." The little black dress that he loved so–that she wore in her bereavement–would become the staple of her line. Before this, women had worn black dresses only when in mourning. Chanel set a new precedent and black became an acceptable color for all occasions.

THE ANDROGYNOUS *CHANEL* LOOK

In the post-war years, young women began asserting their growing independence and tossing aside the constraints of corsets and confining clothing. As the epitome of womanhood, the full-figured look was giving way to the slim and svelte. Quick to capitalize on this trend, Gabrielle Chanel continued designing progressively shorter dresses with a tighter fit and simpler design. Because this style lacked the frills and lace of previous eras, it was regarded by traditionalists as "boyish." The Parisians referred to this style as the *garçonne* look while the English-speaking world called it the *flapper* look. Women who dressed in this style were described as *flappers*. Coco Chanel would later claim, with some justification, that it was she alone who invented the flapper.

Before his death, Boy had introduced Coco to a woman of the arts, Misia Sert, who would become friend, mentor and fan. A Russian intellectual, Sert was enchanted by the Coco's style and chic. On meeting Coco, Misia would confide, "Despite not saying a word, Coco radiated a charm that I found irresistible. I found her totally bewitching." They became friends and Misia opened many doors to the arts and artistic men. It wasn't long before Misia introduced her single friend to Sergei Diaghilev, Igor Stravinsky and Grand Duke Dmitri. All became Coco's lovers and companions, accepting monies from her in exchange for providing her access to upper-class Parisian society. The Grand Duke was put on the payroll of the House of Chanel. It paid huge dividends as this member of the former Russian royalty attracted many wealthy women to the House of Chanel. Even Sert was shocked when Coco endowed Diaghilev with 200,000 francs. But the wily Coco knew how to build a following and money was but a means to that end.

FROM DRESS FACTORY TO OLFACTORY

When Coco turned 40 in 1923, she decided to pay tribute to her first real love, Boy Capel, by issuing her classic perfume, Chanel No. 5. The development of this fragrance involved a great deal of experimenting, testing, rejecting, and retesting. In the end, she had eight samples from which to choose. Coco chose the fifth sample, and called it "Chanel No. 5"–a dramatic, but ingenious departure from conventional descriptive names. Its container, a bottle with a simple rectangular design, was also a departure from the more ornate flasks of the typical perfume containers. When Chanel No. 5 became the world's #1 fragrance, Coco was hailed as a visionary with a Midas touch.

Business was so strong that by 1923, Coco had to expand her premises in Paris, for the House of Chanel now employed almost 3000. Furthermore, the renewed popularity of the French Riviera in the post-war era prompted Gabrielle Chanel to open another shop in Cannes. Business was booming and the world was ready to enter a new celebration of fashion.

In 1925, Coco introduced the Chanel suit for women. It sported a cardigan jacket with no collar; long, tight-fitting sleeves; and a relatively short skirt with simple geometric lines. This suit became a trend-setting classic that launched the "Chanel look" and catapulted Chanel to the top of the world of fashion. The House of Chanel was now offering garments of all kinds for women, including an entire line of sports clothes. Actress Gloria Swanson and Elizabeth Bowes-Lyon (the future wife of King George VI) were now wearing Chanel-designed clothes. In 1927, Chanel opened a boutique in London.

THE GREAT DEPRESSION

As the Roaring '20s came to an end, the excesses of a frenzied decade gave way to the somber pessimism of the '30s. The stock market in New York had crashed and the Depression was well under way. Wealthy Americans fled the playgrounds of the French Riviera and the luxury trade was reeling. Chanel had to cut its prices by half, and even that measure did little to increase revenue. Then Sam Goldwyn, the famous American movie producer, offered her $1 million a year to design for his movies, and she went to Hollywood. Coco was swept to the top of the social register and no salon was closed to her. As her image rose in concert with her fame and fortune, she became more and more paranoid about her past life. She had paid her family to lie about their modest beginnings, but she was having increasing difficulty hiding the truth from herself. Her secrets drove her more deeply into creating fantasies about her past. In these fantasies, the nuns at the orphanage were transformed into Coco's "aunts" and her father became a fortune hunter who emigrated to America to seek his fortune. The truth was far less romantic.

THE LABOR MOVEMENT

On April 26, 1936, the French people voted into power a leftist coalition–the *Front Populaire*. The abject conditions of the Depression had spawned a people's movement that sought social and economic reforms. The "sit-down" and "sit-in" strikes employed by the labor movement in the U.S. were being adopted by the unions in France, who were demanding paid vacations, a forty-hour work week, and higher wages. As these strikes swept through the textile industry, they inevitably reached the House of Chanel. When Coco Chanel arrived at her Parisianne shop one morning to discover her seamstresses staging a sit-down strike, she expressed her outrage (Madsen, p. 215):

> *A sit-down strike on my dresses…Women on their behinds, it's obscene! And don't talk to me about wages. My wages are perfectly proper, and paid vacations!*

Her immediate reaction was to fire 300 of the employees, but these employees refused to leave the premises. When it became apparent that a competing designer, Schiaparelli, had settled with its workforce and were preparing their fall-winter fashion collection, she capitulated.

THE WINDS OF WORLD WAR II

At the closing of the 1930s, it became increasingly apparent that war in Europe was imminent. Then on March 13, 1939, Hitler marched into Czechoslovakia and a few months later, into Poland. On September 2, 1939, Britain and France declared war on Germany. Three months before the end of the decade, Coco Chanel laid off all her staff and closed the House of Chanel. On June 14, 1940, the Germans occupied Paris and within two years, all of France was under German occupation.

Information on Gabrielle Chanel's activities during World War II is spotty and fraught with a mixture of rumor, innuendo and third-party testimonials. It has been alternately suggested that she was a Nazi collaborator, an Ally collaborator, a conscientious objector, and a hedonistic, politically disinterested party animal. Whatever the case, it was clear that she remained in a form of self-imposed exile from the fashion industry until 1953.

THE RENAISSANCE OF THE HOUSE OF CHANEL

At the age of 70, Coco Chanel acquired financial backing from her old distributor, Pierre Wertheimer, and reopened the House of Chanel at 31 Rue Cambon in Paris. Eventually, her new line of couture won favor with the rich and famous. By the mid 1950s, Coco's clientele included such celebrities as Grace Kelly, Lauren Bacall, Ingrid Bergman, Rita Hayworth and Elizabeth Taylor. However, the rapidly changing tastes in fashion made the enterprise less profitable than it had been in past. On May 24, 1954, Coco Chanel sold to Pierre Wertheimer the posthumous rights to everything that bore the name *Chanel* in exchange for a cash settlement and his underwriting of all the costs associated with her fashion house. She continued to focus on her fashion design without the distractions of other business. By 1959, only five years after her re-entry into the world of haute couture, she was at the top again. *Vogue* magazine wrote (Madsen, p. 298):

> *If fashion has taken a turn to the woman, no one can deny that much of the impetus for that turn stems from Coco Chanel–the fierce, wise, wonderful, and completely self-believing Chanel.*

THE FINALE

In 1968, when Coco was 85 years old, *Time* magazine estimated that the annual revenues of her fashion house and royalties from her perfume were about $160 million. But, in her final years, money was not a concern of Gabrielle Chanel. Arthritis began to invade her hands and encumber her dress-designing activities of pinning and fitting models. Most of the people with whom she had shared life's joys and sorrows had passed on. Loneliness was becoming an increasingly pervasive torment, especially on holidays when her employees returned to their families and left her to the desperate solitude of the unloved. She told her grand-niece, Gabrielle Labrunie (Madsen, p. 328):

> *All things told, you're the one who got it right. You've got a husband, children. I've got nothing. I'm alone with my millions.*

On Sunday, January 10, 1971, in her eighty-eighth year, Gabrielle Bonheur "Coco" Chanel called out to her maid, "I can't breathe! Céline, open the window." After Céline attended to her, Coco uttered her last words (Madsen, p. 329), "You see, this is how you die."

Chanel's Decade-by-Decade Climb

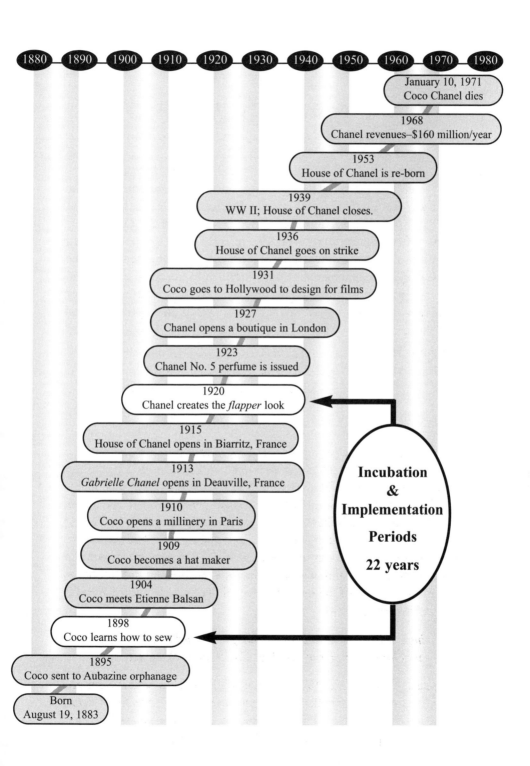

1880 · 1890 · 1900 · 1910 · 1920 · 1930 · 1940 · 1950 · 1960 · 1970 · 1980

January 10, 1971
Coco Chanel dies

1968
Chanel revenues–$160 million/year

1953
House of Chanel is re-born

1939
WW II; House of Chanel closes.

1936
House of Chanel goes on strike

1931
Coco goes to Hollywood to design for films

1927
Chanel opens a boutique in London

1923
Chanel No. 5 perfume is issued

1920
Chanel creates the *flapper* look

1915
House of Chanel opens in Biarritz, France

1913
Gabrielle Chanel opens in Deauville, France

1910
Coco opens a millinery in Paris

1909
Coco becomes a hat maker

1904
Coco meets Etienne Balsan

1898
Coco learns how to sew

1895
Coco sent to Aubazine orphanage

Born
August 19, 1883

**Incubation
&
Implementation

Periods

22 years**

A Personality Profile

COMMUNICATION STYLE: ALOOF AND ARROGANT

Coco Chanel became an icon as the goddess of haute couture. The country girl molded herself into a Parisian sophisticate with a mesmerizing persona that attracted some of the world's most eligible bachelors. The waif from the little village and Catholic orphanage had metamorphosed into her own fantasy. Interested in the occult and the mythical, Coco had an ethereal sense of destiny. Madison Avenue would have been proud of the way she adroitly packaged herself. Her House of Chanel came to represent the epitome of chic. Part of the Coco magic was in remaining aloof and mysterious. One of her ploys to win over sophisticated clientele was to be unavailable, because she believed that those in demand were always hard to reach. Coco would write, "a client seen is a client lost; make yourself available and it will cost you allure." This was her charismatic appeal. Associating with the bourgeoisie was tantamount to becoming one. Consequently, she remained distant and unreachable.

On one occasion, she attended the debutante ball for the daughter of her long-term lover, the Duke of Westminster. After a posh dinner at his British estate, Coco excused herself to change for the ball and never returned. When the concerned Duke sent his manservant in search of his mistress, he found her resting in bed with no intention of attending the festivities. The haughty London dowagers had predicted her demise that night, but she fooled them by not showing up and thereby denying them a chance to demean her. It was Coco's means of controlling what she couldn't control. Just don't appear. She later bragged to the media, "That night I was the queen for not showing up."

True power comes from being special. In Coco's case, "special" meant emerging with style and grace from a chauffeur-driven Rolls-Royce. Emulating royalty in this way was her way of being what she was not and it worked. Her aloofness and outward arrogance belied her humble beginnings and intimidated those who never suspected the truth about her.

INTUITIONAL STYLE

Most entrepreneurial geniuses tend to be Prometheans, i.e., intuitive thinkers. These personality types chase opportunities rather than security. They have short attention spans and seldom like to do the same thing twice. When these types have a penchant for perfectionism, they carry it to the extreme. A visionary such as Coco sees the big picture first and then attempts to give it substance through analytical implementation.

Gabrielle Chanel was highly intuitive on what made sense for women to wear, even when it violated traditional fashions. Close friend Jean Cocteau offered valuable insight in his comment:

> *She has, by a kind of miracle, worked in fashion according to rules that would seem to have value only for painters, musicians, poets.*

In her own words, "The purpose of fashion is to make women look young," and with that in mind she destroyed existing matronly dresses.

Coco Chanel once told *Vogue*, "I've been in business without being a businesswoman." This comment showed that she understood it was intuitive insight, not any ability to organize or manage, that made her unique. Chanel was always convinced that her strength was her female intuition for the demands of feminine appeal that gave her a decided advantage over her male competitors.

"Fashion," Coco said, "is not simply a matter of clothes. Fashion is in the air, borne upon the wind. One intuits it. It is in the sky and on the road." Her legal counsel, Robert Chaillet, spoke of the dichotomy in her. She had no understanding of numbers but possessed an amazing sense for making money. He told the media, "She knew nothing about figures, but never lost sight of the essence of money." Such intuitive insight is the magic of the entrepreneurial genius who chases ideas that lead to money. It seldom, if ever, works the other way.

Intuition differentiated Coco from the pack. It made her and almost destroyed her on many occasions. Never was this more evident than in her contract for the distribution of Chanel No. 5. Never interested in the details of distribution, packaging or the other necessities of such an enterprise, she signed away all marketing rights to Pierre Wertheimer for 2% of the *profits*. That would seem to be both brilliant and stupid. Normally, it is better to make a royalty arrangement based on sales revenues because these are easily verified. However, she tied the royalties to profits that are easily hidden or kept artificially low by creating inflated expenses, especially in a privately controlled company. Her infamous contract made Pierre and his brother extraordinarily wealthy. Coco made money, but a pittance compared to what her business partners earned. In retrospect, it is clear that this arrangement made her name a worldwide brand and led to the multi-million-dollar Hollywood contract with Sam Goldwyn. From this perspective the contract might be seen as a spark of genius. However, interminable legal battles over the original contract resulted, and in the end, Coco received more money than she could ever spend. When she needed the financial backing for her comeback in 1953, it was Pierre Wertheimer who put up half the money. Eventually, the two bitter adversaries became cautious allies.

CREATIVITY

The Chanel approach fits Joseph Schumpeter's definition of innovation as "creative destruction." The maverick destroyed the bauble look of yesteryear. She made the complex simple and it sold. Everything she designed "was terribly sensible." In the words of biographer Madsen, "Coco made black fashionable anytime" (p. 117). Out of the creatively destructive Chanel look came the flapper look in black. She seemed to have the Midas touch: by the 1920s, the name *Chanel* had become an icon and would remain so for six decades.

INTENSITY

Like most entrepreneurial geniuses, Coco was in a hurry. In 1957, *The New Yorker* wrote that she was able to out-work, out-party, out-think and out-smart all those in her circle. They said, "Coco has the unquenchable vitality of a twenty-year-old." She was 74 at the time. Though always in a hurry to get things done, she never hurried a design. This poster girl for the classic Type A personality was meticulous and methodical when it came to creating products for the House of Chanel. If she didn't achieve, she suffered guilt and, like most Type A's, Coco Chanel confused self-worth with achievement.

Overachievers like Chanel are unable to relax on vacation, feeling culpable if not totally immersed in all their undertakings. At the House of Chanel, Coco felt guilty if she were not integrally involved in every nuance of the operation. Two of her boutiques were opened while she was on summer holidays at Deauville and Biarritz and a third while in London cavorting with the Duke of Westminster. Even after she became wealthy, she could be found pinning up dresses and totally immersed in design. At the House of Chanel, nothing happened until the boss showed up around 10:00 a.m. *Vogue* wrote, "Her work habits are relentless. Her creations follow each other at a dizzying pace, Chanel is faster than anyone in fashion."

Style and force defined her. "A woman who doesn't wear perfume has no future," she adamantly told her clientele. Was that true? Of course not, and she knew it, but it fit the image she needed to convey. Pure force of will pervaded her soul. It made her unique and it made her successful. This renegade soul was candid about her mission and her decision not to marry (Madsen p. 183):

> *God knows I wanted love, but the moment I had to choose between the man I loved and my dresses, I chose the dresses. Work has always been a kind of drug for me, even if I sometimes wonder what Chanel would have been without the men in my life.*

One of the most famous quotes of Gabrielle Chanel was her analysis of her priorities in life (Madsen, p. 304), "There is a time for work, and a time for love. That leaves no other time."

SELF-IMAGE

Coco believed in herself long before the world did. In concert with a strong sense of self, Coco was energy incarnate. Underneath her calm resolve was a woman never about to return to her humble beginnings. With obsessive determination, she told the media (Madsen, p. 15):

> *Arrogance is in everything I do. It is in my gestures, the harshness of my voice, in the glow of my gaze, in my sinewy, tormented face, in my whole person.*

Like most other great entrepreneurs, Coco saw herself in a messianic light. When Jacques Chazot interviewed her in August 1969, he observed that she had started a feminine revolution by having women cut their hair. Coco Chanel curtly responded (Madsen, p. 323):

> *I cut my hair, which isn't the same thing...They cut their hair because they saw that I looked attractive. I was the one who changed, not fashion. I'm the one who was fashionable."*

ECCENTRICITIES AND PERSONAL PARADOXES

Coco Chanel's life was a study in paradox. She was a miserly boss in the Dickensian sense, but she gave away millions to unworthy suitors. One long-time faithful employee asked for a raise and was terminated immediately. When her seamstresses went on a sit-down strike, Coco was appalled and responded with outrage (Madsen p. 160):

> *Increase their salaries, are you out of your mind? They are gorgeous girls, why don't they find lovers. They should have no trouble finding rich men to support them.*

Then at the height of the Leftist movement in 1936, she agreed to turn the business into a working cooperative if she could manage it and work for the cooperative as the designer. This was the same woman who financed Cocteau's drug habit and the machinations of artistic gigolos and well-bred parasites like Igor Stravinsky, Duke Dmitri, Vera Bate, poet Pierre Reverdy, Misia Sert, and the Nazi Hans von Dincklage. In one sense she had become what she despised, an opinionated effete snob. This was a woman who hated mercenary relationships but engaged in them regularly.

ACHIEVEMENTS & HONORS

MAGNITUDE OF SUCCESS

Salvador Dali offered validation to Coco's legacy by telling the media "she has the best dressed body and soul in the world" (Wallach, p. 127). *Vogue* wrote about the adoration of the world of couture for her work, saying, "Everything she does makes news." Tenacity and verve were the trademark traits that made her great but none contributed more than her ability to be a sensual female with a male twist. Coco had learned how to synthesize to success by being both what she was and what she was not without sacrificing either role.

The legacies of great people are often measured by what they leave at the party relative to what they brought. Coco certainly left the world with more than she took. Chanel No. 5 became the most successful fragrance in history. How many can say that about a creation? Coco loved to say, "There are people with money and people who are rich." The point is that she was rich long before she had any money. Such a mythical sense of destiny is what makes people great. Coco sensed what women wanted and offered it to them in a fashion statement not found elsewhere. In her own words, "To earn a living in the feminine trade you must know women." It sounds trite, but this reality is often lost on self-important designers who believe that women will follow what is dictated to them.

Testimony to Chanel's success is that the House of Chanel was still reporting $1 billion in sales revenues at the millennium, some ninety years after Coco opened her first boutique and thirty years after her demise. The little girl without a family built an empire named *Chanel*. This uneducated and insecure woman made millions by making other women feel secure. She did it by offering fashions well outside the mainstream that often became trends in themselves. That is her greatest and most lasting contribution to couture.

Chanel would have been hard pressed to define what made her an entrepreneurial phenomenon. It was certainly never money. Money was never important to her except for the doors it opened and the places it permitted her to go. She often said, "It's not money for money's sake that I'm interested in, but money as the symbol of success." Money gave her the freedom to design on her terms, to live iconoclastically, to say I don't need to get married, and to thumb her nose at convention. Coco Chanel often gave away very expensive dresses to women she detested. But the dresses were not gifts. They were marketing promotions even though she may not have understood the subtle nuances of such. One doesn't have to like the rungs on the ladder as long as they lead to the top. Those women she befriended were often distasteful rungs but she took them and they led to fame and fortune.

The pursuit of any dream comes with a price. The ultimate question is always "Is the price worth the journey?" Coco never seemed to question her choice *during* her trek to the top, only after it was all over. The House of Chanel was the most enduring and most sensuous affair of her life. It was her only legacy.

HONORS

Early 20th-century Paris had no middle class: there were the haves and the have-nots, the well-read and the un-read, the well-bred and the ill-bred, the aristocrats and the bourgeoisie, the classes and the masses. A wide gulf separated these groups, making it difficult, if not impossible, to breach the gap. It is remarkable that a woman reared in an orphanage was able to transcend this chasm. The Queen of Couture proved it was possible to go from the poorhouse to the penthouse. The transition was not without travail and heartache to her and to a few ravaged bodies left in her wake.

French writer Andre Malraux gave testimony to Coco's remarkable contributions. He wrote, "From this century three names will remain: DeGaulle, Picasso and Chanel" (Sischy, 1998). In 1957, the Dallas retailer Neiman-Marcus honored her as "The most significant designer of the past fifty years." New Orleans gave Coco the keys to the city that time had forgotten. *Vogue* displayed her work prominently and quoted her for the better part of three decades. One writer said, "It was chic to be dressed by Coco Chanel" (Madsen, p. 116); another commented, "Chanel was the pied piper who led women away from complicated clothes and made them forget tradition." At the height of a volatile career, Coco had become the wealthiest couturier in Paris and probably the most successful self-made woman in history. *Glamour* magazine opined, "She is so seductive." Her fragrance business exploded after screen star Marilyn Monroe purred to the press "All I wear to bed is Chanel No. 5."

LESSONS LEARNED FROM COCO CHANEL

BE WHAT YOU ARE AS WELL AS WHAT YOU ARE NOT

Those who have studied the great artists, writers and leaders have found in them a propensity to flip-flop between opposing behavioral traits. If extroverted, they are able to introvert when needed and conversely. Rationalists are able to have feeling, controlling personalities are able to delegate, and the timorous are able to take significant risks when necessary. In other words, they are highly adaptive.

Research has shown that those capable of adapting, by attacking their worst fears or adopting a chameleon-like persona on command, are especially effective in creative ventures. Many successful politicians and entrepreneurs have been extroverted introverts. Why is this so? Introverts tend to be more reflective, so when they rise to be heard, they are more successful. Such was the case with the highly introverted Adolf Hitler, Mahatma Gandhi, and Howard Hughes. Controlling personalities with the ability to listen or restrain themselves are stronger than if they yield to their natural inclination toward action.

Unless you are willing and able to be what you are *not* as well as what you are, you will never be more than you presently are. While this may sound like convoluted double talk, this statement asserts that what we are at any given time is only a part of what we can be if we develop our full potential. For example, Gabrielle Chanel was an impoverished waif from an orphanage in a remote town of southern France. She lacked formal education and all the graces and training of the aristocracy. Yet, within a decade, she was setting the standard of fashion and elegance for Paris, the world, and all those who might claim entitlement through lineage. By aspiring to be the elegant and "chic" woman with the highest standards of taste, she metamorphosed into that image. The fantasy that she promoted became her reality. Coco Chanel has shown us how someone dealt a hand containing no ace, one face, and few trump, can use the strength of will to draw additional cards from the deck and acquire a winning hand.

STRIVE FOR AN ANDROGYNOUS BALANCE

The term *syzygy* was used by psychotherapist Carl Jung as the conjunction of the male and female within the unconscious mind. It is where macho men give rein to their feminine side, and where highly feminine women tend to express their maleness. Synthesizing the male and female aspects of our personalities is an extension of being what we are and what we are not. Nathaniel Branden spoke of this in *Six Pillars of Self Esteem* (1994):

> *The most creative individuals are those who can integrate both male and female aspects of personality.*

What did he mean? A "macho" man can be more effective by reacting with sensitivity when the situation demands it, and a nurturing female can operate more rationally in an emotional situation by suppressing her natural instinct to protect.

In this book, Chanel is presented as a model for tapping into one's syzygy. This epitome of femininity wore her hair like a man, rode horses like a man, and frequently designed female undergarments by using male underwear as a model. According to close friend Jean Cocteau, Coco was highly androgynous. He said, "Coco has virile appetites," that coincided with her preference for male friends. Male sporting events offered her insight into styles that defied the frilly feminine styles which dominated the tastes of the period. Biographers described Coco as dressing in "defiant femininity." That defiance never waned. In a moment of candor she said, "It's probably not by chance that I'm alone. It would be very hard for a man to live with me unless he's terribly strong" (Madsen, p. 269).

Chanel's climb to the top was one of defiance. She challenged convention with a simple elegance that was mesmerizing to the rich and powerful. Coco had shown that she could be what she was but could also be what she wasn't, and when she married the two she was powerful indeed. The ability to tap into her maleness while maintaining her femininity proved to be synergistic. It was this synthesis of the male and female components of one's being that Carl Jung was referring to in his observation, "In the unconscious of every woman is a hidden male personality."

Coco had impeccable presence, a palate for fashion, an imperious style, and an indomitable will, but most important, she had a highly androgynous persona. Deep within this implacable woman was a renegade spirit with the temerity that few would wish to challenge. Coco came into any negotiation armed to do battle with an inner sense of self that was not to be denied. In business or couture, she married masculine simplicity with feminine elegance.

Recent research offers insight into the magic of marrying our two opposite gender personalities to attain a synergism. The eminent University of Chicago psychologist Csikszentmihalyi wrote in his book *Creativity* (pp. 65-71):

> [Creative individuals]...escape rigid gender role stereotyping and tend to androgyny and seem to harbor opposite tendencies on the continuum between extroversion and introversion.

While the concept of androgyny and its role in the entrepreneurial personality are investigated in more depth in chapter 14, *How Entrepreneurial Are You?,* you will recognize androgenous qualities in the profiles that follow.

Jean Paul Getty

Test the Limits–Big Wins Demand Big Risks

b. Minneapolis, MN   December 15, 1892
d. Sussex, UK   June 6, 1976

"There are one hundred men seeking security to one able man who is willing to risk his fortune."

SELF-DESCRIPTION
"I am a wildcatter at heart."

MOTTO
"I buy when everyone else is selling, and hold on until everyone else is buying."

INNOVATION	Getty's chief adversary at Signal Oil, Garth Young, said, "He could see further than any other guy I knew." He got inside the numbers that set him apart.
UNIQUE QUALITY	A high roller if he felt the deal was right
OBJECTIVE	To be the largest independent oil producer in the world; he reached this objective when in his 60s.
NET WORTH	Getty Trust was sold to Texaco after his death for $10 billion. The Getty Museum Trust bequeathed $2.2 billion
HONORS	French Légion d'honneur (1960)
BIRTH ORDER	Second; older sister died at age 9, prior to his birth
EDUCATION	Graduated from UC at Berkeley; Post-graduate degree in Economics from Oxford, 1914
PERSONALITY	Promethean perfectionist and renegade eccentric
HOBBIES	Art collector; cavorted with entourage of "classy" women
POLITICS	Apolitical
RELIGION	Raised as a Christian Scientist, but never religious
FAMILY	Wives: five Children: five

3
Jean Paul Getty

Test the Limits–Big Wins Demand Big Risks

"I buy when everyone else is selling, and hold on until everyone else is buying."

Overview

The media quest for sensational news about the rich and famous usually yields a distorted view of the personality and character of those who are profiled. The public perception of J. Paul Getty is that of a licentious, money-hoarding mogul who inherited his wealth and indulged his sexual appetite without restraint. He acquired and abandoned wives in a fashion that flouted current social norms. The public learned that he installed a pay telephone in his lavish Sutton Place mansion to avoid paying the long distance tolls of his house guests. His depiction as a modern-day Scrooge was even more dramatically portrayed by his reluctance to pay ransom to the kidnappers of his grandson J. Paul III. After the young man's ear was brutally amputated and sent to the Gettys with a warning that other body parts would follow, J. Paul Getty continued to negotiate the ransom amount before ultimately capitulating. While these events shed some light on the character of J. Paul Getty, they fail to capture the multi-dimensional nature of this complex individual.

The young Getty was a rake and wildcatter who set out to prove to his father that he was able to run an oil business. An oil business is the quintessential risk. More dry wells are drilled than producing ones, and predicting which holes will yield oil is at best a crapshoot. Getty eventually became an oil tycoon not by following a safe, well-trodden path, but by taking calculated risks. He used the numbers to understand the gamble. This methodical man, who became familiar with every nuance of drilling, including the costs of extracting and refining oil and of building rigs, used this to his advantage. He knew more about the costs than almost anyone. When you know how much to bet because you know the odds, it gives you an advantage over those less informed. Getty was also the consummate user of a form of leverage known in business as "other people's money." The young man with the golden touch continually used existing assets to purchase new assets. This intelligent use of leverage was a key factor in his building of the Getty empire.

J. Paul Getty always believed in buying when everyone else was selling and in selling when they were buying. Biographer Robert Lenzner (1985) said of him:

Getty had the vision to go against the grain of economic disaster. It was perhaps his greatest stroke of courage and genius.

This was never more apparent than in his buying spree during the Great Depression. To wrest control of Tidewater Associated Oil Company from the Standard Oil Company, he bought more than 743,000 shares of Tidewater stock at depressed prices. Getty was smart enough to know that the Depression was temporary but oil was forever. The world of machines that Henry Ford had launched three decades earlier needed oil to operate. By 1937, Getty had won a voice in the management of Tidewater. It didn't take long to show how right he was. World War II drove up the price of oil and he was on his way. In retrospect, he looked like a genius.

Jean Paul Getty was a millionaire at 23. By his mid-sixties he was the richest man in the world. Getty Oil was sold to Texaco for $10 billion a few years after his demise. Ironically, it was not money that drove him, it was the challenge to be the biggest and the best, and to beat the big guys at their own game. (Great entrepreneurs are usually more driven to make their mark in the world than to get rich.) Getty confirmed this in his memoirs when he wrote, "I had never been interested in having a lot of money." However, he placed a financial value on everything, later admitting it was the money that drove him–not for money's sake, but as a tool to gain freedom and a gauge to show how well he had done.

Lenzner wrote, "No man in history has left money to so many different women." The irony is that none got what they expected–they received only a pittance of what they earned relative to their role in the billionaire's life. But quantity was important for Getty, leading him to multiple females at his side at all times. These hangers-on put up with the dementia of an aging billionaire, expecting to be repaid in his will. It was not to be.

J. Paul Getty lamented near the end of his life that he had no successor whom he regarded as worthy to rule the Getty empire after his death. His inability to bond with his offspring prevented him from building a family dynasty like the Kennedys or the Rockefellers. It was a price he paid in his struggle to become the world's wealthiest man. In the end, he shocked everyone, including his children, by leaving most of his money to the J. Paul Getty Museum in Malibu, California. It was his only legacy.

The Formative Years

EARLY EXPERIENCES

Getty was the second child of George Getty and Sarah McPherson Risher. Their first child, a daughter, died of typhoid ten years prior to Jean Paul's birth in Minneapolis on December 15, 1892. The older parents doted on their son since they knew he would be their only surviving child. The result was a spoilt and self-indulgent boy who grew into a similar adult. His genteel parents imbued the boy with impeccable manners–manners that later served him well in the art of seduction.

In 1903, when Jean Paul was 10 years old, the family relocated to Bartlesville, Oklahoma where his father had invested in oil wells. Oklahoma was a territory inhabited mainly by Indians, still four years away from statehood. Trips to the oilfields gave Jean Paul a larger-than-life view of roustabouts and wildcatters. He acquired a romantic view of black gold gushing from the earth. To the young and impressionable boy, oil was raw energy that led to instant wealth and power. At 12 years of age, after reading and rereading the exploits of Horatio Alger in *Risen from the Ranks*, Jean Paul began to see himself as an entrepreneur. G. A. Henty's adventure novels also proved quite motivational. Henty was a English Victorian author who preached that hard work and vigilance always led to virtue, honesty, chastity, and heroism. Jean Paul's fantasies may have influenced his move to England later in life.

The future oil tycoon learned the value of leverage when his father, in an attempt to instruct his son on the value of securities, allowed him to buy 100 shares in the George Getty Oil Company when he was 12. George Getty told his son, "You are now my boss." Jean Paul also learned that buying stock on a note was far better than having to pay cash.

As an only child, Jean Paul was doted on and given excessive freedom to roam. He gradually developed into a self-absorbed egocentric man-child with an indomitable spirit. Despite the permissive indulgence of his parents, his father tried to instill some responsibility in him, resulting in a long-running battle of wits. George Getty was a strong-willed lawyer and taskmaster. But he was also cold and distant. Jean Paul's first wife Jeannette told the media, "Jean Paul was terrified of emotion." Why? His parents were never affectionate. They gave him material things but little affection. His mother suffered numerous emotional relapses, and was distant and unemotional with her son. She functioned more as matriarch than mother. Jean Paul and his father shared a love-hate relationship that ultimately made "papa" the major influence in Jean Paul's life.

In 1906, when Jean Paul was approaching 14, the family moved to San Diego and then to Los Angeles where he attended Harvard Military Academy and the Polytechnic High School. As a teenager, Getty gradually became more precocious and more wayward. He once took off in his father's car in the middle of the night to partake in the Los Angeles nightlife. He was subsequently grounded, but the enterprising teen talked his father into buying him the parts from which he would build his own car. Such initiative may have been a harbinger of Jean Paul Getty's ultimate quest to rule his own destiny.

FORMAL EDUCATION

Getty was not a good student. In fact, he was asked to leave a Southern California academy. That led to stints at the University of Southern California and then Berkeley. No school satisfied his defiant and wanton lifestyle. In April 1912, he took a leave of absence from school to tour the Far East, visiting China and Japan. On returning home, he declared that California colleges were below his standards and he wanted to attend Oxford University in England, where the family had visited the past summer and where many of Henty's action scenes had taken place. To reinforce the strength of his application, he talked his father into having then President William Howard Taft write him a letter of recommendation. Getty was admitted to Oxford as a non-collegiate student in 1912. By the winter of 1913, Jean Paul cut classes and took off for continental Europe in his second-hand Mercedes. Getty's auto-biography states that he spent two years at Oxford and graduated in 1914 with a degree in Economics. However, the Oxford record merely shows that he graduated in 1913. Biographer Robert Lenzner questions whether Getty ever really *earned* a degree at Oxford. When he finally returned to America he went directly to Oklahoma and became a wildcatter. This–his baptism of fire–changed his life.

The Climb to the Top

MAKING DEALS IN THE OIL FIELDS

When Jean Paul returned from Oxford at 21, he persuaded his father to finance his initial venture as a wildcatter. The arrangement called for George to continue to pay him as if he were still in college–a crafty but understandable strategy. For his part, Jean Paul would search out lands to lease for oil rights and then seek his father's approval to close the deal. George would finance all the exploration and drilling costs, and he and Jean Paul would share the profits 70/30. This early entrepreneurial experience proved important in training Jean Paul how to bargain with older men. His partnership was based on his finding the wells, negotiating the terms, making the deals, and then seeking his father's permission to close the deal. His expenses were fixed at $100 a month. George insisted on maintaining control, however, and Jean Paul had to work on the condition that no investment would be made unless it had long-term potential, beyond immediate profits. Long-term opportunity was a key to all his investments from that day forward.

THE NANCY TAYLOR ALLOTMENT

Getty had a penchant for going first class from an early age. Living well was important for him and work allowed him that luxury. Learning to buy low and sell high was key to making enough money to support his expanding lifestyle. In his journal he wrote, "Oil is like a wild animal. Whoever captures it has it" (Lenzner, p. 18). But the young Getty struggled in Oklahoma. In the first year he worked diligently with little success. Then he came across an opportunity that offered a large potential gain. It was an oil lease on a property known as the Nancy Taylor Allotment. However, the lease was to be sold at public auction and Jean Paul feared that he would be outbid by the many other competitors who had shown an interest in the property. Marshalling all his courage, the savvy youth went to the local bank and asked them to represent him in the public auction. It worked! The other competitors assumed that the bank must be bidding on behalf of a large company with the resources to outbid them, so they dropped out of the bidding early. Getty won the lease on the Nancy Taylor. At 23 years of age, he had already secured his first big lease. He had learned early that image is everything: using the bank was a ploy that kept the auction from becoming a bidding war. Getty knew that to be big, one had to look and act big. That was often difficult in the early days when he was more bluster than balance sheet.

Those early years in Tulsa provided valuable lessons that would serve him for the rest of his life. On that experience, Getty once commented (Lenzner, p. 21):

> *[I learned that] the one who had the most information was the one likely to get the most information in return...After my experiences in Tulsa I knew all the nuts and bolts of the oil industry.*

Getty had learned from his father to chase only the best and most productive oil leases. "Chasing the best" was a philosophy that he would soon apply to women, clothes, yachts and homes. But all of these (except perhaps the women) had to be acquired at a discount. He never bought at the top no matter how badly he wanted a property. Gradually, he acquired the reputation of a man who would deal. For anyone wanting to make a cash deal, Getty was the guy.

Within two years the Nancy Taylor Allotment lease was producing a few hundred barrels a day and his 30% share made him a millionaire. The impetuous youth decided that he had all the money he would need for the rest of his life, so he left Oklahoma for the sunny beaches of Southern California to retire, *at the age of 24*, to a life of wine, women, and parties.

RETIRING FROM RETIREMENT

Getty's retirement to a life of hedonism lasted less than two years. In his own words, "A total lack of work brought me nothing but boredom, restlessness and a sense of futility." Returning to the oil business to work with his father, Jean Paul Getty had learned at an early age that he thrived on challenge.

By the early 1920s the Getty oil interests had moved into southern California where every drilling seemed to yield a productive well. J. Paul Getty was living the fast life in Los Angeles and frolicking with the Hollywood crowd. He also spent considerable time at Jack Doyle's boxing arena where he worked out on the heavy bag. Teddy Hayes, a trainer of boxing legend Jack Dempsey, claimed that Getty actually sparred three rounds with the champion and "did very well." Apparently the hard manual labor in the oil fields and the training at Jack Doyle's had endowed Getty with the physical constitution and stamina that would sustain him through the conflicts that lay ahead.

ACQUIRING CONTROL OF TIDEWATER

In October 1929, the stock market crashed, launching the Great Depression. On May 31 of the following year, Jean Paul's father, now over 75, suffered a stroke and died. Jean Paul inherited $500,000–a small fraction of his father's estate. His friends and associates advised him to liquidate all his assets and hold his wealth in cash because they believed that the economy was about to collapse. Jean Paul felt otherwise. As expressed in his autobiography (Getty, p. 15):

> *I didn't see things that way at all. I was convinced the nation's economy was essentially sound–that though it might sag lower in the near future, it would eventually bounce back, healthier than ever. I thought it was the time to buy–not sell.*

Jean Paul began buying up oil stocks at 5% of their asset value. He saw the future while the rest of the world was scrambling to survive. This tends to be the economic climate in which so many of life's great opportunities are manifest. Throughout the Depression, young Getty accumulated the stock of the Tide Water Associated Oil Company at a bargain. He used his existing wells, and a few he garnered from his mother (who inherited the bulk of the George Getty estate), to get the needed cash. Between 1932 and 1937, Getty had accumulated 25% of the shares of what was later renamed Tidewater Oil. Even with his ingenious maneuvering, he was never able to buy up what he would have if the cash had been more plentiful.

His objective was control of Tidewater, a Standard Oil holding company. Always living on the high-risk fringe, Getty wanted to invest where he saw unrealized value, while his cautious mother wanted him to follow a more conservative approach. However, Jean Paul seldom listened to anyone, even his mother. After numerous fights he finally convinced her to give him control of the family trust. It was then that he took over Tidewater. That early leveraging during the worst economy in U.S. history led him to become an oil tycoon. Had he listened to his well-meaning mother he would have become only moderately successful. However, through his calculated risk-taking approach, he would later gain control of Tidewater and see its assets reach one billion dollars during the 1960s.

BUYING WHEN EVERYONE IS SELLING

In tough economic times, the world is rampant with distress merchandise and cash is king. One such "distress acquisition" by Getty was the Hotel Pierre in New York City. The Hotel Pierre had a prestigious location at Fifth Avenue and 60th Street, with a full view of Central Park. However, in 1938 the prolonged Depression had taken a severe toll on the revenues of the Pierre. The hotel was in serious financial difficulties, so although Getty had no understanding of or interest in the hotel industry, he knew a bargain when he saw one. Discovering that he could buy the virtually new hotel for one-fourth its original cost, he realized that there was a huge upside potential with very little downside risk. He immediately paid $2.35 million cash and began using it as his East Coast home. Fifteen years later, when friend Frank Ryan called him with an offer of $17.5 million–over seven times his cost–he took the offer on the spot and walked away with a $15-million dollar cash profit. Many such cash deals were made over the years. The more deals he made, the more deals were offered. Garth Young of Signal Oil described his chief competitor Getty as a visionary, a man who "could see further than any other guy I knew" (Lenzner, p. 100).

In acquiring assets in Tidewater, Getty inadvertently obtained some ownership in the Skelly Oil Company in Tulsa. Skelly Oil had a subsidiary, Spartan Aircraft Corporation, that had been manufacturing aircraft since 1928. In February 1942, as President of Spartan Aircraft, Getty undertook to serve the war effort by managing the production of aircraft parts and the training of aircrew. Under his direction, the company reached a peak of 5500 employees and was training an average of 3000 pilots per year. When World War II was over, Getty remained at Spartan until 1948 to help the company in its conversion from aircraft parts to house trailers.

EXPLORING FOR OIL IN THE MIDDLE EAST

World War II accelerated the demand for oil, which depleted the oil reserves in the western world. Oil exploration was reaching out to other areas of the world by the late 1940s. In February 1949, Getty obtained from Ibn Saud, the king of Saudi Arabia, a 60-year oil lease on land in the Neutral Zone. This was an arid stretch of desert land between Saudi Arabia and Kuwait that was relatively unexplored. Since there had been no previous evidence of oil in this region, an oil lease might have been regarded as a triumph of hope over reason. In exchange for granting the right to explore and drill for oil, Getty paid the Saudi Arabian government $9.5 million plus $1 million per year whether they struck oil or not. In telling this story, Getty recalled (Getty, p. 21):

> *It was a gargantuan risk and many people in the petroleum industry once again openly predicted I would bankrupt my firms and myself. Four years and $18 million were needed before we brought in our first producing well in the Neutral Zone. But by 1954, I could relax and enjoy a private last laugh at the expense of those who had prophesied my ruin.*

These rich oil fields turned out to be among the most productive ever discovered, with yields exceeding 16 million barrels a year. Such yields necessitated the construction of huge oil refineries and gigantic supertankers to transport the oil from the Middle East to the Americas. In 1954 the first fleet of supertankers was under construction and by the mid-1950s, oil was being shipped all over the world from the Middle East. During this expansionary phase, Pacific Western became Getty Oil and the Getty Empire was in full flower. In 1957, *Fortune* magazine named him the richest man in America. J. Paul Getty decided, for the second time in his life, that it was time to enjoy his wealth.

THE FINAL YEARS IN ENGLAND

In 1959, at 66 years of age, J. Paul Getty acquired Sutton Place in Sussex, England, from the Duke of Sutherland. It was an opportunity that he couldn't afford to miss. The Duke of Sutherland was unable to maintain the mansion. Sensing his desperation, Getty seized his chance to become a part of the landed gentry by buying the multi-million-dollar estate for the ridiculously low price of $600,000. The upkeep on the property was exorbitant, but the shrewd Getty set it up as part of his European operations and maintained it out of company funds. Even the additional acquisition cost of $140,000 (for land transfer and closing fees) was paid with a check from Getty Oil.

The two things that Getty truly loved were women and oil, and not necessarily in that order. Each of his five wives was certain that oil was #1. Having been raised by a cold mother and business-like father, the only child spent his life in search of love. Unable to give love, he attempted to secure what he was missing through sexual conquest. His money allowed him to buy whatever affection he needed and he indulged his need with a gallery of attractive and sophisticated women.

Getty's palatial estate at Sutton Place became his den of iniquity for the last two decades of his life. His sexual prowess with women was legendary. B. W. von Block, ghostwriter of one of Getty's autobiographies, interviewed women who had been sexually intimate with the charismatic billionaire. They all reported that J. Paul Getty was, indeed, an extremely satisfying lover who ensured that his partner reached orgasm. Furthermore, it was reported from several sources that Getty's physical machinery was well-suited to the task. Lenzner states (p. 135):

> *Turron [a former FBI agent] believed that Getty was "as well hung as any man I sever saw, maybe 8½ inches long in the swimming pool."*

No record of the water temperature in the pool accompanied the estimate of length.

The connection between libido and the entrepreneurial drive is not capricious. In about 1900, Sigmund Freud had suggested that human productivity is a consequence of sublimated sexual passion. In Getty's case, it the sublimation was only partial. Lenzner observed (p. 135):

> *Getty himself felt that success in business and success with women were inextricably connected. He told von Block that "business success generated a sexual drive, and that sexual drive pushed business."*

While Getty's reputation as the world's richest person bought him flocks of females who attended to all his needs, his extreme wealth brought him a host of problems unique to the super-wealthy. In his book that he wrote while living at Sutton Place, *How to be Rich,* he provided an insight into some of these exigencies (pp. 193-4):

> *The effect a rich man's money will have on others is often surprising, sometimes barely believable, and by no means always salutary or ennobling. I've said before that a millionaire is a marked man. There are many who consider him an easy mark as well...I recall one man who tried to sell me what he said was a rare 16th Century tapestry, and for "a mere $45,000." When I told him I wasn't interested, he flew into a rage.*
>
> *"But you've got to buy it!" he shouted, thrusting the tapestry at me. "My wife worked months to make it!"*

J. Paul Getty also mentioned in his book that he received up to 3000 letters per month from strangers, 70% of them requesting money. Among them was a letter from a banker who had embezzled $100,000 and was requesting that sum so he could make good on the money he had stolen. On one particular day, Getty claimed that the requests for handouts exceeded $15,000,000.

Among the worst of the trials and tribulations he faced as a consequence of his wealth was the kidnapping of his grandson J. Paul III. On July 12, 1973 Gail, the mother of Paul III, received a ransom call from hoodlums based in southern Italy who were demanding money for the release of her son. When she approached J. Paul Getty for help in meeting the 300 million lira ($500,000) ransom demand, Getty responded, "I have 14 other grandchildren and if I pay one penny ransom, I'll have 14 kidnapped grandchildren." Cat-and-mouse negotiations with the kidnappers spanned several months. Then on November 10, Paul III's mother received a package containing her son's right ear and a note threatening that other body parts would follow if the ransom wasn't paid. By this time the ransom demand had escalated to 1700 million lira ($3.2 million). After more negotiation, J. Paul Getty finally capitulated and paid the ransom. On December 13, after 6 months of captivity, Paul III was released. The kidnappers, discovered to be part of a ring of drug-dealers, were brought to trial. Of the $3.2 million ransom, only $17,000 was recovered.

Amidst the family traumas and harassment from panhandlers and mercenary acquaintances, Getty continued to focus on building and expanding his empire even as he moved into his 80s. On May 5, 1976, blood tests revealed that J. Paul Getty was dying of prostate cancer. He refused an operation because he did not want to suffer the temporary loss of control that he would experience if anesthetized. He did agree to take female hormones to reduce the cancer growth, but expressed concern about whether this treatment would impair his sexual function.

Then, on June 6, 1976, only a month after his diagnosis, J. Paul Getty succumbed to the cancer–exactly three years to the day after his eldest son George had committed suicide!

Devoted assistant and lover Penelope Kits, displaying the English penchant for understatement, said at his funeral (Miller, p. 302):

He was a true eccentric. Only an eccentric could have achieved what he achieved. He was a genius in his way but very naughty.

Getty's Decade-by-Decade Climb

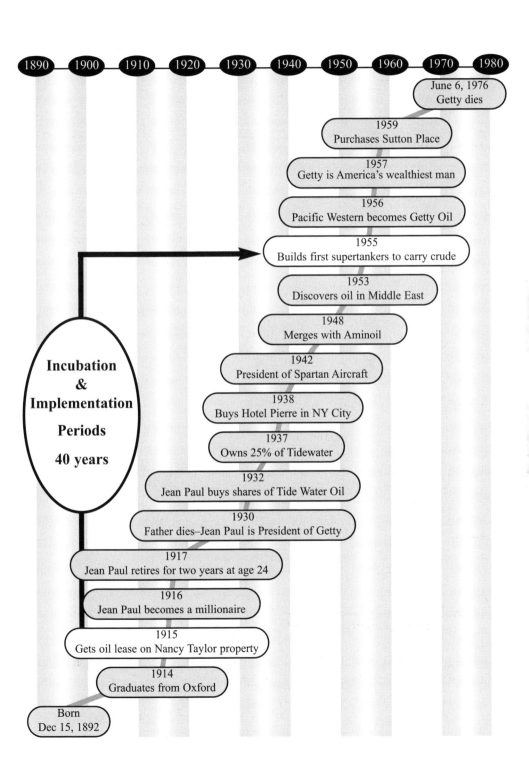

1890 1900 1910 1920 1930 1940 1950 1960 1970 1980

June 6, 1976
Getty dies

1959
Purchases Sutton Place

1957
Getty is America's wealthiest man

1956
Pacific Western becomes Getty Oil

1955
Builds first supertankers to carry crude

1953
Discovers oil in Middle East

1948
Merges with Aminoil

1942
President of Spartan Aircraft

1938
Buys Hotel Pierre in NY City

1937
Owns 25% of Tidewater

1932
Jean Paul buys shares of Tide Water Oil

1930
Father dies–Jean Paul is President of Getty

Incubation
&
Implementation
Periods
40 years

1917
Jean Paul retires for two years at age 24

1916
Jean Paul becomes a millionaire

1915
Gets oil lease on Nancy Taylor property

1914
Graduates from Oxford

Born
Dec 15, 1892

A *Personality Profile*

INTUITIONAL STYLE: INFORMED BY ANALYSIS

Getty was a true Promethean–an intuitive thinker on a grand scale, a man who chased opportunities with passion. From his earliest years, he was using his intuition to decide where he might find oil and where drilling might pay dividends. In commenting on his good fortune in drilling so many successful oil wells, Getty modestly claimed, "I still think my early successes were due mainly to pure luck." However, J. Paul Getty used intuition, enhanced by the information that he was constantly absorbing. In comparing his approach to that of others prospecting for oil, Getty explained (Getty, p. 6):

> There were no secrets, no mystical formulas behind these successes. I operated in much the same manner as did almost all wildcatters–with one important exception. In those days, the science of petroleum geology had not yet gained very wide acceptance in the oil fields...I was among the few who believed in geology. I studied the subject avidly at every opportunity, and applied what I learned to my operations.

Getty's understanding of the need to inform his intuition is evident in his adage, "No man's opinions are better than his information." He further elaborated on the need for a careful assessment of information and its source before making decisions (Getty, p. 65):

> Opinion is never better than the information on which it is based, the qualifications of the person voicing it and his ability to correctly interpret the information at his disposal.

For him information was godly. It made him almost pathologically inquisitive about the most trivial of facts. If he wasn't able to get the numbers on a deal, he didn't do it. His adversary, Joe Cumberland, once observed (Lenzner, p. 117):

> [Getty] could tell you every single well, where the casing was set, what it cost to drill, what it was producing. He had it all in his head, an intricate knowledge of geophysics, engineering. It was really impressive.

RISK-TAKING PROPENSITY

Entrepreneurs like J. Paul Getty test the limits in most things and display a high propensity for risk-taking. One of his most frequently quoted comments was, "The meek shall inherit the earth, but not the mineral rights." He loved to roll the dice on oil ventures and did so with the flair of a high-stakes gambler. But he was always astute enough to hedge his gambles with the numbers. When betting big in his takeover of Tidewater, he was aware it was a win-it-all or lose-it-all game and admitted that if he had failed, he would have been "penniless."

The oil impresario saw risk as key to success and wrote in his memoirs, "There are a hundred men seeking security to one able man willing to risk his fortune." But the media refused to see him as anything but frugal because his eccentricities made better copy. It was true that Getty never picked up a tab if he didn't have to. However, when Getty saw a potential gain, he paid up. Few people understand that frugality has little or nothing to do with risk-taking. Oil exploration is a major gamble from the outset. It is akin to commodities trading where millions are gained and lost daily. It is not a game for the meek and Getty would never have made it in that world had he not been a high roller. Consider the odds in hitting it big in oil. There is a 10% chance of drilling a productive well and a mere 2.5% chance of hitting a gusher on any particular drilling.

Perhaps the most dramatic example of Getty's risk-taking propensity and use of leverage was his investment in the Middle East Neutral Zone oil reserves. After exploring in the "rough outback" of an Arabian desert and finding nothing but dry holes for four years, he found himself teetering on the brink of financial ruin. Yet Getty followed his instincts and persisted until he was finally rewarded with the discovery of a gusher of gigantic proportions. Already about 60 years old, he risked his entire fortune on something that could easily have broken him. At an age when most men would consider a conservative approach to investment, J. Paul Getty was putting all of his cash at risk. He bet the bundle on an intuitive feel that there was a lot of oil in the area and that he would be able to get it out and to a refinery. Getty never did anything half way. He had taught himself to speak some Arabic to better negotiate with the Arabs. The associate who helped him with this deal, Dr. Walton, later said, "He was more interested in the challenge than the money."

It was through his propensity for high risk that the eccentric became a billionaire. He dared what lesser men feared and that set him apart. J. Paul Getty was the consummate Big T (testosterone) personality–those specially empowered by creativity, aggressiveness, risk-taking and a high sex drive. The Middle East venture, clearly his grandest gamble, proved to be his biggest victory. Before his Middle East venture he was merely wealthy; after it, he was the richest man in the world. Such is the nature of pushing the limits.

INTENSITY

Former heavyweight champion boxer Jack Dempsey once described J. Paul Getty as (Lenzner, p. 28):

> *"well built, pugnacious by nature, and quick. I've never met any boy with such intense concentration and will power–perhaps more than is good for him."*

When working on anything, Getty was impatient to a fault. He operated with a kind of kinetic energy that was frustrating and debilitating to those less driven. A flattering description was that Getty was a "man with a mania for efficiency." The purchasing agent for Spartan Aircraft once observed (Lenzner, pp. 82-3):

> *[Getty's] mania was efficiency and more efficiency. He demanded it and he got it. When he was away from Tulsa each manager had to write a daily log of all his activities and these were given to Getty at the end of the week, thus fulfilling his passion for day-to-day control.*

Getty wanted to make the deal and get on with the enjoyment of reveling in what he had accomplished. Like most great entrepreneurs, he was a man on a mission and was not inclined to waste time on those he regarded as losers or inhabitants in the sea of mediocrity.

Getty approached courtship the way he approached a business deal. In this respect, women and oil leases were indistinguishable. Both were useful commodities to Getty and he was relentless but unemotional in their pursuit. He felt marriage should be treated as a business contract, not some romantic liaison. He wrote in *As I See It*, "I felt just because I was married was not a good reason for me to deliberately avoid my other women friends." Getty considered courtship a mundane activity for the masses. He eloped with his first two wives to avoid the time-consuming rituals of meeting parents and planning elaborate weddings. The marriages were short-lived since he had no time to share and therefore received little commitment in return. Consequently, he left a long trail of women in his wake.

Moderation was not a word used to describe J. Paul Getty–personally or professionally. Five marriages attest to this in his personal life and his off-the-wall negotiating tactics substantiate it in his professional life. Most everything he did or desired was in excess. He lived large and he partied large, and if it wasn't a large, flashy work of art, he was not interested. Getty was never content with a lot of money, he had to have the most. He was not content with one adoring woman, he had to have three or four. He was not satisfied with building a small tribute to his life, he had to build (in Southern California) the most grandiose monument since the Taj Mahal. When he got a face-lift, one wasn't enough. He kept at it until he felt he had it right. (Ironically, they made his nose and ears look larger and had the opposite effect intended.) When young, he was not content with being the largest stockholder in Tidewater Associates, Getty had to control the whole company.

SELF-IMAGE: RUGGED INDIVIDUALIST AND EMPEROR REINCARNATE

J. Paul Getty saw himself as a rugged individualist and champion of the free enterprise system. He lamented the inexorable growth of government and its increasing interference in business. He reflected (Getty, p. 141):

I glimpse myself as an anarchist–regretting the growth of government and the ever-increasing trend toward regulation and, worst of all, standardization of human activity.

Getty railed against what he perceived as a trend away from rugged individualism and toward institutional homogeneity. He further asserted that the survival of the free enterprise system resided with the entrepreneurs who could resist the security of conformity and pursue their own visions. He wrote (Getty, p. 151):

There is, however, hope for any person who wants to remain an individual. He can assert himself and refuse to conform. He'll be on his own, that's true, but while he will not have the security enjoyed by those who do conform, there will be no limits to what he may achieve....One needs only to remember that a groove may be safe–but that, as one wears away at it, the groove becomes first a rut and finally a grave.

When Jean Paul's father George died of a stroke in 1930, the Getty Trust was turned over to Jean Paul's mother, Sarah, to administer. George had written, "J. Paul is not to be trusted to run the family business." That comment left a lasting impression on Jean Paul. As noted by *A & E Biography* commentator Peter Graves, "J. Paul Getty spent the rest of his life attempting to prove his father wrong." It wasn't long before he conceived a plan to wrest control of the trust from his aging mother. Later he confided to close associate Howard Jarvis, "I just fleeced my mother." Jarvis was a Mormon and aghast that a man of his wealth would stoop to cheating his eighty-year-old mother.

In spite of his quest to be loved and his struggle to prove his father wrong, J. Paul Getty had a strong sense of self. In speaking about the qualities needed to go against the trend, he observed (Getty, p. 16):

> *In business, as in politics, it is never easy to go against the beliefs and attitudes held by the majority. The businessman who moves counter to the tide of prevailing opinion must expect to be obstructed, derided, and damned.*

Getty was an astute observer of human nature. He understood that playing the role of renegade would bring rejection, but it was also the path to success. Always the inveterate loner, Getty was never one of the crowd, looked upon as a maverick by friends and family alike. Money, in and of itself, never held a high place for him and he chased it for the pleasure of the game and for the notoriety and women that came with it. Had he been less successful in accumulating wealth, history may have written him off as a womanizing sociopath.

The fantasy life he lived came close to the edge in his later years when he came to believe that he was destined for immortality as a Roman conqueror. With this provocative reincarnation in mind, he acquired an Italian villa to enshrine himself as a Hadrian-like Caesar. In his memoirs, he wrote, "I would like to believe I am the reincarnation of Hadrian's spirit and I would like to emulate him as closely as I can" (Lenzner, p. 136). One New York antiques dealer characterized Getty as having a god-like persona. "In his mind Getty came close to being king of the world. He only wanted to buy regal works of art" (Lenzner, p. 178). His fantasies began to intrude upon his reality when he started writing things like "I feel no qualms about likening the Getty Oil Company to an Empire–and myself to a Caesar" (Lenzner, p. 139).

ECCENTRICITIES AND PERSONAL PARADOXES

J. Paul Getty was not only different, but he was so far outside convention in most things that the media labeled him eccentric. That is not unusual for great entrepreneurs. Like many of them, he was also pathologically insecure and, as he admitted in his memoirs, obsessed with the fear of failure. Such people deal with insecurity by masking it with an overriding arrogance. (We observed a similar characteristic in our profile of Coco Chanel.) A close look at the world's most vociferous innovators, such as Pablo Picasso, Adolph Hitler and Frank Lloyd Wright, reveals arrogant overachievers masking internal fears. Their strong sense of self serves to offset inner feelings of doubt. Entrepreneurs like Perot, Stewart and Trump (profiled in this book) also display these characteristics.

In middle age, Getty was on a plane struck by lightning. The experience left such a scar on his psyche that he never again boarded an airplane. Like many successful people, he was highly superstitious. On one occasion a European fortune-teller implied that the next trip across the Atlantic would be his last. He never made that trip, spending the last two decades of his life in England. Such fears kept him from seeing the Getty Museum in Malibu, his glorious tribute to art that cost $17 million.

It is surprising that a man with a penchant for control would leave all his money to total strangers, with no strings attached. This was a man who monitored every penny of his expenditures. He kept track of what he spent on each guest for dinner, and would allot to their entertainment only the amount that was commensurate with their perceived merit. One biographer wrote, "Getty put a financial value on everything including friends and lovers." This comment is reminiscent of Oscar Wilde's depiction of a cynic as one who "knows the price of everything but the value of nothing."

ACHIEVEMENTS & HONORS

MAGNITUDE OF SUCCESS

The splendor of the Getty Museum is living testimony to the grand style and flair Getty had for life. Such opulent and conspicuous consumption dominated his life and his death. Perhaps as an attempt to follow the tradition of ancient pharaohs who were buried in their tombs, Getty requested burial in his mythical mansion with two of his estranged sons lying alongside him.

Getty's main contributions were his discovery of oil reserves in the Middle East and his investment in refineries and supertankers. His enterprise is responsible for bringing to the world huge supplies of oil and gas that, even today, continue to supply the ever-increasing world demand for fossil fuels. The refineries and supertankers also employ tens of thousands of people world-wide. At the time of his death in 1976, he bequeathed to his museum four million shares of Getty Oil, worth $662 million, and the Sarah Getty Trust, owning approximately double that number of shares, worth about $1.3 billion.

The paradox of Getty's life and death can be found in the billions he left to the Getty Museum, all aimed at aggrandizing his life. The Getty Museum is the largest endowment ever made without restrictions on its use.

HONORS

After Getty had donated $20,000 to the Mayor of St. Nazaire, France, where he had chosen to build his fleet of oil tankers, the French honored him with the Légion d'honneur. His $207-million gamble was enhanced when he persuaded the French to subsidize 55% of the cost of these gargantuan ships. The Getty supertankers rendered obsolete the rest of the world's oil-transporting ships. In 1957, *Fortune* named him the richest man in America.

LESSONS LEARNED FROM JEAN PAUL GETTY

Jean Paul Getty has taught us several important lessons by example. Two of the most pervasive in all his business activity are presented below.

THERE ARE NO BIG WINS WITHOUT BIG RISKS

Risk is embedded in the concept of entrepreneurship. However, most people seek risk-free opportunities. In reality, there is no such thing as a big gain without significant risk. Furthermore, risk and reward have a strong positive correlation. That is, the amount of the reward is roughly proportional to the amount of risk involved. Most people allow their fears to dominate their decisions and in so doing, limit the size of their potential rewards. More than a century ago, advisors told Andrew Carnegie to diversify his investments, but he declined, stating in his autobiography:

> *I decided to go entirely contrary to the adage not to put your eggs all in one basket. I determined to put all the good eggs in one basket and then watch that basket.*

That strategy made him the richest man in the world in 1900 with a fortune in excess of $300 million–$10 billion in today's dollars.

J. Paul Getty was a strong advocate of risk-taking, but he insisted on employing a careful assessment of the risks involved before taking the final plunge (Getty, p. 68):

> *The businessman who is able to calculate his risks–and then is willing to take them–has his battle for success nine-tenths won. The remaining one-tenth is the unknown variable, the unpredictable factor that puts the zest and excitement into the game. Without the "x" factor, business would be hopelessly dull, routine and uninteresting.*

In the entrepreneurial world, it is important to live on the edge where your competitors don't dare go. However, like Getty and other high-risk takers, it is essential that you gather as much information as possible before taking the plunge. When competing with older corporations, you have an advantage because their size and need for safety dictate that they behave conservatively. That is why few great innovations come out of such organizations. They mitigate risk, unaware that they are simultaneously mitigating potential. Helen Keller once observed, "Security is mostly a superstition." However, those with substantial assets understandably wish to protect their asset base and invest their money in low-risk ventures. Psychological studies have shown that when people choose between the receipt of a guaranteed $80 or a wager with an 85% chance to earn $100, the majority choose the $80, even though that is not the more mathematically prudent option.

A corollary to the principle of taking calculated risks is the adage, "Buy when everyone is selling." As noted earlier, Getty bought the Hotel Pierre when it was losing money and the general consensus was that its prospects for recovery were dismal. Getty observed (Getty, p. 199):

> *Conrad Hilton started buying and building hotels when most other hoteliers were eagerly scanning all available horizons for prospective buyers on whom they could unload their properties....I, myself, began buying stocks during the Depression when shares were selling at bargain-basement prices and "everyone" believed they would fall even lower.*

A caveat in applying this principle is that timing is crucial. When Getty first began buying common stock in 1930, he bought on margin and near-ly lost everything when shares plummeted. He said later (Lenzner, p. 36):

> *My stock purchases were financed by every dollar I possessed and every cent of credit I could obtain. Had I lost the campaign...I would have been left personally penniless and very much in debt.*

Successful entrepreneurs are willing to bet the farm on their dream, which is why they have led the way in almost all new frontiers. Entrepreneurs like Carnegie, Edison and Ford were always willing to go further than their peers. That is why they died rich and famous.

As I noted in the preface, few people buy into new ideas in the beginning of a venture. That is the dilemma facing the entrepreneur. Most people view new ideas as worthless. This means that the proper time to launch a new idea is when few others see the opportunity. Entrepreneurs tend to represent the 1% of people who see the possibilities lost on the other 99%. Oil tycoon J. Paul Getty observed (Getty, p. 115):

> *All top businessmen I know have made their biggest strides up the success ladder because they were able to see the possible in what others rejected or ignored as the impossible.*

LEVERAGE IS THE FAST WAY TO GROW (AND LOSE) MONEY

When you leverage your existing property for more property, especially in an inflationary environment, the wins can be huge. If you guess right you grow quickly. If wrong, you can lose it all. Getty became a master of leverage. He learned the nuances of leverage as a teenager when his father allowed him to buy an interest in the Getty Oil fields. As a young man he became a wildcatter in the Oklahoma oil fields and once again borrowed money from his father to buy up oil property. It worked and he was a millionaire by 23. The die was cast.

Leverage is a two-edged sword. Using existing assets to buy new ones is one way of growing fast. But in leverage the present assets are as much at risk as the new ones. When you win at this game you can grow exponentially; when you lose it can also be exponential. One of the keys to using leverage is to ensure your ability to service the debt. In other words, you must be willing to lose what you have to win what you don't yet have. That is the bet. And despite what Donald Trump said in his autobiography–that he never gambled–he used leverage to the extreme. You will see this in Chapter 9, Donald Trump's profile. Leveraging your assets is just another form of gambling. It can make you or break you, so you need to calculate the odds carefully.

Entrepreneurs Thomas Edison and Henry Ford exploited leverage to the limit. Did they pay a price for their temerity? Huge! Both went bankrupt and often lived on the edge of insolvency. But both men died wealthy–not because they got lucky or changed their ways, but because of their daring. Rupert Murdoch and Ted Turner were of a similar persuasion. Both media barons were high rollers beyond the pale of most men. Few people would be willing to bet everything–billions in the case of both men–by leveraging their existing properties to buy new ones. Murdoch almost lost it all in the early '90s when his Fox network and other worldwide investments came tumbling down like a house of cards. To his credit he sold off many cherished ventures to survive. Turner did the same with CNN and then a few years later when he tendered an offer for CBS. Both are now worth billions.

J. Paul Getty's understanding of leverage and the principle of using other people's money is captured in one of his most popular quotes, "If you owe the bank $100, that's your problem. If you owe the bank $100 million, that's the bank's problem."

The Wonderful World of Bucky Fuller

The chapter you are about to read enables you to look into the past at the predictions of the world's first "futurist." Fuller's inventions anticipated many of the

advances that have come only recently, as well as others that are yet to come. The picture on the right shows his Dymaxion House, designed in 1929 as a low-cost solution to the public housing problem. Many of its features are now embodied in what is called today, the "smart house."

The picture below shows Fuller's Dymaxion Car, invented in 1933. It had a single rear wheel that enabled it to park in a space four feet shorter than a conventional car and it had an air-cooled V-8 90 hp engine that enabled it to attain a speed of 120 miles per hour. When first shown to the public, it was such a sensation that people swarmed around it causing traffic jams.

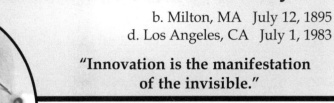

Buckminster Fuller

Chase a Vision, Never Money

b. Milton, MA   July 12, 1895
d. Los Angeles, CA   July 1, 1983

**"Innovation is the manifestation
of the invisible."**

SELF-DESCRIPTION
"I am a design science revolutionary and I'm the
world's most successful failure."

MOTTOS
"Intuition is terribly important to design."
"All of matter is synergistic."

INNOVATION

"We are not going to be able to operate Spaceship Earth successfully nor for much longer unless we see it as a whole spaceship and our fate as common. It has to be everybody or nobody."

UNIQUE QUALITY

Lived outside conventional boundaries, years ahead of his time–an eccentric innovator who predicted the Internet in 1962. Thriving on ambiguity, he defined entrepreneurial success as antiestablishmentarianism.

OBJECTIVE

"To achieve more and more in less and less time." He conceptualized *ephemeralization* as the path to success.

NET WORTH

Never deified money and wrote, "Money is entropic. You can make money or make sense because the two are mutually exclusive."

HONORS

47 Honorary Doctorates; Arthur C. Clarke wrote, "Bucky is the first engineering saint."

BIRTH ORDER

Second born of 4, three years younger than brother, Leslie

EDUCATION

Expelled from Harvard twice for dissident behavior.

PERSONALITY

Raging optimist and visionary, with a penchant for seeing technological opportunities ahead of their time.

HOBBIES

Fast vehicles and fast living in a world too slow for him

POLITICS

"I am transpolitics."

RELIGION

Buddhist

FAMILY

Wife: Anne, Daughters: Alexandra, Allegra

4
BUCKMINSTER FULLER

Chase a Vision, Never Money

"Truth is always approximate. Truth is a tendency."

Overview

Bucky Fuller has often been described as the 20th century's Leonardo da Vinci. He was the quintessential entrepreneur, but so far ahead of his time he never achieved anything close to his potential. Industrialists, Wall Street pundits and other scientists were afraid of him. When the volatile 1960s hit, Fuller was rediscovered by counter-culture intellectuals who loved his off-the-wall wit and erudite sense of the future. By then, he had long since given up trying to sell his ideas to the establishment for mass production. In fact, he had concocted the phrase "Legally Piggilys" to describe those who resisted progressive change, such as the auto firms and oil companies who resisted the production of fuel-efficient cars because they would render obsolete the present vehicles and bring a loss of revenues. He often quoted J. P. Morgan when he was told an invention that would inhibit iron from rusting. J. P. Morgan's response? "Young man, you must be crazy. The more it rusts, the more I sell." The sad commentary on Fuller's life is that many of his most incredible discoveries were never funded and never built because of such vested interests.

The central thrust of Buckminster Fuller's philosophy was to do more with less, a principle he referred to as "ephemeralization." He believed that by optimizing our present resources and using them efficiently, we could raise the standard of living of everyone in the world to that which is currently enjoyed by only the top 5% of the population. Bucky applied his ephemeralization principle to the structure of buildings, the design of cars, and even the design of communities.

The multi-disciplinary nature of his work is epitomized in his majestic geodesic dome for which he is universally known. He reasoned that the tetrahedron, a pyramid with a triangular base, is the strongest geometric solid

A tetrahedron

because it can retain its shape and remain undeformed under extreme external forces. In articulating his first principle of structural design, Fuller stated (Hatch, p. 153):

> *The tetrahedron is the basic structural system, and all structure in the universe is made up of tetrahedral parts.*

To apply ephemeralization to the design of structures, Bucky Fuller used the fact that a sphere has a smaller surface area than any other geometric form containing the same amount of space. Hence, a structure built in the shape of a sphere requires less material than any other structure. Fuller referred to his use of tetrahedra as the building blocks for forming spherical shapes as his "synergetic geometry" (Hatch, p. 97):

> *I use energetic and synergetic geometry–the basic building block of the universe, because it has the greatest strength with the least surface.*

By creating "spherical" structures composed of tetrahedral building blocks, Fuller was able to construct what he called *geodesic domes*. These geodesic domes were extremely strong from a structural standpoint because they were composed of tetrahedra, and extremely efficient from a material standpoint because they were spherical.

Fuller's relentless quest for optimal speed, performance, and efficiency led him to adopt the term *Dymaxion*–a conjunction of the words *dynamic, maximum* and *tension*–to describe the embodiment of these three qualities in a single entity. The Dymaxion concept found its way into a myriad of Fuller's creations that are described in more detail later in this chapter, namely Dymaxion House (1927), the Dymaxion Automobile (1933) and the Dymaxion Map (1943). In spite of his many and varied contributions to civilization, the world remembers Bucky for the geodesic dome that pervades our consciousness each time we walk into EPCOT or watch a ball game at a domed stadium.

The story of Bucky Fuller's recovery from the brink of suicide (after the tragic death of his daughter) to his status as one of the 20th century's greatest intellects, embodies the drama and pathos of the human condition. It will forever stand as one of the great stories of a visionary's struggle against the inertia of conventional thought. As Bucky himself used to say as he launched yet another of his many lectures (Baldwin, p. 2):

> *I'd like to introduce myself as the world's most successful failure.*

The Formative Years

EARLY EXPERIENCES

Buckminster Fuller was born on July 12, 1895 in Milton, Massachusetts, the second of four children. His father, a successful merchant, died prematurely of a stroke when Bucky was ten. He credits his dad for inculcating in him the need for independence and nurturing his Robin Hood sense of values. His father read to Bucky the tales of the altruistic renegade from Sherwood Forest. Bucky led an almost mythical life based on a sense of adventure that he learned from books. He grew up thinking of himself as a new age Robin Hood, defying the power elite in order to bring technological progress to mankind. The following comments from Bucky's own book, *Critical Path*, offer insight into his assessment of that early influence (p. 134) :

> *Robin Hood...became my most influential early-years' mythical hero...In inaugurating my new life, I took away Robin Hood's longbow, staff, and checkbook, and gave him only scientific textbooks, microscopes, calculating machines, transits, and industrialization's tooling. I made him substitute new inanimate forms for animate reforms.*

Young Bucky showed signs of seriously impaired vision that was corrected with Coke-bottle glasses at age 4. After receiving the lenses, he began to excel. By age 6, he had already built his first tetrahedral octet truss out of toothpicks and dried peas. This kindergarten creation was a simplistic model for the geodesic dome that he would perfect forty years later. As a young lad, he was precocious but not well adjusted. Like many other visionaries he was bored with the needless routine and often didn't bother to attend class. By age 12, Bucky was already driving a car and by age 21, he had flown an open-cockpit plane.

FORMAL EDUCATION

Fuller attended Milton Academy and Harvard, the two schools attended by a long line of Fullers. At Harvard, Bucky found a class system that he felt cast him as an outsider. He claimed that he was excluded from the "in-group" because of his lack of wealth and absence of a father to look after him. His friend and biographer Alden Hatch suggests that this explanation was merely a rationalization and that he was ostracized because he was different (Hatch, p. 32):

> *The plain truth is that Bucky was too individualistic, too much of an oddball in thought and appearance, to meet the conformist standards of those young, so-sure-of-themselves aristocrats. He was short, carelessly dressed, with a head much too large for his body. His teeth, which had not then been straightened, were oddly arranged and those enormous magnifying lenses made his eyes look like big pools of amber liquid.*

Bucky's desire for acceptance led him to display excessive "party animal" behavior. On one occasion, he withdrew his stipend that was to be used for tuition, books, etc. and traveled to New York City where he attended the Zigfeld Follies. He threw a lavish party to which he invited half the Zigfeld Follies chorus line. When it was discovered that he had squandered his entire stipend for living expenses and incurred further bills, Harvard expelled him for what they termed "irresponsible conduct."

His mother used influence to get the wayward man-child a job in Canada until the next term, September 1914, when Harvard reinstated him. His performance, once again, regressed to what it had been before and Harvard expelled him for the second and last time for "lack of sustained interest in the processes within the university."

The Climb to the Top

THE CAREFREE NAVY YEARS

When the U.S. entered World War I, Bucky enlisted in the Navy, impelled by a passion for sailing. It was in this more controlled atmosphere that Fuller found his calling. Practical engineering, as opposed to theoretical constructs, held a special fascination for him. Later he would say that his technical education all took place during his time at Annapolis. Highly inquisitive by nature, he jumped into the regimen and educated himself in mathematics, hydraulics, and aeronautical engineering.

During his stint in the Navy, he went through officer training and began to excel in engineering. His time in the Navy transformed his focus and ignited his passion for innovation. He invented two devices that prevented pilots from drowning when they missed the landing strip on the aircraft carrier. On at least one occasion, he experienced the joy of seeing his invention used to save the life of a pilot whose plane had plunged into the ocean.

While on leave in the summer of 1915, Bucky met Anne Hewlett, the daughter of a renowned New England architect. They dated for a year, became engaged in 1916 and married in 1917. Bucky would comment over a half-century later (Hatch, p. 245), "Certainly one of the most beautiful things about our marriage is that each day now it gets more beautiful."

REACHING THE NADIR

After the war, Bucky embarked on a number of professions but each led nowhere. By 1922, he was unemployed and deep in debt. To alleviate a growing feeling of foreboding, he attended a Harvard-Yale football game and spent the weekend rediscovering his party days. On his return home, his wife Anne, sobbing uncontrollably, informed him that their daughter Alexandra was seriously ill with polio. She died a few hours later in his arms—on her fourth birthday. Bucky blamed himself for not being around during her illness and went into a depression.

To forget the heartbreak, Bucky became a whirlwind of frenetic activity. His father-in-law, Monroe Hewlett, had developed and patented an innovative concrete building block that had exceptional strength and insulation features. Bucky felt the product had revolutionary potential in the home-building markets, so he formed a company, called the Stockade Building System, to manufacture these blocks. As President he invited friends and family to invest in the company. Between 1922 and 1926, the company had factories in four locations and was headquartered in Chicago. Determined to alter the world of housing, he and Anne moved to the Windy City where they had a beautiful apartment overlooking Belmont Harbor on Lake Michigan. To his delight, Anne became pregnant again.

It looked as though good times were ahead. Stockade had built 234 homes featuring the innovative fibrous building blocks and Bucky, like most entrepreneurs, had been deeply immersed in every facet of the process. However, the perfectionist in him had led to refinement after refinement without any near-term prospect of profitability. The older and more conservative businessmen on the board were not as interested in altering the world of building as they were in making an immediate profit. Sacrificing near-term profits for long-term potential was not in their plans, so the board held a secret meeting and fired Bucky. He was devastated. Still suffering the agony over his daughter's death four years earlier, and with a newly pregnant wife, he was suddenly unemployed with nothing to show for almost five years of frenetic activity. He called his mother in Boston to seek support, but she offered no sympathy and attributed his problems to his own "flaky" behavior. This exacerbated his feelings of despair and drove him into a deep depression. He later wrote, "I really thought I was some kind of freak." Buckminster Fuller decided to end it all.

On a cold windy winter night in 1927, Bucky walked to Lake Michigan intent on suicide. At the age of 32, he looked in the mirror and concluded,

> *I've done the best I know how and it hasn't worked. I guess I'm just no good, even my mother said I was worthless. I guess she was right.*

Bucky stood at the edge of the frigid water preparing to stop the hurt. He had reached what he later called a "critical detonation point." Before executing his final action, he began reflecting on his predicament. Suddenly, it occurred to him that suicide was a cowardly act and that he certainly wasn't a coward. He knew he loved to chase opportunities and life's possibilities and he knew that most people were not so inclined. What if he was right and the world was wrong? Maybe, just maybe, they were not right. If he perished, he would never know the answer to this quandary. Staring into the frigid waters awakened an inner consciousness; Fuller experienced an epiphany. It suddenly occurred to him that he was different but that the difference might be an asset rather than a liability. Fuller described his transformational experience (Hatch, p. 88):

> *If I am to believe in myself and the validity of my own ideas, I must stop thinking as other people told me to and rely on my own experience.*

With those prophetic words Fuller decided to drop out instead of copping out. For the next two years he would speak to no one except his new daughter Allegra. He walked home, told his wife of his decision, and set out on his journey to contact his inner self. Bucky later wrote:

I decided to unlearn and drop out from conventional thinking. I am going to embark on a new life mission.

GOING BACK TO THE WELL

The new Fuller was on a mission to reinvent himself and in the process try reinventing societal norms. Never again would he depend on values and beliefs of others as his rules for living. There would be no more absolutes, only approximations.

A month after these inner wanderings, he moved Anne and Allegra into a ghetto in south Chicago where they would not be known and where the rent was affordable. The drug-infested mobster hangout proved more than he wanted, but it was a learning experience for becoming what he called "the most unlearned man in the world."

Fuller would "become very suspicious of words." About his enforced silence, he commented:

I gradually regained those precious childish sensitivities to such an extent that I really see and feel very much like a little kid.

What had Bucky done? He had effectively brainwashed himself by wiping out the bad experiential tapes and replacing them with others he could live with. During the sensory deprivation he got in touch with what he called "the metaphysical aspects of the universe" (Hatch, p. 92). Biographer Hatch described his transformation as "an intense period in which he decided that experiences are finite and not related to philosophical innovations."

Fuller's drive and passion were legend. While on his frenetic mission of self-ordained change and reverie, he conceived many of the most powerful and innovative ideas of his life. Although unemployed in the conventional sense, he worked on a variety of design projects aimed at improving human living conditions. Since shelter is one of mankind's most fundamental needs, he sought to design a strong and efficient multi-unit dwelling. Fuller knew from his engineering studies that materials have a stronger tensile strength than compression tolerance (i.e., it takes more force to stretch a steel column than to crush it.) Since a steel column can support a much heavier load suspended from it than on top of it, Bucky designed a multiple housing unit of twelve stories that was suspended by cables from a strong central mast. It exploited the benefits of the dymaxion principle by using tetrahedra as the fundamental building blocks. By using lightweight materials, Fuller made the building easily transportable so it could be delivered and assembled anywhere in the world. He called this new invention the 4D building, to capture the futuristic aura of Einstein's recent formulation of 4-dimensional space-time.

An article on Buckminster Fuller and his 4D building appeared in 1928 in the Chicago *Evening Post*. As his work became public and interest grew, Bucky developed a one-story version of his 4D building that was later nicknamed "The House on a Pole." This futuristic design anticipated many of the features (such as solar heating) of today's "smart house." The entire structure weighed only 3 tons and sold for $1500 (less than $15,000 in today's dollars). A vitally important feature was that it could be mass-produced. As public interest in The House on a Pole increased, those who were more attuned than Bucky to marketing issues suggested that it be called the "Dymaxion House." The article in the *Evening Post* brought investors who provided financial backing to form the 4D Company with Buckminster Fuller as its president.

RE-ENTERING THE EXTERNAL WORLD

In 1929, with the Dymaxion House receiving increased attention, Bucky ended his period of enforced silence. He re-emerged irrevocably changed from his two years of self-proclaimed exile. He had successfully transformed himself into an indomitable individualist. The loner would no longer allow any "external reality" to influence his actions or behavior. "Internal reality" would be his only god, and if external forces didn't see the world as he did, so be it. Bucky swore that never again would another human being control any facet of his life or work.

In September 1929, Bucky relocated his family to Long Island, New York while he spent weekdays in Greenwich Village. He set for himself the surreal objective of unraveling life's great mysteries. During those horrid years in Chicago at Stockade Building System, he had worked double shifts that were frequently followed by all-night vigils. Now, living in Greenwich, he became more reflective, eating and sleeping sparingly and drinking excessively. Though working incessantly, Fuller lived a Bohemian lifestyle and associated with a group of wannabe artists, poets, sculptors, visionaries and entrepreneurs. He later commented (Hatch, p. 120):

*I found myself being followed by an increasing number of human
beings, particularly women, who were beginning to make me into
some kind of messiah. I became a cult, and that was exactly what I
did not want to be.*

Through his trials, Fuller had been reborn into something greater than
before, and he was beginning to receive approbation for his ideas. He was
receiving fees for lectures that he delivered across the country and though
the income was modest, it was enough to keep Bucky and his family
solvent. Fuller needed a forum for sharing his ideas with the public. In
1930, he cashed in his Naval life insurance to buy the architectural
magazine *T Square* and changed its name to *Shelter.*

True to the new, reborn Bucky, he informed the advertisers that he would
no longer run ads in his magazine because he wanted the magazine to pay
for itself by reader subscriptions. He also informed his readership that he
would not specify any dates of issue for his magazine. *Shelter* would be
published only when he had something worthwhile to say and the time to
say it clearly. Hence subscriptions would cost $2 per copy for a fixed
number of copies extended over an indefinite time. Even with this
remarkably unconventional marketing, *Shelter* was a very successful
magazine, having a circulation of 2,500 during the Depression in 1932.
The articles were of very high quality and dealt with hitherto unaddressed
topics such as ecology. From a profitability standpoint, *Shelter* was
marginal and Bucky made very little income from it. However, there was
a growing readership and good profitability was within grasp. Then, near
the end of 1932, Bucky informed his readership that he was about to fold
Shelter and would deliver one last great issue. Fuller had no interest in
profit; he was eager to get on with the next phase of his explorations.

THE DYMAXION CAR

At the beginning of 1933, Fuller was approached by an investor who
wanted to bankroll the creation of a prototype "car of the future." Fuller
signed an agreement to produce one prototype and founded the
Dymaxion Corporation of which he was to be director and chief engineer.
His creation would be called the "Dymaxion Car." Work on the prototype
began on March 4, 1933 and by July 12 of that year it was on public
display. The Dymaxion Car created a sensation. Its "fish-form" lines were
created to give it aerodynamic stability and reduce air friction, thereby
reducing fuel consumption. The air-cooled 90-hp V-8 engine enabled it to
reach a speed of 120 mph, and it had both front and rear-wheel steering

that enabled it to park in a space 4 feet shorter than a conventional car. Many of the features of the Dymaxion car would not be incorporated in American cars for several decades. It embodied both futuristic vision and high functionality.

Bucky was pleased with his creation, but he had agreed to produce a prototype with the idea that he could move on when finished. However, the prototype was so successfully received that the investors and his workers pleaded with him to build more. Reluctantly, Fuller agreed to produce two more. Then in 1933, an English consortium interested in buying a Dymaxion car sent an aeronautical authority to examine and report on the prototype. On the way back to the airport in the Dymaxion car, another car pulled alongside the Dymaxion and challenged it to race. Both cars reached high speeds, then the other car sideswiped the Dymaxion causing it to roll. The driver of the Dymaxion was killed and the aeronautical authority was seriously injured. The other car sped off, leaving the impression with the media that the Dymaxion car was unstable and had merely flipped. Funding ceased and the car was history. After that, other seed monies dried up and the incredible automobile never went into production despite orders from a number of celebrities such as Amelia Earhart. Bucky Fuller always believed that the "accident" had been orchestrated.

NINE CHAINS TO THE MOON

In 1934, Bucky Fuller moved his family to Manhattan so Allegra could attend the progressive Dalton School. There he met Felix and Christopher Morley who became close friends as well as connections to other writers and poets. By 1936, Bucky was working on his first book, *Nine Chains to the Moon*. He had calculated that if the entire population of the world were stretched in a long chain, it would reach to the moon and back nine times. The title was to convey that the ideas expressed in the book were about elevating the quality of life for the entire human race. A considerable portion of the book was dedicated to the scientific and philosophical ideas of Albert Einstein and their practical implications. The book explained Einstein's theories in layman's terms. Bucky's publisher had read that Einstein had previously stated that there were only ten men in the world capable of understanding his theories. Since Fuller's name was not listed among those ten, the publisher told Fuller that he was not qualified to write on Einstein's theories and therefore they could not publish his book. However, in a brief audience granted Bucky by Dr. Einstein, the renowned scientist gave Bucky a full endorsement. The publisher relented and *Nine Chains* was published in 1938. Although it was mainly ignored at that time, it would later become a classic as Bucky rose to the status of revered futurist and guru.

THE PHELPS DODGE CORPORATION

In the fall of 1936, when the Fullers were at yet another penurious stage of their turbulent lives, Bucky was offered a high-salaried job as Director of Research with the Phelps Dodge Corporation. It was Bucky's responsibility to create a research department to determine what copper products the company might produce as it progressed from its original beginnings as a copper mining company. Fuller's formidable creativity yielded a variety of powerful inventions including a precursor to today's disc brakes and a special centrifuge that made it possible to refine a particular type of tin ore. Perhaps the most popular of his inventions was the Dymaxion bathroom that used copper throughout, occupied only five square feet of space and could be made for about $300. Fearing that the plumber's union would object to the reduction in plumbing work that such a facility would bring, one of Phelps Dodge's biggest customers persuaded Phelps Dodge to cancel production. The Dymaxion bathroom, as a commercial product, died.

FINDING FORTUNE

In 1938, a dream job that was made especially for Buckminster Fuller appeared. The managing editor of *Fortune* magazine invited Bucky to join the staff of *Fortune* as technology consultant and writer at $15,000 per year. Bucky worked hard and generated a plethora of ideas, but he wrote few articles. One day during an audit of worker output, the auditor opined to the managing editor that Fuller's output did not justify his $15,000 salary. The editor of *Fortune* replied (Hatch, p. 151):

> *As managing editor I have to have new ideas every single, solitary day, and sometimes I just dry up. So I send for Bucky; and Bucky comes in and talks for about two hours. By the time he leaves I have more ideas than I can publish in the magazine in ten years. He recharges my batteries, and he's worth twice what he's being paid.*

While at *Fortune*, Fuller began the development of what he called *synergetic-energetic* geometry. This was a vector geometry based on the idea that nature has its own unique coordinate system. Rather than the perpendicular axes of the Cartesian system, this vector geometry uses axes angled at 60° relative to one another as do the edges of a tetrahedron.

All other shapes are composed of the tetrahedra that form the "atomic building block" of this geometry. To construct this geometry, he began with a pingpong ball as the model of a sphere and packed other spheres tightly around it. In three-dimensional geometry, a solid with flat polygonal faces is called a *polyhedron*. Fuller found that the solid formed from this packing was a polyhedron of 14 sides. His investigations of other packings of spheres and tetrahedra led him to develop a variety of different kinds of polyhedra. Among these was the so-called *truncated spherical icosahedron* which is a formal name for the shape that is modeled by a soccer ball. Observe that the surface of the soccer ball is composed of pentagonal and hexagonal faces. The "corners" of these shapes are called vertices. If you count the vertices on the surface of the soccer ball, you discover that there are 60 of them. The significance of the truncated spherical icosahedron wouldn't appear until almost a half-century later when a 60-atom carbon molecule with this structure was discovered.

THE FULLER DYMAXION AIROCEAN WORLD MAP

By 1941, the Fullers had reached financial comfort. Bucky gave up the excessive drinking that he had fallen into since 1933 and became a total abstainer. He also developed the practice of drinking thirty to forty cups of weak tea per day to flush his system. As his health became an important priority, he instituted a jogging regimen 30 years before it became trendy. Bucky's life had finally turned around; he was receiving recognition for his inventions which appeared at an ever-increasing rate. Between 1940 and 1942, Fuller developed the Dymaxion Deployment unit (DDU) that the military used during World War II to house its troops.

During the early 1940s, Bucky attempted to develop a world map that he could use to demonstrate the connectedness of the land masses of the earth and identify the most efficient air routes connecting cities. Since the world is a globe, any projection onto a flat surface results in distortions. For example, the familiar *Mercator* projection (invented in 1569) maps the meridians of longitude into parallel straight lines, thereby exaggerating areas near the poles relative to the areas of equatorial regions. Fuller wanted to create a projection of the globe onto a flat surface that would be free of all distortions. In mathematical terms, he wanted areas and angles to be preserved under this new projection.

To achieve this map, Fuller used a polyhedron of 20 flat faces (called an *icosahedron*) to approximate the globe. Then he projected the map from the globe onto the flat faces of the icosahedron. To transform the surface of the icosahedron into a flat map, he cut along its edges and laid it flat, displaying all the land masses with minimal distortion and virtual preservation of areas. He called his creation the *Dymaxion Airocean World Map*. This projection has the advantage that it has no visually detectable distortions in shape. Countries and continents appear as they would on a globe and distances between any two locations on the same face can be calculated using the same scale. The resulting Dymaxion Airocean World Map shown below is accessible on the Buckminster Fuller Institute Web Site at www.bfi.org/map.htm.

icosahedron

Fuller's Dymaxion Airocean World Map ^{TM}

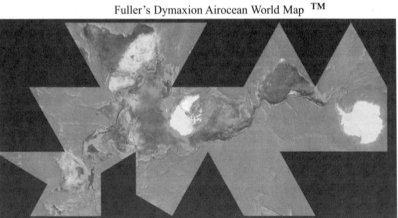

At the time of this writing, the Buckminster Fuller Institute Web Site includes an animation showing the successive transformations that map the world globe into the Dymaxion map.

In 1942, as World War II raged on, Fuller was offered the position of Director of the Mechanical Engineering Division of the Board of Economic Warfare. Bucky had to move the family to Washington D.C. where he carried out his important work. While employed with the government, he agreed to design a "high-powered" car for the industrialist, Henry J. Kaiser, in New York. This forced him to commute almost 1000 miles daily by train so that he could work in Washington by day and New York at night. He slept in snatches on his return trips from New York.

FULLER HOUSES INC.

In 1944, Bucky incorporated the company that later became Fuller Houses Inc., to build the Dymaxion Dwelling Machine, a much-improved version of his earlier 4D house. This futuristic house weighed about 3 tons and would cost only about $6500. The demand for the house was so strong that the shares of Fuller Houses Inc. soared. However, Fuller refused to go into production because he felt the prototype still needed some work and that going into production without properly working out all the glitches in the design would be selling under false pretenses. Conflict arose between Bucky and the shareholders who saw the prospect of large profits vanish before their eyes. Subsequently all the investors bailed out and Fuller closed the company.

THE GEODESIC DOME

Bucky had been disturbed by the earlier criticism of his Dymaxion Airocean World Map as non-rigorous and somewhat inexact because he had not proven analytically that there were no distortions. To master the analytic aspect of mapping a sphere onto a flat surface, Bucky undertook the study of spherical trigonometry during 1947 and 1948. Out of this intense study emerged models of structures that he eventually named the *geodesic dome*. In designing these structures, Fuller exploited the fact that the triangle is nature's strongest polygonal shape because, unlike any other polygon, its shape cannot be altered without changing the length of one of its sides.

The diagram below shows how a rectangle, for example, can be deformed into a parallelogram without any sides changing in length. For this reason the rectangle (or any other polygonal shape *except* the triangle) is not effective as the fundamental shape underpinning a load-bearing structure.

A pyramid having all faces triangular in shape is called a *tetrahedron*. Since all four faces of the tetrahedron are triangular, it is the ideal "building block" in the design of structures that require stability.

Another geometric fact is that the sphere is the most efficient geometric form. That is, a spherical shell is the geometric shape that requires the least amount of material to enclose a given amount of space. Bucky Fuller realized that if he constructed spherical buildings from tetrahedra, he could marry the strength of the triangle with the efficiency of the sphere and create buildings that were virtually indestructible and yet required a minimal amount of material to construct. He called these structures geodesic domes, and it is the geodesic dome for which he is universally known.

However, in early 1949, the geodesic dome was a only a concept; he hadn't proved in reality that it could be constructed and could support its own weight. During a drive to one of his many lectures, Bucky mentioned to Anne that he believed that he could make the geodesic dome a reality, but that he had no money to build it. She had just received a legacy of $30,000 in IBM stock and, in her characteristically supportive way, immediately offered to lend it to him so that he could turn his dream into a reality. Bucky established Geodesics Inc. so that he could subsequently patent the geodesic dome and fund his further work with royalties from the patent. He proceeded to build prototypes and discovered that, indeed, his theoretical models could be translated into real entities. The first large dome was built by Bucky's former students in Montreal, Canada in 1950. It was constructed of a skin over aluminum struts and had a diameter of 50 feet. The geodesic dome created a sensation. Through the 1950s, '60s and '70s, geodesic domes spread like wildfire throughout the world. The United States pavilions at international fairs were inevitably geodesic domes, reflecting America's crowning contribution to architecture. The military used them in a variety of applications including the DEW defense line in the Arctic. Children's playgrounds used simple versions as climbing apparatuses, and many people living outside areas with restrictive building codes incorporated the geodesic dome in the designs of their homes. It is estimated that there are more than 200,000 geodesic domes in the world today. Perhaps the most famous dome is the beautiful structure at Disney's Epcot Center shown opposite. With the ubiquity of the geodesic dome and the recognition of its remarkable features, Buckminster Fuller would eventually receive the recognition he deserved along with his place in history among the great engineers and visionaries of the 20th century.

The geodesic dome *Spaceship Earth* at Disney's Epcot Center showing the silver tetrahedra that cover its surface

THE FINAL YEARS

Bucky Fuller was a human dynamo. He worked at a pace beyond most men half his age. Norman Cousins, a former editor of the *Saturday Review* and a close friend of Bucky Fuller, once observed (Hatch, p. 235):

> *What Bucky demonstrates to me in all this is that the key to longevity is creativity; the notion of degeneration of brain cells beyond a certain age is true only in the absence of creativity...It seems to me that there is a direct connection between creative thought and involvement in life and the production of epinephrine by the adrenal gland. When the challenge stops, the supply is turned off; the will to live atrophies and the body chemistry no longer functions.*

A further discussion of the connection between the will to create and longevity is investigated in more detail in Chapter 13, *The Psychology of Entrepreneurship*. However, the story of Bucky Fuller's last days supports Cousins' conjecture. In June 1983, Bucky's wife of 66 years, was suffering from intestinal cancer and had lapsed into a comatose state. The details of her final moments were provided by her daughter Allegra in a letter to a close friend:

> *I was sitting on one side of her bedside and Daddy was sitting on the other. He was holding her hand.. He suddenly looked up at me, across the bed, and said, "I know she's squeezing my hand!!!!!" He stood up...and it was then that he had a massive heart attack...I was ushered out of my mother's room while the whole brigade of the heart emergency crew of the hospital arrived in her room. He died, but not at her bedside, and about an hour later...But after he had died, he had an exquisitely happy smile on his face. I think he felt that perhaps mother was sort of hanging on the edge because she was afraid to leave without his going too, and that he should usher the way for them both to depart together. It was 36 hours later before she actually did die...Who knows if she knew he had gone ahead?*

It seemed as if Buckminster Fuller, an infinite source of energy for almost 88 years had suddenly willed his own death.

Fuller's Decade-by-Decade Climb

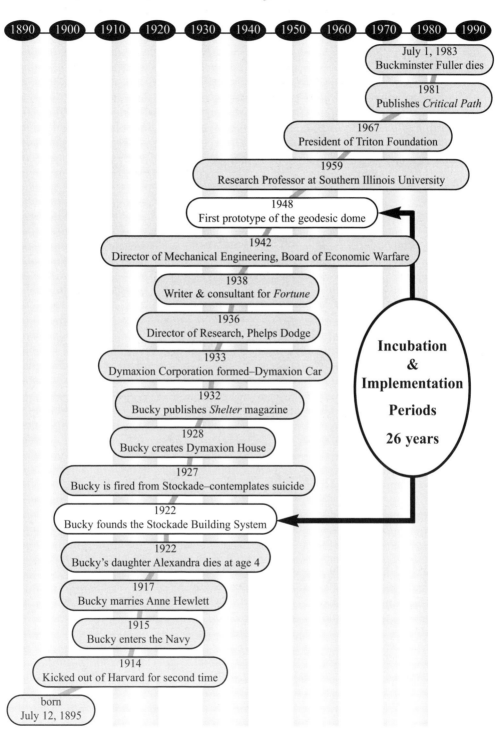

1890 — 1900 — 1910 — 1920 — 1930 — 1940 — 1950 — 1960 — 1970 — 1980 — 1990

July 1, 1983
Buckminster Fuller dies

1981
Publishes *Critical Path*

1967
President of Triton Foundation

1959
Research Professor at Southern Illinois University

1948
First prototype of the geodesic dome

1942
Director of Mechanical Engineering, Board of Economic Warfare

1938
Writer & consultant for *Fortune*

1936
Director of Research, Phelps Dodge

1933
Dymaxion Corporation formed–Dymaxion Car

1932
Bucky publishes *Shelter* magazine

1928
Bucky creates Dymaxion House

1927
Bucky is fired from Stockade–contemplates suicide

1922
Bucky founds the Stockade Building System

1922
Bucky's daughter Alexandra dies at age 4

1917
Bucky marries Anne Hewlett

1915
Bucky enters the Navy

1914
Kicked out of Harvard for second time

born
July 12, 1895

**Incubation
&
Implementation
Periods
26 years**

A Personality Profile

COMMUNICATION STYLE: MACHINE GUN CYBERSPEAK

In 1929, the new Fuller became an evangelist with many intellectual disciples at his side. Whether telling a story, reciting poetry, or philosophizing on the nuances of mankind in a paradigm shift, Fuller could be mesmerizing. The reinvented Bucky made the ordinary exciting and the extraordinary dazzling. Just keeping up with his steady stream of rapid-fire monologues proved a challenge. Bucky's brother-in-law Roger Hewlett said (Hatch, p. 268):

> *Bucky will do anything, including inventing geodesic domes, to make you love him. I think that is why he charms the great and the famous and the powerful like Indira Gandhi.*

The Indian leader hired Bucky to design the Bombay airport despite his lack of formal architectural credentials. Hatch described Fuller as "one of the world's great natural salesman." Bright people gravitated to Fuller, envisioning him as spiritual soul mate against the hated establishment and self-serving politicians.

Bucky's written prose, however, was less clear than his oral discourse. Hatch observed that Fuller "would rather not be understood than be misunderstood." He further observes (Hatch, p. 147):

> *In his meticulous endeavor to be absolutely precise he had evolved a labyrinthine prose style involving the use of esoteric Latin- and Greek-root words that few people could understand;* Time *magazine later christened it "Fullerese."*

An obtuse Fullerese can be likened to today's Cyber-speak–a machine gun rat-tat-tat devoid of grammatical punctuation or structure. Fullerese flowing at its full stream-of-consciousness speed is evident in the following sentence taken from Bucky's *Critical Path* (p. 252):

> *What we count on is political reaction in its bipartisan tail-of-the-dragon function, now flappingly, now snappingly, yielding one way or the other to society's vivid realization of the arrival of historically unprecedented crises and dawning awareness of the availability of possibly effective but unfamiliar techno-physical*

means of coping with the ever-more-frequently-occurring crises as are occasioned by the practical development and availability of hitherto-nonexistent artifacts.

Audiences were spellbound by his passion and intellectual jargon. Two former disciples spoke of listening carefully for fear you would lose out on some gem of genius.

INTUITIONAL STYLE

Fuller felt intuition was the most important dimension of his creative work. He even named his boat *Intuition*. In *Critical Path* he proclaimed, "Innovation is the manifestation of the invisible." In a plea to discourage the deification of the quantitative, he wrote, "All truth is an approximation. Intuitive conversions by the brain are what transform experience into generalized principles." What was he implying? That there are few absolutes in life no matter how much we would like it to be otherwise.

British psychiatrist and writer Robert Ornstein studied the brain relative to creativity and wrote in *The Amazing Brain* (1986), "The artist, dancer, and mystic have learned to develop the non-verbal portion of intelligence and therefore have become creative." In his 1997 work *The Right Mind,* Ornstein said, "Somehow the right-hemisphere (the seat of creative insight) seems to provide the general background of the human worldview" (p. 60). Even more telling are the profound views of Harvard's Burton Klein who wrote on success and economics (Klein, 1977):

> *If the entrepreneur wants to give himself the best chance of putting the law of large numbers on his side, he will use his intuition to leap to new hypotheses. His riches are his hints, but if his hints are not to be squandered he must trust his intuition.*

Intuition was important to Bucky, leading him to say (Fuller, p. 125):

> *I intuited to articulate my own innate motivational integrity instead of trying to accommodate everyone else's opinions, credos, educational theories, romances and mores.*

The Dymaxion House (called The House on a Pole–a doughnut-shaped structure suspended from a central mast, giving optimal space at low cost) was an example of his need for exploration outside the box. When he created the Dymaxion House in 1928, it was so far ahead of its time no one saw the possibilities. After World War II it was transformed into the Wichita House that gained a huge following as low-cost housing for returning GIs, although it was never funded.

CRITICAL THINKING

The iconoclastic Fuller was a visionary extraordinaire. He said, "Life itself is entirely metaphysical–a pattern integrity" (Fuller, p. 342). That insight was apparent in his prediction of the Internet in its present form almost two decades before it was invented (Fuller, p. xxxi):

> *We must integrate the world's electrical-energy networks. I therefore predict that before the end of the 1980s the computer's politically unbiased problem-solving...the world electric grid, with its omni-integrated advantage, will deliver its electric energy anywhere, to anyone, at any one time, at one common rate...All this accounting switchover must also be accomplished before 2000 A.D.*

RISK-TAKING PROPENSITY

In *Critical Path* (Fuller, p. 151) Bucky wrote, "I seem to have made more mistakes than any others I know." That is the price of taking more risks. For him, errors were part of the learning process just as they were for Henry Ford. Fuller thrived on risky ventures: driving fast cars, chasing fast women and flying fast planes. Fear never interceded in his decisions to take on a new opportunity. In the likeness of entrepreneur Howard Hughes, he disdained hiring others to test his ideas. Bucky was almost always his own test driver. Happiest when in the fast lane, the intrepid innovator flew, sailed and drove with abandon. When asked about his proclivity for risk he said he was "rash." Once when testing the maximum acceleration and speed of his Dymaxion Car, he crashed. His daughter Allegra and his wife Anne were in the car at the time, but fortunately were unhurt.

One of the greatest risks that Fuller took was his resolve to live on little or no income. He was committed to the idea that humans should work for personal satisfaction and not to "make a living." Challenging society's implicit assumption that the pursuit of money to sustain oneself is a necessary function, he lived most of his life without any prospect of regular income. It's a risk that most of us would be reluctant to take.

INTENSITY

Bucky was in a perpetual hurry. He believed sleep was such a waste that he devised a plan to eliminate as much as possible. Dymaxion sleep (though he never called it that) allowed him to work for six hours and then nap for thirty minutes, followed by six more hours of work followed by another 30-minute nap. He became so proficient at this he was able to go into a trance-like nap in thirty seconds. Biographer J. Baldwin said this power napping allowed him to "outwork many of his younger colleagues."

Like most of the entrepreneurs profiled in this book, Bucky was possessed of what some psychologists call *hurry sickness*. He did everything as if double-parked on the highway of life. Fuller spoke, worked and thought at warp speed. Difficult tasks were his forte, especially when he saw a chance to make the complex simple. Speed was the most important word in the Fuller lexicon. He believed it was the solution to man's problems, saying "progress meant mobility."

The stories of Bucky's compulsive nature are legion. On one occasion, in his senior years when on a Greek cruise to relax, a fan recognized him and asked if he would say a few words on futurism. Bucky strolled to the lectern without notes and began speaking. He didn't stop for nine hours. This was not unusual. When meeting Indian Prime Minister Nehru, the two exchanged polite bows. Then Bucky launched into a monologue for an hour and a half. When Bucky had finished, Nehru excused himself and left the room without having said a word.

SELF-IMAGE

Bucky knew what the financial power brokers wanted, but had promised himself to never give in to their self-serving needs. That worked to his disadvantage as he made many enemies with his honest arrogance. Friend and biographer J. Baldwin said, "Bucky didn't commit suicide. He committed egocide" (Baldwin, p. 5). An example of his "egocide" was his statement to *Playboy* magazine that infuriated many, "The next most dangerous thing to the atom bomb is organized religion" (Baldwin, p. 82). He was not against religion, for he was highly spiritual, but he detested those who used fear to control their flocks.

Great entrepreneurs require strong egos to carry them upstream against the current of traditional belief. Bucky was no exception. In the fall of

1948, faculty and students gathered at a site where Bucky was about to erect the first geodesic dome. It was the culmination of two year's work and the dome was to rise like the phoenix from the ashes under the increasing tension of supporting cables. To the dismay of Bucky and all the spectators, the colossal structure made it part way into the sky and then collapsed in ruins. Two decades later, Bucky claimed he built it to collapse so that he could find the weak spot. Hatch commented (p. 191):

> *This is typical Fuller after-the-fact rationalizing, and Bucky appeared unconcerned because his ego would never let failure in, any more than infinity–he did not believe in either.*

ECCENTRICITIES AND PERSONAL PARADOXES

Rich and bright mavericks tend to be called eccentric. That was fine with Fuller who referred to himself as a "design science revolutionary." Traditionalists characterized Bucky as "metaphysical" (Baldwin, p. 15). Passion pervaded his life from those early years when he admitted to friend and biographer Alden Hatch that he had slept with 1000 prostitutes (Hatch, p. 84):

> *They seemed the only place where people really talked straight to me; those girls, many of them had babies. I wanted to see them as human beings, to know how they got there.*

Buckminster Fuller was a collection of contradictions and paradoxes. Early in life, he resolved not to talk for two years, yet later in life was known for his proclivity for talking non-stop for nine or more hours in resplendent Fullerese. He eschewed the accumulation of wealth through-out his life, but when he became solvent in his later years, he spent money on lavish hotels, on his living quarters and on acquiring an elegant yacht. Fuller espoused the virtues of spousal faithfulness and yet he claimed to have slept with a thousand prostitutes–many while he was married. During the period from 1933 to 1941 he drank excessively and then he quit and drank no more. Fuller radiated eccentricity in everything he did, but these eccentricities were manifestations of a mind set free from traditional thinking and the rest of humanity were the beneficiaries of his difference.

ACHIEVEMENTS & HONORS

MAGNITUDE OF SUCCESS

Fuller was a Renaissance man with a disdain for financiers whose sole focus was the bottom line. His legacy is a plethora of poetry, mathematical formulas, engineering designs, cosmological insights, inventions, philosophical ideas and numerous architectural monuments to his genius. He held numerous patents and authored 25 books, including his famous *Operating Manual for Spaceship Earth* (1969) and *Critical Path* (1981). One of the first Futurists, Bucky taught us "truth is but an approximation at best."

Bucky became enamored of life's possibilities and worked feverishly to bring his ideas to fruition. The visionary looked beyond the obvious to discover potential in the mysterious. Fuller was an existential philosopher with arcane ideas and a scientific bent tempered with practical sensibilities. He married the magic of the possible with utilitarian values and that will prove to be his legacy.

The culmination of Fuller's work was the geodesic dome. His first prototype was developed in 1948 and he received a patent on it in 1954. The first commercial production of a geodesic dome was in 1953 when Henry Ford II asked him to construct a dome over the circular Rotunda building at the River Rouge Plant. It was to be a tribute to Henry Ford I, another entrepreneur whom Bucky greatly admired. Among the most famous international demonstrations of this new style of architecture were the U. S. Pavilions at the International Trade Fair in Kabul, Afghanistan in 1956 and at the World's Fair in Montreal, Canada in 1967. The dome is a masterful marriage of art and science, form and function; a marvel of engineering elegance optimizing efficient utilization of material, space, cost and esthetics. Scientists have called his invention "perhaps the most significant structural innovation of the 20th century."

A half century after its invention, the construction of a geodesic dome as an exercise in applied geometry has found its way into college curricula. In the photograph shown on the following page, a class of undergraduates at the University of Toronto have assembled–in 22 minutes–a geodesic dome using rolled newspapers for struts and staples for fasteners. By counting the number of edges, faces and vertices of this structure, they are able to verify Euler's Theorem for Polyhedra, discovered by the Swiss mathematician over two centuries ago.

Students in MAT 329 at the University of Toronto assemble a geodesic dome in 22 minutes.

Fuller's entrepreneurial wizardry enabled him to work without expecting rewards. In his own words, "I just invent and then wait until man comes around to needing what I've invented." This reflect his orientation to the future. *PBS* (April 10, 1996) said, "Fuller was an eclectic visionary so ahead of his time, that the times haven't quite caught up to him yet."

HONORS

Arthur C. Clark called Fuller, "The first engineering saint." This recipient of 47 honorary degrees and numerous patents was a college dropout. Paradoxically, in 1959 he was given a department chair at Southern Illinois University at Carbondale, a position he held until 1970. Harvard saw fit to award their radical dropout a chair in poetry–The Harvard Charles Norton Chair of Poetry in 1962. Despite not having a degree, he was named the official architect for the U. S. Pavilion at the 1967 World's Fair in Montreal. In 1972 he was named a World Fellow in Residence at the University City Science Center in Philadelphia. His *Dymaxion Map*–was the first projection of the world ever granted a patent.

We noted earlier that Bucky Fuller had developed models of various polyhedra including the truncated spherical icosahedron having 60 vertices (modeled by a soccer ball). In 1985, two scientists, Harry Kroto and Richard Smalley, proved that a 60-atom carbon molecule (denoted C_{60}) has the shape of truncated spherical icosahedron with one carbon atom located at each vertex. To honor Bucky Fuller who had died two years earlier, they named the molecule *buckminsterfullerene* –subsequently nicknamed *buckyball*. Biographer Baldwin suggests (Baldwin, p. 74) that the scientists might have obtained a subconscious clue of the shape of this carbon molecule from a visit to Fuller's geodesic dome in Montreal–it is a giant truncated spherical icosahedron!

LESSONS LEARNED FROM BUCKY FULLER

Implicit in the behavior of Bucky Fuller are some important lessons for the aspiring entrepreneur.

BEGIN WITH ANSWERS TO END WITH A WORTHWHILE PROJECT

All great entrepreneurs begin at the end and proceed to the beginning. Why? Because knowing where you are headed is prerequisite to mapping out a route to the goal. One can't reach a solution to something not defined. Most people find it difficult to begin with answers, especially answers that are not clearly defined. However, no new innovative idea can be exact. "First approximate an answer, then modify it"; that is the nature of all creative development. It is also the way one writes a book. This was demonstrated by the recent success of J. K. Rowling, author of the Harry Potter series, who told a reporter:

> *My magical characters were not thought up in any methodical way...They normally come fully formed. Harry came very fully formed. I knew he was a wizard, and then it was a process of working backwards to find out how that could be, and forwards to find out what happened next.*

Rowling validated her statement by holding up a manila envelope at the end of the interview and announced that she had already finished the last chapter of the last book–book #7, despite the fact she had just finished book #3. She concluded, "Here is where Harry Potter ends."

Working backwards from a desired destination to a present location to find a route that connects the two is referred to as *inverse creativity*. Inverse creativity comes in many forms. Just as artists and writers begin at the end, entrepreneurs must start with a unique dream and begin working on it to connect the current reality with the desired goal. Picasso began all of his paintings with a philosophical message to the world and then portrayed images to convey his thoughts.

In everything he created, Bucky Fuller began with his vision of the end result–the future. Before he had shown rigorously that a spherical structure could be constructed from a three-way great circle grid, he assumed it was true, and proceeded on that basis to conceptualize the geodesic dome. Even when the special lightweight materials required for his super-domes had not yet been invented, he assumed their existence.

CHASE DREAMS, NOT MONEY

The money paradox says that the more you chase money the less chance you have of getting it; and the more you chase quality the more money you get. Bucky Fuller was fired from his own firm for being too innovative and not driven for quick profits. Fuller never got over such a self-serving mode of operation. In his landmark book *Critical Path* (p. 276) wrote:

> *The drive to make money is entropic for it seeks to monopolize order while leaving un-cope-with-able disorder to overwhelm others.*

Bucky knew that he could make some quick profits if he would only submit to the fast and expedient instead of the innovative. That was something he was never willing to do. Fuller hated designers who created for money or personal aggrandizement. To him they were self-serving and stupid. This led to his statement on money as a motivator (p. 149):

> *You can either make money or do what is right, but when money enters the equation the greed interferes with optimal success in any venture.*

Virtually every eminent entrepreneur profiled in this book had a similar view of money as a by-product, not the goal, in the pursuit of one's passion. Richard Branson wrote, "I have never gone into business purely to make money." Ross Perot said, "Never let money become your goal." And even the frugal J. Paul Getty wrote in his memoirs, "I never enjoyed making money. Money doesn't have any connection with happiness." One of the more profound comments came from Coco Chanel who said, "There are people who have money, and people who are rich. It's not money I'm interested in, but money as the symbol of success." Michael Dell said his success at Dell Computers was a function of pursuing "growth rather than a profit maximization strategy." However, Bucky (unlike the rest) felt that the pursuit of money was a corrupting influence that distracted people from chasing their vision. He dedicated his life to proving that the world's resources, appropriately conserved, recycled and managed, could accommodate the needs of all humans and that "working to earn a living" was not necessary. He believed that the natural human inclination to work for personal fulfillment would yield all the productivity needed to render a high standard of living for all. Indeed, Fuller modeled what he preached, for after his 1927 epiphany, he never again worked to earn a living.

Sam Moore Walton

If It Ain't Broke, Break It!

b. Kingfisher, OK,   March 29, 1918
d. Little Rock, AR   April 5, 1992

"Ignore the conventional wisdom."

SELF-DESCRIPTION
"I am a servant, leader, and a maverick."

MOTTOS
"Keep everybody guessing as to what your next trick
is going to be."
"Our best ideas come from clerks and stock boys."

INNOVATION	Discount retailing empire with $220 billion in revenues in 2001; the largest firm in the world by 2002; astutely built around low cost with all functions aimed at that mission; magic = low cost without a cheap appearance
UNIQUE QUALITIES	Down-home humor with enthusiasm and an unrelenting passion to succeed
OBJECTIVE	"Share your profits with all your associates, and treat them as partners."
NET WORTH	$25 billion at his death in 1992; estimated family wealth over $100 billion (*Forbes,* 2002)
HONORS	Granted the Horatio Alger Award in 1984 Richest Man in America (Forbes, 1985) Presidential Medal of Freedom 1992
BIRTH ORDER	First born; younger brother, Bud
EDUCATION	BA in economics from University of Missouri, 1940
PERSONALITY	Intuitive visionary with a penchant for breaking the rules; never took himself too seriously
HOBBIES	Fishing, competitive tennis, and piloting his own plane
POLITICS	Apolitical, but voted Republican
RELIGION	Protestant; taught Sunday School
FAMILY	Wife: Helen; Children: four

5

Sam Walton

If It Ain't Broke, Break It!

"I have always been driven to buck the system."

Overview

The story of Sam Walton and his creation of the Wal-Mart chain of retail stores out of a mom-and-pop variety store in Arkansas is one of the most fascinating stories in the saga of American entrepreneurship. From his humble beginnings as a boy growing up in the Dust Bowl during the Great Depression, possessed of a fierce competitive drive, and imbued with integrity, tenacity and frugality, Sam Walton created the Wal-Mart behemoth that revolutionized retail marketing. In a David-and-Goliath competition that spanned four decades, Walton challenged the giant retailers Kmart, Target and Sears and ultimately surpassed them all, as Wal-Mart became not only the largest retail chain but America's largest corporation, surpassing General Motors.

The journey to the top of the retail world was not easy for Wal-Mart. Nor did it come without great pain, for it was achieved by breaking some traditional rules of practice. Sam was committed to "marching to the beat of a different drummer" whenever he felt it was good for the customer and not injurious to the company. In his memoirs, he spoke of the long, tough journey from that first five-and-dime store he established after World War II. "Wal-Mart was an outgrowth of everything we'd been doing since 1945," he once observed. He built many five-and-dime stores, but the first Wal-Mart didn't open its doors until 1962, after he had learned what worked and what didn't.

Most great breakthroughs are born on the fringe of accepted practice. Walton was living proof of Bertrand Russell's admonition, "Every opinion now accepted was once eccentric." At a time when the giant retailers–Woolworths, Kresge (later Kmart), Sears and others–believed that department stores could survive only in high population areas, Sam realized that such stores could thrive in less populated regions if they offered significantly discounted prices. His early experiences with variety stores enabled him to build a network of deep discount stores that eventually spread into the high population areas and challenged the giant merchandisers in their home field.

Walton made it to the top by building a "customer-centered" operation while maintaining low costs. In contrast, his chief competitor had remained loyal to traditional merchandising procedures and had not been so passionate about monitoring costs. Executives at Kmart symbolized a devil-may-care attitude toward minimizing expenditures as they traversed the country in expensive private jets. However, when it became necessary to travel between stores in the Wal-Mart network, Sam got his pilot's license, acquired a refurbished pre-war plane, and flew himself to his destinations. Decades later, Wal-Mart reduced the need for expensive air travel by pioneering the use of satellite technology to link all its stores. Sam Walton had realized that subtle differences in expenditures could generate huge differences in profits in competitive environments.

It took Wal-Mart from 1962 to 1991 to win the merchandising war. That was when Wal-Mart passed Kmart with revenues of $32.6 billion to Kmart's $29.7 billion and passed Sears to become the largest retailer in the United States. By the end of the decade, the merchandising war was over. Sam had won. Kmart filed for Chapter 11 bankruptcy protection in 2002, while Wal-Mart, with revenues of $191 billion, nearly doubled Sam's prediction of $100 billion by the end of the millennium.

In the process of revolutionizing the retail world and creating jobs for about a million people, Sam accumulated a huge personal fortune. In 1985, *Fortune* named him America's wealthiest man. The factors underpinning Walton's dramatic success derive from a powerful combination of his prescient insights, his effective business strategies, and his unique personality traits. In his memoirs, *Made in America*, Sam Walton gives his interpretation of the significance of the Wal-Mart story (Walton, p. xiii):

> *As I do look back...I realize that ours is a story about the kinds of traditional principles that made America great in the first place. It is a story about entrepreneurship, and risk, and hard work, and knowing where you want to go and being willing to do what it takes to get there. It is a story about believing in your idea even when maybe some other folks don't, and about sticking to your guns.*

The Formative Years

EARLY IMPRESSIONS

Sam Walton was born on a farm near Kingfisher, Oklahoma, to parents Tom and Nan Walton, on March 29, 1918. World War I, the war to end all wars, was raging in Europe, and survival on the farm presented physical and economic challenges. These challenges did not diminish after the War, but metamorphosed into hardships in the 1920s and early 1930s. Steinbeck's portrayal of the starving share croppers in his novel, *The Grapes of Wrath,* captures the plight of those who tried to farm the Dust Bowl during the Great Depression.

Though Sam's father did not practice farming himself, he worked for his brother Jesse in the farm mortgage business, servicing old farm loans. This meant, particularly during the Depression, that he had to repossess farms whose loans were in default. Years later, Sam reflected on his impressions of his father's work (Walton, p. 5).

> *In twenty-nine and thirty-one, [Dad] had to repossess hundreds of farms from wonderful people whose families had owned the land forever. I traveled with him some, and it was tragic, and really hard on Dad too–but he tried to do it in a way that left those farmers with as much of their self-respect as he could. All of this must have made an impression on me as a kid, although I don't ever remember saying anything to myself like, "I'll never be poor."*

Sam learned to cope early in life. The Walton family were transients, having moved five times before Sam attended high school. Tom Walton was transferred to Marshall, Missouri, then to Shelbina, and eventually in 1933 to Columbia, where Sam attended high school. Such movement is often characterized as bad for children, but in some respects the opposite is true. Helen Walton (his wife) attributed Sam's extroverted nature to these early experiences that required him to make friends or remain a loner. In fact, Sam thrived on social interaction and in 1931, at the age of thirteen, he became the youngest Eagle Scout in the history of Missouri.

Growing up in America's Dust Bowl was to instill survival skills in Walton seldom found in those with a less formidable upbringing. As observed in the chapter on Henry Ford, more is learned from failure than success. Life's hard lessons are learned when life is tough. And when the tough lessons are learned early, the lessons are learned well. The American work ethic was forged out of such hardship, and Sam Walton's success adds yet another testimonial to this truth.

A Study in Enterprise

Since the age of seven, Sam Walton worked a paper route that he maintained even through his college years. When the family was struggling during the Great Depression, his mother started selling milk to earn food money. Sam, her first son, was her salesman and delivery agent. When that venture ended, he worked a number of jobs. In 1938, when many people were standing in bread lines, he earned a remarkable $4000 (equivalent to about $45,000 today) delivering papers.

By the time Sam reached high school age, the family had settled down and after that he changed high schools only once. Along with his income-earning activities, he found time to study and play on state championship teams in both football and basketball. Winning became a way of life and it never left him. The Eagle Scout motto, "I will do my best in all things," became his rule to live by. At Hickham High in Columbia, Missouri, he played quarterback for the football team and led them to the state championship. Later, when explaining his success in retailing, he recalled (Walton p. 18):

> *I never played in a losing football game...I think that record had an important effect on me. It taught me to expect to win...Later on in life, I think Kmart, or whatever competition we were facing, just became Jeff City High School, the team we played for the state championship in 1935.*

Formal Education

Upon graduation from high school, Sam attended the University of Missouri where he majored in business. He was elected President of his senior class. The fraternity newspaper called him "hustler Walton" for his work ethic and competitive nature. To pay his way through college, the driven overachiever delivered papers, waited tables, and served as head lifeguard. He graduated from the University of Missouri with a B.A. in economics in 1940.

EARLY SUCCESS IMPRINTS

When Sam graduated from college, he considered enrolling in graduate studies but chose instead to work as a management trainee at J. C. Penney in Des Moines, Iowa. He earned $75 per month, but it was here that he learned the management techniques that would serve him well in his future career.

When America entered World War II, Sam enlisted, but was refused full service on account of an irregular heartbeat. While awaiting limited service in the Military, he decided to travel to Tulsa to investigate the burgeoning oil business. Sam was staying in nearby Claremore, Oklahoma, when he decided to spend some leisure time bowling. It was there that he met a beautiful girl named Helen Robson, who eventually became his wife and lifelong companion. Helen's loving support would become a key factor in providing Sam with the solid family foundation on which he later built his empire. Her father, Leland Robson, would also have a profound effect on Sam's personal goals and values. Leland was a highly successful lawyer and businessman whose ventures had made him both wealthy and well respected.

It was April, 1942 and Sam had just celebrated his twenty-fourth birthday. As he wrote his memoirs almost half a century later, Sam recalled the remarkable influence that Robson had on his thinking (Walton, p. 7):

> *Listening to L. S. Robson was an education in itself. He influenced me a great deal. He was a great salesman, one of the most persuasive individuals I have ever met. And I am sure his success as a trader and a businessman, his knowledge of finance and the law, and his philosophy had a big effect on me. My competitive nature was such that I saw his success and admired it. I didn't envy it. I admired it. I said to myself: maybe I will be as successful as he is someday.*

Sam and Helen married in 1943 and in 1944, their first child, Sam Robson Walton was born. In the fall of 1945, they moved to Newport, Arkansas where Sam Walton leased a store that was part of the Ben Franklin chain of franchised variety stores. The upfront fee for the franchise was $25,000 (approximately $280,000 in today's dollars). Sam and Helen used their savings of $5000 and a loan of $20,000 from her father to finance the transaction.

The Climb to the Top

THINK BIG, START SMALL

On September, 1, 1945, Sam Walton's career as a retailer was launched with the opening of his 5000-square-foot Ben Franklin variety store in Newport, Arkansas, a town of 5000 people. At age 27, he set the first of many retail-related goals that would define his life (Walton, p. 28):

> *I've always believed in goals, so I set myself one: I wanted my little Newport store to be the best, most profitable variety store in Arkansas within five years.*

Sam did not know at the time that under the previous owner, this store had been losing money. Shortly after signing the lease, he realized that the 5% of sales that he paid as rent for the store was much higher than the going rate. This left him no room to offer discount prices. How would Sam be able to make the store a success, in spite of paying exorbitant rent and overpaying for his franchise? Tedlow (p. 331–332) observes:

> *Much of what was to make [Sam] the great merchant he became was evident from the very beginning. First he learned all the rules. Then he broke all the rules which did not make sense to him—which meant almost all of them. It seems that way because it was. Sam Walton did not become a billionaire because he was a genius (although he was without question smart, shrewd, and astute). The real explanation for his success was that he had the courage of his convictions.*

Butler Brothers, the franchisers of the Ben Franklin stores, had a list of highly restrictive rules that franchisees were expected to follow. Among these was the requirement that 80% of a franchisee's merchandise was to be purchased through Butler Brothers (who had already marked up prices considerably). Such a rule precluded franchisees from selling goods at discount prices. Hence, this became the first of many rules that Sam broke. Walton found cheaper suppliers from whom he purchased his products and then discounted his prices to pass the savings on to his customers. He believed the reduced profit margins would be more than compensated by the increased sales volume. Butler Brothers did not invoke sanctions against Walton because his policies made the store fabulously successful. By 1950, Sam's store had sales of $250,000 and a profit of approximately $35,000. Sam had achieved his five-year goal in becoming the most profitable variety store operator in Arkansas!

At the end of his five-year lease, Sam discovered that he had no renewal clause, even though these were routinely included in such contracts. On observing the store's profitability, his landlord, Mr. P. K. Holmes, chose not to renew Sam's lease, opting to have his son run the store, thus keeping the profits in the Holmes' family coffers. Sam now had no store in Newport and no way to earn a living in retail in that town. Devastated but undefeated, Sam uprooted his family to begin all over again. Years later, Sam referred to this incident as the low point of his business life.

With the help of Helen's father, Sam obtained a 99-year lease on a store in the small town of Bentonville, Arkansas. Though it was part of the Ben Franklin chain, he named it Walton's 5 & 10 store. As one might expect, Sam was starting small again but thinking big. The store sales tripled in a short time and by 1952, Walton opened his second variety store–this time in Fayetteville, Arkansas. Soon after, he introduced self-service in both stores to reduce the number of cashiers needed, and he began to investigate further acquisitions.

In the following years, Walton's variety stores began to sprout like mushrooms in small towns across the country. By 1960 Sam Walton had become America's largest independent variety store operator with fifteen stores and annual sales of $1.4 million. However, Sam was restless. He realized that a strong wind of change was blowing across the country –discounting was becoming the new trend in retail. In 1962, F. W. Woolworth had created Woolco, a discount arm of the company; S. S. Kresge established Kmart; and Bayton-Hudson gave birth to Target. All three companies had seen the trend and the retail wars were under way.

When Sam decided to go into deep discounting, he knew he was first and foremost in a war against Kmart. His chief rival had a significant advantage in seasoned managers, distribution and money. The Kresge chain were also better at merchandising, buying and distribution. In the 1960s, the public was involved in their love affair with Kmart and relatively oblivious to the upstart Wal-Mart. Sam observed the terrain and refused to go head-to-head with the giants, Kmart, Woolco, and Target. During this era, Kmart would not open a store in any market of less than 50,000 people and the southern-based Gibson stores would not open in a market smaller than 12,000. Since they were in the big cities, Sam went to the suburbs. For many years he was the only one in those markets, and learned how to build and operate a profitable retail store. Sam worked to become financially solvent so he could grow once he was ready.

The first store Sam opened to compete directly with archrival Kmart was located in Rogers, Arkansas. That store was to become both the cornerstone of his empire and the crucible for his study of the retail industry. He used his low-cost operations to force Kmart to compete or capitulate. Since Sam had become the master in markets of 5,000 or fewer people, his competition eventually chose the latter option.

GROWING PAINS

Wal-Mart's shift into high gear generated significant problems in its early phases. When the management of the Ben Franklin chain turned down his plan for building a deep-discount store as a prototype, Sam did it on his own. He was a Promethean type who would build a castle, but rather than move in, would move on to build another. In 1962, his new castle was Wal-Mart. During the next eight years he opened 30 more Wal-Mart stores.

Fast growth almost strangled the firm financially. For a number of years the company flirted with insolvency. Sam had lived by the motto, "experiment, innovate and expand." To finance his expansion he used leverage–using existing assets to buy new ones. If it works, you grow fast by using debt rather than equity. However, leverage has an exponential effect–either positive or negative. It lets you grow very fast or plummet very quickly. With typical candor Sam wrote (Walton, p. 119):

> *...Helen and I were also in debt up to our eyeballs–several million dollars' worth...If something happened and everybody decided to call their notes, I kept thinking, we would be sunk. Maybe that's what being raised in the Depression does to you, but I wanted out of that debt in the worst way.*

Wal-Mart's high debt frightened away many potential investment bankers and other traditional credit sources such as Prudential. When he could no longer get people to loan him money, he bought the National Bank in Rogers, Arkansas with its deposits of $29 million, and then used that resource until even it was insufficient to accommodate his fast growth.

In early 1970, Walton was beginning to saturate the smaller southern markets and was looking for a way to expand nationally. His growth strategy demanded larger, and hence more distant markets. That meant going into direct competition with his adversary when he had only 32 stores distributed across Arkansas, Missouri and Oklahoma. He sensed that the time was right to strike and strike he did. On October 1, 1970, Sam took Wal-Mart public to get expansion capital. This would enable him to expand the chain of Wal-Mart stores beyond those three states. In return for about $4 million, Sam gave up 20% of the company. After the offering, his small team maintained 75% ownership in Wal-Mart and Sam's shares were worth $25 million. By the end of 1971, there were 51 Wal-Mart stores generating an annual revenue of $78 million.

STRATEGIC MARKETING PLOY

Before 1972, Wal-Mart was a chain of stores spanning only five states, and none of these stores was in a town or city served by Kmart. Finally in 1972, Sam Walton decided to go head-to-head with the giant. He had observed that the Kmart store in Hot Springs, Arkansas had high prices that reflected the lack of local competition. As his initial entry into the retail war against Kmart, Sam sent Phil Green, a highly respected associate, to open Wal-Mart store number 52 in Hot Springs. To fire the first shot across the bow of the good ship Kmart, Phil placed the largest order for Tide detergent ever received by Procter & Gamble. His strategy was to use this large order to send a message, for that order exceeded the combined volume sold in all of his stores in the United States–3500 cases! Such a large volume purchase enabled Sam to sell a box of Tide for $1.99, while the same product was selling at Kmart for $3.97. Wal-Mart was now the price leader–a title they would never relinquish. Sam told *Fortune Magazine* (June 29, 1992):

> Our strategy, to meet the competitors head on, was one of the smartest strategic decisions we ever made.

After this initial competitive move, Wal-Mart began to grow exponentially. From a start of 52 stores and revenues of $78 million he became even more aggressive, despite the fact Kmart was still ten times his size and had 500 stores generating $3 billion in revenues. But Sam never backed away from a fight. In fact, his fierce competitive spirit merely impelled him more strongly to further expand and grow. Reflecting in his memoirs on his competition with Kmart, Sam opined (Walton, p. 242):

> If our story doesn't prove anything more about the free market system, it erases any doubt that spirited competition is good for business–not just customers, but the companies which have to compete with one another too...We wouldn't be nearly as good as we are without Kmart.

To serve the growing number of stores, Sam built a number of huge distribution centers. The Wal-Mart revenues in 1971 had increased by 77% over the previous year. This got Wall Street's attention and in 1972 Wal-Mart was listed on the New York Stock Exchange. A single share of Wal-Mart stock purchased for $16.50 in 1972 would be worth $116,736 in March 2000, equivalent to a return of about 700,000% on the original investment. Ironically, most of those who owned shares in Wal-Mart were not the shrewd Wall Street investors, but rather Sam's store managers and family friends who saw first-hand what was about to happen.

By 1974, Sam had invested almost 30 years of effort and energy into building the Wal-Mart empire. When not absorbed in his business, he sought leisure in tennis and quail hunting. The former appealed to his tenacious competitive spirit and the latter was a cooperative enterprise with his bird dogs. Now, at 56 years of age, he decided it was time to spend more time in leisure and leave the day-to-day operation of Wal-Mart in younger hands. To this end, he appointed Ron Mayer as chairman and CEO of Wal-Mart and Arend Ferold as president. Sam retained the position of Chairman of the Executive Committee in the hope of maintaining some long-term control of the company's destiny.

In Chapter 3, we reported that J. Paul Getty's attempt to retire to a hedonistic life style at age 24 lasted only two years before the lure of business enterprise drove him back into the oil fields. In what might be considered a predictable chain of events, Sam Walton, a man who lived on the adrenaline rush of competitive discount retail, terminated his retirement in 30 months and resumed his previous position as Chairman and CEO at Wal-Mart. In his own words, (Walton, p. 192):

> *I failed at retirement worse than just about anything else I've ever tried. Actually, I knew it was a mistake almost right after I resigned the chairmanship...Unfortunately, I just couldn't stay away from it.*

In the 30 months that Mayer had been CEO of Wal-Mart, he had hired many new executives and had acquired the loyalty of many other senior officials. When Sam returned to lead the company, Ron Mayer left Wal-Mart and took with him many of the top brass who were loyal to him.

During the next few years, Sam had to rebuild his executive ranks. At the same time, Kmart had responded to Wal-Mart's tossing down of the gauntlet in Hot Springs, Arkansas by building stores in four of the towns served by Wal-Mart. By 1976, the retail war between the "giant" 1000-store Kmart and the miniscule 150-store Wal-Mart was under way.

Realizing he was in a battle of survival, Sam hired a research group to evaluate his discount stores and make recommendations. The consultants' final report criticized every aspect of the Wal-Mart stores including the displays, the pricing, the stock levels and the management of staff.

This harsh critique of the Wal-Mart stores by the research group was later described by Walton as "a turning point in our business." Wal-Mart created a new business plan aimed at the radical overhaul of its policies in three main areas: promotion, merchandising and human resources. Out of these plans emerged a more flamboyant approach to promotion that bordered on outrageous and a more aggressive merchandising practice that reduced profit margins on most items. However, one of the most important developments was a new recognition of employees as partners and business associates. This new vision included a generous profit-sharing plan and professional staff development that elevated the status of the employees from mere wage earners to business partners with a shared interest in Wal-Mart's success.

By 1979, Wal-Mart had expanded to 230 stores with gross revenues of $1 billion. Two years later, Wal-Mart took the next giant step by expanding east of the Mississippi River through the acquisition of Kuhn's Big K stores. After that, Wal-Mart entered a super-expansionary mode, adding over 100 new stores per year. However, in 1983, when Sam Walton was 65 and just four years into this hectic expansion, he was diagnosed with leukemia. He signed up for the experimental drug Interferon and, a short time later, his cancer appeared to be in remission.

When *Forbes* listed Sam Walton in 1985 as the richest man in America, his life changed forever. Interviewers and reporters became enamored with the billionaire who drove a pickup truck. The fact that money had never been important to Sam intrigued them. When queried about his frugal lifestyle he responded, "What am I supposed to do, haul my dogs around in a Rolls-Royce?"

Shortly after Sam reached the age of 70, he was diagnosed with a form of bone cancer known as multiple myeloma. Sam agreed to write his memoirs, *Sam Walton: Made in America (1992)*. In the last chapter, he reflected on his success and its price (Walton, p. 320):

> *Here's how I look at it: my life has been a trade-off. If I wanted to reach the goals I set for myself, I had to get at it and stay at it every day...if I had the choices to make all over again, I would make just about the same ones.*

Walton's Decade-by-Decade Climb

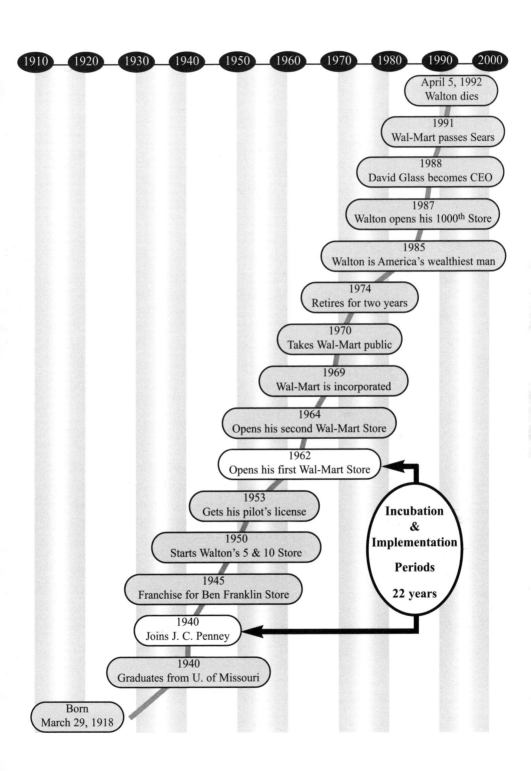

| 1910 | 1920 | 1930 | 1940 | 1950 | 1960 | 1970 | 1980 | 1990 | 2000 |

April 5, 1992
Walton dies

1991
Wal-Mart passes Sears

1988
David Glass becomes CEO

1987
Walton opens his 1000th Store

1985
Walton is America's wealthiest man

1974
Retires for two years

1970
Takes Wal-Mart public

1969
Wal-Mart is incorporated

1964
Opens his second Wal-Mart Store

1962
Opens his first Wal-Mart Store

1953
Gets his pilot's license

1950
Starts Walton's 5 & 10 Store

1945
Franchise for Ben Franklin Store

1940
Joins J. C. Penney

1940
Graduates from U. of Missouri

Born
March 29, 1918

**Incubation
&
Implementation
Periods
22 years**

A PERSONALITY PROFILE

COMMUNICATION STYLE: DOWN HOME

Sam had charisma, but it was the understated charisma of a man whose powerful personality lurks beneath the appeal of an approachable, unassuming demeanor. He did not exude the polish or panache of a highly educated sophisticate, yet he was able to connect with people from all social strata at a visceral level. In his own words, he "never met a stranger." Though he was a billionaire, Sam never thought himself any better than his employees whom he referred to as "associates" and treated as colleagues. This demeanor ingratiated him to all the workers in the Wal-Mart hierarchy and they responded to his generosity of spirit with an uncompromised loyalty.

Charles Kuralt did a retrospective on Walton's life in which he spoke of the "cult-like following" at Wal-Mart. When the big brass shows up in most large firms, employees tend to keep a low profile. That was not the case at Wal-Mart. Sam would have been dismayed at the suggestion that his presence was intimidating to his employees. When he showed up it was time to sit down and discuss what was happening and what should be happening.

A measure of the kind of allegiance that Walton could generate was evident the time he used satellite TV to communicate simultaneously with his diverse network of stores. During the broadcast he led his vast audience of employees in the chant:

> *I solemnly promise and declare that every time a customer comes within ten feet of me, I will smile, look him in the eye, and greet him, so help me Sam.*

Who could not respond positively to such a salutation? Psychologists report that 80% of sales are made to people who like you. And people liked Sam. One of Wal-Mart's first buyers, Claude Harris, said (Walton, p. 69), "He's a very persuasive man; he could charm a bird out of a tree."

Communication was one of the keys to success in Sam's world. He was a cheerleader extraordinaire who was able to communicate his passion in a contagious manner. When Sam drove to a store in his legendary pickup truck, the atmosphere would become electrified. No employee was too far down in the hierarchy for the Chairman to befriend and every store visitation ended in a pep rally. Sam's departure from the store would leave in its wake a more highly charged and motivated staff.

Promotion was Sam's forte, and the more outrageous the better. At his first Ben Franklin store in Newport, Arkansas, he installed a Ding Dong ice cream stand on the sidewalk and people would wait in long lines to get free ice cream. On other occasions, he used a popcorn promotion. As the smell of popcorn permeated Main Street, Sam became known as the king of promotion. What had been dubbed "a *corny* promotional gimmick" by his competitors turned out be a highly effective marketing technique. Customers came just to make sure they weren't missing out on some huge sale or bargain. The store manager across the street who had observed in awe the success of this upstart later commented, "Walton had the personality that brought people in."

From that very first Wal-Mart store in Rogers, Arkansas, Walton had a penchant for promotion that would have done P. T. Barnum proud. In his memoirs Sam wrote, "I have the personality of a promoter." He thought nothing of buying a truckload of watermelons and stacking them on a sidewalk with a donkey ride to attract families. According to Wal-Mart CEO David Glass, who had witnessed this arcane promotion in 1964 (Walton, p. 58):

> It was the worst retail store I had ever seen. Sam had brought a couple of trucks of watermelons in and stacked them on the sidewalk. He had a donkey ride out in the parking lot. It was about 115 degrees and the watermelons began to pop and the donkey began to do what donkeys do, and it all mixed together and ran all over the parking lot. And when you went inside the store, the mess just continued, having been tracked in all over the floor. He was a nice fellow, but I wrote him off. It was just terrible.

The disaster didn't dissuade Glass from eventually coming on board at Wal-Mart.

INTUITIONAL STYLE: PROMETHEAN

Intuition is usually the internalization of prolonged observations, and Sam was an astute observer. Rather than tapping into formal surveys or computer models to make marketing decisions, Sam observed practices in other stores as well as his own. In his memoirs, he stressed the importance of "keeping your ear to the ground" (Walton, p. 285):

> *A computer is not–and never will be–a substitute for getting out in your stores and learning what's going on. In other words, a computer can tell you down to the dime what you've sold. But it can never tell you how much you could have sold.*

Charlie Baum, a colleague of Sam's, provided a vignette that illustrates Sam's talent for transforming observations into revenue (Walton, p. 42):

> *As soon as Sam moved the store from Newport to Bentonville, he had a nice big sale, and we put barrels of stuff all around the floor. Those elderly ladies would come in and bend way down over into those barrels. I'll never forget this. Sam takes a look, frowns, and says: "One thing we gotta do, Charlie. We gotta be real strong in lingerie." Times had been hard and some of those under-things were pretty ragged.*

Several decades later Sam reported that Wal-Mart had sold, in 1991 alone, enough socks and underwear to outfit every person in America. In this sense only could Sam Walton be dubbed "America's greatest under-achiever."

When he chose to go into discounting on a grand scale, Sam was regarded by his family as a radical who would squander the family's money with his wild, impetuous scheme. In his memoirs he wrote (Walton, p. 62):

> *Everybody who knew I was going ahead with the discounting idea on my own really thought I'd completely lost my mind.*

But Sam "felt it in his bones" and such acute instincts are germane to most gifted entrepreneurs. Some things "feel" right. No matter who demeans their ideas, they follow their passion and pursue it with a vengeance. As the Greek philosopher Aristotle observed over 2000 years ago, "There is no great genius without a mixture of madness." In Sam's case he never did anything half way. When he decided to launch, he moved at full throttle no matter how formidable his adversaries. He later described his zeal (Walton, p. 314):

> *I think I overcame every single one of my personal shortcomings by the sheer passion I brought to my work. I don't know if you're born with this kind of passion, or if you can learn it. But I do know you need it... and pretty soon everybody around you will catch the passion from you.*

The entrepreneurial genius tends to see the answer first and then reverts to the beginning to verify that the answer makes sense. Such people have a holistic view of a concept, envision it functioning in its complete state, and then set out to ensure that they can transform that vision into a reality. Such was the intuitive mentality of Sam Walton. He wanted to create the largest retail operation that could provide the best service at the lowest prices. Though he did not realize his vision overnight, it ultimately became a reality–a reality that superceded the realities of Kmart, Target and Woolco.

The idea of visualizing a desired result and striving to achieve it has become very popular in athletics. Professional golfers describe how they prepare to sink a putt by first visualizing the path of the ball as it travels to the hole and drops into the cup. This vision helps them execute the shot with greater consistency and increases the probability of achieving the desired result. Tennis players also use visualization techniques to enhance their performance. Entrepreneurs need to do the same.

CREATIVITY: DARING TO BE DIFFERENT

Great entrepreneurs like Sam Walton are different from most of us. Moreover, they tend to be eminently successful merely because they dare to be different and do things traditional executives would be loathe to consider. The entrepreneur gains a significant advantage by rushing in where others fear to tread. When an entrepreneurial boss like Sam Walton enters the scene and encourages managerial innovation, one of two things happens: the manager either fosters creativity or creates chaos. The difference resides in who is given such latitudes. This is precisely why most creative breakthroughs come out of the eccentric fringe of society. The eccentrics are almost the only ones who dare challenge the system. In Sam's case it was the reason his Wal-Mart venture became the most pervasive and largest retailer in the world. He not only broke prices, he broke with tradition in order to compete with operations that had an edge in every other quarter.

RISK-TAKING PROPENSITY: HIGH

CEO David Glass gave Walton the ultimate compliment when he wrote, "Sam Walton is less afraid of being wrong than anyone I've ever known." Even Sam sensed that he was different in this regard saying, "I see myself as being a little more inclined than most people to take chances." (Walton, p. 253). Like most great entrepreneurs, he had a higher tolerance for risk than others, though he seldom took foolish chances. While running the company, he personally owned eighteen different planes and piloted them long after he could have easily afforded to hire a pilot. He often flew lower than the law allowed. Sam's son Rob added to the Walton mystique when he told A&E *Biography*:

> *My dad liked to fly low to look for real estate deals. The FAA would radio and say, "You can't go that low" and dad would reach down and turn off the radio.*

The depiction of Sam Walton as a high flyer applied more to his business ventures than to his aviatorial practices.

In the early days of Wal-Mart, Sam's daughter Alice confided to a school chum, "My daddy owes so much money and he won't quit opening stores" (Walton, p. 86). Nothing seemed to scare him; even close brushes with death in his plane. One day in Carthage, Missouri, while landing with a prospective executive, a student pilot pulled out in front of his twin-engine Beach Baron. Sam later called it the closest he ever came "to being killed in an airplane" (Trimble, p. 4). Telling the story in his own words, Sam recalled:

> *I gave the plane full throttle, raised the nose, and tried to get back into the air, yanked the yoke to my chest in a massive effort to get the plane to fly above the other plane.*

The Beach Baron barely missed the Piper. Sam was 51 at the time.

INTENSITY: FUELLED BY A PASSIONATE IMPATIENCE FOR RESULTS

In the early days of Wal-Mart, Sam's passionate and impatient desire for results set a frenetic pace that permeated the company and its stores. His easy-going personal demeanor belied the hard-driving intensity that drove him to succeed. He played tennis with a similar controlled aggression that seemed to suggest the world would end if he didn't win. Sam successfully communicated the need to beat Kmart no matter the cost. This mission was core to the firm and pervaded the conscious everyday activities of the Wal-Mart employees. The Wal-Mart corporate culture clearly reflected the competitive fervor of their leader. As Sam explained (Walton, p. 15):

> *I have always pursued everything I was interested in with a true passion–some would say obsession–to win.*

After Sam became successful and the media wanted to know how the country boy had beaten the big boys, Sam attributed that success to his passion to compete. He fostered a spirit of positive, rather than negative competition. In his own words, "We're really not concerned with the competition or what they are doing wrong; we're concerned with what they are doing right." His passion proved contagious. "If you love it, then showing enthusiasm is easy," he told the media.

A stroll today through the Bentonville, Arkansas offices would make it quite apparent that the ghost of Sam is still there in spirit. His ethical standards, frugality, honesty, and sincere respect for others still carry Sam's imprint–so also does his legendary need for speed. A classic story of Sam's everpresent sense of urgency was his decision to create a policy manual. Formal administration was anathema to Sam, but he capitulated and hired an executive who had just finished the same job for Kroger's. That project had taken Jack Shewmaker about one year to complete. Sam gave him 60 days. Shewmaker commented, "Sam never wants to wait for anything. He has no patience."

Sam Walton's perpetual sense of urgency spawned an acute intolerance of delays. He made impulsive decisions so he could move on to conquer other worlds. For him speed was key. The faster you made it to a target, the better the edge you had over the competition–an advantage that would translate into lower cost. Speed was integral to his strategy whether chasing tennis balls or battling Kmart. Be fast and be good was his slogan. Do it now was his style. His executives knew this and made sure that when he asked for something it was delivered. His personal secretary for 25 years, Loretta Boss Parker, wrote (Walton, p. 148):

> *His mind works ten times faster than everybody else's. I mean he just gets going and stays two or three jumps ahead and he's quick to go with what's on his mind.*

The intensity of Sam's drive was evident in 1992 when his doctors told him he was dying. Within two weeks of receiving this devastating news, he opened 35 new Wal-Mart stores in a single day. Nothing, not even life-and-death issues, could dissuade him from moving into new vistas.

SELF-IMAGE: AN INCURABLE OPTIMIST

When you believe in a dream, your dream can become contagious. One high school classmate remembered Walton as an athlete who was "optimistic all the time." Walton admitted, "I've never been one to dwell on reverses. We just got after it and stayed after it."

Such remarkable confidence can prove infectious–even when the belief is delusional! We find strong delusional beliefs in the arrogant convictions of Napoleon Bonaparte, Frank Lloyd Wright, J. Paul Getty, Henry Ford and Adolph Hitler. Their megolamaniacal perspectives spawned a passion that overcame other shortcomings.

Never was this more apparent than the day Sam called his brother Bud and told him to meet him at the local airport. When Bud arrived, Sam was considering the purchase of a small airplane. His bewildered brother reminded Sam of something that he must already have known, "Sam, you can't fly." With characteristic confidence, Sam announced, "But I can drive, so I'll learn how to fly." Sam purchased the plane on the spot.

How many people would buy a plane without any indication that they could fly or make it through flight school? Such a positive demeanor is the life force of the entrepreneurial genius. Optimists tend to be so enamored of life's opportunities that they often ignore details.

CRITICAL THINKING AND ICONOCLASM

Profiles of high achievers suggest that normal people are normally suc-cessful and abnormal people are abnormally successful or abnormally unsuccessful. They have abnormal confidence, abnormal vision, abnor-mal passion, abnormal diligence, abnormal tenacity, and an abnormal risk-taking propensity. They show a natural disposition to challenging the status quo and breaking rules. Research on the gifted reveals that they are intolerant of blind conformity.

Walton matched the profile of the abnormal person in all of these traits. He didn't care that something was running smoothly. If a new promotion could improve revenues, he went for it. That was a characteristic of his entrepreneurial genius. Sam Walton encouraged his store managers to think creatively and to break the rules whenever it would lead to higher profits. Mistakes were part of the game for Sam. At Wal-Mart, to err was human, to attempt to hide the error was a sin and to do nothing was a mortal sin. Sam's willingness to challenge the rules enabled him to make new breakthroughs in retailing.

ECCENTRICITIES AND PERSONALITY PARADOXES

It is paradoxical that the unassuming Sam Walton, who had a lifelong disdain for money, accumulated more wealth than anyone in history. Sam stated, "Money never has meant that much to me, not even in the sense of keeping score." His associate Charlie Baum observed, "I believe that money is, in some respects, almost immaterial to him. What motivates the man is the desire to absolutely be on top of the heap. It is *not* the money."

While Bill Gates remains the world's wealthiest individual, the Walton family together has a net worth in excess of $100 billion. To his credit Sam put all of his stock in Wal-Mart in his wife's, children's, and family trusts from the beginning. What can we learn from this about wealth building? In a nutshell, don't chase money. Chase dreams and chase them relentlessly, and the money will come in trucks.

Most visionaries are focused on results and show impatience with inconsequential details and what they regard as irrelevant "paperwork." An indication of Sam's disdain for paperwork came from his first retail boss at J. C. Penney's who said, "I'd fire you Walton if you weren't such a good salesman." (Walton, p. 23). Sam's long-term secretary described him as unpredictable and completely disorganized. Such characteristics are typical of great entrepreneurs. They operate with a kind of *pragmatic perfectionism.*

Sam disdained grandiose job titles, posh offices, chauffeurs, yachts, country clubs, and all the trappings that were flaunted by the CEOs of his competition. He vowed never to allow such behavior to creep into Wal-Mart, and to this date, it has not. Consequently, Wal-Mart has consistently reported the lowest overhead in the retailing industry. Some felt that Sam's frugality reached excessive heights when he insisted that store managers stay two or more to a hotel room when attending a conference or industry trade show. Walton admitted, "I'm a pretty conservative guy but I'm driven to buck the system."

ACHIEVEMENTS & HONORS

MAGNITUDE OF SUCCESS

It is hard to truly assess or put into perspective the unbelievable success of Wal-Mart. One way is to use the numerical indicators that Walton eschewed. By the end of the millennium, Wal-Mart was the largest retailer in the world. They closed 2002 with 4000 discount stores: over 1800 Wal-Mart stores, nearly 1000 Supercenters, 500 Sam's Clubs and 20 Neighborhood Markets in the United States plus another 1000 in other countries. As this chapter is written, Wal-Mart revenues are nearing $300 billion and climbing, with new stores opening daily in such diverse markets as Argentina, Brazil, Canada, China, Germany, Korea, Mexico, Puerto Rico and the United Kingdom. The once small-city retailer now has in excess of one million employees. In September 2001 they proudly announced they had sold more American flags in two days than in their prior history. Sam would have been proud.

The juggernaut Sam Walton put in motion never stopped growing. As noted in the overview, in 2002 Wal-Mart went from the world's largest retailer to the world's largest company. Their annual profit is approaching $10 billion. They are way out in front of their nearest rivals and are growing much faster. This meteoric Wal-Mart growth, displayed in the table below, is unprecedented in the annals of U. S. retailing.

Wal-Mart Growth in Stores, Sales, & Profits 1960–2001

	1960	1970	1980	1990	2000	2002
Number of Stores	9	32	276	1528	3000	4000
Sales in Dollars	$1.4M	$31M	$1.2B	$26B	$191B	$300B
Profits in Dollars	$112K	$1.2M	$41M	$1B	$6.3B	$7B

Note: 1960 figures represent the five-and-dime stores.

Sam would have been pleased to have seen the 2001 Walmart.com Internet service offering of $9.95–half the price charged by AOL. The promotion was aimed at the mass markets of young buyers, giving them the lowest web-service pricing in the industry; something that had always been near and dear to Sam's heart. Finding new ways to give customers the best value was the Walton way. Wal-Mart still regards that mission as sacrosanct. Sam spoke passionately and often about swimming upstream to find the biggest fish. He got the biggest fish in retail, ending his career as the quintessential retail genius of the 20th century.

HONORS

When Wellington observed, "Napoleon on the field of battle was worth 10,000 men," he was complimenting his mortal enemy. In much the same way the founder of Kmart, Harry Cunningham, said of Sam, "Walton is the greatest businessman of this century."

In 1984 Sam was given the Horatio Alger Award for entrepreneurship. In that year, he also made the Forbes list of richest persons. In 1989, *Financial World* voted him the CEO of the Decade and at the millennium Wal-Mart was listed #1 in the *20th Century's Greatest Business Dynasties*. Charles Kuralt paid tribute with a television feature, calling him the greatest merchant in the last half of the 20th century.

On March 17, 1992, President George Bush and the First Lady traveled to Bentonville to pay tribute to Sam who was in a wheelchair and incapable of projecting his normal charisma. Sam accepted the Medal of Freedom, the nation's highest civilian honor, that bore the inscription:

> *This unassuming original never doubted his ability but never flaunted his success. He is the consummate retail genius.*

Sam later referred to this honor as the "highlight of our entire career."

On his death in 1992 at age 74, a *USA Today* headline characterized Sam Walton as a "pioneer who changed the face of retailing." Management guru Tom Peters wrote:

> *With the possible exception of Henry Ford, Sam Walton is the entrepreneur of the century.*

LESSONS LEARNED FROM SAM WALTON

How did Sam Walton go from a mom-and-pop retailer to the largest in the world? In his memoirs (Walton, p. 314–17), Sam outlined the following ten rules or maxims that he believed to be the pillars on which his success was built:

Rule 1: Commit to your business. Believe in it more than anybody else.

Rule 2: Share your profits with all your associates, and treat them as partners.

Rule 3: Motivate your partners. Money and ownership alone aren't enough.

Rule 4: Communicate everything you possibly can to your partners.

Rule 5: Appreciate everything your associates do for the business.

Rule 6: Celebrate your successes. Find some humor in your failures.

Rule 7: Listen to everyone in your company.

Rule 8: Exceed your customers' expectations.

Rule 9: Control your expenses better than your competition.

Rule 10: Swim upstream. Go the other way. Ignore the conventional wisdom.

These rules can be combined and consolidated into the five prescient principles described in the paragraphs that follow.

PLAN FOR LONG-TERM GAINS

The fact that there was a 17-year hiatus between Sam's opening of his first variety store and his first Wal-Mart store is testimonial to his focus on the long term. Sam knew from the beginning what Henry Ford had discovered several decades earlier–decreasing margins yields higher sales volume and higher revenues. In Sam's words, "charge less and make up the difference in volume." If you do not have volume, you are less flexible and have few options. This policy allowed Wal-Mart to pass the defensive players as if they were stuck in neutral on the nation's retailing freeway.

Sam's quest to build a discount chain with lowest costs and hence lowest prices drove him to implement any procedure or mechanism that would increase efficiency. For example, he revolutionized retail distribution by building a spoke-and-wheel system of store distribution to gain an edge and become the lowest cost retailer. He built huge efficient warehouses central to his target markets. Then he carefully planned and executed the construction of his stores. He was sufficiently astute to understand that in a billion-dollar business, a streamlined distribution system can save pennies per item that generate huge profits when sold by the millions. The first such distribution system opened in Bentonville, Arkansas in 1969. On that date, the wide chasm between giant Kmart and little upstart Wal-Mart began to close.

While Kmart was busily building stores helter-skelter to capture near-term profits, Sam was content to bide his time and build the system before building the stores. "I was never in anything for the short haul," he wrote. Quick gains are seldom manifest in long-term rewards in any venue.

PRESS FOR FIRST MOVER ADVANTAGE

Sam understood that mid-size towns of small population could support a single store the size of Wal-Mart, but not two stores of this size. Therefore, being the first to build such a store excluded all competitors who would have to risk a substantial investment in an environment where failure was highly probable. This strategy, known as *first mover advantage*, has been widely applied in the computer field where building early brand loyalty to a specific piece of software or hardware establishes market dominance that is hard to displace. Sam's understanding of this concept helped fuel his sense of urgency during Wal-Mart's expansion.

SHARE OWNERSHIP AND ENCOURAGE INNOVATION

Another innovative tactic that led Wal-Mart to become the world's largest organization was Sam's decision to make his managers part owners. If a new manager didn't have the money to invest, Sam loaned him the money. The manager was in charge, and so a manager who wanted to try some radical new promotion could try it without asking anyone's permission. This was not possible at Kmart.

Placing full responsibilities on the shoulders of the manager was a highly successful strategy that led to many innovative shopping promotions. Among these were the "buy American" slogan, the "satisfaction guaranteed exchange" policy, the Shopping Cart Bingo, and the still popular people-greeters. Walton never got stuck in traditional ways of doing anything. He believed that to be good you had to be unique. That entailed trying all kinds of bizarre stunts to attract customers, even if it meant bucking the system. And more importantly, Sam was never too arrogant to learn from his managers or competitors.

One of the reasons that Sam could trust his store managers to improvise was that they were owners with an owner's mentality. He insisted they buy stock from day one. If a problem cropped up on Sunday afternoon he knew they would be there to solve the problem (unlike a nine-to-five employee with no stake in the store's success). The result was that Wal-Mart managers saw their jobs as twenty-four-hour-per-day commitments spanning seven days per week. Such convictions are critical in an industry operating seven days on two shifts. Sam was convinced that good service and low prices would win in the long run. In his words, "Give them superb service, at the lowest prices possible, and guarantee every sale." The strategy worked and allowed the roughly-hewn Oklahoman in a pickup truck to build a dynasty. Because sharing the wealth was important to Sam, all store managers from the very beginning were not employees–they were his partners. In this way, he generated total loyalty and his goals became theirs. That was the Walton magic.

CHARISMATIC LEADERSHIP IS A PRIME MOTIVATOR

Many first-born children become leaders. Some psychologists conjecture that serving in a leadership role in their sibling relationships imbues them with a predilection to leading rather than following. First-born Sam was no exception. In any situation, Sam adopted a "take charge" approach and led the field into battle. However, his personal leadership style was informal and his persona, one of the keys to his success, was that of down-home boy, ol' Sam.

Sam Walton had many talents that brought his success, but he saw his ability to motivate others as his predominant gift (Walton, p. 17–18):

> *I guess I was just totally competitive...and my main talent was probably the same as my best talent as a retailer–I was a good motivator.*

In spite of his growing wealth and power, Sam remained unpretentious and highly approachable. Upon entering a Wal-Mart store, one of his first actions would be to seize a microphone and invite the employees to come forward and speak. Moving into his role as cheerleader, he would yell into the mike, "Give me a W;...give me an A!..." and he would call out the letters until his enthusiastic following had spelled W-A-L-M-A-R-T.

When the firm achieved an unprecedented 8% return on sales in 1984, Sam had to honor a promise that he would do the hula down Wall Street if he achieved that return. At the time of his promise, he had thought he was safe because the retail industry was typically yielding about 3%

return on sales. Wall Street rejoiced in his entrepreneurial flamboyance, and applauded as the 66-year-old Walton, attired in a hula skirt and adorned with leis, danced the hula down Wall Street and warmed the hearts of New Yorkers.

Much of Wal-Mart's phenomenal success can be attributed to Sam's allowing managers to engage in wild stunts as long as they attracted customers. His managers dropped balloons containing frozen pizzas off rooftops and engaged the customers in Shopping Cart Bingo. Such stunts enticed customers into the store in the hope that their lucky number might yield a free cart full of items. Walton culminated 25 years of such antics with the World Championship Moon Pie Eating Contest where they sold the most Moon Pies in history. The real win was the huge publicity that helped build brand loyalty toward the Wal-Mart name.

Swim Upstream: Break the Rules to Find Better Ways

Although Sam Walton was a devout Christian and a family man, he was also both radical and defiant. In his personal life, he was conservative and god-fearing; in business, he was just the opposite. The Walton way in business was to forget convention and break all the rules if it meant improvement. Nothing was sacred to Sam except giving customers the brand-name products at the lowest prices. This was his contribution to retailing–if it ain't broke, then break it, and only then will you be able to dominate your industry. Sam was not only willing to break what wasn't broken, but he relentlessly endeavored to reconceptualize anything and everything in pursuit of what worked best.

Walton was candid about his philosophy of breaking what was not broken. In his memoirs he wrote (Walton, 1992, p. 34):

> *As good as business was, I never could leave well enough alone and in fact, I think my constant fiddling and meddling with the status quo may have been one of my biggest contributions to the later success of Wal-Mart.*

In order to gain insight into the strengths of competitors like Kmart and the Price Club, Sam would jump into his truck and visit their stores. Often he was discovered in disguise wearing dark glasses to avoid being recognized. On occasion, he could be found on his hands and knees crawling around and peering under Kmart's counters. Such industrial espionage is not illegal, and it is certainly one method of discovering new ways that work. Sam saw it as a duty to his managers and shareholders to learn as much as he could about the effective practices of the competition. The Walton children later reported how their dad would drive off highways to visit a competitor–even when they were on vacation.

One of Sam's favorite haunts was the The Price Club in San Diego. The revolutionary warehouse club was unique and fit the Walton model of innovative marketing. He wrote:

> *I guess I've stolen more ideas from Sol Price as from anybody else in the business. I really liked Sol's Fed-Mart name, so I latched on to it.*

On one information-gathering trip, Sam was stopped by the Price Club security guard. His tape recorder was confiscated and he was taken to the office as an interloper. Fortunately, Sam knew Sol Price and an incident was averted.

The strong egos of many executives would prevent them from undertaking such demeaning tasks. However, Sam asserted, "Whenever you get confused, go to the store. The customer has all the answers." When he found a competitor doing something well, he imitated them. When he found them under-selling him, he reduced the prices in his stores. His plagiarizing was never more blatant than when he copied Sol Price's innovative *Price Club*, and opened his own division called *Sam's Club*.

The ability to innovate made him special. His motto had always been, "buy cheap, sell low and pass the savings on to the customer." The idea of maximizing profits by minimizing the cost to the customer had been atypical in retailing where most marketing managers strive to create generous profit margins that maximize the return on investment. When he documented his rules for success he admonished readers to pay particular attention to "Rule 10–Swim upstream" (Walton, pp. 314, 317):

> *Swim upstream. Go the other way. Ignore conventional wisdom. If everybody else is doing it one way, there's a good chance you can find your niche by going in exactly the opposite direction....I always prided myself on breaking everybody else's rules, and I always favored the mavericks who challenged my rules.*

And then Sam advised, with characteristic iconoclasm (Walton, p. 314):

> *So pay special attention to Rule 10, and if you interpret it in the right spirit–as it applies to you–it could mean simply: Break All the Rules.*

Hugh Marston Hefner
Start with the Answer–Reality or Fantasy

b. Chicago, IL   April 9, 1926

"I believe in health through hedonism."

SELF-DESCRIPTION
"I never intended to be a revolutionary. My intention was to create a mainstream magazine that included sex."

MOTTO
"Once I had the money, I bought my Shangri La–Playboy Mansion, and once I moved in, I became the Playboy depicted in my magazine."

INNOVATION HMH Publishing founded in 1953 to publish *Playboy* with a bank loan of $600 plus another $8000 in equity capital. Name changed to Playboy Enterprises in 1971

UNIQUE QUALITY Fantasy escapes into movies; the Playboy philosophy – hedonism gone amuck; money was only a vehicle for living life on his terms–the true sybaritic lifestyle

OBJECTIVE "My intention was to create a magazine for the urban male that would combat the repressive anti-sexual, anti-play and anti-pleasure aspects of our puritan heritage."

NET WORTH Estimated at $200M (based on various resources)

HONORS Magazine Hall of Fame, 1998

BIRTH ORDER First born; younger brother, Keith

EDUCATION BA in Psychology from University of Illinois in 1950; One semester grad school in Sociology

PERSONALITY Control freak and perfectionist; every detail of his *Playboy* empire is approved by him; intuitive introvert; libidinally-driven visionary–lives by his passions

HOBBIES Sexual antics and films; loves games including Monopoly, backgammon, and pinball.

POLITICS Libertarian–if it doesn't hurt anyone, then it's O.K.

RELIGION Agnostic from early age despite Puritan upbringing

FAMILY Wives: Two, Children: Four–two from each marriage

6
Hugh Hefner

Start with the Answer–Reality or Fantasy

"I never intended to be a revolutionary."

Overview

Great entrepreneurs start with a prescient vision and then work passionately to make it happen. Hugh Hefner is our poster boy for such an approach. Hef sensed a market need and filled it without regard to dissenting opinion. His temerity made him rich and famous. Many great entrepreneurs have taken a similar path, for example, Thomas Watson Sr. of IBM fame said (Gerber, p. 69):

> At the very beginning I had a very clear picture of what the company would look like when it was finally done. I had a model in my mind of what it would look like when my vision was in place. From the outset IBM was fashioned after the template of my vision.

All revolutions begin with a superb idea, accompanied by the passion to see it fulfilled. Similarly, all breakthrough products begin with a vision and then become a reality through a champion who makes it happen. That was the magic behind the creation of the *Playboy* empire. When he decided to create the quintessential "girlie" magazine, Hugh Hefner wanted to make a philosophic statement rather than merely titillate the male appetite for female nudity. Hef's vision was to create an intellectual magazine of quality, aimed at altering the mores of what he saw as an uptight world.

From the beginning, Hef contended that *Playboy* magazine was not created principally for money. He claimed it was a way for him to assuage the inner guilt that had plagued him as a youth growing up in a puritanical environment. The *Playboy* philosophy was that there was nothing evil about sexual fantasy as long as no one was hurt in the process. In essence, his conception of a magazine that would indulge male sexual fantasies was a rebellion against "the anti-sex, anti-play, and anti-pleasure aspects of the Puritan heritage" (Telese, p. 576). Though Hefner was never against family values or normal romance, he fought vehemently for the right of the individual to choose. The magazine was his vehicle for expressing this philosophy. Of course, Hef's rebellion also turned out to be remarkably lucrative, because he tapped into a market that was ready to indulge by joining his revolution. Hugh Hefner's net worth has been estimated to be between $100 million and $200 million. This is no meagre reward for his quest for the naked truth.

How did Hef launch such a successful sexual revolution? His genius was not only in his timing, but also in his artistic taste. What made *Playboy* special was Hef's idea that nude female photographs would be only *one* of the delights that a young sophisticated male should enjoy without shame. To create this aura, *Playboy* magazine also featured interviews with people of intellectual substance and articles from celebrated authors–all on glossy, coated paper. This elevated tone set *Playboy* apart from its tawdry "skin magazine" competitors whose bawdy models, displayed on yellowed newsprint, reminded the reader that he was doing something "dirty."

After the launch of his first issue in December 1953, it was apparent that *Playboy* magazine was an idea whose time had come. Hugh Hefner began living the fantasy that he promoted in his magazine–a life of affluence and self-gratification, driving a 300SL sports car and living in a Chicago Victorian mansion. In 1960 he observed, "I had come out from behind the desk and become the playboy depicted in my magazines. I had become the model of my magazine's fantasies, donning a robe and smoking a pipe."

Through the 1960s and '70s the *Playboy* empire flourished, expanding into entertainment clubs throughout the United States and internationally. By the 1980s and '90s, the social climate had changed. The excesses of the hedonistic life were no longer a novelty, and the *Playboy* empire went into a gradual decline. By the end of the millennium, as its founder approached the age of 75, the *Playboy* empire was immersed in the process of reinventing itself.

In late 2001, Hugh Hefner was roasted on his 75th birthday in New York City. The quintessential playboy showed up with no less than seven 20-something blondes on his arm. The event was a huge success, causing the father of all playboys to quip, "I can't remember when I've had this much fun sitting up." One New York pundit offered some insight into Hef's life and work when he said, "Hefner personifies why the World Trade Center terrorists hate us."

The Formative Years

EARLY EXPERIENCES

Hugh Marston Hefner was born in a Chicago suburb on April 9, 1926. His accountant father, Glen, worked for an aluminum company and was seldom home. Both parents were distant and cold but his mother, the former Grace Swanson, was the primary influence in his early life. His brother Keith was born two years after Hef. Keith would later work for the Playboy Clubs as Training Director. Both boys led sheltered uneventful lives, but were subjected to a puritanical upbringing. Hugh Hefner described his early life as providing a great deal of intellectual freedom but little ethical freedom. He later commented:

I first withdrew into fantasies. I collected all kinds of butterflies and animals. Later I escaped into fantasy by writing and drawing.

He grew up to be a reclusive introvert with a need to express himself through his artistic renderings.

Hef's 4th-grade teacher called his mother one day complaining, "All he does is draw." By age 12, Hugh was attaching words to his vast number of cartoons. Between twelve and fourteen, he drew more than 70 different comic strips, binding them meticulously into neat volumes for future publication. An early character was *Cranet*–his alter-ego. As a teenager, Hef wrote 45 short stories and a novelette on the supernatural. Most of his writings were fully illustrated with cartoon characters that were later used in *Shudder* magazine that he sold for 5 cents each. By age sixteen he had begun work on his autobiography, titled *Comic Autobiography*. In this cartoon spoof he portrayed a frustrated male fighting for survival. It was a theme that would recur often throughout his life.

Throughout his teenage years, Hef had illusions of being seduced by beautiful women, but these fantasies never saw any reality beyond his imagination. This too poor, too shy, too mid-western, and too bright kid with a raging libido would not have seemed a likely candidate for changing the sexual mores of the society in which he lived. Little did Hefner think at the time that within ten years he would bet everything on his vision and become an instant publishing phenomenon. His personal transformation into a playboy would take longer. Hef would be thirty-three before he owned that 300SL and sported that button-down Ivy

League look with a sexy blonde on his arm. He later told the *Saturday Evening Post* (Apr. 29, 1962):

> *I began to work on* Playboy *with everything I had, and for the first time in my life I felt free. It was like a mission–to publish a magazine that would thumb its nose at all the restrictions that had bound me.*

FORMAL EDUCATION

When Hugh Hefner was in grade school, his teachers sensed that he was gifted and tested him. Hefner had an IQ above 150. In high school, he wrote for the school paper and drew countless comic strips, with one autobiographical episode known as *Goo-Heffer and His Misadventures at Stinkmuch High*. He graduated 45th in a class of 212 from Steinmetz High in 1944 where he had excelled as President of the Student Council. He was also voted Class Humorist, One of the Best Orators, One of the Most Artistic, One of the Most Likely to Succeed, and One of the Most Popular.

Upon graduation, he was inducted into the Army. During his service, the voracious reader was always seen with a book in his pocket. His all-time favorite was Fitzgerald's *The Great Gatsby*. Jay Gatsby's opulent lifestyle was intriguing and he fantasized about his hero for many years. Once he had the money, his own life dwarfed that of his hero.

On release from the Army in 1946, Hef enrolled at the University of Illinois in Psychology. While attending university, he discovered the Kinsey Report, *Sexual Behavior in the Human Male*. Reading the statistics presented in this report, he felt he had been misled by the church, his parents and the American establishment to feel guilt for sexual urges that were innate in the human species. With this realization came the emancipation of the young man who would become the "Prince of Pleasure." He would never again have a blind faith in accepted mores.

Hefner graduated from the University of Illinois with a Bachelor's Degree in 1949, the same year that he married college sweetheart Millie Williams. In his first job he lasted but a few months, quitting in disgust over the provincial attitudes at the firm. In search for social meaning, he enrolled in graduate school at Northwestern University in Evanston. His first research paper was titled *Sex and the U. S. Law*, for which he received a B–not for the content, but for his liberal conclusions that ran counter to those of his professor. That incensed Hef so much he quit grad school and took a job at Carson, Pirie, Scott as an advertising copywriter.

The Climb to the Top

BEGIN WITH A DREAM

It was at Carson, Pirie, Scott that Hugh found symbiosis with a group of young bright guys, including one named Leroy Nieman. These colleagues offered encouragement when he began working on a cartoon satire of Chicago. To gain recognition in his chosen profession, Hef felt he needed to be published. He wrote a book titled _The Toddlin' Town_. After numerous rejections from publishers the intrepid writer borrowed $1000 from friends and family members. He then located a printer and self-published 5000 paperback copies. This initiative proved to be an important learning experience, because it taught him that publishing, not writing, would prove to be his forte. His book was reviewed by the _Chicago Tribune_ and described as an "irreverent satire." In true entrepreneurial style, Hef hawked the book at every bookstore in and around Chicago and sold direct by mail order at $1 per copy until the entire inventory was sold out. However, this sales effort took so much time from his "day job" he was fired from Carson, Pirie, Scott after only five weeks.

Shortly after leaving Carson, Pirie, Scott, Hef got a job with _Esquire_ magazine as a promotional copywriter. However, this was just a typical office job and had none of the glamour he had imagined from reading the magazine. When _Esquire_ moved its headquarters to New York in 1951, Hef decided to remain in Chicago and was once again unemployed.

After a short hiatus, Hefner landed a job as promotion manager at the Publishers Development Corporation (PDC) at $80 per week. PDC published what were called "seedy skin magazines" that featured nude pin-ups, but PDC escaped prosecution for obscenity by masquerading as "art" or "naturalist" periodicals. It was while working at PDC that Hugh verbalized his intention of becoming a publisher of his own magazine. To turn his dream into a reality, he contacted two former colleagues at _Esquire_ and together they created a mock-up of the first issue of a "girlie magazine" that they called _Pulse_. However, they were unable to raise the necessary funds to launch _Pulse_ and this new enterprise died on the vine.

At this point, it seemed that Hugh Hefner was approaching the low point of his life. Biographer Russell Miller reported (Miller, p. 31):

> *...it was during this time that he [Hefner] began slipping out in the middle of the night and taking long, contemplative walks along the lake shore, looking up at apartments where the rich lived and wondering miserably if he would ever get a chance to taste the good life.*

While Hef struggled with his dream, wife Millie continued to toil at her teaching job to contribute to the dwindling family coffers. Then in 1952, Millie gave birth to daughter Christie Ann Hefner. Although delighted by his new fatherhood, Hefner continued his unrelenting quest to fulfill his desire to publish a sophisticated "girlie magazine." In early 1953, he wrote (Miller, p. 32):

> *I'd like to produce an entertainment magazine for the city-bred guy–breezy, sophisticated. The girlie features would guarantee the initial sale, but the magazine would have quality too.*

LAUNCHING THE DREAM

In 1953, Hefner was working as circulation director of *Children's Activities* magazine. In his free time after work, he and his old friend, Eldon Sellers, worked on rough layouts for a magazine of the kind that Hugh had envisioned, and they planned to call it *Stag Party*. However, he had no money and virtually no collateral, forcing him to get a $400 loan on his new furniture. Lake Shore Bank loaned him $200 in the summer of 1953 and Hugh talked his conservative parents into investing $1000. Keith Hefner invested another $500 and friend Eldon Sellers bought $2000 worth of stock. These loans were insufficient to bankroll the first issue of *Stag Party*, so in July, 1953, he, Millie, and Eldon incorporated HMH Publishing Company as an Illinois corporation. Friends and relatives of both Hef and Sellers bought shares in HMH, yielding enough money to fund the first issue of *Stag Party*–a total of $10,000, all of which Hef had personally guaranteed. If that first issue failed, Hef would be wiped out and insolvent for many years to come.

With some money now in hand, Hugh Hefner started looking for the hook so critical to any new venture. For a magazine, the hook is the cover story or picture. In his search, Hefner came across a firm in Chicago that owned the rights to the Marilyn Monroe calendar nudes–photographs taken before Marilyn became a big star. One of them had never appeared before. Hef was determined to buy it for his magazine and successfully negotiated the rights for $500. This was a huge amount of money to him since he also had to arrange for the cover artwork, stories, printing, delivery and payroll and wasn't quite sure how he was going to do it. But his biggest risk came when he quit his job, on September 11, 1953 at *Children's Activities* magazine while his newly pregnant wife (carrying son David) and daughter Christie were at home and depending on him as sole provider.

At the eleventh hour, just before the launch of the first issue of *Stag Party*, Hef received legal notification that a field-and-stream magazine named *Stag* objected to the title of his new girlie magazine, saying it might confuse the market. In a last-minute brainstorming session, Eldon Sellers suggested the title *Playboy*. The new title was instantly accepted.

The unfolding of events following the launch in October 1953 of that first issue of *Playboy* has become an often-told success story in the history of publishing. From the time it first hit the newsstands, it was clear that *Playboy* would be a resounding success. Hef calculated that he needed to sell 30,000 copies of that first issue just to break even. When the sales were tallied, he discovered that the first issue had sold 53,991 copies!

Hef had realized that *Playboy* might be a failure and so had decided to hedge his bets. He had decided not to assign a date to his first issue, though it was published in October, and he did not put his name on the masthead as publisher in case the first issue were a dismal failure. Fortunately, the success of the first issue obviated the need for such caution. By January 1956, circulation of *Playboy* had reached 500,000 and by 1959, it had surpassed *Esquire* magazine and reached 1,000,000!

Surprisingly, before 1953, virtually no American male had even seen a nude female in color in any mass medium. Hef's mission would be to ensure that any man who was so inclined would be able to indulge his interest with some degree of overt attention and no shame. Hef told *Look* magazine (Jan. 10, 1967):

> *My naked girls became a symbol of disobedience, a triumph of sexuality. To publish* Playboy *was like waving a flag of freedom, like screaming rebellion under a dictatorship.*

In those pre-Viagra days, Hefner was motivated to (in his own words) "give the American male a few extra laughs and a little diversion from the anxieties of the Atomic Age. [If successful], I will have justified our existence." As expressed by biographer, Russell Miller (Miller, p. 47):

Playboy *was welcomed as a guidebook to this new "good life."* Playboy *told its readers what to wear, what wine to drink with what meals, what records to listen to, what movies to see. Its authoritative tone soothed their anxieties that they might inadvertently wear the wrong necktie or mix a cocktail incorrectly. In particular,* Playboy *espoused sex as a healthy and enjoyable activity, free from guilt.*

FINDING PLAYMATES

The centerfold of *Playboy* featured what became known as the Playmate of the Month. The Playmate also became the centerpiece of the magazine, endowing it with a personality and a persona that fired the fantasies of the young male readers. Her depiction as the "girl-next-door" was enhanced by a description of her daily habits as well as her likes and dislikes in food, sports, theater and men. Although these mini-biographies were often more fiction than fact, they fed the sexual fantasies of young American males who showed their collective approval by purchasing *Playboy* in ever-increasing numbers.

Hef desperately wanted to tell the world that it was okay for nice girls to be sexy and for normal men to give in to their voyeuristic tendencies. In 2002, Hef told A&E, "What set *Playboy* apart was that the girl next door can be sexy. Sex does not have to be dirty." All his enormous energies and talent were spent making that vision a reality. That is the essence of entrepreneurial genius. Hef's liberal message was a huge gamble in the mid '50s. But the gamble paid spectacular returns. Furthermore, the victory allowed Hef to sate his own fantasies as the quintessential playboy. Even now in his late 70s he can be seen flaunting his success with a bevy of beautiful women whose accessibility is beyond the wildest dreams of most American males.

As happens with successful ventures like *Playboy*, it grew far beyond his original plans for it. Hef had wanted to publish a sophisticated slick magazine with intellectual articles and artwork. However, *Playboy* was released when social mores were on the cusp of transition. Elvis was changing music with his gyrations and his whitebread version of black rock. The existential Beat movement was rampant in San Francisco, and the movie, *Blackboard Jungle*, featuring Bill Haley's *Rock Around the Clock* music was in the theaters throughout America. It was a time of change and *Playboy* was riding the wave. HMH Publishing Company began to spawn a variety of new ventures that sought to present its basic philosophy through an assortment of new venues.

PLAYBOY'S PENTHOUSE

It was into this environment of unfettered optimism that Hugh Hefner attempted the publication of another magazine, *Trump*. This venture was to be a full-color humor magazine that would resemble the very popular *Mad* magazine, but would eclipse it in style and sophistication. The first issue of *Trump* was launched in January 1957 but it never seemed to catch on. After substantial delays in the release of its second issue, it died a natural death that carried with it significant financial losses.

The year 1957 was also dismal from a domestic standpoint. In the summer of 1957, Hugh Hefner acknowledged in his diary that his marriage to Millie had been eroded by their time apart and they initiated the separation that culminated in divorce in April 1959. Now divorced and sexually unencumbered, Hugh Hefner launched into another venture that would extend the *Playboy* empire. On the suggestion of two television producers, Hef decided to present the *Playboy* lifestyle on television in a program called *Playboy's Penthouse*. The idea was to televise a live party at the Playboy mansion that would showcase a bevy of beautiful women and a cast of showbiz celebrities enjoying "the good life" in a high style. Hugh Hefner would be the host of this party and would portray a suave bachelor surrounded by an entourage of beautiful, fawning, young women. The hint of unfettered sexual freedom and unlimited debauchery was designed to capture the envy and interest of healthy young males with less exciting social lives. *Playboy's Penthouse* debuted on black-and-white television on October 24, 1959, featuring celebrities Ella Fitzgerald and Nat King Cole. It ran for 26 weeks until it ran out of steam and vanished without adoption by a network.

While *Playboy's Penthouse* was playing out its life as television entertainment, Hef and his friend Victor Lownes III were conceiving a "real-life" nightclub version of *Playboy's Penthouse*. Whereas *Playboy's Penthouse* presented an opportunity for libidinous young men to enjoy vicariously the pleasures of a party with beautiful people in lavish surroundings, the new Playboy Club would enable men to purchase a membership giving them access to a prestigious night club. This club would offer a sophisticated atmosphere to those special members who possessed a "key of entitlement." The creation of this club would provide an opportunity to promote *Playboy* magazine. In turn, *Playboy* magazine would promote the Playboy Club. In late 1959, Playboy Clubs International was incorporated. The first of many such establishments, and situated in Chicago, it would serve as the template for the others.

THE BIRTH OF THE PLAYBOY BUNNY

To add an erotic touch to the image of the Playboy Club, Hef and Lownes conceived the idea of hiring a hand-picked collection of gorgeous cocktail waitresses adorned in what were called "bunny outfits." The rabbit had been adopted for the *Playboy* logo as a symbol of sex and fertility, so the costumes of the waitresses were designed to serve this motif. These seductive uniforms featured loose fitting tops, fashioned to reveal cleavage, and tight fitting shorts that exposed the upper thighs. The addition of collar and cuffs was included to provide an aura of respectability that would elevate the Bunny above common rabbit status. To top off the bunny outfit, the waitress sported a pair of ears on her head and a small puff ball on her bottom–the latter to serve as the infamous "bunny tail." The Playboy bunny subsequently became a ubiquitous symbol of male sexual emancipation and arguably one of the world's most recognizable logos. This was Hefner's unwavering vision and the reason his empire flourished despite bitter attacks from the religious right, congressional do-gooders, and competing skin magazines that lacked Hefner's loftier ideals. (Ironically, the Playboy corporate jet with the rabbit logo on its tail fin was a frequent occupant of the Chicago airport named *O'Hare*!)

In January 1960, Playboy Clubs International began recruiting their Playboy bunnies. Auditions were held and the successful applicants were given a rigorous training in proper Bunny deportment. A strict Bunny code of behavior was laid out in a 44-page manual that included such admonitions as "Always remember your proudest possession is your Bunny Tail. You must make sure it is white and fluffy." Bunnies were also forbidden from dating patrons after working hours because Hefner wanted to convey an air of respectability and avoid possible charges of solicitation. The first Playboy Club opened its doors on February 29, 1960 and by 1961 it had 106,000 members (called keyholders).

The Playboy venture worked so well and Hugh Hefner got so caught up that he became his own fantasy. Near the end of 1959, Playboy purchased for $370,000 an elegant property in downtown Chicago. Renovations that eventually added an additional cost of more than $3 million created a palace of luxury that became known as the Playboy Mansion. All-night parties became frequent occurrences at the mansion and Hugh Hefner was the ever-present host who was always accompanied by one or more beautiful young women. By the age of 34, Hef was living his life's dream and there was no end in sight to this exotic fantasy. One biographer commented (Miller, p. 113):

For most of the sixties, Hefner remained closeted in the Playboy Mansion with the windows shuttered and the curtains drawn, heedless of day or night or the passing of the seasons. Sometimes he would not see daylight for months on end.

THE PUBIC WARS

As the sixties decade came to a close, serious competition in the girlie magazine market began to threaten. *Penthouse* magazine, an imitator of *Playboy* that had been published and distributed in Europe, announced plans to expand to America by September 1969. *Penthouse* was more daring than *Playboy* in its depiction of its female nudes. The British magazine exploited the more liberal attitudes of the Europeans toward nudity and displayed pubic hair–a practice that was hitherto forbidden in American skin magazines. To retain market share, *Playboy* risked obscenity charges and followed the *Penthouse* lead. This action launched what Hefner facetiously called the "Pubic Wars" (a play on words relating to the Punic Wars of ancient Greece). As the publishers escalated the Pubic Wars, the nudes became increasingly more seductive and more exposed. Another magazine called *Hustler* entered the market and strived to outdo them all in its lewd depiction of women as they would appear from the gynecologist's vantage. Eventually, *Playboy* realized that it was being drawn away from its original vision and retracted to its earlier position on the high road, leaving the low road to the others.

FROM PUBIC TO PUBLIC

In 1971, Playboy Enterprises was building a luxury resort hotel in New Jersey called Great Gorge. The building costs had escalated beyond projections, resulting in cash flow problems for the corporation. Reluctantly, Hefner decided to generate more cash through a stock offering. Playboy Enterprises went public on November 3, 1971, offering its shares at $23.50. Hef's ownership of the company dropped from 80% to 71.1%, taking his personal net worth to approximately $157 million.

During the first two decades of its existence, *Playboy's* circulation grew steadily. By January 1974, on the occasion of *Playboy's* 20th anniversary issue, monthly circulation was approaching 6 million, down slightly from its peak of 7 million copies a month. There were also 23 Playboy Clubs throughout the world, serving the Playboy philosophy to a world in transition. Young males had needed a fantasy escape from a world fraught with Vietnam and a Cold War and, in the early '70s, Hef had given it to them with progressive jazz served by cotton-tailed Bunnies with push-up bras. However, by September 1974, it was apparent that the Playboy empire was in decline. The 1974 Annual Report revealed that profits were down 48% from the previous year. The share price of Playboy stock had plunged from its initial value of $23.50 in 1971 to $2.87. The Pubic Wars had taken their toll, and the IPO had made Hef accountable to a Board of Directors and therefore more restricted in his decisions. It seemed that Hugh Hefner was losing interest in the enterprise he had founded two decades ago. Russell Miller commented (Miller, p. 229):

> *The consensus in Chicago was that Hefner had more money than he knew what to do with and only wanted to enjoy life. His efforts to keep himself informed by the media meant that he became less and less well informed about what was going on in American life. The richer he got, the more insulated and more irrelevant he became.*

REORGANIZING TO CONTAIN COSTS

In October 1976, Hefner took action to stem Playboy's hemorrhaging losses. He hired Derrick Daniels as president and Chief Operating Officer of Playboy Enterprises Inc. to restructure the company. Daniels wasted little time in cutting wasteful expenditures. By the end of 1977, Daniels had pruned the payroll by 10%, sold the Playboy record business, and closed the Playboy movie theatres and eight Playboy Clubs. Daniels also appointed Hefner's daughter, Christie, as Vice President of Playboy Enterprises Inc. She had graduated summa cum laude from Brandeis University in 1974 and had been elected to Phi Beta Kappa. Hef had asked Daniels to train her as the future CEO of the company.

Daniel's cost-cutting measures, combined with strong profits from the Playboy casino-hotel in London, restored some health to Playboy's bottom line. As the decade of the '70s drew to a close, Playboy recognized that its greatest profit potential resided in hotel-casinos rather than in the publication of its magazine. (This high profitability of casinos had also been recognized by Donald Trump around the same time. See Chapter 9.) In March 1979, anticipating future receipt of a gaming license, Playboy Enterprises Inc. began construction of a $135-million hotel-casino on the boardwalk in Atlantic City. However, during this period, the renewal of Playboy's gaming licenses in London was being challenged on account of alleged violations of the gaming laws. A lot of internal politics in the ranks of the Playboy senior executives interfered with Playboy's ability to defend itself adequately, and on October 5, 1981, Playboy lost its gaming license in England. Playboy shares dropped from $8.48 to $5.75. The next month, Playboy Enterprises sold all its UK gaming operations for $24.8 million dollars (less than two-thirds the current year's profits).

Perhaps the most severe consequence of the loss of the gaming licenses in the UK was its impact on their application for a license in Atlantic City. The granting of a license had seemed like a mere formality, but now the application was revisited with a new focus. On April 7, 1982, the Casino Control Commission of Atlantic City released their verdict. The Playboy gaming license would be approved only if Hugh Hefner was not at the helm of Playboy Enterprises. Faced with this ultimatum, Playboy declined the offer and, in so doing, were denied a gaming license in Atlantic City and excluded from the most lucrative part of their business. This was the nadir in the history of the Playboy empire.

A NEW ERA IN THE PLAYBOY EMPIRE

On April 28, 1982, Christie Hefner, at the tender age of 29, became the President of Playboy Enterprises Inc. From the moment she took office, she implemented major cost-cutting measures including major firings in the executive ranks. Threatened employees termed it "the Reign of Terror." In spite of these extensive measures, Playboy Enterprises lost $17.5 million dollars in the 1983 fiscal year.

Gradually under the leadership of Christie Hefner, Playboy Enterprises divested itself of the unprofitable branches of its business. The last of the Playboy Clubs closed in 1991. By 2002, *Playboy* magazine and the Playboy Channel (a pay-television channel established in 1982) remain the two profit-making products of Playboy Enterprises. The circulation of *Playboy* magazine has stabilized around 4 million. The programming for the Playboy Channel has evolved in tandem with the increasingly permissive attitudes towards sex, so that at the time of this writing, the program content is about as sexually explicit as the market demands. Consequently, the Playboy Channel remains profitable.

Seven years after Christie took over the management of Playboy Enterprises, Hugh Hefner decided to have another run at domesticity. In July 1989, he married the young beauty Kim Conrad. The marriage lasted nine years and then ended in divorce. Hugh re-opened the Playboy Mansion and returned to his playboy life.

Hefner's Decade-by-Decade Climb

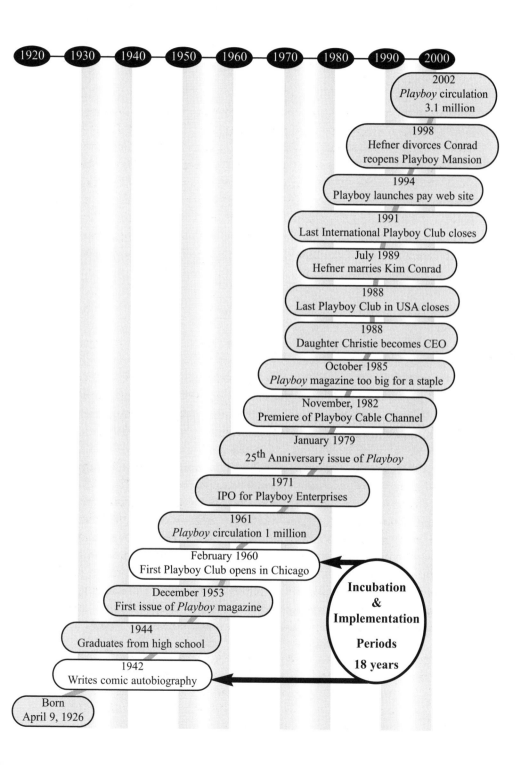

1920 — 1930 — 1940 — 1950 — 1960 — 1970 — 1980 — 1990 — 2000

2002
Playboy circulation
3.1 million

1998
Hefner divorces Conrad
reopens Playboy Mansion

1994
Playboy launches pay web site

1991
Last International Playboy Club closes

July 1989
Hefner marries Kim Conrad

1988
Last Playboy Club in USA closes

1988
Daughter Christie becomes CEO

October 1985
Playboy magazine too big for a staple

November, 1982
Premiere of Playboy Cable Channel

January 1979
25th Anniversary issue of *Playboy*

1971
IPO for Playboy Enterprises

1961
Playboy circulation 1 million

February 1960
First Playboy Club opens in Chicago

December 1953
First issue of *Playboy* magazine

1944
Graduates from high school

1942
Writes comic autobiography

Born
April 9, 1926

**Incubation
&
Implementation

Periods

18 years**

A Personality Profile

COMMUNICATION STYLE: IMAGE PROJECTION

Hef's world is a fantasy world that has modeled life in the fast lane for the young libidinous male. Anything that projected this image was brought into service, including progressive jazz, sports cars, and sexy women. His Playboy Mansions (east and west) were dens of iniquity that fed the fantasies of millions of males who read in *Playboy* about raunchy parties attended by high profile celebrities in lavish luxury. These mansions became the symbol of decadence, displaying at the entrance the Latin inscription *Si Non Oscillas, Noli Tintinnare* which translates as "If you don't swing, don't ring."

Hefner has understood the power of communicating through symbols. The bunny logo personifies the rabbit–a prolific and sensuous animal –onto which *Playboy* projected the image of sophistication and style. The Playboy Big Bunny, the corporate black DC-9 jet replete with elliptical bed, sunken Roman bath and dance floor, bore the bunny logo on its tail fin and also promoted the unfettered luxury that accompanies "the good life" of the playboy.

All of Hefner's toys were aimed at furthering the image that he wanted the world to envision. None were so wickedly symbolic as the round bed of the Chicago mansion. This bed was the centerpiece of Hef's Pleasure Palace. A headboard master control panel could cause it to vibrate, to rotate 360 degrees, and to stop at any number of desired locations such as a fireplace, stereo, TV, phone or drink station. With such an imagination, Hef set out to become all that he had been denied in childhood. Many have regarded him as a man fixed in adolescence.

Image was so important to Hefner's projected fantasies that he turned down millions in advertising revenues for breath mints, athletic foot powders, acne medicines and hair restoring agents. Those products were inappropriate for use by a *real* playboy. Hef also emanated a personal charisma of sophisticated charm for his own seductive purposes. When he met the beautiful Barbi Benton, he was 43 and she was an 18-year-old UCLA freshman. Hef asked if she would consider having dinner with him. Barbi demurely commented, "I've never dated anyone older than twenty-four." Without hesitating, Hef responded with a sheepish grin, "Neither have I."

INTUITIONAL STYLE

Hugh Hefner was in tune with his instincts and allowed them to influence his many decisions at *Playboy*. Early *Playboy* editor Lee Gottieb said, "We never did feasibility studies, we were a gut-reacting company." Hugh Hefner sensed that a few million young men wanted a magazine to excite their sexual fantasies and to provide them with intellectually honest articles about sex. The Kinsey Report had made him aware that women were also interested in sex and that illicit affairs and pre-marital sex were much more prevalent than society would admit.

RISK-TAKING PROPENSITY

The fact that Hugh Hefner had a high propensity for risk-taking is evident in the way he gambled body and soul in his quest to found *Playboy*. When Hefner decided to leave his steady employment at Children's Activities, the general manager warned him, "If you fail, you won't even have a shoestring left." In spite of this warning, Hef left the security of employment and struck out on his own. In the wake of several early failures, he persisted relentlessly, risking everything while his wife, Millie, continued teaching to provide for the family. To raise money for *Playboy*, Hefner indentured himself so heavily that if the enterprise failed, he would have been in debt for his foreseeable future.

INTENSITY

Hef's first wife, Millie, characterized Hef as "obsessive." Mr. Playboy once wrote a 38,000-word memo–equivalent to a small book–to Don Myrus, the head of the Playboy Book Division. No detail was ever too small for the boss and no time too precious to spend on getting every nuance perfect. Deadlines always took second place to perfection. He once turned down 500 photos of a Playmate centerfold, presented by *Playboy* photographer Dwight Hooker, before accepting one. On another occasion, when editing a new magazine layout, he wrote a 15-page memo to a highly experienced professional staff on the nuances of "punctuation, commas and semicolons." Hefner made it to the top by being on top of every little detail of his magazine. Only when that stopped did his empire begin to crumble. However, until then, nothing was done in moderation in his life or his work.

Another aspect of his intensity was his desire to be in control. Hefner was a "control freak" in his need to have everyone organized into tight compartments with him at the helm. Though he delegated power in some areas, he reserved for himself the ultimate authority on most of the company decisions.

Hef's compulsive nature was particularly evident in his promiscuity. The Prince of Pleasure acted as if he were trying to compensate for the late start in his sex life. He spent hours each day engaged in the art of seduction and for months never wore any clothing except pajamas. Even today, in his seventies, he can be found running around southern France with a bevy of eighteen-year-olds.

Like most compulsives, Hefner was a workaholic. After the success of his first issue of _Playboy_, Hef began work immediately on the second issue. By this time his marriage was irretrievably lost. In the words of biographer Russell Miller (p. 45):

> _Hefner, who thought nothing of working thirty-six hours without a break, bought a bed for his office and soon took to staying overnight...At first, he diligently returned to the marital home on weekends, but neither Millie nor marriage interested him as much as his magazine and his weekend visits became less and less frequent._

Hef began restoring energy with the consumption of a case of Pepsi daily. Later the Pepsi was supplemented with amphetamines. He once commented, "I was obsessive and seldom left the Playboy offices. There were times when I didn't leave for weeks at a time." One biographer wrote (Telese, p. 102):

> _He kept his clothes in the office, had food sent in, girls sent in, made love there, and created the Playboy legend there._

When Hef was up he was way up and when he went down he hit the bottom. The workaholic stayed up all night, and after he moved into the Playboy Mansion, seldom hit the office until four in the afternoon.

SELF-IMAGE

Hugh Hefner saw himself as a genius of sorts with a messianic mission. His intent was to share his philosophy with the world. Because his intellectual horizons were limited, he seemed unaware that many of his philosophical ideas had been stated by others in previous centuries. Biographer Miller describes how Hugh Hefner, while being filmed as the subject of a documentary, commented about himself (p. 136):

Genius is a funny kind of word...I suppose by definition I consider myself one, both intellectually and in terms of creativity.

In commenting to *Time* magazine on his own television show, *Playboy After Dark,* Hef revealed his somewhat self-serving and inflated view of his own talents, "It's better than the Johnny Carson Show and I do a better job of hosting than Ed Sullivan does."

ECCENTRICITIES AND PERSONAL PARADOXES

Hef is a paradox. He cannot swim, yet swimming pools adorn his mansions. He is a social animal yet reclusive, a true visionary yet an obsessive perfectionist in all things. Part of his paradoxical persona has him working for a children's magazine at the very time that he was launching *Playboy,* a magazine that challenged the sexual mores of the time. Here was a man with a flare for human nature and a profound insight into what makes people tick, yet he so often made poor hiring decisions that staffed Playboy Enterprises with a large number of redundant and incompetent executives.

The competent executives were sometimes questioned and ridiculed, while those of limited insight were often trusted and promoted. Hefner's need to believe in the unbelievable–that right-brain vision of what might be–is what made him so creative, yet it is also responsible for his buying into grandiose plans that were ill-conceived.

Despite Hef's reputation as a detail freak–Playboy executives described him as a pathological perfectionist–he only spent time on those things he deemed important and relegated important financial matters to others. On one occasion, Hugh Hefner spent all night responding to a letter to the editor, but another time he went two years without ever setting foot in the *Playboy* offices.

Hef believed that he had great philosophical insights and yet he read very little about the ideas of others. As one biographer noted (Miller, p. 119):

> *As a philosopher, Hefner's views were hardly revolutionary and not particularly original (John Stuart Mill said much the same a hundred years earlier in his essay, On Liberty), but he presented them with a touchingly triumphant air, as if stumbling across astonishing truths previously concealed.*

ACHIEVEMENTS & HONORS

MAGNITUDE OF SUCCESS

Beyond opening the door to free expression and paving the way for the Pubic Wars, *Playboy* showed that a dream can be transformed into a reality. The Playboy empire is now a vast enterprise encompassing the web, music, publishing, TV, and video sales and rentals. It includes an international multi-media operation of DVD production and sales, Playboy On-line, Playboy.com, Playboy Cyber Club, Cyberspice, Critic's Choice Video, and Collectors' Choice Music. It also derives income from licensing the Playboy logo for consumer products from the *Playboy* magazine, and from the Spice catalogs and Networks. Playboy Enterprises generates close to $400 million annually and Hef still owns 71% of the outstanding stock.

Even Hefner's greatest detractors admit *Playboy* has many redeeming qualities. Biographer Russell Miller wrote, *"Playboy's* most important contribution to American journalism is the *Playboy* Interview" (Miller, p. 124). Examples of the magazine's sophisticated writing include the interviews with Martin Luther King, Bertrand Russell, Ayn Rand, Jean Paul Sartre, Fidel Castro, Albert Schweitzer and President Jimmy Carter. Notable entrepreneurs interviewed were Akio Morita of Sony (1982), Donald Trump (1990), Bill Gates (1991) and Ted Turner.

Playboy was for many years the most widely-read male magazine in America. It began as one-of-a-kind but was soon copied by *Penthouse*, *Hustler* and a host of other copycats. For a long period, it was an intellectual vehicle for free speech and the *Playboy* Philosophy was presented as a challenge to puritanical dogma. The public offering of Playboy Enterprises stock that took place during the white heat of rebellion in 1971, rendered Hefner's stock certificates, adorned with a watermark of a Playboy centerfold nude, less controversial than the institutional investors who had deemed them politically incorrect. Some 20,000 investors purchased at least one share of stock for the privilege of owning a symbol of sybaritic sensuality. At the millennium, Playboy Enterprises celebrated its 29-year rollercoaster ride as a public company, enjoying during its brief history a volatile growth, a host of nefarious employees and fluctuating potential.

After the IPO, Hugh Marston Hefner was worth more money than he dreamed existed. No matter what happens in the future, *Playboy* and its creator have transformed our conceptions of nudity, obscenity and sexual pleasure. *Playboy* led the way in creatively destroying social norms that had grown in Hef's opinion to be too straight, too puritanical and too oriented to sexual repression. From the moment that Hef first encountered the *Kinsey Report*, he decided to tell the world the truth about sexual repression. *Playboy* was merely the vehicle, his *Playboy* Philosophy the message. It was meant to sow the seeds of revolt and it did. His timing was impeccable. By the early sixties America was becoming malcontent. Within a decade it was fully at war with convention. Youth would no longer accept the myth that they would go blind if they touched themselves. Many used Hef's philosophy to violate established norms, often with bumper stickers extolling the virtues of sex, drugs and rock'n' roll. Freedom from restraint had been Hef's message and the youth loved it. Many adopted him as a role model. Like Hef a decade earlier, they were no longer willing to live life as a lie.

Hefner's legacy will be his revolutionary onslaught against sexual repression. At 27 Hef wanted desperately to be a playboy and by his early 30s he had achieved his dream. His fantasy was played out for the world to see in the pages of his brainchild, *Playboy* magazine. Hef has demonstrated that life is too short to dance to the tunes written by others. In liberating himself, he liberated us all.

HONORS

In 1968, Hefner was inducted into the Magazine Editors' Hall of Fame, something he regards as his greatest honor. This living icon of free sexual expression is a symbol of the consummate hedonist. Hef's bunny is one of the world's best-known logos and it also celebrates the pursuit of free sexual expression. In 1979 he was given the Award of Free Expression for his interminable fight for First Amendment rights of free speech.

LESSONS LEARNED FROM HUGH HEFNER

Some of the lessons presented here represent lessons learned from Hefner's successes, while others are derived from his mistakes.

Tap into the Customers' Psyche and You'll Own Them

Making young libidinous males believe they could be special and be surrounded by bevies of beautiful women, hanging on their every word, was the magic that made *Playboy* work. That was the message conveyed in every aspect of *Playboy*–pictures, advertising and subliminal graphics. The goal was for every reader to see himself as a dashing raconteur with women admiring his sports jacket, sports car, stereo and macho wardrobe. The *Playboy* male came replete with blazer, blonde and flashy Corvette. Remake the nerd into a debonair 007 and he is yours. Such was the surreal image concocted by Hef that would offer consolation to young males who had just been turned down by a college coed for some "cool" guy with wheels. Hefner looked into his inner soul where a super-charged libido raged and found the iconic lexicon that would become *Playboy*. His magic was in discovering the hot button of the typical young male and pushing it with words and pictures. Hef knew how to tap into the young men's psyche and when he did, he owned them. (In Chapter 8, we will learn how Martha Stewart tapped into the psyche of the women she sought to capture.)

Always Dance With Who Brung Ya

With all success stories, there is a downside. For Hef it was trying to go where he had no expertise, getting into ventures beyond his ability to manage, and forgetting the core competencies that were born of *Playboy*. Hef should never have made movies or become a hotelier, nor ventured into the casino business. Even though the Playboy Clubs made sense as a component of his business empire, they should have been franchised or licensed for others to run. However, relinquishing these ventures never fit the controlling nature of Hefner and he paid dearly for it. Every enterprise outside his core competency failed miserably. Had he occasionally left his lair at the Playboy Mansion, these ventures may have fared better. *Playboy* lost millions. Of his various business initiatives, the core enterprise in the Playboy empire remains the one that he originally created–the *Playboy* magazine.

In 1973, Playboy Enterprises earned a staggering $22 million, while every venture other than the casinos and *Playboy* magazine in his growing conglomerate lost money. When he focused on what he did well, he was hugely successful. When he didn't, he failed big time. A prime example was the Lake Geneva Resort Hotel & Club. It cost Playboy $18 million and went through fourteen managers in ten years. Great Gorge in New Jersey was even worse: it never once made a profit and cost the company $33 million. The moral? Do what you do well–focus on your core competency. When outside your area of competence, hire professionals in that arena and let them do what they do well. Hef stopped dancing with the *lady who brung 'im* and it cost him dearly.

NEVER UNDERESTIMATE THE MARKET FOR FANTASY

Hef's success at *Playboy* had less to do with nudity than it had to do imagery. Few understand that simple fact. The magazine told men they were okay and that it was normal to have voyeuristic urges that needed resolution. More important than the visual and intellectual messages were the subtle subliminal and vicarious communications embedded in the slick ads for sports cars or cigarettes, showing men on yachts being served exotic liqueurs under palm trees. Electronic toys were as sexy for some subscribers as the centerfolds, especially when they were being hawked by a svelte blonde with seduction in her eyes. The ads were the most important part of his illusion, not only for the revenue they generated, but because they conveyed a subliminal message that seduced the male reader. Hef was quick to exploit his insight into the male ego.

Hugh Hefner mastered the art of portraying men in surrealistic settings of pure fantasy–he instinctively knew that fantasy sells better than reality. The magical myth created by the Bunny magazine promoted virility and strength. Hef was offering males the right to be masculine. His fantasies were delivered with panache and style, but his timing may have been the most powerful factor in exploiting the sexual revolution for which he was a catalyst. Hef launched his revolution when society was on the cusp between the conservatism of the fifties and the pending rebellion of the sixties. It was a time when America elected a father-figure president in Dwight Eisenhower. It was the age of the nuclear family, Lassie and Little Orphan Annie. No legitimate magazine would attempt what he did, and that made him a pioneer whom entrepreneurs need to study. Hef understood and lived sexual fantasy, and he knew that a similar need for fantasy must be shared by a multitude of other males. That was the market he tapped into, and the results were–for want of a better word–*fantastic!*

Henry Ray (Ross) Perot

Believe & the World Will Follow You–Anywhere

b. Texarkana, TX   June 27, 1930

"I would just as soon run for king."

SELF-DESCRIPTION
"I see my vision as solving problems"

MOTTO
"Business should be pursued with the same positive spirit one brings to an athletic contest."

INNOVATION
"People didn't want computers, they wanted results" –the genesis of computer leasing and billion dollar industry led by EDS

UNIQUE QUALITY
Arrogant philanthropist ($120M) with "can do" attitude.

OBJECTIVE
To be the very best he can be no matter the venue

NET WORTH
$3 billion (*Forbes*, July, 2001)

HONORS
President of Jr. College Class and Naval Academy Class
Elected to the Business Hall of Fame in 1988

BIRTH ORDER
Third; older sister Bette and older brother who died

EDUCATION
Graduated from the U.S. Naval Academy in 1953

PERSONALITY
An abrasive control freak and intuitive thinker

HOBBIES
Jet boats, skiing, and cabin cruisers

POLITICS
Republican turned independent 1992
Reform Party nominee for President in 1996

RELIGION
Devout methodist

FAMILY
Wife: Margot
Children: Ross Jr., Nancy, Suzanne, Carolyn and Katherine

7

Henry (Ross) Perot

Believe and the World Will Follow You–Anywhere

*"Business should be pursued with the same
positive spirit one brings to an athletic contest."*

Overview

Electronic Data Systems (EDS) was Ross Perot's baby. He created the company and nurtured it to a dominant player in an industry that he helped computerize–in spite of the fact that he could not write a single word of computer code! The EDS annual revenues of about $5 billion and its 48,000 employees attest to the magic of the Perot confidence and validate his entrepreneurial genius. What can we learn from his success? For one thing, he believed when others didn't, and that is vital to building an empire in any discipline. Furthermore, he ignored the advice of experts and that helped him in his climb to success.

Perot's "can-do" attitude inspired confidence in those who knew of his reputation for getting things done. In 1969, the war in Vietnam was raging and the Nixon administration sought his help in securing more humane treatment for the American POWs. To this end, Perot, at his own expense, chartered two jets and filled them with Christmas dinners and presents for the 1420 known POWs. This 3-ton cargo was then flown to Vientiane, Laos while permission to enter North Vietnam was sought. When the North Vietnamese refused entry, the food and gifts were disseminated to orphaned children in South Vietnam. At some risk to himself and his family, Perot spent considerable time and money during the next four years visiting North Vietnamese and Viet Cong POWs in Saigon until the war ended in 1972. It was later learned that Perot's initiative had enhanced the treatment of the American POWs by their captors.

In 1979, when two EDS employees were taken hostage by the Iranian government, Perot conducted a dramatically successful rescue mission to free the hostages–an operation that was subsequently lionized in the best-selling book, *On Wings of Eagles*. Within the next three years, Perot was asked by two successive governors of Texas to help in domestic matters.

In the first instance, Ross Perot recommended new laws aimed at reducing the use of illegal drugs in that state. In the second instance, he led efforts to reform the public school system in Texas.

Ross Perot sold his creation, EDS, to General Motors in 1984 for $2.5 billion. This made him the largest shareholder of GM and a member of the board of directors. Perot's disagreement with the way that the GM President Roger Smith was running the company led to battles that were aired in the media. Subsequently, GM bought out Perot's shares for $740 million to get rid of him. The buyout carried a $7.5-million penalty clause should either party speak to the press. Perot violated the agreement before it was a few days old with these acerbic remarks to *Ward's Auto World*:

> *The first EDS-er to see a snake kills it. At General Motors, the first thing you do is organize a committee on snakes. Then you bring in a consultant who knows a lot about snakes, then you talk about it for a year.*

On June 1, 1988, when the non-compete clause of the GM buyout agreement expired, Ross formed Perot Systems, Inc.–a competitor of EDS.

On February 20, 1992, Larry King of CNN asked Perot during an interview whether he would consider running for President of the United States in the 1992 elections. Perot responded by saying:

> *If you, the people, will on your own register me in 50 states, I'll promise you this: between now and the convention, we'll get both parties' heads straight.*

Perot's supporters registered him in all 50 states and within a few months he led both President Bush (senior) and Bill Clinton in the polls. When the election was over, Perot had spent about $60 million of his own money and garnered about 15 million votes, representing 19% of the popular vote. This was more than any other independent candidate since Theodore Roosevelt in 1912, but a distant third behind the incumbent President George Bush and the President Elect, Bill Clinton.

In 1995, Perot formed the Reform party to run against the Republicans and Democrats in the 1996 election. Then in 1996, as a member of the Reform Party, he ran for the U.S. Presidency a second time. However, the greater public exposure that he had enjoyed during the 1990's had convinced many that his style of leadership was not what the country needed or wanted and he won only 8% of the vote. As is the case with many entrepreneurs, the skills and personal qualities that bring great success in business are sometimes counterproductive in a political context.

The Formative Years

EARLY EXPERIENCES

Ross Perot was baptized Henry Ray. At age twelve, his name was changed to Ross after his father and a deceased older brother. Perot was the only living son of cotton broker Ross Sr. and Lulu May Ray. From an early age, Ross was expected to become a leader. Lulu May, a schoolteacher, was the one responsible for instilling in him a strong Christian ethic. His father taught him how to break horses and how to negotiate deals. It was from his father that he learned the art of selling, bartering, and toughness. During the 1992 Presidential race, Ross told the media, "My Harvard Business School education was learned in my father's cotton office."

When not working, Perot could be found immersed in inspirational Horatio Alger books. (These same adventures had inspired J. Paul Getty almost four decades earlier.) In those books success arose out of diligence, hard work, and fair dealing. From these readings, Ross acquired a strong sense of heroic adventure. Manhood to him was defined in terms of fighting and defeating stronger adversaries. This conception would be played out many times during his volatile career in the Navy, during his involvement in the Iran rescue mission, during his battle of wits with Roger Smith at GM, and during the Presidential campaign when he wanted to take on the entire American political system.

Where did Ross Perot acquire such temerity and arrogance? Certainly some inspiration can be attributed to his Horatio Alger readings but most of his spunk may have derived from observing his diminutive father who took no prisoners in his job repossessing Texas farms during the Great Depression. (Recall Sam Walton's similar formative experiences described in Chapter 5.) Perot later described how his family struggled through the Depression and recalled how his father once sold his favorite horse to buy Christmas gifts for the family. Additional learning took place in his teen years spent hitch-hiking across Texas and Oklahoma. On one occasion the intrepid warrior hitchhiked all the way to Mexico. Research indicates that early challenges in life imprint temerity and self-sufficiency and Perot's life adds further evidence to support that principle.

At age 7, Ross sold Christmas cards, bridles and saddles, and the *Saturday Evening Post*. Breaking horses left an indelible imprint on the young Perot. It taught him that you were in control or you were controlled. It showed him the value of maintaining an edge over your adversary. It instilled in him the courage to fight and not to back away from confrontation. During his first run for President he recalled breaking those horses for $1 each. His sister Bette contributed, "I can't remember how many times he broke his nose." Ross said of the experience (*U.S News & World Report,* June 29, 1992, p. 26):

> *I was small, but at seven I was a good rider. That experience is why my nose is so jagged. I was always getting knocked out.*

At age 12, Ross Perot became a Cub Scout and within 13 months he became an Eagle Scout. When he was 13, Ross applied for a paper route. When he was told there were none available, he offered to create a route in the dangerous area of his hometown, Texarkana, where there had been no delivery before. Because of the danger involved, he was able to negotiate double the normal rate. Then he proceeded to deliver his papers on horseback or bicycle to avoid any potential muggings. This showed an early-acquired resolve to meet challenges head-on. A few years later, the paper's executive decided to change his special rate, but Perot appealed successfully to the head of the paper to maintain the current arrangement.

FORMAL EDUCATION

Both Ross and older sister Bette attended the Patty Hill school–a private elementary school in Texarkana. In high school, Ross excelled in making money, but was only average in making grades. His natural proclivity to lead, that had helped him achieve Eagle Scout status, also resulted in his election as President of three different school classes.

Upon graduation from Texarkana Junior College in 1949, Ross's father and his father's political friends secured his entry to the U.S. Naval Academy at Annapolis. Although he graduated 543 out of a class of 925, his fellow students elected him the best all-around midshipman and class president for life. He also distinguished himself as an excellent debater. While a midshipman at the Naval Academy, he met and dated his future wife, Margot Birmingham, who came from Greensburg, Pennsylvania.

On graduation from the Naval Academy in 1953, he was obligated to serve four years in the military. Although he attempted to escape this obligation, his petition was refused and he spent the next four years at sea. Perot served on an aircraft carrier and a destroyer just as the Korean War ended. In 1956, when he was 26 years old, Ross Perot married Margot.

The Climb to the Top

AN EMPLOYEE AT IBM

Ross Perot received his honorable discharge from the Navy in 1957. He and Margot moved to Dallas, Texas, where Ross took a job as a salesman in the data processing division of IBM. He quickly distinguished himself as IBM's most successful salesman and was given two of IBM's most lucrative and most challenging accounts: Southwestern Life Insurance Company and Texas Blue Cross. Southwestern had just realized that their newly purchased $1.3 million IBM 7070 had more capacity than it needed and were considering returning it to IBM. To encourage Southwestern to retain the 7070, Perot found another company that would lease computer time on the 7070 from Southwestern. This initiative enabled Ross to save a potentially lost sale, so that in the first three weeks of January 1962, Ross had already met his annual quota for sales for that year!

Inspired by the Southwestern experience, Perot conceived the innovative idea of selling a computer to a customer and leasing back the spare time to other firms unable to afford their own computer. Following established protocol, he presented the idea to his boss at IBM. When the boss turned down the idea as inappropriate, Ross became frustrated and despondent. Then, one day while sitting in a Dallas barber shop thumbing through a *Reader's Digest* he came upon the quote by Henry David Thoreau, "The mass of men live lives of quiet desperation." This was the inspiration that Perot later described as an epiphany that changed his life. Reflecting on Thoreau's observation, Ross decided to become the master of his fate and resigned from IBM on June 27, 1962–the day he turned 32. At the time of his resignation, he was IBM's top salesman and could have settled for a comfortable and lucrative career. However, that was not the Perot way. Ross Perot's decision to leave IBM was the genesis of what would later become EDS. About his decision to leave IBM, Perot later mused (*The Washington Post Magazine*, April 12, 1987):

> *If I'd stayed at IBM, I'd be somewhere in middle management getting in trouble and being asked to take early retirement.*

A NEW LEASE ON LIFE: THE FOUNDING OF EDS

According to Perot, "Starting EDS was months of terror because we didn't have any money and we didn't know what we were doing." With only a check for $1000 borrowed from his wife Margot, a school teacher, Ross set out on a quest to build his computer leasing idea into a business. Being a fearless competitor, he took pride in building EDS as a provider of a superior service rather than as an innovator offering highly sophisticated software. Ross envisioned leasing computers to companies and helping them with their data processing functions, and was willing to bet his job and his money that there was a market for this service. In the beginning, EDS was a one-man company. The idea was to sell a computer and lease back the second or third shifts and then find someone to rent that time. In essence, EDS was initially serving as a broker for computer time.

Since Texas Blue Cross had been a client of Perot's when he worked at IBM, he offered to continue to serve their needs as a data processing consultant in exchange for compensation of $20,000 per year (just under $100,000 in today's dollars). He also negotiated an office in their Dallas headquarters from which he could operate EDS for a nominal rent of $100 per month. Perot began building EDS by leasing computer time from his previous client Southwestern Life Insurance and then contacting over 100 companies that used IBM 7070s to offer them additional computer capacity.

Gradually, EDS began to include software with the computers that they leased back. This evolved into customizing software to accommodate the needs of clients. Since Ross had no training in writing computer code or programming, he hired others to perform these tasks. He carefully recruited employees with strong positive optimism and "can-do" attitudes. He also sought self-starter types who were innovators rather than followers. To this end he used recruiting slogans like, "Eagles don't flock." He believed that these qualities were more important than technical skills that could be learned later. However, Perot also realized that it cost about $10,000 in the early 1960s to train a person in data processing, so he recruited employees from IBM and Texas Instruments who were already trained. To induce prospective employees to leave the higher compensation offered by those companies, Perot included shares of his company in the compensation package. In 1963, Perot gave the wife of every male employee 100 shares of EDS stock as a gesture of appreciation for their forbearance during the building phase of EDS. (Those 100 shares would be worth in excess of $200,000 by 1992).

A Period of Healthy Growth

At first, the EDS clients were small companies. However, as EDS developed more sophisticated software, it acquired bigger clients such as the potato chip company Frito-Lay. By December 1964, EDS had become a company of about a dozen employees generating a net profit of $4100 on gross revenues of $400,000.

Then in 1965, the newly-created Medicare and Medicaid programs generated the need for computerized medical-claims processing. Southwest Medical signed a contract with EDS that was contingent on the latter's ability to automate the Medicare system. Under Perot's direction, EDS developed the necessary software. By the end of 1965, it had become a major subcontractor for Blue Cross/Blue Shield. At that time, EDS was computerizing the Medicare and Medicaid billing systems for 11 states. On June 28, 1966, EDS signed a lucrative three-year contract with Texas Blue Cross/Blue Shield to supply the with computer time. The contract omitted a standard clause that would grant the government the right to inspect the books of EDS to ensure proper billing. Since Perot had been employed as a consultant by Texas Blue Cross and the contract had been signed without solicitation of competitive bids, the Social Security Administration complained that there was a conflict of interest. However, the missing clause in the contract prevented it from inspecting the EDS books to determine whether the billings by EDS had been exorbitant. A congressional hearing in 1971 revealed that the federal government paid EDS a total of $36 million between 1966 and 1971, and government analysts estimated that EDS profits were over 100%. However, Perot argued that the billings were comparable to what other companies would charge and if profit margins were large, it was a consequence of EDS's extreme efficiency in minimizing its costs. It was clear at this point in Ross Perot's career that he was highly skilled in negotiating contracts that anticipated benefits and advantages long before their implications were clear to others. His deal-making abilities that were manifest when he negotiated his paper route commissions as a boy, were once more surfacing. This was just the beginning.

An IPO for EDS

Ross Perot's next move was the one that catapulted him into the billionaire's club. By 1968, EDS had become the preeminent Medicare systems provider in the country and in that year had a pre-tax profit of $2.4 million on revenues of $7.5 million. The phenomenal profit margins and revenue growth impressed investors who were buying into a bull market in high-tech stocks. It was an ideal environment for launching an IPO and Ross Perot was not one to overlook such an opportunity. Though most stocks were trading at 10 to 20 times their annual earnings, the remarkable performance of EDS enabled the underwriter to issue the stock at $16.50–an extraordinary 118 times the 1968 earnings per share! (These rates were rarely seen until the heady days of the late 1990s.) When the shares came on the market on September 12, 1968, investors, eager to buy into the EDS success, drove the share price up to almost $23 at the market close. In a single day, Ross Perot's net worth had catapulted to $230 million. Within a year and a half, the share price had climbed to $162.50 and Perot's net worth reached $1.5 billion–he had become an "instant" billionaire! *Fortune* magazine later referred to this successful IPO as "the greatest personal coup in the history of American finance."

AN UNHOLY ALLIANCE

Ross Perot's new-found wealth brought him to the attention of the public and the captains of industry. Among these was Donald Kendall, the chairman of PepsiCo. Kendall introduced Perot to the Republican presidential candidate Richard Nixon to advise the aspiring politician on how to use the computer in his presidential campaign. This was the beginning of an association that would later develop between Perot and the Nixon administration. In late 1968, Ross Perot contributed seven EDS employees and substantial funds to help with the Nixon campaign. After Nixon was elected, Perot and his seven employees attended the inaugural celebration. In the years between Nixon's first election and his resignation, both parties in this association traded markers.

Late in 1969, the Nixon administration sought Perot's assistance in establishing a pro-Vietnam Committee that would unite the various groups who supported the prosecution of the war to a "peace-with-honor" conclusion. Perot agreed to serve as a member of the committee, but eventually, as he thought of ways to promote public enthusiasm for this cause, he formulated his own plan. He would fly to North Vietnam in a jet loaded with food and Christmas presents that would be distributed to American POWs. When North Vietnam refused entry of the jet, Perot planned to show good will by turning the food over to the orphans in North Vietnam, using Russia as the intermediary. The Nixon administration, concerned that such action might be used by propagandists as America's admission of guilt over the war effort, asked Perot not to pursue this plan. Against the wishes of the Nixon administration, Perot persisted until ultimately Russia and North Vietnam thwarted his plans. (The food and gifts were eventually distributed to the orphaned children in South Vietnam.)

Perot's insistence on pursuing such initiatives in his own way, in spite of the government's objections, alerted the Nixon administration to the fact that Perot was his own man and could not be contained. This was the first major initiative that created a public persona for Ross Perot as a "can-do" person. It was the beginning of an image that would serve him well in a future bid for public office.

TAKING THE BULL BY THE HORNS

The raging bull market in which EDS had issued its IPO in 1968 had seen such record high volumes that the brokerage firms could not keep pace in processing the stock trades. This necessitated the closing of the New York Stock Exchange on Wednesdays to allow the brokerage firms to catch up with their paper work. Perot recognized an emerging opportunity to create and sell a computerized system that automated the data processing of stock transactions. By 1969–70 the bull market had metamorphosed into a bear market. Investors stayed away from the market in droves and many brokerage houses, witnessing steep declines in their commission revenues, either declared bankruptcy or entered into mergers. Francis I. du Pont & Company, the third largest brokerage firm in America at the time, was on the verge of bankruptcy after its loss of $8 million in 1969. Seizing the opportunity, Perot paid $3.8 million to purchase the subsidiary of du Pont that did its data processing. Then EDS signed an 8-year contract with du Pont to perform its data processing for $8 million per year. In the meantime, a Crisis Committee of Wall Street executives had been formed to salvage the brokerage firms and avert a collapse of the market. The Committee, recognizing that Perot had a vested interest in the survival of du Pont, approached the Nixon administration and asked that they encourage Perot to make a bailout investment in du Pont.

On December 16, 1969, Ross Perot gave du Pont a $10-million loan with the stipulation that if du Pont was unable to raise an additional $15 million to establish solvency, EDS would receive 51% of du Pont shares. On May 14, 1970, a 51% controlling interest in du Pont reverted to EDS–eventually EDS owned it entirely. Despite little knowledge of the stock brokerage business, Perot thought he could show the sophisticated New Yorkers how the problem could be solved–Texas style. The two cultures clashed and the salvage operation failed. In 1974, du Pont filed for Chapter 11 bankruptcy protection. Ross Perot lost $70 million in the process and suffered his first public failure.

FLIGHT TO IRAN ON THE WINGS OF EAGLES

In his perpetual search for new markets, Ross Perot discovered the remarkable opportunities for computerized data processing in Europe and the Middle East where the use of computers had lagged that in the United States. By the end of 1976, EDS had secured lucrative contracts in Saudi Arabia and Iran. Profitability was high and times were good. Then on December 28, 1978, Ross received a frantic telephone call informing him that two EDS executives stationed in Teheran were taken hostage by Iranian revolutionaries in the wake of the fall of the Shah of Iran.

Ross Perot first approached the U.S. Government for help in freeing the hostages, but it seemed to Ross that the Government did not appear to share his sense of urgency. Perot then sought volunteers who would help him in a private rescue mission. A testimonial to his recruiting techniques at EDS was the fact that seven of the volunteers who agreed to participate in the rescue mission were EDS employees. The actual rescue was led by retired Colonel Bull Simons, the leader of a military team that had raided a North Vietnamese prisoner camp to free American POWs. The rescue mission, dubbed Operation Hotfoot (acronym for Help Our Two Friends Out of Tehran) was planned and rehearsed by January 8, 1979 –just 11 days after the kidnapping.

Perot then chartered his own plane and boldly flew into Tehran disguised as an NBC reporter. His intention was to attempt one last negotiation for the release of his two employees. When it was clear that such efforts would prove futile, Perot visited his two employees at Gasr prison to boost their morale and ensure them that help was imminent. However, on viewing the heavily guarded ramparts and tight security, Perot and Colonel Simons realized that the commando-style raid that they had planned would not succeed. Perot flew out of Iran and in the weeks that followed, pursued other avenues of approach such as bribery or ransom to free his employees. Finally, on February 11, in the wake of Ayatollah Khomeini's return to Iran from Paris, riots erupted and Gasr prison was stormed in a manner reminiscent of the storming of the Bastille almost 200 years earlier. The prisoners were freed, including the two EDS employees, who followed the operation Hotfoot plan and scurried to the Hyatt House where they were met by Colonel Bull Simon. From there, they were taken overland in a Range Rover across the border to Turkey where they met up with Perot. NBC later televised a miniseries that described this event, albeit somewhat dramatized to enhance the entertainment component. Perot's public persona had reach a zenith.

Two Wars in Texas

In January 1979, Ross Perot was asked by the Governor-elect of Texas to help stem the escalating use of illegal drugs in that state. Serving as chair of the War on Drugs Committee, Perot dedicated himself to publicizing to the youth in Texas the dangers of using drugs. He organized community groups to help spread anti-drug messages. He spent in excess of $2 million of his own money to educate the public through symposia in which experts on the drug problem involved the public in open discussion. Using a carrot-and-stick approach to the problem, Perot followed the educational component of his anti-drug campaign with the formulation of five new draft bills that his War on Drugs Committee presented to the Texas legislature. These bills proposed tightening the control on the sale of drugs by pharmacists and introducing mandatory sentences and tougher penalties for those caught selling drugs near schools. In 1981, after much fanfare and lobbying by Perot, the bills were passed into law by the Texas legislature.

In 1983, just two years after his anti-drug campaign, Perot was once again called upon by the Texas government to champion a public cause. This time, the Governor invited Perot to chair his Select Committee on Public Education (SCOPE). Texas had ranked forty-fourth out of the fifty states in academic achievement and there was widespread consensus that educational reform was urgently needed. Perot jumped into the task with his characteristic unfettered desire to introduce reforms as he saw fit. Taking his perceptions of the weaknesses of the public education system as his starting point, he set about garnering the support of public groups and the business community. His concern that resources had been allocated to football at the expense of academics prompted him to say (Posner, p. 157):

> *I thought I was living pretty good until I found a school system that had towel warmers and towel coolers for the football team...Do you want adult entertainment, or do you want kids to learn?*

Perot's efforts to increase the emphasis on academics by diverting resources from extracurricular activities infuriated millions of faithful Texan football fans. Football is a sacred cow in many small Texas towns that value cattle, and when Perot sounded the slogan, "No Pass, No Play" it was tantamount to heresy. He added further insult to injury when he referred to Texas students who were studying to become teachers as "the dumbest in college." Perot was perceived by many to have crossed the line from change agent to egocentric power monger. Virtually every teacher, athlete, and coach resented him with a passion that was expressed on a multitude of bumper stickers proclaiming, "I don't brake for Perot."

In spite of much opposition from various sectors of the public, Perot continued to push his reform package by hiring the best lobbyists and by applying arm-twisting techniques to those who threatened to vote against it. Ross admitted to operating in a style that would have impressed Machiavelli (Posner, p. 159), "[We had to play] pure hardball. It wasn't pretty, but we got it done. That's the way it works down here."

Perot's package was passed by the Texas legislature as House Resolution 72. Senator Leedom, who had opposed the bill and voted against it commented (Posner, p. 159):

> *I know plenty of legislators who were not supporters of the bill, but they were intimidated by Perot's machine and afraid of going against him. He makes a contest out of everything, and people are afraid of getting crushed if they are on the wrong side.*

Perot's inclination to "make a contest out of everything" would surface again and again as he became increasingly more public in his battles. As an epilogue to this educational contest, it may be noted that when Perot ran for the Presidency in 1992–just 8 years after the passing of the resolution–Texas had moved up only one position in educational achievement to forty-third out of fifty states.

THE GM BUYOUT

The exponential growth in Perot's personal wealth rose sharply in 1984 with his sale of EDS to General Motors for $2.5 billion. Part of the purchase was paid in shares of GM, making Perot a member of its board and its largest independent shareholder with 5.5 million shares. (Perot's shares had a total value of $700 million and he personally received $930 million in cash.)

Roger Smith, Chairman of General Motors, had realized that his company needed to computerize its data processing functions and had courted Ross Perot and EDS. However, shortly after the beginning of his tenure as a Director, Ross began to criticize publically how management was running General Motors. In one show of candor he told *Fortune* magazine what was wrong with GM (March, 1988), "Anyone who needs a

chauffeur to drive him to work is probably too old to be on the payroll."
With such insults, the Texas entrepreneur alienated virtually everyone at
General Motors and others who didn't even know him. Major conflict
between Perot and Roger Smith about the running of the company broke
out and escalated steadily during the next two years. Perot's public verbal
attacks on Roger Smith's running of GM led GM to offer Perot a buyout.
On December 1, 1986, Ross Perot and GM parted company. The buyout
agreement required GM to pay Perot $742.8 million for his shares of GM.
It contained a "non-compete" clause that forbade Perot from competing
with EDS for at least 18 months. In addition, it contained a "no publicity"
clause that imposed a penalty of $7.5 million on either party who
criticized the other publically. Although Perot violated the latter clause
before the ink on the agreement was dry, GM did not invoke the penalty.

THE FOUNDING OF PEROT SYSTEMS INC.

On June 1, 1988, exactly 18 months after the signing of the GM buyout,
Ross Perot founded another company, Perot Systems. Like EDS, it
offered data processing services. This company would grow to a value of
$3.6 billion by 1999, showing once again that Perot had the Midas touch.

Through the publicity he received for his highly visible adventures in
Vietnam and Iran, Perot had become a celebrity and a popular presence
on television talk shows. Americans were impressed with his "can-do"
and aggressive take-charge attitude that produced results. By the end of
the 1980s, Perot was on the move again, but this time he was intent on
moving into the ultimate public arena.

THE FIRST RUN AT THE PRESIDENCY

On February 20, 1992, Larry King (the host of CNN's *Larry King Live*)
asked Ross during an interview whether he would consider running for
President of the United States. As noted earlier, Perot responded that he
would run if the people took it on themselves to register him as a
presidential candidate in all 50 states.

The telephones at the television studio were deluged with callers
volunteering to participate in the Perot 1992 campaign for President. In
the early months following his entry into the race, Perot led Bush and
Clinton in the polls. Ross's reputation as a person who can get things
done appealed to a vast number of voters who were seeking change in
government. However, as the campaigns progressed it was evident that

there was disarray and a lack of coordination in the Perot election campaign. Public support gradually diminished and on July 16, Perot announced the withdrawal of his candidacy for family reasons. However, his supporters ignored his withdrawal, continuing to register him in various states. Then, on the urging of his followers, he re-entered the race on October 1, 1992.

This time, he ran his campaign in his own way rather than leaving it to the "spin doctors" who had sent his first effort into a tailspin. He began by purchasing television infomercial half-hour time-slots for $380,000 from CBS and from ABC for $500,000. (Eventually this run for the top office in America cost Perot $60 million of his own money.) During the campaign, Ross Perot broke every rule in the book on how to seek electoral support and blatantly said, "Elect me and I'll shake up Washington." Jack Perkins on *A&E Biography* said, "Perot ran the most unorthodox Presidential campaign in modern times."

In the world-wide televised debates with incumbent President George Bush (senior) and Democratic candidate Bill Clinton, Perot came across as a sincere business man with a let's-get-at-it attitude. Supporters loved his confrontational style; adversaries feared his extreme need for control. Political pundits saw him as a ticking bomb and far too volatile to be running the nation. One wag described him as a loose cannon with a bad haircut. Others portrayed him as a fraud and railed against his radical tactics. But Perot hit an anti-government nerve and when all was said and done he garnered 19% of the popular vote as an independent.

THE SECOND RUN AT THE PRESIDENCY

Perot's failed attempt at securing America's top job did not spell the end of his public life. On the contrary, in the true spirit of a rodeo rider tossed from a bronco, he climbed aboard for another rough ride. He continued to maintain a high visibility on television talk shows, and in 1993 established a group called *United We Stand America*. Its purpose was to monitor the actions of the federal government and to campaign for financial reform and deficit reduction. In 1995, *United We Stand America* became the Reform party with Ross Perot as its presidential candidate. This time, prolonged exposure had hurt Perot, as the public began to fear that his remarkable ability to get things done might be somewhat compromised by an operating style that was more autocratic than democratic.

Perot's Decade-by-Decade Climb

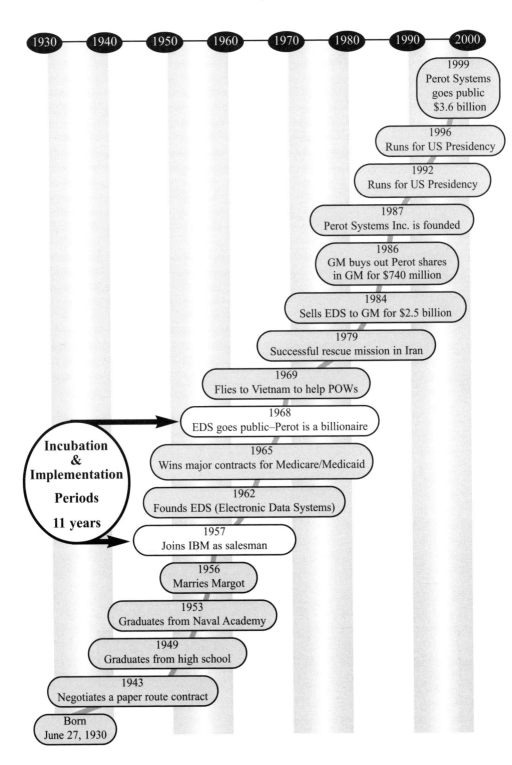

A Personality Profile

COMMUNICATION STYLE: A FLAIR FOR THE DRAMATIC

Perot's flair for the dramatic was legendary. Biographers spoke of his ability to find newsworthy events for self-promotion. Among these was the acquisition of a signed copy of the Magna Carta for $1.5 million that he immediately donated to the National Archives in Washington, DC, with great hoopla. *Fortune* (1988) suggested he had "an instinct for the dramatic." Close associates knew that Ross seldom went into anything without a larger agenda that the media would describe as a cause célèbre.

His quest for media coverage was evident in his disclosure to the press of the details of his non-disclosure agreement with General Motors–before the ink on the contract was dry! The Texas Tiger virtually dared GM to file a lawsuit. In all the wars he waged, Ross Perot sought media exposure and used it as a vehicle for obtaining leverage in his bargaining.

Ross regarded television as the most powerful medium for promotion and he advertised extensively in it. In 1969, he offered to help Nixon boost his image by contributing $50 million to purchase television time. In his own presidential campaign he invested large sums in television infomercials. The Perot bravado was often disguised in the trappings of humility. In the televised debates with the other presidential candidates, Perot's clever use of homilies projected a straight-talkin', straight-shootin' Texan image that endeared him to many voters. When challenged on his lack of government experience, he retorted, "I don't have any experience in running up a $4-trillion debt." When opposing the NAFTA (free trade) agreement, he talked about the "big suckin' sound south" to describe the flow of jobs from America to Mexico that would ensue. He played on the fears of the American public to generate support for his position.

Perhaps the pièce de résistance in Perot's quest for dramatic appeal was his spectacular 1979 rescue mission to Iran. The entire episode played out as a coup of dramatic proportions, involving intrigue and danger. Ken Follett, who wrote *On Wings of Eagles* and consulted with Perot on the details of this rescue, observed, "There were times Perot might put in more drama than was absolutely necessary." When NBC created a miniseries based on Follett's book, Perot secured final approval on the script to ensure the story was presented as he wished. When challenged about his excessive use of literary license, he responded (Posner, p. 121):

Now, in creating a miniseries, there is always a little dramatization–little things that are not exactly the way they happened.

Perot was remarkably successful in achieving his goals and was known as a man who got things done. Although this reputation was well earned, its magnitude was enhanced by Perot's penchant for communicating through the media in a style that was a delightful mixture of melodrama and bravado.

INTUITIONAL STYLE

Ross learned at his father's knee the psychological games involved in horse trading. He internalized these experiences as an intuition that served him well in his bargaining and his conflicts. In negotiating his buyout with GM, he understood that the negative publicity resulting from his public criticism of GM made his silence an urgent necessity for GM. As biographer Posner observed (Posner, pp. 181–2):

[Perot] knew, from his days of watching his father trade horses in Texarkana, that the person who needs the sale the most will eventually pay the price.

Perot used his intuitive understanding of this principle to push for a most lucrative settlement in the GM buyout.

During the 1992 election campaign, Ross admonished his team to think creatively. One of Perot's former secretaries explained (Posner, p. 258):

One of the things that Perot had told us over and over again was that we should always think outside the box...that we should never do things just because that's the way they had always been done.

Pat Horner, President of Perot Systems, told the press, "Ross is not a manager. He's a leader." He was trying to convey the difference between Perot and other executives: managers work on details; leaders work on philosophical vision. Perot would admit that he never worked on things, only on visions and missions. Horner says, "Perot challenges you to reach your highest potential. It's the antithesis of micro-management." Perot told *U.S. News & World* (June 1992), "Leadership is having goals, a vision; getting it done, and then go on to the next one."

RISK-TAKING PROPENSITY

The Perot propensity for risk-taking is evident in everything he does. From the earliest age, he was breaking broncos. Then, as a 13-year-old, he delivered newspapers in a part of Texarkana where no one else would dare to tread. He conducted a risky mission of mercy into Vietnam and another dangerous rescue mission into Iran. Ross Perot thrived on risk and adrenaline.

Throughout his life, Ross Perot has been eager to sacrifice the safe present for the unknown future. He quit a big job at IBM and gambled on his dream. When his bosses at IBM told him that leasing back computer time from key customers was not viable, he ignored them and went ahead on his own, using a $1000 loan from his wife. Through such tenacity in his quest to succeed, he prevailed and his enterprise, EDS, flourished.

Perot's appetite for risk carried over into his recreation. Speed has always been one of his passions. He owns fast boats and planes and often races them in competition with his sons. The Texas Tiger is an avid water skier, alpine skier, and surfer. His preference is for high-speed cigarette boats that spear through the water at 100 mph. This insatiable need for speed led him to install two jet engines at a cost of $500,000 in one of his boats in order to race his son Ross Jr. across Lake Texoma at 135 mph. Ross was well into his 60s when Leon Derebery told *Newsweek* (June 29, 1992), "Shoot, you can't scare him. He just puts on his goggles and hangs on." Meanwhile, Perot's son flies overhead in a helicopter, racing his dad to the finish line.

INTENSITY

A high-school girlfriend characterized Ross as "driven and very intense" (Posner, p. 14). Patience never was one of Perot's qualities. This Type-A overachiever was on a mission to conquer anything and anybody who crossed his path. This was evident in his dealings with the U.S. Naval Academy. Those attending the Naval Academy are required to serve a minimum four-year stint for receiving a free first-class education. After two years, Perot decided he didn't want to stay in the service despite his agreement. He began a tirade of calls and letters to the power elite in an attempt to get an early release. Perot railed against the Navy, charging that they were "promoting mediocrity." He asserted, "They have no incentive for competition. The motivation is time and grade instead of capability." In another letter he said (Posner, p. 20):

I would prefer to make my life's career in a field where men are more self-reliant and the threat of disapproval is not the paramount consideration when making decisions.

The Navy refused to yield and remained adamant about Perot serving out his time.

His wife Margot said that when she and Ross went on vacation from IBM, he filled thirteen pads with his scrawled plans for a new company. He planned a staff that operated as a meritocracy that rewarded performance and achievement rather than formal education and seniority. He later reflected on his approach to hiring at that time (Posner, p. 29):

I wanted people who are tough, smart, self-reliant, absolutely honest...people who have a history of success since childhood and people who love to win. After that, bring me people who hate to lose.

One EDS executive characterized him as "having an incredible level of intensity" that caused more than one of his employees to suffer from burnout. That executive went on to explain (Posner, p. 92):

We used to say, only half joking, that a lot of the time it was as though Ross asked you to go climb a sheer ice glacier and report back to him. Then you would go ahead, climb the glacier, almost kill yourself in the process, and report back. And he would say, "Okay, now do it without gloves."

During the late 1970s, Texas Medicaid had been a major client of EDS with billings of $4 million per year. However, by 1980, Texas Medicaid had grown tired of what they perceived as a lack of support from EDS and gave their business to a New York competitor, Bradford. This small firm went after the account and agreed to things EDS had denied. When Perot first heard of the loss he exploded. In London at the time, he caught the next plane back, called key executives together, and announced, "Pack your bags. We're going to war." *Inc* magazine in 1989 described the incident, "It was Perot as classic SOB. He came screaming out of the sky, talons bared, and ripped their eyes out." Apparently, the Texas Tornado told EDS Vice President Ken Riedlinger (Posner, p. 136):

I am going to kill those guys, then I am going to bury them, and then I am going to dance on their graves until the stench gets so bad I can't stand it.

Perot subsequently hired private detectives, called on his contacts in the Governor's mansion, implored the legislature not to allow such a valuable contract to go out of state, and actually threatened state employees. He vowed to win or bring everyone down with him, and that is exactly what happened. The state decided he was just too much to contend with and refused to do business with either firm. He so infuriated state officials that the court threw out Bradford's and EDS's bids and awarded the contract to a third firm. When it came to conflict, Perot was often seen as a "high testosterone" personality with a Machiavellian style of leadership.

Ross's sale of EDS to General Motors made him a multi-billionaire. He had a yacht, a ranch in Texas and lavish estates in Vail and Bermuda. He could have retired to a life of leisure, but that would not satisfy his restless spirit. Once the non-compete clause had expired, he opened Perot Systems, trying to take business away from his old firm.

SELF-IMAGE

When Ken Follett was working on the best-selling book and movie on the Iranian rescue, he asked Perot if he would consider running for the Presidency of the United States. Ross confided, "If I could run for king, I would do it", reflecting the magnitude of his ambition driven by a strong ego. A top official in the White House who had been approached by Perot for help in the rescue of the POWs in Vietnam asserted (Posner, p. 64):

He actually thought he knew what to do, better than anyone else. He never considered the possibility that anyone else could be right.

Perot maintained that mindset throughout his election campaign. While delivering one of his unabridged, straight-talkin' speeches, his campaign team watched in horror as Ross ran afoul of the rules of political sensitivity. One of the consultants in his campaign headquarters opined (Posner, p. 282):

It confirmed to all of us that this guy is just not going to listen to anyone. He is not going to let anyone write a speech. He is just going to keep doing it his way until he implodes.

During the short period that he served on the board of GM, Ross made no fewer than thirteen proposals for radical change. GM's Elmer Johnson said, "I have never seen a guy who likes to fight as much as he does."

In an attempt to define this super-wealthy Texan, *Fortune* magazine (March 24, 1988) wrote:

> *Perot is a creative genius with business acumen, entrepreneurial talent, flair, a touch of exhibitionism, old fashioned patriotism, and an old-boy down-home persona.*

Those words capture the many dimensions of Perot's complex personality. Disciples love him and detractors hate him: with Perot, there is no middle ground. He knew that image is everything in politics and that branding an image was critically important to his political future. To this end, he spent tens of millions on television commercials in his bids for the presidency. Brux Austin, editor of *Texas Business,* said, "I have never encountered a CEO of his stature [who was] that sensitive about his image."

ECCENTRICITIES AND PERSONAL PARADOXES

Biographer Gerald Posner called Perot "complex and contradictory." The truth is that Ross Perot is an anomaly to most people. What seems paradoxical to many is how this superior judge of character, a man who was eminently successful hiring and motivating top people, could be so easily hoodwinked by some of the most arcane charlatans whom he put into top positions at EDS. Other entrepreneurs like Hugh Hefner had a similar propensity. They were both bright, opinionated hard-liners, but those who understood them could manipulate them as puppets.

Despite a strong ethical sense, Perot could be a screaming tyrant. While preaching openness and freedom, he frequently used polygraphs and repeatedly tapped the phones of key executives and adversaries. If he suspected an executive of having an affair or acting unethically, the executive was summarily dismissed without remorse and without severance. In many ways, Perot resembled Henry Ford. Both men were highly moralistic and attempted to monitor the moral turpitude of their employees. Both also spied on their employees to ensure that they remained faithful to their wives and that they avoided alcohol.

Paradoxically, Perot had a reputation among his employees as a very supportive leader. Posner observes (p. 96):

> *Indeed, the image most workers [at EDS] had of Perot was of a gifted motivational leader who cared about their welfare.*

The same man who had risked a fortune and his life to release prisoners held hostage in Iran would, for no apparent reason, castigate employees for daring to challenge his authority. Former employees described Perot either as a god or an SOB. The supporters and detractors were alike only in the intensity of their feelings.

When Perot ran for the U.S. Presidency, he vowed to eliminate Washington's profligate spending, but was at the same time negotiating single-source contracts for himself that were incompatible with this promise. According to biographer Posner, Perot had overcharged government agencies millions.

Although Ross enjoyed confrontations at any level, he was extremely paranoid about his personal safety. He drove around in armored cars with bulletproof windows. One associate reported that Perot would have his secretary book reservations on several different airlines to a destination so that no one would know which one he was on–yet he would eat lunch at Dickey's Barbecue in full public view. Another executive at EDS described how this highly personable extrovert would eat alone in the company cafeteria and refuse to speak to anyone. This seemed strange behavior for a man who prized camaraderie and promoted teamwork.

Perot has been described as everything from "an indignant prude" by his navy buddies to a "dangerous egocentric and fraud" by the media. Unquestionably, the bronco buster from Texarkana marches to a different drummer and says what he thinks no matter the consequences. During the debates in the 1992 Presidential campaign, it was suggested he not use graphic charts to illustrate his points on national TV. His advisors told him he was not in a board meeting and would appear stiff and insufferable. Perot ignored his advisors. Even in an interview with Larry King, he insisted on holding up his infamous charts. Many observers thought he projected the image of an intransigent bully.

Perhaps Perot's greatest eccentricity is his insatiable need for control. If he isn't the center of it all, he refuses to play. Even in philanthropy, he refuses to give unless he dictates where the money is spent. When he was attending his first General Motors Board meeting, Roger Smith asked him not to pass out his favorite management book, *Leadership Secrets of Attila The Hun.* Perot apparently suffered a minor "meltdown" and vowed to bring down Smith. Ken Follett conjectured (Posner, 117):

> *The reason he doesn't drink is that he wouldn't enjoy that slight feeling of loss of control.*

ACHIEVEMENTS & HONORS

MAGNITUDE OF SUCCESS

After graduation from the U.S Navel Academy, it was onward and upward for Ross Perot. He quit IBM in 1962 and built EDS with a $1000 loan. Within five years he had taken the firm public, becoming a multi-millionaire in the process. A little more than a year after his IPO, he was a billionaire. In 1984, when he sold EDS to General Motors, he was worth almost $3 billion. The take-charge man from Texas was suddenly the largest stockholder in the largest corporation in the world. Eighteen months after selling EDS, Perot founded his next corporation, Perot Systems, and in 1999, took it public. After that IPO, Perot Systems Corporation was valued at $3.5 billion.

During his rise to the top of the corporate world, Perot has conducted two dangerous missions and helped the State of Texas enact laws. Perot has been a ubiquitous presence in the United States and has stood as a model of what can be done by anyone with enough energy and tenacity to conceive a vision and pursue it relentlessly. He describes one of his proudest moments as the time his son, Ross Jr., was chosen as one of America's Most Outstanding Young Men and he invited his dad to sit beside him at the awards ceremony. Ross Perot wrote (Posner, p. x):

> He is "big Ross." I am "old Ross." I live in my son's shadow, and there is no better place for a father to live.

HONORS

So far, Ross Perot has received more than sixty awards. Among these is the Medal for Distinguished Public Service from the Department of Defense for his work on behalf of the POWs in Vietnam between 1969 and 1972. In 1988, Perot was named to the Business Hall of Fame as a tribute to his contribution to the world of enterprise. His popular success in the Vietnam and Iran ventures and his ubiquity as a television talk-show personality resulted in his nomination as a candidate in the 1992 and 1996 Presidential elections.

At this writing, Perot is a respected philanthropist who has donated over $120 million to worthy causes. Clearly, the drive and ambition that led him to billionaire status have not waned.

LESSONS LEARNED FROM ROSS PEROT

Egomaniacal personalities like that of Ross Perot antagonize many people, but even his most strident detractors must acknowledge the remarkable success he has achieved in his endeavors. From these successes we can learn many important lessons. Two of the most prominent are presented here.

ATTITUDE, NOT APTITUDE, IS THE KEY TO SUCCESS

Berkeley research scientist Mark Rosenzweig found "Positive experience alters IQ, brain size, and learning ability." Eminent psychologist Eric Erikson wrote:

> *Study after study has shown that children with superior intelligence but low self-esteem do poorly in school, while children of average intelligence, but high self-esteem, can be unusually successful.*

Other studies have shown that success is a function of the way you think more than a consequence of innate talent. Even one's health is highly dependent on one's state of mind. If the doctors believe you will recover, your chances improve dramatically. If they believe you are terminal, their influence can prove disastrous. Many studies show that students who believe they are gifted, even if they are not, do superior work and achieve high grades.

Ross Perot is the consummate example of belief leading to success. Perot revolutionized an industry in which he had little formal training. Executives at EDS said he never learned to program and was lost in the technological world of writing computer code. Yet writing code was the essence of the business at Electronic Data Systems. That deficiency did not deter Perot from his mission. He knew he could hire people to do the programming and that would free him to undertake the business end. He recruited and hired people who shared his same aggressive "can-do" attitude toward achievement. For him business was war and he advised his personnel to "Do business with the same positive spirit as an athletic contest."

The magic of the Perot experience is to believe that you are good or worthy of success *prior* to the proof. But where does such a strong belief originate? It is usually an early success imprint. For Perot, it happened when breaking horses at age 7. He leaned that to win, you had better not give in to failure. A strong sense of self and optimism armed him to deal with life's adversities. In fact, a positive attitude derives from a strong sense of self–the next lesson to be learned from Ross Perot.

A STRONG SENSE OF SELF IS A PREREQUISITE FOR SUCCESS

In the words of former President Woodrow Wilson, "All the extraordinary men I have ever known were chiefly extraordinary in their own estimation." Entrepreneurs appear to be in more need of a strong sense of self than the normal population. Even if deluded, they need powerful self-confidence to make it to the very top. When you find yourself out in front of the pack, you have few life-support systems and must believe faithfully in your own sense of destiny. Every one of the great entrepreneurs profiled in this book had strong egos.

If you don't believe in yourself, it is best to get a job where your sanity is not questioned daily. Ross Perot worked for IBM but when he told his boss his idea about buying computers and leasing back time to sell to others who couldn't afford one, his boss scoffed at such a silly idea. He was told to just keep doing his job and not rock the boat. But Perot had been a boat rocker since he was a kid. Confidence to the degree of arrogance is common among entrepreneurs and Perot fits the profile. His sense of superiority can be grating at a personal level, but in the real world it is key to survival.

Pundits have often referred to Perot as having a little man complex: an inflated ego to offset an inner sense of inferiority. Even if it is true it is not all bad. History has provided a long list of such overachievers like Napoleon and Picasso at 5′3″ and Bucky Fuller at 5′2″. Ross Perot is 5′6″ and not prone to take prisoners in business dealings.

Martha Kostyra Stewart

Passionate Perfection is the Path to Power

b. Jersey City, NJ   August 3, 1941

"If you love it, buy it."

SELF-DESCRIPTION
"I'm eclectic, demanding, and a perfectionist."

MOTTOS
"If you love it, buy it."– she bought not one but two East Hampton estates.
"I'm extremely curious and have a goal to learn something new every single day."

INNOVATION	"Martha Stewart has become a brand," Kirstin Feldman of Morgan Stanley
UNIQUE QUALITY	A perfectionist homemaker image that belies the truth: she is really an overachieving entrepreneur with a need to be the very best or die trying.
OBJECTIVE	"I am a commitment to a kind of lifestyle; that's what I am."
NET WORTH	An IPO (public offering) in October 1999 gave her a net worth of $1.27 billion.
HONORS	Branded the Diva of Domesticity by 1990 media "Best Dressed College Girl" for *Glamour* while at Barnard First national exposure: cover of *Country Living* (1979)
BIRTH ORDER	Second born of six; first daughter and father's favorite
EDUCATION	B.A. in art history from Barnard College in 1963
PERSONALITY	Obsessive-compulsive and intuitive thinking visionary
HOBBIES	Alaskan ice hiking and other eclectic ventures
POLITICS	Democrat
RELIGION	Roman Catholic upbringing–spiritual; into astrology
FAMILY	Husband: Andy (since divorced), Children: Alexis

8
Martha Stewart

Passionate Perfection is the Path to Power

"I plan to be rich and famous."
(Stewart's promise at age 20)

Overview

What makes us is often what breaks us: our greatest strengths become our mortal weaknesses. This theme that threads through the great Shakespearean tragedies has never been more apropos than in the life and work of the paragon of perfection, Martha Stewart. The "diva of domesticity" pervaded the public consciousness throughout the roaring '90s with her ubiquitous persona as a model of homemaking and hostess perfection. Martha had become throughout the western world the standard to which many women would aspire in their attire, their homemaking, their gardening, and their entertaining.

In 1997, the "daytime dynamo" formed a conglomerate named Martha Stewart Living Omnimedia Inc. in order to buy back from Time Warner her rights to *Martha Stewart Living* magazine. The move was pure genius and would become the vehicle that would make her a billionaire. Martha insisted on including all her media enterprises under the umbrella of Omnimedia. This action made her name the leading commodity in her vast empire and led to underwriters insisting on a $122-million insurance policy on her life. Why? She was the company.

Martha's celebrity as the arbiter of American taste superceded her role as CEO of Omnimedia. She and her persona became a dominant presence on the web, network TV, magazine racks, direct-response catalogs and even in syndicated radio. Many experts felt she would over-saturate. But the astute businesswoman knew better. There seems to have been no limit to the demand for her work. She continued to spin her magic in a phantasmagoria of domesticity resembling in magnitude that of Ralph Lauren in menswear and McDonald's in hamburgers.

By the end of the millennium, Martha had come a long way from an attractive middle-class girl in Nutley, New Jersey to become a billionaire celebrity and one of the 50 most powerful women in America. She had burst into the public consciousness through her plethora of TV shows, books, magazines, talk-show guest appearances and product offerings at Kmart. Then suddenly, the very thing that made her rich and famous, threatened her demise.

In June 2002, shortly after she had reached the billionaire status, her meteoric rise to fame and fortune plummeted into a downward spiral of scandal at a greater speed than the ascent. What *Newsweek* (July 1, 2002) profiled as "Martha's Mess" was her flirtation with disaster in her alleged insider trading of shares of a biotech company called ImClone Systems Inc. In December of 2001, Martha Stewart had sold off a mere 3928 shares of ImClone stock just prior to that firm losing FDA approval for its cancer drug Erbitux. When the media learned that prior to making the sale, Martha had telephoned her personal friend, ImClone CEO Samuel Waksal, a media feeding-frenzy fomented. Because the loss of the FDA approval had not been announced publically, it appeared that Martha had received and acted upon privileged information–a violation of insider trading rules.

The public has a love-hate relationship with the rich and famous: it admires their celebrity and wealth, but envies their privilege. Like Madame Defarge calling for the heads of the aristocracy by guillotine, the public was particularly outraged by the alleged crime and called for blood. In a predictable sequence of events, the media exploited the public need for retribution in a deluge of muckraking and conjecture. The Justice Department became involved and eventually, Stewart was forced to resign from her seat on the Board of the New York Stock Exchange.

On June 4, 2003, Ms. Stewart was indicted and charged by a US federal court on nine criminal charges. These charges pertained, not to insider trading, but rather to her alleged attempts to conceal her insider trading activities by destroying or falsifying evidence. In addition, she was charged with securities fraud pertaining to her own company Martha Stewart Living Omnimedia Inc. The indictment claims that Martha, as CEO of her company, had made false statements about her ImClone trade to protect the share price of her stock. As a result of the formal charges against her, she resigned her position as CEO and Chairwoman of Omnimedia, although she remains the majority shareholder of that company's stock.

During the year-long probe into the ImClone trade, the share price of the Omnimedia stock continued to erode and on the announcement of the formal criminal charges it plummeted from $11.20 to $9.52–a drop of 15% in a single day! Shareholders realized that Martha Stewart was Omnimedia Inc. Martha lamented that in the year between the initial public announcement of the alleged insider trading and the laying of criminal charges by the U.S. attorney for the Southern District of New York, her personal equity had dropped by almost one-half a billion dollars–about 2000 times the amount involved in the infamous stock transaction!

Had she sold after the public announcement about Erbitux, her stock loss on ImClone would only have been $43,000. Furthermore, if she had merely donated the proceeds of her sale to a charity, it would have cost her $227,824 and the scandal could have been averted. However, her reluctance to part with approximately a quarter of a million dollars–a mere pittance for a billionaire–ignited a public outcry that injured her public image and invited potentially devastating criminal charges.

In addition to the financial losses Martha has sustained in her Omnimedia stock, she also faces a civil lawsuit for insider trading launched by the Securities and Exchange Commission. Martha Stewart has pleaded not guilty to all criminal charges and is expected to be embroiled in a long court battle to exonerate herself and her public image. Even if she succeeds in her legal fight, Martha will not escape unscathed from the scandal and loss of credibility.

Martha's reluctance to sustain a loss, no matter how miniscule, may be the source of much of her recent travails, but it is also what has enabled her to build such an all-pervasive empire and elevate her to the status of the rich, famous, and powerful. In spite of what people may believe about her, it must be acknowledged that she is one of the great entrepreneurs of the 20th Century, and perhaps a tragic heroine in the Shakespearean tradition. Richard III's final words, as depicted in Shakespeare's play (*Richard III*, Act V, Scene 4) were a desperate call, "A horse, a horse, my kingdom for a horse!" Referring to this quote, a poet mused:

> *For want of a nail, a shoe was lost,*
> *For want of a shoe a horse was lost,*
> *For want of a horse, a kingdom was lost,*
> *All for the want of a horseshoe nail!*

The Martha Stewart kingdom hangs in the balance pending the outcome of her trial–the consequence of a horseshoe-nail telephone call.

The Formative Years

EARLY EXPERIENCES

Martha Kostyra was born on August 3, 1941 in Jersey City, New Jersey. Her dad, a pharmaceutical salesman, was considered quite bright and known as "Eddie the dictionary" because of his extensive reading. But Eddie Kostyra felt his status as a Polish immigrant had hindered his ability to get ahead. It led him to groom his favorite child for a better life as the consummate, wholesome girl-next-door type. He was the primary influence in her life. Martha once commented to the media:

> *My father gave a lot to me. I think I was his favorite because I would do anything for him since I was his first daughter...I go to see every production of Death of a Salesman because that's my father–Willy Loman.*

Martha's mother had been educated as a teacher but never taught because she was busy raising a brood of six children.

Eddie Kostyra was well-meaning in his fanatic need for order and perfection. In an effort to please her dad, Martha tried desperately to be the very best she could be, but that was never quite good enough. This unrelenting struggle to satisfy her father's demand for perfection left an indelible mark on the psyche of Martha Kostyra. It also left her with few boy friends during her school years. To be loved, Martha felt she had to be perfect. Eddie's legacy, good or bad, was that he taught his daughter to strive for excellence–this would become her obsession and her hallmark. High school friend, Barb Howard, commented, "Martha did nothing half way. She was highly ambitious and competitive."

When she was thirteen, Martha's favorite TV show was the sitcom *Father Knows Best*. To her, it was the model of an idyllic family life that she never knew in Nutley. But in Martha's mind Eddie was Robert Young, her mother was Mrs. Anderson and she was Betty Anderson–the perfect daughter, in the perfect family, with the perfect home. That is the imagery that still pervades the work of Martha. However, the reality in Nutley stood in stark contrast to the Andersons' family life as depicted on television. Eddie, unlike Robert Young, was an obsessive autocrat and her mother a submissive domestic. Both parents were distant and had no time for coddling or loving relationships. Affection in the Kostyra household was sparse or non-existent–achievement was everything and love was given only for performance. A high school classmate told biographer Jerry Oppenheimer, "Martha always had a need for admiration and attention and was unable to stand rejection."

Martha Kostyra's fear of her father's wrath caused her to try to avoid making a mistake. Consequently, she grew up in constant fear of failure and Eddie's retribution. If she weren't perfect she wouldn't be loved and this molded her into a perfectionist fanatic and a driven overachiever.

By the time Martha had passed through puberty, the "princess of perfection" was both physically and psychologically developed. Boys who would normally be attracted to her statuesque beauty were intimidated by her aloofness and lack of receptivity to their overtures. Her former schoolmates from New Jersey describe her as a girl who was bright, pretty, and perfect to the point of intimidating all potential suitors. The attractive blond model had fewer dates than almost anyone in high school.

FORMAL EDUCATION

In elementary school, she befriended a teacher, Irene Weyer, who became a role model. Fashionable, fastidious and highly feminine, she was worldly and dressed with the elegance of a professional, in sharp contrast to Martha's matronly mother who never left the kitchen. Weyer was everything Martha aspired to be and she became a surrogate mother figure to Martha throughout her school years.

Her father had told her that she would have to earn her own way through college. By age fifteen, the long-legged blonde was catching the train into Manhattan and modeling for Clairol, Lifebuoy and Bonwit Teller. Her first national exposure came in a Lifebuoy Soap ad for Bonwit Teller that aired on the popular television program *Paladin*. In the 1950s the clean-cut girl-next-door look was in fashion. With her fresh pretty face, Martha was in vogue on Madison Avenue and she got plenty of work. Having been weaned on the Veronica Lake pinup look, and she mimicked the Hollywood star.

In 1959 at age 17, Martha graduated from Nutley High School where she excelled in academics and social activities. She entered Barnard College on the campus of Columbia University in New York City. During her college years, Martha earned a total of $30,000 modeling, and that income combined with a partial scholarship enabled her to pursue her studies in art history. Her good looks and meticulous attention to detail in her dress kept her in strong demand as a model, and in her sophomore year at Barnard, she won *Glamour* magazine's Best Dressed College Girl.

During the spring of her freshman year, Martha Kostyra went on a blind date with a man named Andy Stewart, a sophomore at Yale Law School. Most college-age men were intimidated by her beauty and brightness, but not the well-traveled Andy. He had seen the world with globetrotting parents and was equally at home in Europe as America. The handsome, stylish six-footer swept Martha off her feet and they became inseparable. Eventually he asked her to marry him and move to Connecticut while he completed his law degree. Upon his graduation, she could return to finish her education. Martha agreed and they married in July 1961, when she was 19. Martha returned to Bernard a year later and graduated in 1964 with a B.A. in Art History.

The Climb to the Top

RIDING THE BULL

Nothing and nobody could dissuade Martha Stewart from her unrelenting drive to move up in the world. Her marriage to Andy was part of the plan that biographer Jerry Oppenheimer described as an "egotistical and imperial" study in contrasts. Testimony to Martha's demand for more and more came when Andy surprised her with a diamond engagement ring that the struggling college student had bought from world-famous jeweler Harry Winston. On receiving the ring, Martha told Andy, "I don't like it and I don't want it." At that moment Andy might have suspected that his future wife was strong-willed and self-absorbed. Then Martha asked Andy if she could pick out her own ring. He capitulated, and in so doing, established a pattern that would recur throughout their marriage.

After college, Martha modeled until the birth of her only daughter Alexis in 1965. Two years later she began a career as a stockbroker with the brokerage firm Monness, Williams, and Sidel, and quickly became a star performer earning as much as $135,000 a year in the late '60s. In her mid-twenties Martha would stroll down Wall Street, adorned in hot pants, and presenting a striking figure in that bastion of male power. At the time, she worked with Brian Dennehy who later became an accomplished actor. Style and grace, combined with a take-no-prisoners attitude for selling securities, made her very successful prior to the downturn in 1970. Biographer Jerry Oppenheimer wrote that men did business with her for the chance to lunch with her. During those torrid years of hot pants and free spirits, a gorgeous female with intelligence and drive was able to do well. Her Machiavellian methods didn't hurt. However, her employer promoted the sale of some very risky stocks, such as Levitz Furniture that eventually went bankrupt. Many of Martha's clients, including some of her friends who had invested with her, lost money on these stocks.

THE UNCATERED AFFAIR

In 1973, Martha hit bottom when the stock market popped her bubble of invincibility. She was unable to handle the defeat and rejection. When friends and family sustained losses from stocks she had touted, the stress took its toll. Martha crashed along with the market and retreated quietly to her country estate at 48 Turkey Hill Road South in Westport, Connecticut that she and Andy had bought in 1971. Martha suffered an emotional breakdown.

After a period of recovery, Martha's drive and talents took her in another direction, inspired by a visit from Norma Collier, a friend from Martha's early career in modeling. Norma and Martha chatted about possible enterprises that they might undertake together, now that their modeling careers were behind them. Out of this chat emerged the idea of providing a local catering business. By 1974, the feminist movement had created opportunities for women to pursue professional careers. In an upscale community like Westport, professional women didn't have the time available to do the detailed planning and preparation necessary for formal entertaining. In the words of biographer Christopher Byron (p. 72):

> *Into this turmoil stepped Norma and Martha, offering a service that instantly set them apart from every other catering business in town...a catering service set up to look as though the woman of the house did all the work herself!*

Martha and Norma opened The Uncatered Affair, a 50/50 partnership. The idea was that Norma and Martha would prepare the meal in their own homes and then arrive at the client's house before the formal dinner, place the dinner in the oven, set the table and decorate the dining area. When the guests arrived, they would see the hired servers delivering the meal to the table, but would assume that the hostess had done all the preparation. The Uncatered Affair had anticipated a market that was, as yet, untapped. Martha bought a commercial oven and she and Norma began catering upscale parties and weddings. Martha's clientele was to be Westport and Norma's, the nearby New Canaan. Among the neighbors for whom they catered parties were celebrities such as Paul Newman, Beverly Sills and Robert Redford. Martha's talents and her perfectionist attention to detail were ideally suited to chic upscale events for the discriminating tastes of the affluent community around Westport.

Within a few months, friction began to emerge between the two partners. Norma felt that Martha was attempting to upstage her in public and to quietly squeeze her out of the partnership. When Norma discovered that Martha had been booking catering on the side and not sharing the profits, she confronted Martha. The ensuing conflict led to a dissolution of their enterprise in early 1975, just six months after it had been formed. Norma and Martha ceased to be friends, and Norma retained bitter feelings toward Martha ever after. Martha continued catering and opened a shop called The Market Basket, that offered many of the dishes and desserts that she had prepared in her catering business. This enterprise became an immediate success and on January 1, 1977, she incorporated her business under the name Martha Stewart Inc. Martha was on her way up.

THE PRINT MEDIUM

Meanwhile, husband Andy had moved from assistant in-house council for a publishing company to CEO and President of Harry Abrams Publishing Inc. It is said that success is what happens when readiness meets opportunity. Martha Stewart was certainly ready in 1980 when Andy asked her to cater a big Manhattan party for the launch of one of his books. Attending was the President of Crown Books, Alan Meiken, who was taken with Martha and her ability to cater. He suggested she write a book on the art of catering and entertaining. An inexperienced writer, Martha hired a ghostwriter, Betsy Weinstock. The book, titled *Entertaining,* took two years to come to fruition. Martha exercised full control over the entire project and never acknowledged Weinstock's contribution as ghost writer.

When *Entertaining* was published in 1982, the culinary critics criticized it, charging that many of the recipes had been stolen from Julia Child's classic cookbook, *Mastering the Art of French Cooking.* The critics also claimed that many of the recipes contained the wrong proportions of ingredients. In spite of these complaints, *Entertaining* became a best-seller with sales exceeding 500,000 copies. Martha had understood what women in the early '80s needed was–not a cookbook but a fantasy about gracious "home-and-hearth" living. In the words of biographer Christopher Byron (p. 91):

> *[Entertaining]* wasn't actually a cookbook at all, but a celebration *of a certain kind of tinselly, nouveau-grandeur that was seeping into American life as the 1980s began.*

The success of her first publication encouraged Martha to write more books for the same market. She followed with *Quick Cook* in 1983, *Hors d'Oeuvres* in 1984, *Pies & Tarts* in 1985, and *Weddings* in 1987. These books were not only successful from a sales and marketing standpoint, but they also served to catapult Martha Stewart to the status of the reigning guru on cooking and entertaining. Like Richard Branson, Donald Trump, and other modern entrepreneurs, Martha was coming to understand the role of public persona in establishing a "branding" marketing strategy. The name *Martha Stewart* was becoming a commodity.

ATTENTION KMART SHOPPERS

Martha's growing reputation led to a telephone call in February 1987 from Barbara Loren-Snyder. On behalf of Kmart, Barbara was seeking a spokesperson for their enterprise who would enhance their public image. Kmart's reputation as a discount retail store had seriously curtailed their share of the growing yuppie market. To capture this more affluent group, Kmart needed to have its merchandise endorsed by someone known for "discriminating taste." What better figurehead than the "Diva of Gracious Domesticity"? After several meetings and six months of negotiations, Martha Stewart signed a 5-year contract with Kmart as their "consultant." The contract was to pay her $200,000 per year plus $3000 per day for each of the 30 days that she was required to represent Kmart at various functions. Eventually, Martha manoeuvred Kmart into investing heavily in her enterprises, leveraging much more money from them than was called for in the original contract.

TROUBLE IN PLEASANTVILLE

While Martha was launched on her climb up the entrepreneurial ladder, her relationship with husband Andy was gradually deteriorating. The stress of fixing up and maintaining their 19th-century vintage home and maintaining a horrendous business schedule was manifesting itself in unrelenting abuse of her husband. She found fault with everything he did and launched into tirades when things were not done as she wished. Those who knew Martha prior to her move to Westport commented favorably about her, but friends who socialized with them subsequently described Martha as a Jekyll-and-Hyde personality who would launch into a Ms. Hyde routine when things didn't go her way. Meanwhile, it was rumored, though not confirmed, that Andy was having an affair. The years of Andy's growing anger and resentment finally erupted on June 19, 1987, when Andy, after almost 26 years of marriage, left Martha once and for all. He filed for divorce. After protracted litigation and much vitriol, the divorce became final in 1990. Andy subsequently married Martha's assistant, Robyn Fairclough.

FROM BOOKS TO MAGAZINES

Martha continued to escalate the time and energy that she poured into her work. She negotiated a contract with Time Warner to create a magazine called *Martha Stewart Living* that featured her on virtually every page. The men at Time Warner were skeptical about the market potential of a magazine that resembled an infomercial on Martha. However, Martha's intuitive understanding of what women wanted was correct again. The test issue of the magazine in November 1991 sold out and about 100,000 subscription orders resulted from a direct response mailing!

FROM THE PRINT MEDIUM TO TELEVISION

By the early 1990s, Martha was making frequent appearances on television. She became a familiar face on *Live with Regis and Kathie Lee* and the *Today* show, and was making plans for her own show. Martha had become an American icon (*Byron*, p. 195):

> *[Martha] had become ubiquitous, the face of the age. She had become so famous that, as the* New York Times *rightly pointed out, she no longer needed a last name. She had become simply "Martha"–a kind of Cher, or Madonna, or Jackie.*

On January 19, 1993, a contract was signed with Group W Productions to syndicate a television series called *Martha Stewart Living*. When the pilot episode was aired, there was considerable skepticism among the syndicators regarding viewer reaction to the show. It was initially judged to be rather vacuous and trite by some of the male marketers. However, it was such a roaring success with the predominantly female audiences of morning television that its original half-hour format was extended to a full hour. By early 1996, *Martha Stewart Living* had become the most popular women's program on morning television. By 1998, it had moved from a weekly to a daily program. Once again, Martha had demonstrated that she knew her market better than anyone else.

ONWARD TO A CROSS-PLATFORM MEDIA MONOLITH

Early in 1997, Martha incorporated all her enterprises under one umbrella company, named Martha Stewart Living Omnimedia. This company was one of the first so-called *cross-platform* companies that have acquisitions in several different media, such as print, television, and Internet using one medium to sell products rooted in the other media. In February 1997, with the help of Sharon Patrick, a brilliant financial advisor, Martha bought *Martha Stewart Living* magazine from Time Warner in an agreement that required her to pay $48 million and issue Time Warner 6.3% of the unregistered shares in her new company's stock. The purchase price was reported in the *New York Times* as $85 million. The payment of $48 million called for $18 million immediately plus $30 million over four years. To meet the $18 million obligation, Martha used $16 million she received from Kmart in another deal and only $2 million of her own money! To repay the $30-million loan, she conceived a clever plan. She would take her new company public in an IPO and pay the remainder in shares.

Through 1998 and 1999, the stock market had been strongly bullish. The NASDAQ Composite Index had shot up 80%. Initial public offerings (IPOs) for the dot.com sector companies were hot. The share price of stocks in an IPO offering would often triple or quadruple by the end of the first trading day. Investors' fear of missing large profits induced them to buy in a feeding frenzy that drove prices into the stratosphere. It was in this environment that Martha Stewart decided to take Martha Stewart Living Omnimedia public.

At 9:30 a.m. on October 19, 1999–exactly a dozen years to the day that the market "crashed"–Martha Stewart struck the opening bell at the New York Stock Exchange to open trading on her IPO at $18 per share. If her stock were to sell out at this price, her net worth would be $614.7 million. However, the share price immediately soared to $37.25 and her net worth vaulted to $1.27 billion. She was a billionaire!

Martha was at the pinnacle of her career. Her company had a spectacularly successful IPO and she was now one of the wealthiest women in the world. Furthermore, she was now able to repay Time Warner the $12 million that she owed them by transferring shares of her common stock. Christopher Byron opined (p. 269):

> *[The purchase of* Martha Stewart Living *magazine from Time Warner] was easily the greatest financial coup in the history of American publishing...for when she finally took Martha Stewart Living Omnimedia public in her October 1999 IPO, the company's stock price nearly tripled during its first day of trading, giving the one-time Connecticut caterer a personal net worth of more than $1 billion...for which she paid out of her own pocket a mere $2 million.*

Stewart's Decade-by-Decade Climb

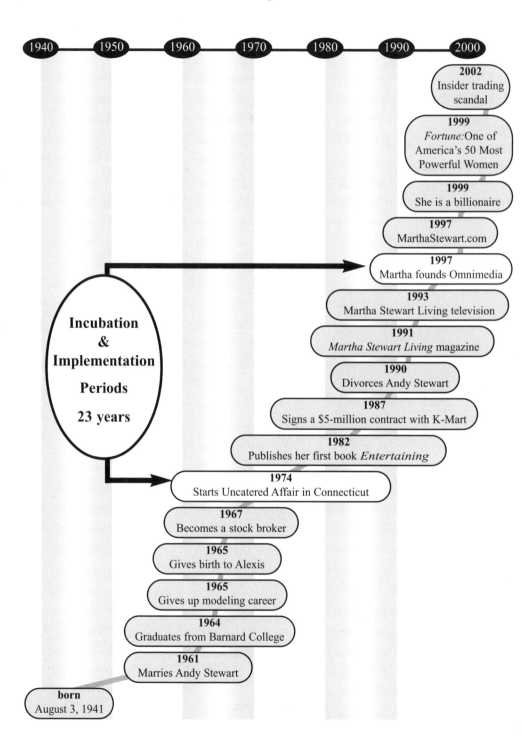

1940 — 1950 — 1960 — 1970 — 1980 — 1990 — 2000

2002
Insider trading scandal

1999
*Fortune:*One of America's 50 Most Powerful Women

1999
She is a billionaire

1997
MarthaStewart.com

1997
Martha founds Omnimedia

1993
Martha Stewart Living television

1991
Martha Stewart Living magazine

1990
Divorces Andy Stewart

1987
Signs a $5-million contract with K-Mart

1982
Publishes her first book *Entertaining*

1974
Starts Uncatered Affair in Connecticut

1967
Becomes a stock broker

1965
Gives birth to Alexis

1965
Gives up modeling career

1964
Graduates from Barnard College

1961
Marries Andy Stewart

born
August 3, 1941

**Incubation
&
Implementation

Periods

23 years**

A Personality Profile

COMMUNICATION STYLE: APPEAL TO FANTASY

Martha is a dream-maker–one of those people who embellishes the truth to make a sale. Donald Trump called it "innocent hyperbole." Such a keen sense for sensationalism is a strong asset in the media world. Martha has a gift for making the mundane seem more attractive; the fine, wonderful; and the special, grandiose. She notes in one of her books that Wendy, her college roommate at Barnard, hailed from Shaker Heights, Ohio, when in fact she actually came from the far less glamorous Steubenville, Ohio. If she thinks an audience needs to be titillated, she titillates.

Most of Martha's daytime television audiences are not from the carriage-trade set, yet she exploits their fascination with the lifestyles of high society by creating fantasy-based portrayals of how the Kennedys and the Vanderbilts entertain. Though she delivers a product that is beyond the purview of middle-American audiences, it is so meticulously presented and surreal that it sells. That is her magic. Her keen sense of the dramatic, an appealing approach, and superb delivery satisfy the fantasy needs of those women confined to the house during the daytime, as well as the women who work outside the house and love to fantasize about upscale gracious living at home.

On one television episode, Martha showed her audience how to make their own soap. Commenting on the fact that soap is an unexciting commodity, TV host Larry King posed the question, "But Martha, soap is three for $5.00. Why would they want your soap kits?" Martha waxed passionately:

> *Women are into crafts, and mine is a craft. And besides it's not the money, it's the opportunity to buy something better that is affordable.*

In the early '90s, the networks had expected that her show would be what is called a *oncer*–a one-time viewing fad that would soon disappear. To the amazement of veteran producers her ratings remained high despite the impracticality of her ideas. The daytime diva would take her audience into a reverie on decorating for a party that they could only imagine. Such a vicarious experience would leave them spellbound and demanding more. That unrelenting demand enhanced the television ratings and the cycle repeated. Martha proved that daytime TV is entertainment first and dissemination of information second. To her viewers, Martha Stewart is merely an escape into that fantasy world of the rich and famous. In the 1980s and '90s, Martha tapped into the fantasies of the American female the way that Hefner had, three decades earlier, captured the secret fantasies of the American male. When originally told that she was making no sense, she ignored the advice and was rewarded with phenomenal success.

INTUITIONAL STYLE: PROMETHEAN

"I consider myself a visionary," said Martha in the summer of 2001 when Larry King asked her to divulge the secret of her success. Like many insightful women, Martha has always had an intuitive sense of what works. Similar to other entertainers, such as Oprah, Martha has a special talent for sensing what the audience wants and giving it to them. Her legal counsel Allen Grubman saw this attribute and commented, "Martha's approach to business is almost on an intuitive, creative basis."

Stewart is a Promethean personality. She is an intuitive thinker who listens to her instincts yet operates rationally on what she hears. Passion and perseverance have also helped her achieve fame and fortune. Once she grabbed hold of that brass ring, she didn't let go no matter how hot it got. The amazing thing about Martha Stewart is not just that she became rich and famous, but that she did so by building a following among people with whom she has absolutely nothing in common. Is it likely that she ever once, in her adult life, sat and watched daytime television? The standard of excellence she promotes is not practicable and is therefore pure fantasy, and yet she appears to execute it as if it were pure reality. Few women in her audience can afford to or would dare attempt her entertainment, decorating or food preparation suggestions.

CREATIVITY: FUELLED BY PASSION

A myriad of precedents offer credence to the idea that passion is the panacea for performance. Mihaly Csikszentmihalyi, in his best-selling book *Flow*, described passion as a state:

> *In the Flow state people are so involved in the activity that nothing else seems to matter; the experience itself is so enjoyable that people will do it even at great cost and risk.*

The founder of Virgin Atlantic, Richard Branson, was another passionate overachiever who said, "I have always thrived on havoc and adrenaline." In *The Paradoxes of Creativity* (1990), Jacques Barzun wrote:

> *Mad passion or passionate madness is the reason why psychopathic personalities are often creators and why their productions are perfectly sane.*

Passion with purpose has no peer in its ability to promote high productivity, superb performance and ultimately peace. Martha has an impeccable record of producing flawless shows. This is a direct consequence of her passion for perfection. But although Martha Stewart comes across the airwaves as a warm and fuzzy charmer, that image belies the truth. Within her lies an inner anxiety that is the magic mover for her achievements. When the lights go dim, the smiling Martha turns into an impatient boss in a hurry to conquer some new world. Her staff is well aware it is Martha's way or the highway. Ever since her teens she has been a woman on a mission.

Mistress Francois Gilot said of Picasso, "I was seduced by his magnetism. He had a passion for work and sex." Many people confuse passion with sex. They are not the same–passion is inner drive, sex is a physical act. Without question, some passionate people have a high sex drive. However, others fall into what Sigmund Freud called "*sublimating* sexual energy into work energy." Freud's most creative output occurred after he was forty, a time when he had already stopped having sex with his wife. Leonardo da Vinci, Joan of Arc, Nikola Tesla and Mother Teresa were also highly passionate, but they too sublimated their sexual drives into their work.

All those who have known Martha Stewart professionally attest to her strong passion, while those who have known her on a more intimate level claim that her passion does not translate into a sex drive. The Diva of Domesticity appears seductive and can be unbelievably charming but has also been described as a cold fish by friends. Passionate people are often difficult to get to know or get close to. One of Martha's critics, Margaret Talbot, told the *New Republic* (Sept. 16, 1996), "Martha is a kitchen-sink idealist. She scorns utility in the name of beauty." That is the essence of Stewart, a woman on a mission for the perfect and the beautiful. Few people are able to relate to such drive.

Why has Stewart been so maligned? One reason is her inability to back off and live life as others do. Those who live life in the slow lane have a hard time relating to those passing them at 150 mph in the fast lane of life. For the same reason, few people liked Leonardo da Vinci or Sigmund Freud. The same negative reactions can be found in commentaries on Margaret Mead, Margaret Thatcher, and Madonna. The line is long. Those with a raging libido or psychic energy must learn comfort as loners or be candidates for a life of subliminal stress. External energy or zeal is an outward manifestation of a seething inner drive for perfection.

RISK-TAKING PROPENSITY

Entrepreneurs live on the edge and Martha is no different. She loves to climb mountains in Africa and go fishing in Alaska, and is "seldom scared or nervous about anything." While vacationing in Maine, she fell in love with and bought a majestic 61-acre estate located on Mount Desert Island. Built in 1925 by Edsel Ford, it included an imposing 50 rooms and 23 bedrooms that prompted her to comment to a reporter, "People were afraid of this place, but I never feel like it's overpowering."

Fear has never prevented Martha Stewart from moving forward on anything. On July 1, 1986, Martha and Andy purchased, for $535,000, the neighboring "Adams House" that Martha wanted to renovate on her television show. However, she and Andy were splitting up and she needed to buy out his share in case the property became encumbered in the divorce process. She risked all by persuading Kmart to buy the house as part of their publicity campaign, while not disclosing that it was she who owned the house. Had Kmart found out at the time, it could have jeopardized her contract with them as well as her television project.

Martha has a penchant for doing what works, no matter the cost. Perfection is far more important to her than the bottom line. On her road from catering to multi-media queen, she had to cross many chasms and left a number of bodies in her wake. Such is the path of entrepreneurial genius. Those unwilling or unable to jeopardize valued relationships to win the game seldom make it to the very top. Big risks, both professional and personal, are the price of big gains. Martha was always willing to destroy valued relationships to win the war. That has not endeared her to many, but it has allowed her to go where the timid never tread.

INTENSITY: DRIVEN BY PASSIONATE PERFECTIONISM

Like many successful entrepreneurs, Martha is not easy to work with or live with. Such people are loners, and Martha is no exception. She has been unmarried during a good part of her trip to the top. Everyone who works for her clearly understands who is boss; if they don't, they are gone. In her first catering business, when she was in partnership with Westport friend Norma Collier, it was soon apparent that it would not work. Collier described Martha's intensity as "debilitating." Other quotes from former associates described her as "like a missile with a live warhead."

Martha's obsession with perfection began early when she had to satisfy a father who was intolerant of failure. If it wasn't right in the Kostyra household there were dire consequences. Martha's father was a heavy drinker and a textbook example of a driven personality. He continually told her, "You can do anything you put your mind to, all you have to do is try." (Byron, p. 300). Since reaching the top, she no longer has to satisfy her father's expectations, but those inner demons remain. She is unable to change her need to be the very best at every little nuance in her life. She must make the best pâté, the best flower arrangement, the best magazine and the best show. This demonic overachiever is incapable of resting on her laurels. More begets more for Martha, the driven woman who begins and ends each conversation with the word I. Such people are difficult to please–for others and for themselves.

Passionate perfectionists are unable to just be good; they must be precise and flawless in all things. And no one had better try to mess with their creations which might make them less than exact. Dr. Seuss once turned down eighty shades of green for a parrot picture. Dostoevsky was never satisfied with a book no matter how perfect. When he finished writing his masterpiece *Crime and Punishment* he said, "My dissatisfaction amounts to disgust." Those with such passion for their work are dealing with a raging insecurity and their self-worth is inextricably tied to positive achievement. They must be right or feel emotionally distraught. Consequently, their impeccable production is what makes them feel worthy. In this book, Martha Stewart is used to exemplify two things: the path to perfection is passion, and such passion also exacts a cost for the perfectionist and those around them. Passionate perfectionists are prone to obsess over their work and become compulsive workaholics to ensure they don't fail. Intolerance of mediocrity in themselves or others is a quality that makes them difficult to work with and for.

Passionate people tend to be workaholics because they are driven to get more and more done in less and less time. Holiday Inn founder Kemmons Wilson once said, "I work only half a day. It makes no difference which half–the first 12 hours or the last."

Time for workaholic entrepreneurs has no meaning. They will call you at midnight or 7:00 a.m. to discuss business. Martha's unrelenting orientation to work on a 24/7 basis was evident when the Chairman of Time Warner got a call from her on Sunday. No one dared call him on a Sunday. But zealots like Martha are not keyed to days but to action. When he pulled up in her Connecticut driveway to let her know that calling him on Sunday was out of order, she was shocked. And when he told her, "You know, maybe you should just buy the company back," his displeasure was lost on Martha. Ironically, his suggestion proved to be the act that launched her move to buy back *Martha Stewart Living* magazine through Martha Stewart Living Omnimedia. The rest is history.

Martha is manic and a lifelong insomniac. She has many of the traits of a bipolar personality. Such people get a lot done in a short time but drive others mad in the process. Martha's intensity is without peer. Hypomanics are known to juggle many things at the same time without dropping any; Martha qualifies on both fronts. Such people are called polyphasic–a multi-tasking talent. She told Larry King, "I don't need a lot of sleep. I sleep about four hours a night but can get by on much less. I still work seven days a week and sometimes 24 hours a day."

Even when first married, Martha got up at 4 a.m. to clean her house. Most women were fast asleep, dreaming of a romantic interlude on a beach, but not Martha. When this fastidious woman cooks, everything is precisely orchestrated. When she plans a picnic, every detail must meet her exacting standards. Passion is her master. Impeccable in dress and implacable in spirit, she is in charge or she won't participate. Family members and former employees describe her as an intense, driven, workaholic.

From an early age Martha was programmed to be special. Special doesn't equate with normality, but as previously noted, normal people achieve normally and abnormal people achieve abnormally–you must be different to make a difference. Martha certainly is different and that difference is exactly what makes her unique. Former protégé Vicky Negrin saw her creativity, but also told biographers that she became Martha's "slave" at the Market Basket venture early in Martha's career.

SELF-IMAGE

Martha believes she is right even when she is wrong. (In the previous chapter, we observed a similar trait in Ross Perot.) An arrogant egotism dominates her actions and confidence permeates every move. Hints of these personality traits come across on television though they are somewhat softened by an external charm. Behind the scenes, she is the omniscient one and god save the one who crosses her! At her firm, Martha rules dictatorially. At social events for the firm she is center stage; when she leaves the event is over. When she isn't center stage at a party, she finds a different party. Such people attract disciples and, as in Martha's case, have legions of fans. When entrepreneurs have a vision, armies of protégés climb aboard for the adventurous ride. The entrepreneur often radiates a can't-miss persona that belies any underlying limitations of their vision. Charismatic power is contagious and people like Martha have it.

The other face of charisma is often a controlling, domineering nature dedicated to forcing compliance to serve the vision. That was the case when Andy told Martha he could only spare two days to help her publicize her book *Entertaining*. His offer was generous considering Andy was president of a publishing firm with significant European commitments. The messianic Martha threw a tantrum. While they were driving to Connecticut she flew into a hysterical rage and jumped from the moving car in what constituted a failed suicide attempt. Her ploy worked. The guilt-ridden Andy took off work for a week, but the event was one more hitch in a marriage not destined to last. Biographer Christopher Byron commented (p. 277):

> *[Martha] dealt with such problems the same way Eddie [her father] had attempted to deal with his frustrations–by yelling and vituperation, hoping, it would seem, to intimidate and thereby subdue the people who lay outside her circle of authority and control.*

In one interview on *Live with Larry King*, Martha declared, "I'm extremely curious and have a goal to learn something new every single day. I have a strong urge to get things done." (Feb. 2, 2000). Martha often used the need to accomplish things as an excuse for going for the jugular when conflicts arose.

ECCENTRICITIES AND PERSONAL PARADOXES

Though the tendency to throw tantrums is not unique to high achievers, the tantrums for which Martha has become famous are exceptional in their intensity. In the1970s when she and her friend, Jill Bowser, planned a family picnic in Westport, Martha prepared, with painstaking care, spectacular picnic baskets with food fit for a king. When Jill got in her car to leave, she backed up over the baskets. Martha, in an emotional meltdown, tore into her friend with a verbal vengeance. According to Bowser (Oppenheimer, p. 173):

> *Martha was a raving psychopath, shrieking at the top of her lungs,*
> *"You stupid fucking idiot! You dumb fucking bitch."*

Needless to say, they never spoke again. Bowser characterized her as a "very schizophrenic kind of person."

Like many passionate entrepreneurs, when Martha is up, she is way up and when she is down, she is way down. Such volatility leads to wide swings in which she can morph in a minute from a mesmerizing lady to a wild, raving, mean-spirited woman. Men are easily bewitched by her charms and women are entranced. One Westport friend described her as "a brassy and ballsy businesswoman." Typical of such bipolar personalities is their volatile mood swings that range from euphoria to depression.

When you are really good like Martha, you can be really bad and get away with it. It certainly has worked for her. Former employee Marinda Freeman described her as a Dr. Jekyll and Mr. Hyde. Ex-husband Andy described her as "Martha A–Nice, and Martha B–Nasty." He said when she was normal she was wonderful but she could be "lethal," and "could turn into a snake." Friend Janet Horowitz said, "Martha's need to control was so dominating she would do almost anything to get what she wanted." (Oppenheimer, p. 315).

When interviewed by Andy Rooney on the *60 Minutes* television show, he suggested she not use eggs when making ice cream. When she ignored his sage advice he commented in his inimitable style, "Martha isn't difficult," and laughing, "She's absolutely impossible." In *Vanity Fair* magazine, Matt Trynauer described her with great insight saying, "She's calm, commanding, and at times imperious, at other times ebullient. She is focused as a bullet in flight."

Stewart is a study in contrasts and paradoxes–a personable and charming woman with a penchant for aggression when things don't go her way. It is paradoxical that while in high school, the future "Diva of Domesticity" detested anything associated with domesticity and made fun of her mother as a slave to a kitchen. Martha once told her home economics teacher (Oppenheimer, p. 4):

> *All my mother does is stand in front of a hot stove cooking. And what does she have to show for it? She works like a peasant. I want more out of life and I'm going to get it.*

The ultimate paradox in Martha's persona is that she projected on television the image of a Stepford Wife–the idyllic housewife (from Ira Levin's book, *The Stepford Wives*) who dotes on her husband and is devoted to making him happy at any cost. She is the perfect hostess, perfect entertainer, and perfect friend. However, in real life, Martha never aspired to be anything remotely resembling a Stepford Wife. According to biographer Jerry Oppenheimer, she began her marriage as a submissive wife and evolved into a "domineering, imperial, cynical, and the classic ball-breaking bitch." Past friends describe their marriage as something less than idyllic with Andy playing the submissive husband to her role as dominatrix. Martha's brother Frank Kostyra lived with the couple for some time and told friends, "Martha treats Andy like a dog." According to most accounts Andy was a devoted husband, but was unable to tolerate her badgering and domineering ways. When she was on tour in 1987 promoting *Martha's Weddings*, a book ironically dedicated to him, Andy left a note saying he was leaving her and would not be back. When Martha returned to find him gone, she launched into a tirade. Live-in caterer, Vicky Negrin, feared Martha might attempt suicide and suggested she seek psychiatric help. The indomitable Stewart said (Oppenheimer, p. 6):

> *They don't work for me. I'm different. I'm always smarter than the shrink. I can always outsmart them.*

Negrin said that Martha was an engaging personality, but with a dark side and a need for control. She told Oppenheimer, "Martha can be a tyrant, very critical and unscrupulous." Biographers describe Martha's behavior as alternating between erratic and psychopathic.

ACHIEVEMENTS & HONORS

MAGNITUDE OF SUCCESS

Even Martha's most ardent adversaries would admit she has made an incredible impact on the American lifestyle. Her trek to the top was no over-night phenomenon. It really began in 1973 when she left Wall Street to set up a catering business out of her Connecticut home. But the genesis of her fame really began in 1982 when she published her first book *Entertaining*–now in its 30th printing with over 500,000 copies sold. By 1990, she had made her mark on television and in a wide range of publications. The Stewart brand is ubiquitous and includes 34 books in print in what she labels "synergistic products." Numerous products and services operate under the umbrella company Martha Stewart Living Omnimedia, with head office in a stylish Manhattan complex–her Cathedral of Commerce.

The darling of domesticity was in the throes of an emotional breakdown in 1973 when she launched that catering business. Oprah Winfrey describes Martha's move up the ladder as a climb from cookie baker to billionairess. From those humble beginnings, she has built a titan that she described in her 1999 Annual Report as a solar system of companies depicted by planets surrounding the sun. Of course, in this metaphoric tribute, it is Martha who is represented by the sun. Those planets orbiting Martha include *Martha Stewart Living*, *Martha Stewart Weddings*, *Martha Stewart Kids*, and *Martha Stewart Baby* along with others that enjoy a combined circulation of 10 million. In 2002 she was still appearing on two daytime television shows with 1.6 million viewers. The human dynamo has two syndicated newspaper columns that appear in 233 newspapers, a syndicated radio show airing over 227 stations, a web site (marthastewart.com) with 1.7 million registered customers, and *Martha by Mail* featuring 3000 products in a high profile catalog in which she offers an exclusive line of Wedgwood Drabware. Capping off her influence are the 5000 products that were doing $1.7 billion in revenue for *Martha Stewart Everyday* at Kmart. Since the Kmart bankruptcy her *Everyday* line is in limbo.

The Martha Stewart name permeates the airwaves to such an extent that Madison Avenue has described her as a brand. Personal friend Charlotte Beers of J. Walter Thompson calls Martha "the greatest knowledge seeker I've ever met." (Tyrnauer, p. 399). The spoils of such passion can be witnessed in her posh estates in East Hampton and Turkey Hill Farm. In addition she now owns an island estate in Maine known as Skylands and two other less flamboyant habitats. Her seven homes are adorned with 21 kitchens. All this from her kitchen catering business that served the likes of neighbors Paul Newman, Robert Redford, and Ralph Lauren.

Martha Stewart Living magazine is still the cornerstone of her still burgeoning empire. When *Martha Stewart Living* hit the newsstands in the 1980s, it was an instant success and is now the flagship of her multimedia empire. The charismatic ex-model has come full circle. Her first job as fashion model in her teens has resulted in her daily exposure on a wide array of shows. Beauty, brains and passion opened many doors during that trek to the top. For a short time she was an editor for *House Beautiful* and parlayed that into a national phenomenon. *Martha Stewart Living* is seen as the standard bearer for conventional living. The irony is that its founder is an unconventional woman whose legal counsel Allen Grubman says, "has an unorthodox style."

HONORS

The Princess of Perfection promised herself to become rich and famous when she was growing up in Nutley, NJ. She dreamed of having servants but never dreamed of having a houseful. The wannabe success has appeared eight times on *Larry King Weekend* on CNN. King refers to her as Miss Handy. *Saturday Night Live* hasn't been so kind and has performed numerous spoofs on her mania for perfection. National exposure has made her a household name across America. That journey began with her modeling for Lifebuoy soap while in high school. A few years later she was named the Best Dressed College Girl for *Glamour* while a student at Barnard. The first national media exposure came in the late 1970s when *Country Living* placed her on their cover. By the eighties, Martha Stewart had become a regular on many shows and her books and magazines were best-sellers. Through the 1990s she built her empire and became recognized not only as a gifted business woman, but as a tycoon and a force to be reckoned with. In 1999, *Fortune* magazine listed her as one of America's 50 Most Powerful Women.

LESSONS LEARNED FROM MARTHA STEWART

To date, Martha has not published any formal guidelines on how to be a successful entrepreneur. However, in her climb to success, she has modeled many positive behaviors that reinforce lessons already learned from other entrepreneurial geniuses and shed light on some new dimensions.

KNOW YOUR MARKET

Martha Stewart was successful with almost everything she touched because she knew her market. Westport in the 1970s was described as a community in which you could sell slow moving products more quickly by merely increasing the price, thereby creating the illusion of greater worth. Martha recognized this opportunity in her market. She was selling homemade pies at the time and decided to increase their perceived value. As Byron observed (p. 76):

> *Realizing no doubt that it wasn't the product itself that was inherently that "good," but rather the illusion of quality embedded in the high price that made the product desirable–Martha quickly hit on a way to increase her sales.*

She achieved this by increasing her output and the price of each item. Her baking enterprise thrived. The same was true when she wrote books and when she created her television shows. In all cases, she had an uncanny sense of what the market wanted.

SELL THE SIZZLE INSTEAD OF THE STEAK

An old marketing slogan advises, "sell the sizzle instead of the steak." In essence, this recognizes that in sales, it is often an effective marketing ploy to sell a dream rather than the product, because the former is often greater than the latter. Martha Stewart knew this better than almost everyone she worked with. She knew that many of her crafts were impracticable and that some of the recipes didn't work. However, she continued to write books that reached beyond what was realistic because she knew that her audience was reading her books not for information but for the fantasy.

When the *Martha Stewart Living* television pilot was about to be released, one of the male syndicators previewed the program with horror, deeming it too sophisticated for its target audience. As reported in a biography (Byron, p. 212):

> *He turned to Martha. "I'm not sure I can sell this…I mean, look, the people in the cities where we have to sell this show are in urban environments. They're working-class people. These people don't have gardens."*

> *Martha looked back at him. Her voice was even and cool, conveying the total confidence in her words as she said, "Yes, but they want them."*

SYNTHESIZE TO SUCCESS: TAPPING INTO YOUR OPPOSITE

Associates and friends describe Martha as charming, strong, talented and gracious, but a cold bitch. In her defense, a male with similar qualities might not be demeaned to the same degree. Such a male might be called an aggressive overachiever. Women aren't expected to come on as strong or be quite as ferociously aggressive. However, it was Martha's aggressive, damn-the-torpedoes attitude that got her to the top. Of course, she is paying the price for tapping into her male side that Jung had called the syzygy. Other strong females, such as Margaret Thatcher and Madonna, have paid a similar price. Coco Chanel did the same and was criticized in the media as androgynous. Whether such behaviors are "good" or "bad" are, of course, personal value judgments. The important point here is that the aggressive pursuit of one's goals is vital to their attainment, though such behavior may also exact a price. Conversely, a male might enhance his effectiveness in business by tapping into, on occasion, his opposite (i.e., his feminine side). This might involve showing a more nurturing or empathetic side to his dealings with associates and employees.

As CEO of a diverse enterprise, Martha has had to be a tough negotiator in a business that eats wimps. Her television appearances give the impression that she is relaxed and easygoing, but that is a façade. From her early role as a vivacious girl-next-door type, she has successfully evolved into a very strong autocratic executive, a woman who gets her way or doesn't continue to play. Sources speak of her controlled aggression. She tends gardens with a gentle whip, prepares gourmet picnic dinners with smiling ferocity, or decorates homes with brutal aggression. Tapping into her opposite has worked for Martha. She has developed a Machiavellian approach that kicks in when she believes it serves the best interests of her business. Former social friend Kathy Tatlock told the media, "To Martha, the end always justified the means."

PERSONAL BRANDING: A POWERFUL MARKETING TOOL

In the chapters on Branson and Trump, we will observe that establishing a public persona is an important and powerful marketing ploy. None of the entrepreneurial geniuses understood this better than Martha Stewart. Her name has become synonymous with tasteful, gracious living, both inside the home and out in the gardens around it. Once her public persona as the "Diva of Domesticity" was established, she was able to parlay that image into a position as spokesperson with Kmart, and from there into billionaire tycoon. As biographer Byron reports (p. 101):

> *[Martha] quickly began to extend her "brand" in any direction she could. "I'll do anything to get my name in the papers," she once had told Norma Collier, and she began to show what she meant. She had already been featured in Bon Appetit and House & Garden's arch rival publication, House Beautiful. Meanwhile, she had begun giving lectures on cooking all over Connecticut, and was soon making appearances in Washington D.C., as well.*

In describing a producer's reaction to how Martha had conceived her television show *Martha Stewart Living*, Byron writes (p. 208):

> *It was brilliant...[The producer] began thinking of her as well–as Martha Stewart the genius...It was awesome! A commercial inside an infomercial. It was even better than that, for the infomercial would be promoting Martha...who would be cross-promoting the magazine...that would be carrying the ads...of the companies that would be advertising on the show! An arrangement like that could spiral into outer space.*

The ubiquity of the name, *Martha Stewart*, and the power of her name in creating brand loyalty have shown us the importance of "branding" in elevating the perception of a product beyond its reality. If we were ever to doubt the power of personal branding, we need only look at the plummeting share value of Omnimedia Inc. when Martha Stewart was indicted on criminal charges. Martha Stewart *is* Martha Stewart Omnimedia Inc.

Donald Trump

To Be Big, Think Big–Real Big

b. Queens, NY   June 14, 1946

"I like making big deals."

SELF-DESCRIPTION

"I always buy distress merchandise and try to turn it around."

"The worst of times often create the best opportunities."

MOTTOS

"Business is just a big game."

"I believe in the power of positive thinking."

INNOVATION — "My attention span is short, and probably my least favorite thing to do is to maintain the status quo. I get impatient and irritable."

UNIQUE QUALITY — "I like thinking big because if you're going to be thinking anyway, you might as well think big…That is my advantage."

OBJECTIVE — To become a tycoon and live like a king. Mar-a-Lago and the $10-million-dollar Trump Tower suite are a testimony to his grandiose lifestyle.

NET WORTH — $1.7 billion (*Forbes,* July, 2001)

HONORS — The Hotel Federation of New York named him Hotel and Real Estate Visionary of the Century (October 2001)
Wharton Hall of Fame: Entrepreneur of the Year 1994

BIRTH ORDER — Middle child of five

EDUCATION — High School: New York Military Academy
Post secondary: Fordham for two years; graduated from Wharton School of Business

PERSONALITY — Brash, brilliant, flamboyant, combative, confrontational

HOBBIES — Boxing, baseball and tennis

POLITICS — Democratic roots

RELIGION — Protestant; his Minister was Norman Vincent Peale

FAMILY — Wives: Ivana and Marla
Children: Donald Jr., Ivanka, Eric and Tiffany

9

DONALD TRUMP

To Be Big, Think Big–Real Big

"I think big and it gives me a big advantage."

Overview

To excel at anything, one must have a dream and pursue it with passion and panache. It cannot be pursued in moderation or with reticence if one wants to be highly successful, just as a ballplayer cannot hit a home run without focusing his full intention and power. It takes a big effort to be big, and no one exemplifies more emphatically a go-for-broke attitude than Donald Trump. In his own words (*Trump: The Art of the Comeback*, p. 9):

...[In 1989], I felt I could do no wrong, that I didn't know how to hit anything less than a grand slam home run.

He usually swings for the fences, and though some of his big swings have led to strikeouts, they have often resulted in home runs.

This chapter is about betting big to win big, and no one bets bigger than Trump. Though he has built and owned several casinos, his gambles are not wagers on games of chance, but calculated risks on real estate developments and ventures. At the heart of these gambles is Donald's penchant for leveraging his assets to acquire new ones. He has often asserted that it's just as easy to dream big as it is to dream small. Furthermore, he dreams relentlessly, and always in color. Trump told *Forbes* (Dec. 2001):

I'm never satisfied. I don't know if I'm capable of being satisfied. There may be a momentary pleasure, but then it's off to the next victim.

Trump not only invests in a big way, but he has a penchant for grandiose display and extravagance to the extreme. This was evident in December 2001 when he hosted the LPGA Championship at his posh Palm Beach resort spa, Mar-a-Lago–the former Meriwether Post estate. He posted $1 million in prize money to entice the top 30 women professional golfers to participate, and used this event to showcase this opulent facility to the aristocracy who live in the lavish land of linen and lace. This spa, designed for the rich and famous, caters to its 250 members who pay an initiation fee of $350,000 and annual dues of $12,500. The LPGA event was just the opening hit in what Trump planned to be a series of out-of-the-park homers.

HITTING HOME RUNS IN THE 1980S

In the 1970s, when New York City was teetering on the brink of bankruptcy and real estate was in decline, Donald Trump saw the intrinsic value in some of New York's greatest properties that had fallen into disrepair. In a series of acquisitions that displayed his remarkable creativity in dealmaking, he was able to obtain these properties at significantly discounted prices. Furthermore, by using cleverly constructed leverage techniques, he financed these acquisitions using very little of his own money. During the 1980s, "The Donald" (as he was called by his wife, Ivana) revitalized or constructed on these sites audacious new buildings known for their opulence and grandeur. Among the most famous are the 68-story Trump Tower on Fifth Avenue and the Grand Hyatt Hotel. He also obtained a New Jersey gambling license and subsequently developed the Trump Castle and Taj Mahal gambling casinos in Atlantic City. In 1987 Donald co-authored his bestselling book, *Trump: The Art of the Deal*, in which he trumpeted with characteristic candor the details of his successful dealmaking. As the 1980s came to a close, the billion-dollar Trump Organization owned or controlled several key hotels and upscale condominium projects in New York City, the most opulent casinos in Atlantic City, the Trump Shuttle Airline, the grandiose Mar-a-Lago estate, and the 25-million-dollar yacht, the *Trump Princess*.

THE HITTING SLUMP

Early in 1990, it was evident that an economic downturn was under way. Declines in property prices, accompanied by interest rate increases, sent the carrying costs of the Trump properties into the stratosphere. Furthermore, the casinos were generating significantly less than anticipated revenues, creating a disastrous cash-flow problem. Donald

Trump was faced with the greatest business crisis of his life. The leverage that had enabled him to parlay relatively small sums of money into a huge fortune was now operating in reverse and threatening to force the Trump Organization, and Donald himself, into personal bankruptcy. In March of 1990, Donald swallowed his pride and announced to Wall Street that, for the first time in its history, the Trump Organization might miss a payment –its $43-million payment of principal and interest on the *Trump Castle* casino in Atlantic City. The ensuing uproar in the financial community ultimately led Trump to convene a meeting to which he summoned his creditors to report his illiquidity and solicit their help. The Trump Organization had several billion dollars in loans of which $975 million had been personally guaranteed by Donald. Had his loan been called, bankruptcy would have been inevitable.

THE COMEBACK

In 1997, a decade after his best-selling *Trump: The Art of the Deal*, Donald co-authored his third book, *Trump: The Art of the Comeback*. In this book, he described the depth of his poverty in 1990 (p. 11):

One day, while walking down Fifth Avenue, hand in hand with Marla, I pointed across the street to a man holding a cup and with a Seeing Eye dog. I asked, "Do you know who that is?"

Marla said to me: "Yes, Donald. He's a beggar. Isn't it too bad? He looks so sad!"

I said, "You're right. He's a beggar, but he's worth about $900 million more than me."

She looked at me and said, "What do you mean, Donald? How could he possibly be worth $900 million more than you?"

I said, "Let's assume he's worth nothing (only from the standpoint of dollars)–I'm worth minus $900 million."

In a marvelous display of deal-making, Trump was able to use his special insights into human motivation and his talent for negotiation to obtain new loan repayment concessions from his creditors. Through the 1990s, he strived to rebuild his empire and re-establish his reputation. By June 2001, *Forbes* estimated his personal net worth at $1.7 billion, making him one of the world's richest men. By staging a comeback from minus $900 million, Donald Trump had, indeed, hit a grand slam home run!

The Formative Years

EARLY EXPERIENCES

Donald John Trump was born on June 14, 1946 in Queens, New York, the second child of Fred and Mary Trump. His father was a very successful builder and real estate developer. Most of his property was located in Queens. Donald was brought up to fend for himself and learned the real estate business at his father's knee. While growing up, Donald was expected to work and was given jobs in his father's firm sweeping floors, running bulldozers, and just hanging around. His father made sure he understood the value of money and if he was going to get money he had to earn it. Fred once refused to buy Donald a baseball mitt because it cost $45. Donald never forgot that lesson.

Donald's older brother Fred, who didn't like the real estate business, eventually moved to Florida where he became a professional pilot and flew for TWA (Transworld Airlines). Subsequently, Fred developed a drinking problem and died prematurely at the age of 43. Witnessing his brother's tragic decline has prompted Donald to abstain from alcohol and cigarettes throughout his life.

In his first book, Donald describes his relationship with his father (Trump, 1987, p. 71):

> *...I was never intimidated by my father the way most people were. I stood up to him, and he respected that. We had a relationship that was almost businesslike. I sometimes wonder if we'd have gotten along so well if I hadn't been so business-oriented as I am.*

Donald's father had encouraged him to learn survival in the street. Trump told A&E Biography (1994), "By my teens I knew everything about constructing buildings." Fred had Donald accompany his rental collection agents in Queens. The experience persuaded him that this was not how he wanted to spend his life, for it showed him the seamy side of the human struggle. In the process, he learned some lessons in "street smarts," such as "Don't stand in front of a door when knocking to collect the rent," because some tenants answer a knock with bullets. In his first book, (Trump, 1987, p. 65) he wrote, "I learned a lot from my dad about toughness in a very tough business." The lessons were not wasted, for eventually Donald would follow in his father's footsteps by taking over the business and expanding it by several orders of magnitude.

FORMAL EDUCATION

Donald Trump describes himself as assertive and aggressive from his earliest years. He tells how he was nearly expelled for giving his grade-two music teacher a black eye when he decided that the teacher knew nothing about music. Donald was clearly out of harmony with the accepted rules of behavior in the educational institution. He was cocky and belligerent with strangers and his four siblings. His sister said he was a troublemaker, "He could drive you nuts," she told A&E Biography. By the time he was thirteen, his father, fearing Donald would end up in reform school, enrolled him in the New York Military Academy in upstate New York. In this structured environment, aberrant behavior was not tolerated. The imposed structure worked, Donald learned to live within rules, and he excelled. He was voted the neatest student and Captain of the baseball team. Trump told the media, "That is where I learned discipline and channeled my aggression into achievement." After graduation in 1964, Trump attended Fordham University in the Bronx. After two years he entered the prestigious Wharton School of Finance at the University of Pennsylvania where he learned the nuances of business. He graduated in 1968 with a major in business finance.

EARLY ENTERPRISE

While attending Fordham, Trump was always seeking opportunities that he could take on with his father's backing. He was interested in showing his dad that he could perform, and this led to a foreclosure opportunity in Cincinnati, Ohio. Trump learned from his father that buying low and selling high was good. He wrote, "Never pay too much even if that means walking away." The foreclosure was for a two-year-old rental housing project of 1200 units called Swifton Village. It had fallen on hard times on account of poor management, high vacancies, bad aesthetics and marginal tenants. These were things Trump could resolve. The property was built for $6 million but was available in foreclosure for $3-million. Donald talked his father into letting him cut his teeth on the deal by putting up no money but leveraging his assets and guarantees. This resulted in a $3 million loan that covered the total acquisition cost so there was no money at risk. This would become his operating style. Fred Trump put his son in charge of turning it around and selling it, all for a piece of the action. Donald fired the management, renovated the property, and resold it for $6 million–yielding close to a $3-million profit–using none of his own money! After this success, he was on his way.

The Climb to the Top

THINKING BIG

In his own words, Donald Trump expressed the philosophy underpinning his success story–a story that reads like fiction (Trump, 1987, pp. 46-7):

> *I like thinking big. I always have. To me it's very simple: if you're going to be thinking anyway, you might as well think big. Most people think small, because most people are afraid of success, afraid of making decisions, afraid of winning. And that gives people like me a great advantage.*

In 1971, at age 25, Donald moved to a tiny, dingy apartment on Third Avenue in Manhattan where he began his trek to the big time. One of his first steps in building the contacts that would later serve his interests was joining the prestigious and exclusive Le Club. Achieving this first step required a level of tenacity and persistence that would have deterred most mortals because membership at the snooty Le Club was by invitation only and Donald knew no one there. After repeated attempts and some wining and dining of the club President, Donald succeeded in gaining membership on the condition that he would not attempt to steal any of the older members' wives.

On July 29, 1974, when Donald Trump was just 28 years of age, he obtained an option to purchase several key waterfront sites owned by Penn Central for $62 million with no money down. There followed four years of public debate, controversy, and politicking about whether or not one of these sites should be used as the location of a new Convention Center for the city. New York City ultimately paid Penn Central $12 million for one site as the location for their new Convention Center and Donald received $833,000 for releasing his option.

While the debate was raging about the appropriate use of the Penn Central waterfront sites, Donald entered another bold venture with another Penn Central property. He acquired the defunct Commodore Hotel for $10 million and then sold it within a week to the city of New York for $1–not exactly the "buy low, sell high" philosophy that his father had taught him. On the face of it, this was a financially disastrous transaction.

The sale of the Commodore Hotel to New York City was contingent on receipt of a 99-year lease on the property and tax abatements worth $120 million over the next forty years. Armed with this contract, Donald Trump set out to find a classy hotelier to build a hotel on his property. He was 28 when he began this quest and wouldn't get the hotel built until he was 33. In the intervening years, the impetuous prodigy negotiated a contract with Hyatt Hotels for the Trump Organization to build and operate it. Now that a hotel was to be built on his property he had enough collateral for an $8-million mortgage to renovate the building and make it into the Grand Hyatt. At the time, Trump had built nothing in his young life and didn't know if he was equal to the challenge. When the Grand Hyatt was finally opened in September 1980, Donald was a 50% owner of the Hyatt flagship hotel.

In August, 1976, when Donald had just reached thirty years of age, he went to the Summer Olympics in Montreal, Canada. There he met a beautiful model, Ivana Winklmayr, who had been an alternate on the Czechoslovakian ski team at the Sapporo Winter Olympics. She was a dignified and intelligent woman who displayed the poise and elegance worthy of a wealthy tycoon's attentions. They courted, and were married in the following year. Ivana would eventually become his business partner and the mother of their three children, Donald Jr., Ivanka, and Eric.

Like virtually every great entrepreneur, Donald Trump began his quest for the brass ring early in his career. Much of his success came as a result of his arrogant and aggressive nature. His temerity, derived from his need to be special, was an important factor in his ability to fight the Manhattan bureaucrats and win.

THE TRUMP TOWER

The signature building that Donald describes as the flagship of the Trump Organization is the famous Trump Tower located on Fifth Avenue and 56th Street. This magnificently opulent building with its six-story pink marble atrium and its 80-foot waterfall has become one of the landmarks of New York City. Negotiation for this site had been initiated in 1978, but the deal did not close until 1979 and construction was not completed until 1983. As usual, the time delays in obtaining the necessary zoning requirements were responsible for the gap between the dream and its realization. The city was staunchly committed to his constructing a small inelegant building on his site. The thought of such a thing appalled

Trump. In order to get his building constructed, it would be necessary to get variances approved. To achieve this, he called an architect and gave him his standard line. "Don't tell me it can't be done. Tell me how we can do it." Then he told them to design two buildings that *he* (not the architect) would present to the city. One building design was to meet city specifications and be the world's ugliest building. The other design was to be the most elegant building possible, but require the variances needed to pass inspection. Trump presented both designs and insisted that he would build either building. Though he never intended to build to their specifications, he told them it was in their hands. Needless to say, Mr. Trump got unanimous approval for his elegant building. The city was trumped, and it wouldn't be for the first or last time.

Meanwhile, Donald had used the time delays to his advantage. During that hiatus he employed a variety of promotional techniques to bring his lavish apartments to the attention of the public and to sell them at premium prices. He had also leased the commercial suites in this building at rates that covered his costs and left him with a tidy profit. By his own calculations, Trump Tower was a financial success of the highest order (Trump, 1987, pp. 191-2):

> *The way I figure it, the entire project...cost $190 million. The sales of apartments have so far generated $240 million–meaning that even before including revenues from the stores and offices, we've earned a profit of approximately $50 million on Trump Tower.*

The Trump Tower was completed in 1983. By the end of that year, Donald, Ivana, and their children moved into one of the 12,000-square-foot penthouse triplexes on the top floors.

ATLANTIC CITY AND THE CASINO VISION

Not long after the Trump Tower coup, Donald saw the opportunity to become a player in the big stakes at Atlantic City. His motivation for switching his focus from Manhattan was financial (Trump, 1987, p. 196):

> *Now, for the first time, [after learning that the total profit of Hilton's 150 hotels was about the same as the profit on its two Los Vegas casinos] it occurred to me that even if I finally got my hotel built and it became a major success in the greatest city in the world, it still wouldn't be nearly as profitable as a moderately successful casino hotel in a small desert town in the southwest.*

In that venue also, Trump would go big or not go at all. Anticipating his construction of an empire of gambling casinos, he began in 1980 by buying some small properties in key locations along Atlantic City's boardwalk. Then he obtained legal help to assist him in his application for a gambling license. (Hugh Hefner's Playboy Casino was already under construction and licensing approval was pending.) Knowing that licensing approvals take time, Trump began making arrangements for financing, designing and building a casino. Finally, on March 15, 1982, the Casino Control Commission of New Jersey granted the Trump Organization a gambling license and a few weeks later, refused a gambling license to the Playboy Casino (see Chapter 6). The first Trump foray into the gambling world of Atlantic City was about to be launched.

Shortly after receiving the license, Trump was approached by Mike Rose, Chairman of Holiday Inns, to enter into a joint venture on his Boardwalk site. Trump and Rose shook hands on a deal that required Holiday Inn to obtain the financing and the Trump Organization to build the hotel. Though ground had not yet been broken on the site, Trump had left the impression that construction on the property was well under way. His reputation in New York had preceded him. Rose knew that building in Atlantic City was difficult at best and impossible at worst. He called Trump and indicated that the Holiday Inns Board of Directors would hold their meeting in Atlantic City so they could see the construction progress. To ensure approval, Trump reported (Trump, 1987, pp. 214-5):

> *I called in my construction supervisor and told him that I wanted him to round up every bulldozer and dump truck he could possibly find and put them to work on my site immediately. Over the next week, I said, I wanted him to transform my two acres of nearly vacant property into the most active construction site in the history of the world. What the bulldozers and dump trucks did wasn't important, I said, so long as they did a lot of it.*
>
> *The supervisor looked a little bewildered. "Mr. Trump," he said, "I have to tell you that I've been in the business for a lot of years and this is the strangest request I've ever gotten."*

The ploy worked and Holiday Inns approved the deal. On May 14, 1984, the Holiday Inn Casino-Hotel opened, signifying Trump's entry into gambling casinos at the tender age of 37. In February 1986, Trump bought out Holiday Inn's interests and the Casino was renamed the Trump Plaza Hotel and Casino.

TRUMP CASTLE

In February 1985 while still in the throes of negotiating a buyout of the Holiday Inn Casino-Hotel, Donald Trump learned that Barron Hilton had been turned down for a gambling license for his new casino-hotel on which he had nearly completed construction. He called Barron Hilton personally and set up a meeting. Trump made a cursory attempt to negotiate a price but Hilton was adamant about recouping his investment of $320 million. On the spot and without even walking into the nearly finished hotel, Trump said "yes." Why would the man, who prided himself on negotiating hard and heavy, suddenly capitulate? He felt it was the largest and most prestigious location on the boardwalk, one that he could not afford to lose. Later Trump confided to a friend, "If I told my father, he would have said I had lost my mind." But Donald knew best, and when he closed the deal on June 15, 1985, Donald added Trump's Castle to his Atlantic City gambling empire.

THE TAJ MAHAL

Trump's next contribution to the glittering world of gaming hotels was the grand Taj Mahal, designed to be the most lavish and spectacularly ostentatious hotel-casino in the world. However, its founder died when the project was only half-completed and considerably over budget in its construction. In 1987, after closing the deal that gave him ownership of his third casino, Trump discovered that there were flaws in its original design. Reconstruction entailed such heavy additional costs that by the time the Taj Mahal opened in 1990 it had become a money pit. Though it was, in fact, the most dazzling, and opulent hotel-casino in the world, it was also the most expensive ever built at the time.

As the decade of the 1980s came to a close, the Trump billion-dollar empire reached its zenith. In addition to its three Atlantic City Casinos, another casino in Indiana, and the Trump hotels and condo developments in New York City, it also owned the Trump Shuttle Airline, the *Trump Princess* yacht, the exquisite Mar-a-Lago estate and the New Jersey Generals AFL football team.

CRACKS IN THE TRUMP EDIFICE

Near the end of 1989 and by early 1990, cracks began to appear in the financial structure of the Trump Organization. The problem was a cash flow squeeze that resulted when the huge carrying costs on the lavish Trump hotel-casinos exceeded the revenues they were generating. When Donald announced that he would miss his March payment on the Trump Castle, the financial world erupted in a frenzy of fear and ferment. Word spread like wildfire through the financial community, with widespread conjecture that the Trump Empire might be insolvent. In an act aimed at damage control, Donald convened a meeting of all the creditors and suffered the personal humiliation of expressing his "mea culpa" to an angry collection of bankers and financiers.

Trump recognized his personal vulnerability as well as that of the Trump empire. By calling his loans, the creditors could force him into personal bankruptcy because he had personally guaranteed many of the debts. However, he knew he had an advantage–forcing him into bankruptcy would yield the creditors only a fraction of what they were owed. It was in their best interest to give him some latitude and help him regain solvency so they would recover the full amount of their loans. In a skillful application of this insight, Trump asked for an additional line of credit of $65 million. After an initially hostile response and a long period of negotiation, the creditors granted Trump the line of credit he requested on June 30, 1990, and deferred all principal and interest payments on his properties for a period of five years. They also agreed not to lay any claims against him personally for the same period. In return, Donald pledged his three casinos as security and agreed to divest himself of his biggest losing enterprises, including The Trump Shuttle, the Plaza Hotel and his yacht, the *Trump Princess*. Donald subsequently described that agreement as the biggest gamble of his life (exceeding his purchase of Barron Hilton's property).

THE ART OF THE COMEBACK

As 1990 came to a close, the news for Donald continued to worsen. The recession in real estate was deepening and declining property values were reducing his equity in the casino-hotels. The whiplash effect of reverse leverage was escalating the debts of the Trump empire exponentially. Furthermore, the Taj Mahal ended the year with huge losses. Ivana's uncontested divorce from Donald was granted on December 11, 1990, and the settlement agreement, which would require a huge cash payout, was scheduled for the following April. Donald Trump seemed to be approaching the nadir of his personal and business lives. He later wrote (Trump, 1997, p. xii):

I was up against a wall. So I sold a few assets to stay afloat. Then, after being pummeled by my bankers, Ivana turned around and sued me for $2 billion. Life, I thought, looked bleak. Then, one day around Christmas of 1990 I said to myself, Donald, it's time to fight back. So I got down to work.

On March 26, 1991, *The New York Times* and *The Wall Street Journal* carried front page stories predicting the collapse of the Trump Organization. In his book, Donald mused (Trump, 1997, p. 4):

[These newspaper] stories were picked up by radio and television and blasted throughout the world. This was by far the worst day of my life.

However, the economy began to strengthen again, the casinos resumed their profitability, and Donald gradually reduced his indebtedness. When the debt:equity ratio for his casinos reached an acceptable level, Trump formed the company Trump Hotels & Casino Resorts, and issued an IPO (Initial Public Offering) that raised $2 billion. Donald was finally able to repay his creditors and return to solvency.

It had been a long and emotionally draining climb back to financial comfort, but Donald was not about to rest. In 1994, he began negotiations that ultimately led to a partnership with GE in constructing the exclusive Trump International Hotel and Tower that would ultimately see completion in the year 2000. In 1996, he bought the building at 40 Wall Street–the second-tallest building in Manhattan–for less than $1 million. He spent $35 million in renovations and named the new structure the Trump Building at 40 Wall Street.

To what does Donald Trump attribute his successful comeback? In his own words (Trump, 1997, p. 223):

Passion is [a] key ingredient to success and perhaps even more so to coming back. ...Passion is the essence of life and certainly the essence of success. If you work hard without passion, you're just wasting lots of energy. You really have to want to do something important.

ONWARD AND UPWARD

Throughout the late 1990s and into the 21st century, Donald Trump continued to make deals and promote his acquisitions and himself with characteristic flamboyance and grandiosity. He has developed a world-class resort spa at the plush Mar-a-Lago property in Palm Beach, Florida and the Trump International Golf Club near the Palm Beach International Airport. Donald is presently renovating his newest acquisition, the $115-million New York Delmonico Hotel, purchased in early 2002. He intends to put another $100 million into a renovation that would turn the 72-year old hotel into luxury condominium suites.

In the past decade, Donald Trump has stimulated a lot of copy in the tabloids with his marriage to Marla Maples on December 20, 1993 and his subsequent divorce three and a half years later (shortly after his purchase of the Miss Universe pageant in 1996). Rumors of his aspirations for the Presidency of the United States emerge from time to time, but they have not yet translated into action. Similarly, plans to build tall buildings in Chicago, Toronto and elsewhere often dissipate amid the noise of other grandiose dreams and aspirations. What we know for sure is that the Donald is a man with a gift for big dreams and the ability and courage to bring them to fruition. He is larger than life and continues to show us that even the most unlikely dreams are attainable if they are matched in magnitude with tenacity, skill and commitment. His rise, his fall, and his subsequent comeback have the makings of a Hollywood film that will inevitably emerge as he moves toward the later phases of his life.

Trump's Decade-by-Decade Climb

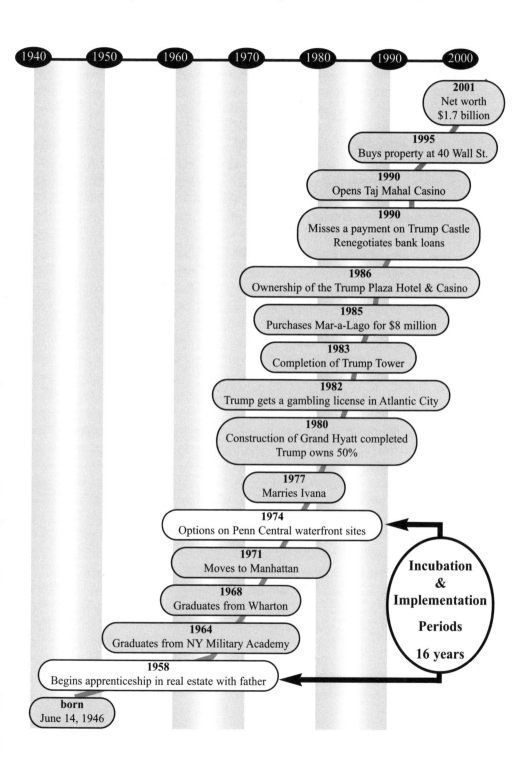

1940 · **1950** · **1960** · **1970** · **1980** · **1990** · **2000**

2001
Net worth
$1.7 billion

1995
Buys property at 40 Wall St.

1990
Opens Taj Mahal Casino

1990
Misses a payment on Trump Castle
Renegotiates bank loans

1986
Ownership of the Trump Plaza Hotel & Casino

1985
Purchases Mar-a-Lago for $8 million

1983
Completion of Trump Tower

1982
Trump gets a gambling license in Atlantic City

1980
Construction of Grand Hyatt completed
Trump owns 50%

1977
Marries Ivana

1974
Options on Penn Central waterfront sites

1971
Moves to Manhattan

1968
Graduates from Wharton

1964
Graduates from NY Military Academy

1958
Begins apprenticeship in real estate with father

born
June 14, 1946

**Incubation
&
Implementation

Periods

16 years**

A Personality Profile

COMMUNICATION STYLE: BRAVADO

Donald Trump is the master of hype and promotion. In his own words (Trump, 1987, p. 58):

> *The final key to the way I promote is bravado. I play to people's fantasies. People may not always think big themselves, but they can still get very excited by those who do. That's why a little hyperbole never hurts. People want to believe that something is the biggest and the greatest and the most spectacular. I call it truthful hyperbole. It's an innocent form of exaggeration–a very effective form of promotion.*

The name "Trump" carries with it an aura of unfettered ostentation and unparalleled luxury. Donald Trump, like Branson and other flamboyant entrepreneurs, understands the power of establishing a reputation and then endowing all products with that image by labeling or "branding." In Donald's case, he chose to brand his buildings and casinos with the imprint of "the biggest and the best." He observed (Trump, 1997, p. 154):

> *I believe in doing things big. I tell my kids: If you're going to do it, go for it. Make it the biggest, make it the best.*

Donald understood that publicity was a more effective and financially superior way of gaining exposure than buying advertisements. He observed (Trump, 1987, p. 57):

> *If I take a full-page ad in the New York Times to publicize a project, it might cost $40,000, and in any case, people tend to be skeptical about advertising. But if the New York Times writes even a moderately positive one-column story about one of my deals, it doesn't cost me anything and it's worth a lot more than $40,000.*

In his *Trump: The Art of the Comeback*, he wrote (p. 55):

> *Just as you can create leverage, you can enhance a location through promotion and psychology...as I did with Trump Tower by promoting [it] as something almost larger than life.*

Promotion was key to his rise to the top. Biographer Jack O'Donnell noted, "With Trump, publicity took precedence over finance–always."

INTUITIONAL STYLE: VISION FIRST, DETAILS LATER

Like all great entrepreneurs, Donald began with a vision and then dealt with the details later. His sister, Judge Maryanne Barry, told the media, "Vision is his genius." Maryanne went on to tell A&E Biography that her brother only builds something that is special. Anyone can build buildings, but Donald's world must be garnished with a special caché or he passes. For verification of this, just step into the lobby of the Trump Tower in midtown Manhattan and take a look at the atrium of pure marble. Everything he touches is elegant and spectacular, testimonies to a huge ego and the demands of being the biggest and the best in all things. No matter what one thinks of Trump's tough operating style, no one has ever accused him of thinking small.

When choosing properties, he relied on an intuitive sense of what could work and what couldn't. Had he consulted with lawyers and CPAs as traditional executives do, he would not have bought his best properties. He told A&E Biography, "I buy distress properties and try to turn them around." Entrepreneurs tend to be adventurous spirits who play the game for the thrill and the ability to go where others fear. The financial numbers are only a means of keeping score for how they did. They are never to interfere with the game. The CEO of a large company, however, must satisfy a board of directors with a bottom line focus and therefore operates with a more restricted vision. Intrepid warriors like Trump are free to negotiate from the hip, like the gunslingers of the old west. It is what makes them tick and makes them rich. Leverage is the fuel that drives them. They thrive on what others fear. That is how they grow.

CREATIVITY: THINKING OUTSIDE THE ENVELOPE

Most epiphanies are innate responses to inner knowing. They seem to emerge from a brain that has absorbed a great deal of information and from which emerges a kind of subconscious intuition. Some of Trump's revelations in the area of real estate investment seem to have derived from his total immersion in that area. In 1975, while listening to his car radio en route to a meeting, he heard that an impending strike at the Hilton casinos in Las Vegas had caused the Hilton stock to fall precipitously. "I was stunned," he said (Trump, 1987, pp. 195-6):

> *How was it possible that the stock of a company that owned at least a hundred hotels worldwide could be hurt so badly by a strike against just two of them? ...[later] it took only a small amount of*

research to determine that Hilton's two casino hotels in Las Vegas accounted for nearly 40% of the company's net profits. By comparison, the New York Hilton accounted for less than 1%.

This insight led to Donald's entry into the Atlantic City casino business five years later. Much of Donald Trump's "instinct" for good real estate investments is a result of incessant gathering of information that is subsequently processed in the subconscious and revealed as insight.

RISK-TAKING PROPENSITY

Successful entrepreneurs like Trump are renegade risk-takers who gather information over a period of time and then, when opportunities arise, they move quickly. In a nutshell, their adage is: *plan long–move fast*. Unlike those in the more academic disciplines, the Trumps of the world have short attention spans. Furthermore, they are impatient to a fault and are intolerant of mediocrity. Leverage is their most treasured tool, since it allows exponential growth through the use of existing assets to acquire new ones.

Donald Trump likes to push the envelope of risk. He spent $22 million for the USFL football team the New Jersey Generals, signing Heisman Trophy winner Herschel Walker to a multi-year contract. At that point in his life he was convinced that he had the golden touch. But that contract was the beginning that almost led to his demise. It was soon followed by a TV game show *Trump Card*. Then he bought the Eastern Shuttle that ate cash so fast he was forced to sell it within months. This was followed by a helicopter crash that claimed the lives of his three top executives. As the roaring '80s came to a close, the Plaza Hotel in Manhattan was in the red and the ill-fated Taj Mahal brought down his house of cards. By 1989 he was billions in debt and Trump Castle was losing money. His elegant toys like the *Trump Princess* yacht and his 727 Boeing airplane were money sinks that contributed to his downfall.

By 1990 he was $2 billion in debt and was unable to pay $900 million in notes that were due. Then he defaulted on $73 million in bonds. The banks were alarmed and brought in a new CFO and took away Trump's ability to sign checks. They forced him to slow down and liquidate non-profitable assets. During this debacle Trump kept up a positive demeanor despite the fact he was going through a sensational divorce from Ivana. Often the larger-than-life people live life surreally and begin to think they are invisible if not invulnerable. Twice on Aspen Christmas ski vacations he ensconced girlfriend Marla Maples in a private apartment while he and his family stayed with Barbara Walters. That is a risk beyond the pale of most men.

In *Trump: The Art of the Deal*, Donald wrote (p.48-49):

> *People think I'm a gambler. I've never gambled in my life. To me, a gambler is someone who plays slot machines. I prefer to own slot machines. It's a very good business being the house…If you go for a home run on every pitch, you're also going to strike out a lot. I try never to leave myself too exposed, even if it means sometimes settling for a triple, a double, or even, on rare occasions, a single.*

But if bringing your girlfriend on a ski trip with your wife and kids is not a gamble, then what is? Trump gambles, but doesn't recognize the risk involved in his actions. Such behavior is common to many entrepreneurial geniuses. Trump once asserted, "The New York Stock Exchange is the biggest casino in the world." In this context, Trump qualifies as more of a trader than an investor. Traders buy and sell to make a quick score and often sell short. That is Trump's style.

When Barron Hilton was turned down for a casino license, Donald made what he characterized at that time as the "biggest gamble I'd ever taken in my life." He shook hands on a deal for $350 million when he didn't have that much money, and claims to have had no inkling how he would raise such a sum. There is little question that Donald Trump lives on the adrenaline boost of high-risk ventures, though he attempts to mediate risk with creative deal-making.

INTENSITY: A RELENTLESS QUEST TO ACHIEVE

Donald Trump is the consummate overachiever. In his latest book, he admitted, "My attention span is short." This is a classic trait of the larger-than-life entrepreneur. Such people are in a mad dash to achieve. In that dash they have a tendency to leave a lot of bodies in their wake. Such is evident in the turbulent life of Trump–both professionally and personally. In his books, he exudes many of those very qualities common to other successful business owners. He wrote:

> *My least favorite thing to do is to maintain the status quo. Instead of being content when everything is going fine, I start getting impatient and irritable.*

The phrase "a New York minute" has come to stand for a shorter period of time than a normal minute, because New Yorkers are seen to be more impatient to get things done quickly. The phrase could be renamed "a Trump minute." One-time employee, the President of Trump Plaza, Jack O'Donnell wrote, "He is hard to keep up with even when walking. He walks so fast." Speed has been his ally and his foe. The magnitude of his impulsive behavior was evident when he bought the St. Moritz Hotel in Manhattan for $70 million. He didn't need a hotel, didn't know how to run one, and bought it on a whim. Three years later he sold it, as impulsively as he bought it–for more than double what he paid. Donald Trump is the kind of boss who thinks lunchtime is wasted time. And since he doesn't take time to eat lunch, he expects those who work for him to follow the same regimen.

Trump's on-going sense of urgency is merely a manifestation of his quest to achieve results. He states (Trump, 1987, pp. 47-48):

One of the keys to thinking big is total focus. I think of it almost as a controlled neurosis, which is a quality I've noticed in many highly successful entrepreneurs. They're obsessive, they're driven, they're single-minded and sometimes they're almost maniacal, but it's all channeled into their work. Where other people are paralyzed by neurosis, the people I'm talking about are actually helped by it.

SELF-IMAGE: A BIG EGO

Biographer Jack O'Donnell said that when he met Donald, his new boss said (O'Donnell, p. 16):

I'm America's most successful businessman...I've done things nobody thought could be done. And I've got big plans.

At that time he was still under forty and yet to get into serious trouble.

Trump's acquisitions offer testimony to his need for recognition, celebrity and power. He lives in the most stylish and lavish penthouse in Manhattan. When the snobbish Plaza Hotel came on the market he bought it without looking at the operating costs or even walking inside to check out the rooms. He had been there, but more importantly it fit his need for image above all else. Form exceeds function in the life of Donald Trump and permeates all that he owns. This was his motivation to make a deal to build in the Chicago Loop. The chance to have the name *Trump* adorn the world's largest building was just too important an opportunity to pass up. He would have done it, even if the project had proved marginal.

Trump's preference for form over function might also apply to his choice of female companion. Donald arrives at parties with the best-looking femme fatale. If she isn't spectacularly gorgeous, he comes alone. His desire for the ultimate in form can be found in the lavish lobby of the Trump Tower, the flashy opulence of his casinos, the elegance of the *Trump Princess* yacht, and his glorious Palm Beach vacation retreat Mar-a-Lago. Donald not only wants to ride first-class, he wants to be seen to be riding first-class.

CRITICAL THINKING: A CONTRARIAN

Even Donald's father, Fred, thought his impetuous son had exceeded reasonable limits when Donald challenged the city in his quest to convert the defunct Commodore Hotel in mid-town Manhattan. On signing the deal for the Commodore Hotel property, his father told him, "Buying the Commodore at a time when even the Chrysler Building is in receivership is like fighting for a seat on the Titanic." Trump was running counter to prevailing wisdom and swimming upstream. (He was applying Sam Walton's *Rule 10* with a vengeance.) In the late 1970s, the City of New York had defaulted on $100 million in bonds, was functionally insolvent and was a rather dubious business partner. True to his intrepid nature, Donald didn't listen to his father or anyone else. He was 28 at the time. The hotel had been closed for some time, but its location next to Grand Central Station was the real value that Donald saw. Sane developers would not touch the rat-infested property. One pundit wrote, "He didn't know enough to know he shouldn't have, so he did." When Trump succeeded, his reputation was won and his future path was smoothed. Forever more he was seen as someone who could do the impossible. Had he taken a safer route with equal success he would never have become the mystical tycoon he is today. In his third book, he expressed the importance of a contrarian approach (Trump, 1997, p. 225):

> *Going against the tide is often a very clever thing to do. While it can involve unbelievable risks, and while I cannot say that it's a primary factor for success, often going in the opposite direction can lead to the highest level of achievement.*

ECCENTRICITIES AND PERSONAL PARADOXES

Although Trump is adversarial and sometimes hostile in his negotiations, he can be spontaneously generous on a personal level. This abnormal magnanimity surfaced when his limousine broke down on his way home from Atlantic City. An unemployed mechanic seeing Trump's plight pulled off the road, repaired the vehicle and upon refusing payment, disappeared into the night like the Lone Ranger. It is reported (though I have no documented evidence of this) that a bouquet of flowers were received by the mechanic's wife the next day with a certified letter indicating that their mortgage had been paid in full.

One of Trump's most obvious idiosyncrasies is that he never carries a briefcase. He sees it as a symbol of needing information to operate. Donald feels he needs no one and prides himself on being free of such trivial encumbrances as a briefcase.

Two obsessions in Donald's life are winning and cleanliness. He told A&E Biography, "I'm a cleanliness freak." He washes his hands immediately after shaking hands with strangers. As he noted (Trump, 1997, p. 176):

> *The only good thing about the act of shaking hands prior to eating is that I tend to eat less. For example, there is no way, after shaking someone's hand, that I would eat bread. Even walking down the street, as people rush up to shake my hand, I often wonder to myself, why? Why risk catching a cold?*

Trump aspires to sartorial splendor with impeccable attire. If his key employees don't show up dressed appropriately in dark suits and white shirts with matching dark ties, he doesn't hide his outrage. His early military training may be a factor in his meticulous attention to detail in his selection of clothing.

In spite of his dominant presence in the world of casinos and gambling and his preoccupation with his net worth and profitable transactions, Trump told the world, "Never let money become your goal." He understood what most entrepreneurs must–that those who chase money never get it in any great amounts. Those who chase their visions make lots of money. Dr. Demming opined, "The corporate world's obsession with profits is misplaced." For Demming, the direct pursuit of money was equivalent to driving forward by looking through a rear view mirror–not the best way to travel safely or effectively.

ACHIEVEMENTS & HONORS

MAGNITUDE OF SUCCESS

The magnitude of Donald Trump's success is manifest in the many high-profile structures and ventures that bear his name. From his first project–the transformation of the dilapidated Commodore Hotel into the luxurious Grand Hyatt Hotel–he has enhanced the skylines of New York and New Jersey. Then he followed in rapid sequence with a series of eponymous edifices: the Trump Tower, the Trump Plaza, Trump's Castle, The Taj Mahal, Trump Parc, and the storied Plaza on the Park. In the wake of these successful projects (all launched in the 1980s), the Trump Organization appeared to be an unstoppable juggernaut in full throttle. While executing these architectural feats, Donald purchased the yacht he christened the *Trump Princess*, the spectacular Mar-a-Lago estate in Palm Beach, and the floundering Eastern Airlines from which he created the Trump Shuttle.

Following his flirtation with bankruptcy in 1990, Donald took a brief sabbatical from development. On his re-entry into the fray, he opened Riverboat Casinos in Indiana. The Trump Spotlight 29 Casino opened in 2002 near Palm Springs. Having lost ownership of the Empire State Building in the early 1990s, he periodically announces plans to build the largest building in the world. This building was originally to be located in Chicago, but the terrorist attack on the World Trade Center has postponed that project to the indefinite future.

Trump's fall and subsequent comeback is a tribute to his tenacity and survival skills. He told the media "You can retreat or fight." He fought! Although he didn't emerge unscathed from the debacle in the early 1990s, he managed to keep his flagship properties Trump Plaza and Trump Castle, Mar-a-Lago and his $10 million penthouse in the Trump Towers. He was forced to sell off the Trump Shuttle he had purchased for $25 million and to divest himself of the *Trump Princess*, his personal 727 jet and the $35-million Connecticut estate that went to Ivana in their highly publicized divorce settlement. In spite of all the volatility of his fortunes, he has been able to claim a recent net worth of over $2 billion, and is one of the richest men in the world. Donald Trump's vision and his personal intensity promise to bring many more architectural triumphs in the decades to come.

HONORS

In 1994, the city of New York named him *Entrepreneur of the Year*. His alma mater at the University of Pennsylvania has entered him in the Wharton School Hall of Fame. In October 2000, Trump was named the "Hotel and Real Estate Visionary of the Century" by the Hotel Federation of New York. In late 2001 Ted Turner released a retrospective on Donald Trump that purportedly cost $3 million to produce. An additional honor he should receive is "Comeback Entrepreneur of the Century!"

LESSONS LEARNED FROM DONALD TRUMP

In his first book, *Trump: Art of the Deal*, Donald Trump presents ten recommendations for deal-making that he calls "trump cards." These trump cards can be generalized beyond the context of real estate to apply to almost any area of entrepreneurship.

TO BE BIG, THINK BIG–REAL BIG

Donald's first admonition–to "think big"–has been visited earlier in this chapter, but it characterizes (probably more than any of his other lessons) his personal style. The following paragraph captures the essence of his philosophy (Trump, 1987, p. 47):

> *I wasn't satisfied just to earn a good living. I was looking to make a statement. I was out to build something monumental–something worth a big effort...It's nice to build a successful hotel. It's a lot better to build a hotel attached to a huge casino that can earn fifty times what you'd ever earn renting hotel rooms. You're talking a whole different order of magnitude.*

A common trait shared by all those profiled in this book is the tendency to think and plan on a grand scale. Mere success is not good enough. The goals must be sensational or they're not worth attempting. All that follows results from the entrepreneur's dedication to this belief.

TAKE CARE OF THE DOWNSIDE, THE UPSIDE WILL TAKE CARE OF ITSELF

When investing in casinos in Atlantic City, Donald Trump was careful to delay his construction of the casino until after he had received his gaming license. Once he received this license, Holiday Inns offered to repay all his original costs, to finance the construction, and to guarantee him against losses for five years–all for a 50% ownership of the casino. Trump reported (Trump, 1987, p. 49):

My choice was whether to keep all the risk myself, and own 100 percent of the casino, or settle for a 50% stake without putting up a dime. It was an easy decision.

Of course, he chose the latter, eventually bought out his partner, and renamed his establishment the Trump Plaza Hotel and Casino. This was but one of many instances when Donald Trump structured deals to minimize his liability and his vulnerability.

MAXIMIZE YOUR OPTIONS

Trump recognizes that most deals are never consummated. Hence, he recommends that prospective deal-makers have several proposals percolating at once. Such an approach not only provides entrepreneurs with alternatives when a deal falls through, but it prevents them from caring too much about the outcome of a particular proposal. This disinterested position enables the entrepreneurs to bargain hard because losing a deal is not perceived as tragic. Trump warns (Trump, 1987, p. 53):

The worst thing you can possibly do in a deal is seem desperate to make it. That makes the other guy smell blood and then you're dead.

KNOW YOUR MARKET

This aphorism applies to any business. One of Trump's remarkable strengths was his insight into the markets for which he was building. Instead of listening to so-called experts, he did his own informal market research by asking questions, talking to people, and developing instincts for what people wanted. By profiling the prospective buyers of his properties, he was assured that he could charge top dollar for his condominium suites and pre-sell all the units before construction was completed. Trump's approach was similar to Michael Dell's in that he invested substantial time in designing products to match what the prospective actually customer wanted rather than what he imagined they wanted.

USE YOUR LEVERAGE

This maxim refers to psychological leverage rather than the financial leverage discussed earlier. Donald advises (Trump, 1987, p. 53):

Leverage is the biggest strength you can have. Leverage is having something the other guy wants. Or better yet, needs. Or, best of all, simply can't do without.

In almost every deal that Donald Trump consummated, there was clear evidence of leverage in his favor. When negotiating with Holiday Inns to buy out their share of the casino, he became enamored of the firm's potential and began buying up their stock. They had two profitable casinos. Trump's plan was to take over the firm, keep the casinos and dump the rest of the company. His strategy called for selling his New York properties to complete the takeover of Holiday Inns. During this time, he bought one million shares of Holiday Inns stock and says he was willing to put up a billion to complete the takeover. Fearing his hostile takeover, Holiday Inns capitulated and offered him their portion of the casino at a bargain price. Donald abandoned his attempts to acquire Holiday Inns. Issuing his own modification of an old Amex commercial, Trump admonishes, " Leverage: don't make deals without it."

ENHANCE YOUR LOCATION

The most famous aphorism in real estate states that property value depends on three factors: location, location, location. Donald makes the observation that you can actually enhance the value of a location if you attract the right people. He cites as an example how he built the Trump Plaza on Third Avenue, a less prestigious location than Fifth Avenue, but enhanced its value using the money he had saved by building on the less expensive site. The added luxuries enticed an upscale clientele, which ultimately elevated the Third Avenue location to a higher status than it had previously. With this increased status came a higher property value. In this maxim Donald Trump has shown that both price and value must be considered relative to one another in determining whether a price is a bargain. A high-priced property in an excellent location may represent less value than a lower-priced property in a less desirable location. If a location can be enhanced, it offers greater potential for profit than an expensive property in a high-rent location. This aphorism applies also to the stock market where price must always be assessed relative to real and potential value.

GET THE WORD OUT

There is no question that Donald Trump is the guru when it comes to promoting a product. He has launched each of his projects with press releases, outrageous claims, and copious amounts of media coverage. Whether the publicity is positive or negative, it increases exposure and that leads inevitably to sales. In his own words, "You need to generate interest and you need to create excitement."

To bring attention to the one hundred acres of land that he acquired on the West Side, Donald announced that he was going to build the world's tallest building on that site. He received immediate media attention from the *New York Times*, from *Newsweek* and on the television evening news. Consequently the location was regarded as prime territory and its value increased substantially. Donald Trump takes the old maxim *Don't hide your light under a bushel* to a whole new level and encourages us to shine our light in the public face.

FIGHT BACK

Trump says, "Lawyers delay deals instead of making deals. They settle rather than fight. I'd rather fight than fold." When asked about his confrontational style he says, "My image is as a flamethrower. I'm not. But nobody pushes me around." Donald Trump is clearly a person who could not work for someone else. He told the media, "I love to have enemies. I fight my enemies. I like beating my enemies to the ground."

One instance occurred in the late '80s when he outfoxed Bally Corporation in a Greenmail scheme. Greenmail is a transaction whereby a firm pays a stockholder a premium for their stock to prevent their mounting a hostile takeover. With Trump's reputation as a fighter with the resources to do battle, he is able to transact such deals. He began buying up Bally stock in the '80s and pocketed millions when they bought him out to just get rid of him. The Bally executives weren't sure whether his accumulation of stock was aimed at a hostile takeover, but they were not about to take a chance they might be working for Trump. So they paid. He wrote, "These idiots, they caved in." Once you have gained a reputation as a fighter, it is easier to negotiate favorable terms in any kind of deal.

DELIVER THE GOODS, BUT CONTAIN THE COSTS

Trump, like all the entrepreneurs geniuses, understands the importance of maintaining quality in your products. He observes (Trump, 1987, p. 60):

You can't con people, at least not for long. You can create excitement, you can do wonderful promotion and get all kinds of press, and you can throw in a little hyperbole. But if you don't deliver the goods, people will eventually catch on.

This is perhaps the fundamental maxim of any business. If there is no quality, there will be no long-term business. However, the quality should not be obtained by unlimited expenditure. If costs aren't controlled, then the product will have to be priced too high for the market to bear. The result is disaster. In spite of the cash-flow squeeze that threatened Trump, he was diligent in controlling his costs in most of his projects and in protecting his downside. His near-bankruptcy was a consequence of overestimating the revenues he would receive relative to his costs.

HAVE FUN

No one can charge that Donald Trump violated this maxim. His life story reads like the adventures of a rich boy in a candy store. Toys make Donald happy and the bigger the boy, the bigger his toys. He indulged himself with a 282-foot floating palace–the $25-million *Trump Princess.* Then came the $8-million Boeing 727 to sport him around the country and to his Aspen ski lodge. For a mere $2 million, he acquired a 47-room weekend cottage in Greenwich, Connecticut. But his most ostentatious purchase was undoubtedly the 118-room Palm Beach estate once owned by Meriwether Post, known as Mar-a-Lago, that he "stole" for $8 million.

Since the mid-1980s he began to add women to his list of hobbies. He was seen courting model Marla Maples in Atlantic City and at Aspen. While still married to Ivana, the flamboyant Trump sat with Marla Maples at ringside at a nationally televised fight as if he were invisible. After many ups and downs with long-term friend Marla Maples, the two were married on December 20, 1993. Shortly after, they celebrated the birth of their daughter Tiffany, Donald's fourth child. His marriage to Marla Maples also ended in divorce. Is Donald Trump having fun? In his own words (Trump, 1987, p. 63):

The real excitement is playing the game. ...If you ask me what the deals all add up to in the end, I'm not sure I have a very good answer. Except that I've had a very good time making them.

Sir Richard Branson
Image Is Everything in Branding
b. Shamley Green, England   July 18, 1950

"I have always thrived on opportunity and adventure."

SELF-DESCRIPTION

"I have always thought rules were made to be broken."
"My biggest weakness in life is that I can't say no."

MOTTO

"I'm an adventure capitalist."

INNOVATION	Founded Virgin Records mail-order business as a teenager; in 1984 launched Virgin Atlantic Airlines on a whim, with no plan and no financial backing
UNIQUE QUALITIES	"I never had any interest in being a businessman." Made *Guinness Book of World Records* three times for wild stunts.
OBJECTIVE	"My interest in life comes from setting myself huge, apparently unachievable challenges and trying to rise above them."
NET WORTH	Billionaire tycoon before age 40; $3.3 billion by 2001
HONORS	Awarded a knighthood by the Queen in the New Year's Day 2000 honors list for entrepreneurship
BIRTH ORDER	First born; younger sister, Vanessa
EDUCATION	Tenth-grade dropout–dyslexia contributed to his hatred of school
PERSONALITY	Renegade risk-taking adventurer who thrives on living on the edge in business and personal life; an eccentric
HOBBIES	Fast boats, fast cars, fast women and dangerous balloons
POLITICS	Apolitical
RELIGION	Agnostic; raised as a Protestant
FAMILY	Wives: Kristen Tomassi and Joan Templeman Children: Sam and Holly

10

Richard Branson

Image Is Everything in Branding

"Let's call it Virgin, since we're such virgins at business."

Overview

*B*randing is a marketing term. Its outer manifestations may be a trademark or a logo adorning a product. Its purpose is to engender a trust or *brand loyalty* that will cause the consumer to purchase and repurchase a particular product over a long period of time. Though we normally associate branding with inanimate objects, the modern media have made it possible to promote products by associating them with particular traits of public personalities. For years, golfing celebrity Arnold Palmer, who was a symbol of trustworthiness and rugged masculinity, endorsed Toro lawn mowers, and in so doing imbued the product with an aura of rugged trustworthiness. Through the 1990s, Dave Thomas projected a friendly guy-next-door persona that engendered a brand loyalty in patrons of Wendy's. In Chapter 8, we observed that personal branding has reached heroic proportions with Martha Stewart. The diva of daytime has so pervaded the media that she has become a trademark for a large variety of different products. However, the consummate expert on branding oneself is the "king of branding"–Richard Branson.

Sir Richard Branson, the CEO of Virgin Atlantic and a myriad other ventures, became rich and famous through nerve, verve and hype. Classical approaches to building brand awareness and brand equity were never high on Branson's list of promotions. He was far more interested in headlines through personal daring and bravado. Branson used shameless self-promotion to put the Virgin name in front of the public and got funding for his ventures through pure hype. Rather than spending marketing dollars and using more conventional channels like direct mail, media stories or trade shows, he preferred to take a more sensational route.

The genesis of the Virgin Airline business was quite interesting if not bizarre. The free-spirited Branson was on a holiday in New York City with his future wife Joan Templeman. In an attempt to impress her and at the same time get a free trip to the British Virgin Islands, he concocted a crazy scheme to get it all for free. It was 1979, and Branson was still struggling to survive in his volatile recording business. He telephoned a travel agent and explained that he was interested in purchasing an island. He had heard that prospective buyers of such expensive real estate were flown first class to such destinations and given complimentary hotel accommodations on the beach. As he later wrote in *Losing My Virginity*, "We could be put up for nothing in a grand villa and they would fly you all around the Virgin Islands by helicopter."

A short time later, the flamboyant Branson and Joan Templeman were flown first class to Necker Island, listed for a mere £3,000,000 (about $6 million). At the time Branson didn't have 3 million pence. After the first helicopter ride, the sales agents became suspicious when Richard talked about a price of £150,000 or just 5% of the asking price. They checked out his credentials in England. When the cavorting couple returned to their posh villa by the sea, they found their luggage waiting for them on the curb.

As one might expect, the vagabond couple had no way back to England. Once they made their way to the airport, the adventurous Branson inquired how one might get out of the small island and back to Puerto Rico. The only flight was a charter that would cost $2000. In vintage Branson style, Richard said, "I'll take it." He had no money, but borrowed a blackboard and some chalk, and started walking around the airport offering flights to Puerto Rico on Virgin Airways for $39. Within an hour he had booked all the seats, collected the cash, paid for the charter and was the impresario of his first airline operation. When the plane landed in Puerto Rico a passenger turned to him and said, "Virgin Airways isn't too bad. Smarten up the service a little, and you could be in business." Branson retorted, "I might just do that," and laughed.

Using flamboyant promotional stunts and shameless publicity events, Richard Branson was able to build brand awareness in every one of his many entrepreneurial ventures that included an airline, a music company, a soft drink company, a travel business, a financial enterprise and a host of other initiatives. By combining his flair for the dramatic with a high propensity for risk, Sir Richard has risen to the top of the entrepreneurial world. By age forty, Branson was a billionaire; by fifty, he was a multi-billionaire. Who else would float down to his wedding in a parachute? He has a sense that image is everything, and in the mass markets it is.

The Formative Years

EARLY UPBRINGING AND ITS IMPACT ON LATER SUCCESS

Branson was the first-born child of lawyer Glen and iconoclastic mother Evette. His mother was the dominating influence in his life, molding Richard into a wild risk-taker in both his personal and professional lives. Eve was a renegade in her own right. One of the first female members of the Royal Air Force during World War II, she later became a pioneer flight attendant for Transatlantic Commercial Aviation. Eve was on the first flight outside Britain and later flew gliders–before most women dared drive cars. Fearing her son would grow up timid in the tranquility of rural England, she set challenges for him throughout his early life. Eve taught him to live life on the edge and went to great lengths to help him acquire powerful survival skills. Her methods might challenge current social norms, but Eve clearly understood that the only way to deal with fear is to stare it down and persist through it until it is conquered.

When Richard was four, Eve drove him to a remote park outside Shamley Green in Surrey, dropped him off and then instructed him to "find your way home" as she drove off. The young lad was found wandering near a farm and the family was called to retrieve him. Through such experiences, Richard learned early how to deal with danger and avoid panic. He has subsequently found himself cast adrift in such diverse environments as the Sahara Desert and the Canadian ice cap, but he has always found his way to safety.

At eight years of age, Richard was sent to boarding school to learn self-reliance. When he was ten, his mother raised the ante in yet another move to prepare her son for life's challenges. On this occasion she drove him 50 miles from home but provided him with a map, a sandwich, and a bicycle before driving off to let him find his way back. In his memoirs he spoke of finding a relative's house and spending the night on the trek across the English countryside (Branson, p. 14):

I remembered walking back into the kitchen like a conquering hero, feeling tremendously proud of my marathon bike ride.

In his memoir, Branson also spoke of the adult conversations in which he engaged his father on legal issues and his mother on such matters as student unrest and human diversity. In Branson's home, intellectual dialog took place on a wide range of controversial issues from pornography to the legalization of drugs. The house was always full of people, providing an ideal environment for the nurturing of the young inquisitive extrovert.

FORMAL EDUCATION

In spite of his early facility with spoken language, Branson was slow to acquire written language. He admitted, "At age eight I was still unable to read. I was dyslexic." While at his boarding schools, first at Scaitcliff Prep and then Stowe, he displayed significant athletic prowess in cricket and soccer. However, an injury to his knee at Stowe ended his sports career. After that, school held little interest for him. Branson wrote, "I realized I'd be hopeless at studying, so I quit to do something I knew I could do and which interested me." He told Keith Hammonds of the *New York Times* in 1984, "I didn't like school, but I wanted to put the world right." His justification for dropping out of school was to launch a counter-culture magazine called *Student*. The entrepreneurial world, well suited to his competitive nature, would become his next field of battle.

Richard dropped out of school after completing the equivalent of the 10th grade. The headmaster at Stowe was not surprised at Richard's decision to leave. On hearing the news, he told young Richard, "Congratulations Branson. I predict you will either go to prison or become a millionaire." Both predictions came true.

A STUDY IN EARLY ENTERPRISE

Branson had begun entrepreneurial ventures quite early in life. At seven, he and buddy Nik Powell decided to get rich by growing and selling Christmas trees. Dreams of early wealth evaporated when the trees died from a parasite attack. Later the two aspiring entrepreneurs became partners in a parakeet mating business. That enterprise may have been improperly consummated, for it met with a similar end. His third venture, the creation of *Student*, was to be a much more successful endeavor.

In 1965 when he turned fifteen, Richard joined the growing tide of dissent that had been bubbling up among the young throughout the mid-sixties.

The appeal of launching a counter-culture magazine to tell the world how students felt became an avocation. *Student* was dedicated to informing the adult world that it was acceptable for students to be different. The magazine was launched with pal Jonny Gems, but the two teens had little comprehension of the magnitude of the task they were undertaking. The two boys exhibited the naïve optimism of youth described over two centuries earlier by the great English poet Alexander Pope (*Essay on Criticism*, c. 1751):

> *Fired at first sight with what the Muse imparts,*
> *In fearless youth we tempt the heights of arts,*
> *While from the bounded level of our mind*
> *Short views we take, nor see the lengths behind...*

Passion was their main attribute, for they were devoid of money, experience, employees and customers. Business plans were beyond their grasp and neither had the skills nor the theoretical bent to construct such a document. However, few men or boys were better suited to transforming such a fantasy into a reality. The two young entrepreneurs were following their instincts on what would work and what would not. *Student* reported mainly on sex, drugs, rock 'n' roll, pregnancy, and abortion. As only an indomitable spirit could do, the irrepressible Branson picked up the phone, called the corporate headquarters of Coca Cola and blatantly told the VP of Sales, "I have just sold an ad to Pepsi but the back page is still available" (Branson, p. 34). Coca Cola bit and *Student* was launched by the two ex-students.

Imagine the audacity of an impetuous sixteen-year-old with no office, no funding and no draft of a first publication, selling advertising to major corporations! Richard even surpassed this feat by convincing Vanessa Redgrave to sit for an interview for his first issue of *Student*. When all was said and done, they had sold an astounding 50,000 copies–about the same number as Hefner's first issue of *Playboy*. Branson also persuaded Jean Paul Sartre and James Baldwin to write articles for various issues of his magazine. Being oblivious to the high probability of failure in some of the challenges he faced enabled him to leap over hurdles that others would regard as unattainable. "I was too young to contemplate failure," he would later write. In 1969, *Student* had revenues of $20,000. After three years it had run its course but had taught Branson a great deal about operating his own venture.

The Climb to the Top

TRANSFORMATION FROM PUBLISHING TO RETAILING

Two factors altered the direction of Branson's quest to become the next Lord Beaverbrook or Rupert Murdoch of the publishing world. The mail-order magazine business was becoming tedious and Richard was looking for other worlds to conquer when, in 1970, the British government abolished the Retail Price Maintenance Agreement. Always one to seize a new opportunity, he realized that the abolition of this regulation meant he could sell records through mail-order *at a discount*! Using his large mailing list of students and exploiting the new opportunity to offer discounts, young Richard decided to compete with the English music shops. In the last issue of *Student* he ran a huge advertisement for discount records that resulted in a "flood of orders." He wrote, "That issue brought in more cash than we had ever seen." The boy wonder was on his way.

Now steeped in selling, billing, hiring, firing, managing, winning and losing, he set out to conquer the burgeoning world of British rock and roll with his new enterprise known as Virgin Records. The name Virgin had been selected when the founders of the company looked at each other and acknowledged that they were virgins at this enterprise. The name was not only catchy but laced with sexual imagery that had always appealed to the young entrepreneur with a raging libido. It also fit the turbulent times.

In its first year, Virgin Records' mail-order record sales did well. Then a second crisis emerged that would alter his life forever. In January 1971, a British postal strike that showed no signs of abating, threatened to end Virgin Records' short life. Branson rose to this challenge in a way few rational people would even entertain for a moment. With no money or assets, he decided to open a retail store. It seemed not to occur to him that he knew nothing about running such a store or about the up-front costs associated with establishing such an enterprise. In fact, he had no money for the first month's rent or even a deposit. But the intrepid entrepreneur strolled down Oxford Street where he found an empty second-story shop–a decidedly unsuitable location for an impulse product like records. He convinced the owner that he was the best possible tenant by arguing that all Virgin Records' customers would be walking past the owner's store downstairs. The increased traffic, he argued, would more than compensate the landlord for the rent that Virgin Records could not afford to pay. The landlord, who felt he didn't have a lot to lose, was persuaded and Virgin Records survived.

Such was the genesis of the first Virgin Record store–one that would soon be a multi-million-dollar worldwide enterprise. Within two years the fearless entrepreneurs were cutting their own labels. Mike Oldfield was their first coup with his huge hit *Tubular Bells* that sold 17 million copies. It was on the soundtrack of the movie *Exorcist* and its success eventually led to Branson's signing of the popular rock stars Boy George, Phil Collins, The Sex Pistols, the Rolling Stones and ultimately Janet Jackson. By 1984 Virgin Records was earning $15 million in profits. All this success was the by-product of an inopportune postal strike.

Today Virgin Megastores can be found in Manhattan, Paris, Tokyo and London. The Virgin Records store on the Champs Élysées, in Paris, set a record for sales with 7 million customers spending $130 million in the period from its inception to 1997. Branson later wrote (Branson, 1998):

> *If we hadn't reinvented ourselves we would have gone bust. There was no choice. I can draw a straight line between that tiny shop and the Virgin Megastores in Paris and New York. It's just a matter of scale–but first you have to believe you can make it happen.*

ADVENTURE CAPITALIST AND BRANDING GURU

By the mid-1980s, Richard Branson had launched the real Virgin Atlantic Airlines. He had received a call soliciting his interest in taking over the London-New York route that had become defunct with the demise of Freddie Laker's airline. Branson said (Branson, p. 175):

> *I was mesmerized by Freddie Laker (a distant cousin) and his independence and was determined to do something similar to what he had done.*

His business partner and cousin, Simon Draper, accused him of being "crazy, mad and a megalomaniac." Everyone at Virgin Records was aghast. How could they compete with British Airways? Simon walked out and never returned. His closest friends told him he had no chance of competing and if he leveraged what he had, he would lose it all on this wild scheme. As usual, he had no budget, no plan and insufficient money. As usual, Branson listened to no one but his instincts. He purchased a 747 jet on credit from Boeing and became an airline executive. Now he had to let the world know the benefits of using his airline.

Branson found himself in a regulated industry demanding huge working capital and a large loyal customer base. With no monies for advertising and little chance of getting any, he decided to use publicity to raise the public awareness of Virgin Airlines' existence. In typical Branson style, he instituted first-class service for all passengers. Other amenities included free limousine service to and from the airport, free massages, free champagne, free movies, and stewardesses with a difference. The customers loved it. An innovative flair combined with his live-on-the-edge nature left his employees stunned, his family fearful, and the media enthralled. Virgin Atlantic emerged with a special aura, and eventually made its mark on that one route.

In order to raise public awareness of Virgin Atlantic, Branson realized that he would have to concoct a dramatically risky and truly spectacular stunt that would be a blockbusting media event. He had heard that a thirty-eight-year-old Swedish hot air balloonist, Per Lindstrand, was looking for a sponsor for the world's first transatlantic flight in a hot-air ballon. Branson saw immediately the opportunity he was seeking. He approached Lindstrand with the offer to sponsor him, on the condition that he accompany the expert balloonist on the flight and receive primary exposure as the captain in this record-setting venture. An agreement was reached and Branson trained with Lindstrand in preparation for a departure from Sugarloaf Mountain, near Boston, in May 1987.

Inclement weather caused postponements of the departure date, but this provided Richard Branson with the opportunity he needed to promote the event and raise the media hype to a frenzy. Finally, on July 2, 1987, Per Lindstrand and Richard Branson were launched on their thirty-hour voyage with the full media pomp and ceremony of an interplanetary space launch. After twenty-nine perilous hours, the two adventurers reached the west coast of Ireland, reminiscent of what Charles Lindbergh had done in his thirty-three-hour solo airplane flight to Paris sixty years before. However, the most perilous part of the journey–the landing–was still to be achieved. As Lindstrand prepared to jettison the fuel tanks, a gust of wind tossed the balloon to the ground where it momentarily touched down before rising rapidly into the air. In the process, the balloon cables twisted and the *Virgin Atlantic Flyer* was flying out of control over the ocean. Lindstrand called to Branson to bail out, but by the time Richard realized his predicament, the balloon was aloft and Lindstrand had parachuted into the ocean, leaving Branson to navigate the balloon alone. A little later, Richard crashed into the Irish Sea and nearly lost his life. After he was unceremoniously plucked from the turbulent waters, he announced, "Those last two hours were the most frightening of my life." What price brand awareness! Most people are unwilling to risk their lives to set a world record, let alone to establish brand equity. But Branson was and is a high-order risk taker, and his antics have brought him the notoriety he needed to brand Virgin Atlantic.

PROMOTING VIRGIN ENERGY AS AN APHRODISIAC

When Branson decided to introduce Virgin Cola, he knew he was entering the big leagues of marketing. The infamous Cola Wars between Coke and Pepsi, which had raged during most decades of the 20th century, were high stakes games in which even a one-percent market shift meant billions of dollars in revenues. He knew he was up against multi-million-dollar advertising budgets and would never compete effectively without the help of the media. The two titans, Coke and Pepsi, dominate most markets in the world. Virgin Cola had to have an edge and be perceived as not only different but better. That led to one of his famous off-the-wall inspirations. Branson decided to suggest on the label that Virgin Energy, one of his soft drink,s was an aphrodisiac. His lawyers advised him against this because there was no research to substantiate this claim. Not easily dissuaded, Branson went ahead and printed his own promotional slogan on the cans, *Despite what you may have heard, there is no scientific evidence that Virgin Energy is an aphrodisiac.* Branson's natural instinct for marketing was reflected in his solution to this quandary. Such promotion contributed to Virgin Cola's success in the United Kingdom, where it bypassed Pepsi within a few years.

BUILDING EMPLOYEE LOYALTY

Branson disagreed with the conventional model in business that dictates that Shareholders are #1, Customers #2, and Employees are #3. In his company he says (Branson, p. 352):

> *Virgin does just the opposite. For us, our employees matter most. It just seems common sense to me that if you start off with a happy well-motivated workforce, you're far more likely to have happy customers.*

Branson is loved and respected by his employees like few other captains of industry in history. His belief that a contented employee means a happy customer and happy customers translate into increased profits has worked for the Virgin Group. The largest privately held firm in England, its net worth has been estimated at $1.5 billion. And this all came about through the power of promotion by a risk-taking entrepreneur.

Branson's Decade-by-Decade Climb

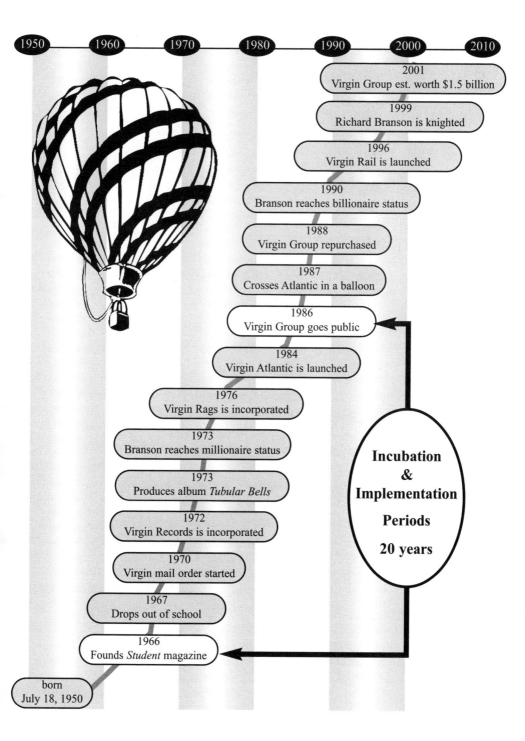

1950 1960 1970 1980 1990 2000 2010

2001
Virgin Group est. worth $1.5 billion

1999
Richard Branson is knighted

1996
Virgin Rail is launched

1990
Branson reaches billionaire status

1988
Virgin Group repurchased

1987
Crosses Atlantic in a balloon

1986
Virgin Group goes public

1984
Virgin Atlantic is launched

1976
Virgin Rags is incorporated

1973
Branson reaches millionaire status

1973
Produces album *Tubular Bells*

1972
Virgin Records is incorporated

1970
Virgin mail order started

1967
Drops out of school

1966
Founds *Student* magazine

**Incubation
&
Implementation
Periods
20 years**

born
July 18, 1950

A Personality Profile

COMMUNICATION STYLE: EXHIBITIONIST

Branson's boyish charm is not only infectious, it has been inspirational to his employees. His image as a dashing raconteur has led to his being touted for Mayor of London. The British appear to be disenchanted with the "old boy network" and Branson would never need to prostitute his views for political advantage. However, the apolitical renegade is probably unsuited to politics and would likely cause chaos in any political chamber. Echoing the sentiments of Donald Trump (see previous chapter), Sir Richard asserted (Branson, p. 343):

> *Fun is the secret of Virgin's success. Fun is at the core of how I like to do business, and it has informed everything I've done from the outset.*

In defense of such hedonistic bravado, Branson states:

> *If I don't do the things to make Virgin the best, why should anyone in my company do it? You must lead by example. Excite them, care for them, and they will perform for you.*

Not many corporate executives would dare launch a new venture named Virgin Bride let alone show up dressed in one of the wedding gowns. But the brash Branson reveled in such stunts. They appealed to his childlike sense of adventure and gained him widespread media attention. In 1996 the bold Brit sought media attention for his Virgin Cola soft drink by renting a military tank and, while dressed in full military regalia, driving the tank audaciously down 42nd Street to Times Square in New York City–not far from where Sam Walton, 12 years earlier, had danced the hula in a grass skirt. The tank trundled along the mecca of American commerce leaving crushed Coke cans in its wake and sending a metaphorical message to American consumers. In 1999, he launched Virgin Mobile by popping up in a London square with nude models. The marketing maven has displayed the Midas touch in promoting his numerous companies without incurring the high advertising costs of his competitors. Such outrageous stunts built Virgin into a worldwide empire.

INTUITIONAL STYLE: A TRUE PROMETHEAN

Virgin co-founder Nik Powell said, "He was always willing to run losses for a considerable period when others would have given up" (*Forbes,* July, 3, 2000). Like most great entrepreneurs, Branson adhered to his basic instincts more than to accepted practice. He wrote in his memoirs (Branson, p. 152):

> *I rely on gut instinct more than researching huge amounts of statistics. Due to my dyslexia, I mistrust numbers.*

Like most great creative minds Branson is right-brain dominant with a rational proclivity–a Promethean personality type. His keen intuition prompts him to operate differently from the traditional leader. In a contrarian approach to a world in the throes of merger mania, where bigger is always better, Branson has argued that bigger is problematic. He believes that a large firm has lost touch with itself and with the customer, and adamantly maintains, "Small is better." A principle pervasive at Virgin is:

> *If you don't known everyone in the operation, then it is too large and should be broken up.*

He told the media (*Success,* 1992):

> *Once people start not knowing the people in the building, it starts to become impersonal and it's time to break up the company.*

CREATIVITY: INNOVATIVE RESPONSES TO CRISES

Employing the British penchant for understatement, Branson told *Success* magazine (April 1998), "Editors have to put pictures in their publications; we try to make their job a little easier." The "pictures" to which he referred were photographs of the sensational promotional stunts that he used to get free publicity. These included shots of him in the hot-air balloon, in women's clothes and in semi-nude poses. His creativity was evident in the way he turned adversity into opportunity when he capitalized on the postal strike and used the repeal of the Retail Price Maintenance Agreement to sell discounted records. It is said of the charismatic Brit that he has never seen a stunt he didn't like. Whatever the cost, the media coverage has made the Virgin brand a household name.

PROPENSITY FOR RISK: VERY HIGH

Harry Smith of A&E Biography (June 2001) observed:

> *Branson had a flair for flamboyant self-promotion. He was a daredevil who risked his life to promote the Virgin brand.*

Richard Branson's larger-than-life persona communicates a sense of adventure that is almost mystifying. His heroics have attracted millions of Brits who admire him for daring what others only dream. The British press labeled Richard a "Hippie Businessman." They were intrigued by his childish sense of adventure that was often scary if not downright crazy. Scrapes with death were his weekly antics when he was involved with around-the-world hot-air-balloon trips and skydiving exploits. On one occasion he accidentally disconnected his chute and was saved by a skydiver in mid-air. One of the wild antics of the founder of Virgin's far-flung empire was to show up at his wedding to long time live-in Joan Templeman suspended from a helicopter. The Brits love his stunts and have coined the phrase *bransonesque* to describe a flamboyant lifestyle.

"Business is about survival," says the man who often lives like he has a death wish. He wrote in his memoirs, "I have always thrived on havoc and adrenaline" (Branson, p. 146). An example of his unusual temerity occurred in 1980 when he was near bankruptcy. Finding himself millions of dollars in debt and losing $2 million annually, he didn't retrench, as many would have, but expanded by purchasing Necker Island in the Virgin Islands. In his own words (Branson, p. 245):

> *I have always believed the only way to cope with a cash crisis is not to contract, but to expand.*

Testimony to his live-on-the-edge style was his impulsive purchase of two nightclubs–Roof Garden and the Heaven, a gay club–in 1980. Virgin was functionally insolvent at the time and a million pounds in debt. Both clubs were owned by a British brewer that was interested in divesting itself of the properties to an experienced operator, so they offered them with nothing down. That is not something the leverage king Branson can turn down, even if he doesn't need the business or even understand it. The only contingency was the new owner sell that brewer's beer. Branson bought both clubs on the spot. His partners were livid. The deal made eminent sense to him–leverage with all the beer you could pour–it was a heady transaction. The gambler in him saw the chance to use the club's assets to bail himself out of his other problems. They also offered a venue where he could review his music and entertainers. When his childhood friend Nik Powell, the operating executive for Virgin Records, discovered the purchase, he quit. Powell was furious with Branson for making an impetuous and unilateral decision. That ended the long relationship between Branson and his long-time entrepreneurial friend. As the high-risk-taking entrepreneur is wont to do, he used leverage for the purchase, paying full price but nothing down. He used the cash businesses to pay off nervous creditors and was able to survive a temporary cash crisis. Such is not the operating style for the faint of heart. Sir Richard once reflected (Branson, p. 168):

> *I have always been unable to resist taking on formidable odds. I must push myself to the limits.*

Daredevil exploits almost cost him his life on numerous occasions. Once, when five, he almost drowned in a valiant attempt to win 10 shillings from his aunt. In his memoirs he recalled the event and wrote, "Only by being bold do you get anywhere." A&E's Harry Smith described him as a man who "got rich by taking risks."

In addition to his exploits in hot-air balloons, the CEO of Virgin is an avid skier, speedboat racer and skydiver. His hobbies, like those of many entrepreneurs, are not for the timid. But such a lifestyle does not sit well with his investors. The financial world cringes every time he makes a decision to risk his life. They want him running the show, not being the show. But the Big T–high testosterone and high-octane nature of Branson–is what makes him special.

Further testimony to Branson's love affair with risk is how he was able to sign Mike Oldfield to a recording contract. This was his first real coup in the recording business. Branson desperately wanted to sign the reclusive Oldfield but anything he said fell on deaf ears. In a final move to land the singer, Branson invited him to take a ride in his new prized Bentley that was a wedding present from his beloved mother. When negotiations reached an impasse, the impetuous one turned to Oldfield and said, "Mike, would you like to have this car as a present?" Aghast, Oldfield said, "Come off it. Your mother gave this to you as a wedding present." Then Branson knew he had him. He wrapped up the deal and Oldfield drove off in his cherished car. For Branson the Bentley could be replaced, but he had a contract that would afford him the opportunity to succeed and to replace it. Within months *Tubular Bells* sold 13 million copies and

Virgin Records was an overnight sensation. Branson's reputation as a promoter of music was launched.

Brushes with death have been routine in Branson's tumultuous life. But once in Mexico he almost didn't live to enjoy the thrill. It was on a trip with first wife, American Kristen Tomassi. Ironically, they were trying to find a common bond and found themselves out in the raging waters of the Gulf of Mexico in a hurricane. The captain advised all parties to sit tight as they would ride out the storm despite the fact they were just a few miles from shore. The couple were young, athletic, and excellent swimmers. They jumped off the boat for an adventurous swim to shore in hurricane-whipped waters. They crawled onto shore exhausted, but the boat they had departed was never found. Their marriage was also stormy, but unlike the participants, it did not survive.

Branson's second marriage almost never happened. The couple had a volatile relationship that had produced two children. Branson was 39 when he finally capitulated and married the mother of his children after a 14-year affair. The two have opposite personalities with Joan never understanding Richard's need to push the limits and risk his life. In 1980, while attempting to keep Virgin afloat, Joan walked out on him leaving a note, "I am pregnant. I am afraid to tell you. I have run away from home. If you miss me, call me at Rose's." He called and his daughter Holly brought the couple closer together.

INTENSITY: DRIVEN BY ADRENALINE

The pragmatist in Branson, coupled with his risk propensity, makes him well suited for the entrepreneurial lifestyle. Looking within, he wrote, "I never enjoyed being accountable to anyone else or being out of control." Although most would say he is perpetually out of control, he meant that he had to maintain control. Despite his capricious style the magic man has survived longer than most and has as many winners as losers in his stable of business ventures. His entrepreneurial prowess allows him to enter new businesses where he has no experience, and to survive on pure adrenaline. In his memoirs he spoke of his adventurous nature (Branson, p. 154):

My interest in life comes from setting myself huge, apparently unachievable challenges, and trying to rise above them.

Branson was always in the fast lane whether driving, fly business (Branson, p. 146):

I have always thrived on havoc and adrenaline. I make up , ...na
about someone within 30 seconds. I do enjoy going fast. I love
powerful boats.

After one aborted balloon trip he told the media that speed was critical to Virgin's success. The media has described Virgin Enterprises as pervaded by the "impatient attitude of its leader." The successful entrepreneur typically is in a hurry and is willing to fail, recoup and move on. It was never in Richard Branson to say "I'll have to check with my lawyer and CPA."

SELF-IMAGE: AN ETERNAL OPTIMIST

Many of Branson's long-term business partners quit when he ventured outside convention–and he did venture often. One associate told him, "Richard, we've been friends since we were teenagers, but if you do this I'm not sure we can carry on working together." When Branson insisted on entering the airline business his close friend and colleague quit on the spot. Once Branson makes up his mind, he is impossible to change. Despite being under-financed, inexperienced and understaffed and with one plane on one route, he entered the airline business. In retrospect he admitted, "We launched the airline on a wing and a prayer and when the engine blew up on our test flight it could have been over before it had begun." In mid-2001 he announced upper-class service on his airline featuring fully reclining seats for sleeping, a bar, beauty stations with massages, aroma therapy, facials and manicures, and a menu including gourmet cuisine.

Branson has been accused of many things but never moderation. Excess is his god–personal and professional. Unabated passion is ever present in words and deeds. Every stunt pushes the limits of rules and decorum. This has been his style since his teens. Breaking the rules began with his counter-culture magazine and going halfway was never an option. If it can't be done big he doesn't want to play. "I find it impossible to stop my brain from churning through all the ideas and possibilities" (Branson, p. 92). *Business Week* (1998) wrote, "No wonder it is a standing joke among Branson's top aides that they're paid to curb some of their boss's wilder schemes." When Branson would propose some off-the-wall idea, Virgin Atlantic CEO Steve Ridgeway would attempt to nip the idea in the bud with the admonition, "Down Richard." However, most would admit it has been Branson's penchant for excess that has been responsible for Virgin's incredible success. Without Branson, Virgin Atlantic would be just another airline. He personally came up with such promotions as seat-back videos, upgraded Business Class, curbside check-in, and access to the Internet for upgrading onboard sleeping accommodations.

INITIATIVE: AN UNRELENTING QUEST FOR CONTROL

Entrepreneurs have a different operating mentality than conventional executives. Since they do not have to worry about being fired, they need only make the venture work well enough to survive. Shareholders are there to monitor results, not to dictate means or methods. Most executives place the shareholder at the pinnacle of importance because the security of their job depends upon pleasing the board. However, Branson put the shareholders last in his priority ranking. This was particularly evident when he took Virgin private rather than deal with shareholder demands that he believed to be short-term expedient but long-term imprudent. Mary Kay Ash took her firm private when an irate stockholder told her to stop wasting funds on the stupid pink Cadillacs. Both entrepreneurs saw the forest rather than getting lost in the trees.

A disgruntled former employee told the media, "Branson ran the operation as a benevolent dictatorship." That was his way of saying that Branson was a control freak. It is true that Richard Branson never operated by the book. Rules for him were only there to be broken and never to be followed. And he broke them with abandon. In his memoirs he wrote (Branson, p. 73):

I have always enjoyed breaking the rules–school or general.

ECCENTRICITIES AND PARADOXES OF SUCCESS

Money was never important to Branson except for the freedom it offered and the lifestyle it permitted. In his own words (Branson, p. 43):

I never really worried about how much profit Student made. We really saw it as much more a creative enterprise than a moneymaking enterprise.

Ironically, he seemed to love to travel the world without any cash in his pocket. He assumed that credit would be readily available no matter where he was. Branson has been bailed out of bizarre jams so many times that he fully expects someone to be on hand to save him. When *Forbes* (July 3, 2000) asked him about profitability, he answered somewhat diffidently:

> *Profits in a private company are not only unimportant, they're actually damaging in that you have to pay taxes on them.*

In his autobiography *Losing My Virginity* (1998), Branson wrote, "I can honestly say I have never gone into business purely to make money." Yet, the Virgin King of kinky hype made a billion dollars before he turned forty despite being a high school dropout and ignoring every rule of business. In his early years, Branson had no money to spend on advertising and admits that he wouldn't have known how to spend it if he had, so he just went off and garnered publicity with his off-the-wall antics. The maverick entrepreneur grew his firm faster than most by daring what most would not have considered.

During the early years, Virgin Records was perpetually insolvent. One time when facing bankruptcy Branson concocted a scheme to export records. Virgin was £15,000 pounds in debt when they began importing and exporting illegally. When custom officials caught up with the scheme he spent one night in jail and was fined severely. The debacle cost him £60,000 pounds but taught him the cost of exceeding certain bounds. He learned his lesson and vowed to never again spend a night in jail. An executive at Virgin characterized his operating style saying, "At Virgin, we don't lie. We complement the truth."

Honors & Achievements

MAGNITUDE OF ACHIEVEMENTS

Virgin Enterprises is a complex entanglement of privately held firms under the Virgin label. The Virgin empire includes such diverse businesses as Virgin Atlantic (airplanes), Virgin Rail (trains), Virgin Megastores (music stores), Virgin Cola and Virgin Vodka (drinks), Virgin Cinemas (theaters), and Virgin Direct (investment funds). Each entity is run by an individual entrepreneur reporting to the irrepressible Branson. The brash "man-on-the-move" is passionate to a fault and his sense of dangerous flamboyance has left him with a net worth of about $3 billion.

The firm employs approximately 24,000 people in 150 separate ventures that have revenues of about $5 billion. The companies are diverse operations in the travel, music, rail, wedding, finance, web, hotel, entertainment, and a myriad of other industries. Virgin Travel and Virgin Entertainment are the largest companies in the group, representing close to 50 percent of total revenues. Branson boasts of having in excess of 200 Virgin Megastores in the world, most in large metropolitan markets like Paris, New York, Miami, and Tokyo. Virgin Atlantic, his airline, is the backbone of the Virgin group with routes to America, Asia and Europe. It took the horrific World Trade Center debacle to cause Branson to cut back on expansion for the near term.

HONORS

Aside from his honors earned as a business tycoon and founder of the Virgin Group, Richard Branson has accumulated an impressive resumé of daredevil records. In 1986, his boat, _Virgin Atlantic Challenger II_, crossed the Atlantic Ocean in the fastest time ever recorded. The following year his hot-air balloon, _Virgin Atlantic Flyer,_ reached speeds of 130 miles per hour to become the first hot-air balloon to cross the Atlantic. In 1991, Branson completed the longest flight to date in a hot-air balloon in a 6700-mile Pacific Ocean crossing from Japan to the Canadian Arctic. During this journey, his balloon reached speeds of 245 miles per hour. These daring achievements reflect the high risk-taking he has employed in his business world transactions.

Even staid old England has been charmed by the flamboyance of the Virgin King. On March 30, 2000, the Prince of Wales knighted Branson for his entrepreneurial contributions. A British consulting group KMPG has repeatedly listed Branson as Britain's best business leader. The British public has long been enamored by the Branson sense of danger and off-the-wall style of promotion. Many believe he could win any public office he sought. In fact, his reputation for wild heroic deeds led the conservative _Economist_ magazine to write in 1995 that he could be elected Prime Minister were he so inclined. An issue of _Business Week_ in 1999 described Branson as "the new daredevil CEO type."

LESSONS LEARNED FROM RICHARD BRANSON

USE FLAMBOYANT PROMOTION TO CREATE BRAND EQUITY

Virgin's success is testimony to Branson's will. This intrepid charismatic entrepreneur was always willing to tread where others feared. His press-worthy treks helped imprint the Virgin brand on the psyche of the public. Branson never saw a promotional opportunity he didn't like and often concocts them to get ink for his ventures. Consistent with his penchant for style, he runs his empire from a London villa in Holland Park and at times from an Oxford estate. And in one of life's great ironies he vacations on Necker Island in the Virgin Islands that he now owns. (This is the island he and Joan had visited as opportunistic vagrants and from which they had been unceremoniously evicted.)

What will be Branson's legacy? In his quest for publicity and brand recognition it is his unique ability to go into socially forbidden territory and do it with an unabashed style that has given him a marketing advantage. Promotion and sensationalism are what made him and will prove to be his heritage. Branson has played on the edge and survived many debacles. His survival instincts have been a hallmark of his success.

Brand equity refers to the added value a product acquires through its association with a charismatic person or trusted company. A positive brand image can make it easier to raise seed monies or gain key support for launching a product. Image is everything in that world where the distinction between image and reality is blurred. The firm with the strongest image and the most resources typically wins the war of market share. Branson has proven that he is a master in that world. Those capable of building image without spending huge sums on advertising are destined to win the battle of the brands. For the fledgling entrepreneur a positive brand image is crucial. The right image will bring in capital as well as customers; the wrong one will chase both away. Aspiring entrepreneurs must be very careful of how they are seen for that is how they will be treated.

In the early days of any enterprise, shelf space is crucial. A product cannot move off a shelf until it gets on the shelf. That is why gaining access to shelves is the most important goal in the early days of a product launch. In that world image is key. Research provides some suggestions as to what behaviors can be used to build a positive image and gain product acceptance. The following table offers a few insights into the qualities and traits of the charismatic personality, exemplified by Branson, that can be used to generate shelf space for your products.

	Branding and Imagery Techniques	
1	Be off-the-wall.	Differentiate yourself–be irreverant!
2	Use swagger.	Be arrogant about your ability to provide benefits.
3	Empathize.	Identify with the target market and customer.
4	Be passionate.	Provide powerful messages about your power to perform.
5	Be persistent.	Stay the course and reinforce imagery via communications.
6	Be very good.	The masters execute effectively with style and panache.
7	Be on-the-edge.	Risk-taking is vital to new ventures: test the limits.
8	Innovate.	Creative destruction is the secret of all branding.
9	Chaos is good.	Greats thrive while others panic–trauma is opportunity.
10	Have commitment.	Remain focused and persevere in the face of naysayers.

Jeffrey Bezos
Avoid Instant Gratification
b. Albuquerque, NM   January 12, 1964

"We intend to lose lots of money for a long time."

SELF-DESCRIPTION
"Work hard, have fun, make history."

MOTTOS
"Get Big Fast"–mantra on the way to the top
"Ideas are easy; it's execution that's hard."

INNOVATION	"Our mission is to invent and innovate on behalf of our customers."
UNIQUE QUALITY	"Our secret is that we have not been competitor-obsessed. We have been customer-obsessed."
OBJECTIVE	In 2000 he was still saying, "This is day one. We're not even a teenager yet."
NET WORTH	$8 billion in 1999, down to $2 billion in 2001
HONORS	Person of the Year 1999 and "king of cybercommerce" (*Time* Magazine)
BIRTH ORDER	First born with younger brother and sister
EDUCATION	Stood first in his class at Miami Palmetto H. S. Graduated summa cum laude in Computer Science at Princeton and Phi Beta Kappa.
PERSONALITY	Bright, intensely competitive, intuitive perfectionist. "His personality is what has saved Amazon." (Spector 2000)
HOBBIES	Reading and playing computer games
POLITICS	Apolitical
RELIGION	Roman Catholic upbringing
FAMILY	Wife: Mackenzie, Children: son, Preston

11

Jeff Bezos

Avoid Instant Gratification

"Sacrifice the present for a better future."

Overview

In early 1994, when shopping on the Internet was virtually unknown, Jeff Bezos was a million-dollar-a-year Vice President of D. E. Shaw & Company in Manhattan, and the market for books was dominated by two bookstore chains–Barnes & Noble and Borders. Within four years, Amazon.com launched a web site that would effectively change the way people shopped for and purchased books. This revolutionary approach to bookselling threatened the dominance of the giant bookstores by offering the book-buying public greater convenience, faster service and even some previously unavailable information.

As Amazon.com expanded its product line from books to CDs and beyond, the Amazon web site became a model for e-commerce, an Internet-based shopping network that would enable consumers to purchase a variety of goods and services on-line while also gaining access to unprecedented amounts of information about the products.

Bezos, the gifted, nerdy wunderkind who grew up on Star Trek and science exploration, introduced the world to the power of the Internet as a vehicle for shopping, and in the process, fashioned Amazon.com into the dominant e-retailer in the world. His childhood dream of becoming an astronaut was never realized, but through his ability to use technology to sell, he has altered retailing more than anyone in history. The 30-year-old who quit a million-dollar-a-year job to chase a dream was a billionaire by the time he was 34.

The story of Jeff Bezos is a glowing example of what can be achieved if an individual is bright, driven, passionate, and tenacious. As the millennium approached, *Forbes* magazine waxed philosophical about Bezos saying, "Amazon is the first shining ray of the new commercial millennium. It's the shape of business in the next century." Biographer

Robert Spector characterized him as "charismatic" and says he has the potential to be a cult leader on account of "an enormous amount of personal power."

In its first half-year of business in 1995, Amazon sold over $500,000 in books. In its second full year (1997) it had revenues of nearly $150 million–a substantial 300 times growth rate. By 1999, the industry had taken notice as the audacious start-up reached revenues of $1.6 billion. Amazon quickly got the attention of Barnes & Noble.

During those early years, Bezos flirted with bankruptcy often and was functionally insolvent much of the time. Jeff had not anticipated the astronomically high up-front costs that typically plague software development companies and Amazon chewed through cash as quickly as a hungry school of Amazonian piranhas. However, consumer acceptance encouraged his strategic marketing moves, though raising money to implement them continued to present a challenge. When web mania hit in 1997, Amazon was struggling to pay the bills. Bezos, always the consummate optimist, was shocked at the growth and admitted there were many times when the firm was 45 days from extinction. By 2001, Amazon had revenues of $2 billion on sales to 35 million registered customers. Revenues in 2002 were projected to reach $6 billion with no end in sight.

In spite of the remarkable growth of revenues and the customer base of Amazon.com, it lost increasing amounts of money in each of its first five years. These losses brought criticism from shareholders and those in financial circles who began to question whether Amazon.com would ever turn a profit. However, Bezos was not interested in short-term profit. Instead, he focused on expanding the use of technology to enhance the shopping experience and consumer choice. Amazon's adversaries have subsequently grown less vehement in their criticism, for at the time of this writing, Amazon is achieving profit margins comparable to that of Wal-Mart. David Ponneman, one of the financial analysts who believes in the Amazon dream wrote,

> *I believe Amazon has the potential to become one of the most successful retailers in the world.*

Having survived the recent pitch and toss of the stock markets in the seas of consumer confidence and fear, Bezos has bankrolled a company *Blue Origin LLC* dedicated to designing a spacecraft that will carry people into orbit at the edge of the earth's atmosphere. Bezos will have fulfilled his desire to live life on the edge–literally!

The Formative Years

EARLY EXPERIENCES

In 1962, with only two shirts and a pair of pants to his name, Miguel Bezos fled Castro's Cuba just before the Cuban missile crisis. His travels eventually took him to the University of Albuquerque where special scholarships were offered to Cuban refugees. To help support himself during his university years, he worked the night shift as a clerk at the Bank of New Mexico.

Meanwhile, on January 12, 1964, two weeks after she turned 17, Jackie Gise Jorgensen, a high school student in New Mexico, gave birth to a son Jeffrey Preston. Within 18 months, her marriage to husband Ted Jorgensen had ended and Jackie became a single mom and sole provider for her son. After graduating from a community college where she studied business, she was hired as a bookkeeper for the Bank of New Mexico. It was there that she and Miguel met and fell in love. They married in 1968 when Jeff was 4. Miguel adopted Jeff, thereby changing his legal name to Jeffrey Bezos. (Jeff never met his biological father and says that he regards Miguel as his *real* father.) Within the next two years, siblings Christina and Mark were born to Jackie and Miguel.

Miguel was a role model for Jeff and the person to whom Jeff's later obsession with work might be attributed. As Jeff Bezos later said of his father, "He is the least lazy person I know." Through hard work and intelligence, Miguel was able to work his way through college to become an Exxon executive. Miguel's job with Exxon often required the family to pick up roots and move.

As a precocious toddler of 3, Jeff insisted that he should have a bed instead of a crib, but Jackie denied his request. A short time later, his mother discovered him with screwdriver in hand, dismantling his crib and transforming it into a real bed. Jeff attended a Montessori pre-school where he became so engrossed in each project that he had to be picked up–chair and all–and moved to the next activity.

His elementary teachers in Houston, Texas, recognized immediately that Jeff was a gifted child. At age 8, he was enrolled in the pilot program for gifted students at River Oaks Elementary School. In one of his more ingenious moments, he and some fellow students used a modem to connect a teletype machine to a mainframe computer and used it to play a *Star Trek* game. On another occasion, he created a makeshift buzzer for his bedroom door to sound an alarm when his younger siblings trespassed on his territory.

Jeff became one of the prized exemplars for the gifted program at River Oaks. In 1977, his intelligence prompted author Julie Ray to feature Jeff as the subject of a chapter in a book she was writing, titled *Turning on Bright Minds: A Parent Looks at Gifted Education in Texas*. In it she described him as a bright student of "general intellectual excellence." However, his elementary teachers assessed him as "not particularly gifted in leadership." (Teachers of the exceptional tend to admire the intellect and creativity of their gifted students, but typically find them to be difficult because of their intolerance of conformity and their need to push against limits.)

The cyber-king loved science and adventure as a child. Jackie Bezos encouraged him with electronic do-it-yourself kits purchased from Radio Shack. While at River Oaks, he saw his first Infinity Cube–a cube with motorized mirrors that could be adjusted to create multiple reflections that appear to extend to infinity. The visual magic of the Infinity Cube ignited Jeff's imagination and he asked his mother to purchase the $20 item for him. When Jackie explained that this toy was too expensive, Jeff proceeded to purchase all the parts at a fraction of the price and assembled his own Infinity Cube. As Jeff commented at the time, "You have to be able to think…for yourself."

From age 4 to 16, Jeff spent each summer on his maternal grandfather's Lazy G ranch in Cotulla, Texas, about 90 miles west of San Antonio. Jeff's maternal grandfather, Preston Gise, proved to be an important mentor and hero for the precocious boy. Preston was retired from the Atomic Energy Commission where he had overseen a staff of 26,000 and administrated a large budget. Highly intelligent and hardworking, he introduced his beloved grandson to the world of high-tech. Together they invented contraptions such as an automatic gate opener that functioned without electricity. His grandfather, whom he later described as "his best friend," taught Jeff how to weld, to fix the D6 Caterpillar tractor and to castrate cattle. (One might say that they had established together a "geld-and-weld" operation.) Jackie would later say (Spector, p. 5):

> One of the things [Jeff] learned [from the ranch experience] is that there really aren't any problems without solutions. Obstacles are

only obstacles if you think they're obstacles. Otherwise, they're opportunities.

Preston Gise also expanded Jeff's tolerance for failure by playing checkers with him and defeating him relentlessly, until the young protégé had sufficiently honed his skills to defeat the old man with regularity. Years later, Jeff would pay homage to his "best friend" and mentor by naming his son Preston.

FORMAL EDUCATION

After Jeff's elementary school years, the Bezos family moved to Pensacola, Florida and then on to Miami. Miami was the Latin city where twenty years before, Jeff's Cuban immigrant father had been lonely and broke. However, Miguel was now an executive at Exxon, and the Palmetto section of Miami where they bought their four-bedroom house was an upper middle class area. Palmetto High School, where Jeff enrolled, had been described as a school where the cars in the student parking lot outclassed those in the faculty lot.

Travel and moving had molded him into a self-sufficient adult who was comfortable with unknown environs. He later told a biographer (Spector, p. 35):

Moves always invigorated me. There's really something very cleansing about it. Every move is an opportunity for spring cleaning.

A youngster faced with making new friends and dealing with strange new cultures learns to cope early. (Recall that Sam Walton also regarded his frequent moves in early life to have been an asset.) Later in life, when Jeff was out in front of the pack (as Jeff would become at Amazon), those early experiences paid substantial dividends in helping him survive the lonely loft at the top. It is not surprising that when Jeff Bezos encountered new opportunities years in e-commerce years later, he would quit and take off to work in a new city, an unknown market. He had no idea if he would ever again receive a paycheck. He had already traveled that same road as a child and found it exciting and empowering.

By high school, Jeff was already a techie who loved science fiction. As an avid fan of Star Trek, he was enamored with the idea of inhabiting outer space. His favorite book was *Stranger in a Strange Land* by science-fiction writer Robert Heinlein. Generally regarded as "uncool" by his classmates, he eventually abandoned attempts to fit in, choosing instead to hang out with a clique of the intellectually elite students. At Palmetto High School, Jeff won the school's *Best Science Student* award in each of his sophomore, junior and senior years and the *Best Math Student* award in his junior and senior years. He served notice on his fellow students that he was planning on becoming the valedictorian of the class of 1982, and this promise became a reality when he stood first out of 680 students. His valedictorian speech spoke of colonizing space and he told the *Miami Herald* of his intention to build hotels and amusement parks there.

When Jeff was a junior at Palmetto High School, he met Ursula "Uschi" Werner, a senior, who became his first serious girlfriend. Ursula's strength was literature and they played the word game *Boggle* together, challenging the legitimacy of each other's words. Uschi was an intellectually stimulating companion for Jeff and when she graduated from Palmetto High in 1981, she was the valedictorian of her class. After graduation, she attended Duke University while Jeff continued into his senior year at Palmetto.

In the summer of 1982, Jeff and Ursula formed a business partnership in a summer-education camp that they named the DREAM Institute. (DREAM was an acronym derived from its full name, the Directed REAsoning Methods Institute). This Institute was located in Jeff's bedroom and had an enrollment of five students between grades 4 and 6. The parents paid $150 for each child for this two-week program that ran for three hours each morning. The curriculum involved a series of readings from books ranging from *David Copperfield* and *The Matchmaker* to *The Lord of the Rings* and *Dune*. When interviewed by the *Miami Herald* that summer, Jeff described the program in his own words, "We don't just teach them something. We ask them to apply it."

When it came time to prepare for college entry, Jeff applied only to Princeton University. His rationale was simple, "Einstein was there, for goodness sake!" He entered Princeton with impeccable scholastic credentials and majored in theoretical physics to follow in the footsteps of Albert Einstein and Stephen Hawking. However, a short time after arriving at Princeton, he discovered that for the first time in his life he was not the most gifted student in the class. Biographer Mark Leibovich reports an interesting turning point in the direction of Jeff Bezos' career path (Leibovich, p. 78):

One night during his freshman year, Bezos was struggling over a partial differential equation he had to complete for a quantum mechanics class. After a few hours of frustration, he and his study partner visited the dorm room of a classmate, who glanced at the equation and said, "Cosine."

"After we expressed some incredulousness," Bezos says, "he proceeded to draw three pages of equations that flowed through and showed that it was cosine." It led to a realization: There were people whose brains were wired to process abstract concepts in a very graceful way, and Bezos was not one of those people. "It was initially devastating," he says, "very, very, troubling."

This realization prompted him to re-direct his focus. He changed his major to electrical engineering and computer science. Once again, he excelled in the cognitive courses buttressed by abnormal intensity, competitiveness and a strong work ethic. He graduated summa cum laude in 1986 with a B.S.E. degree in electrical engineering and computer science and was subsequently elected to Phi Beta Kappa.

Before proceeding on to the next phase of Jeff Bezos' meteoric climb to success, we digress to observe that Bill Gates had experienced the same kind of "troubling" concerns in the rarified atmosphere of the exceptionally gifted. Describing his decision to abandon mathematics research as his career, Gates said (Wallace & Erickson, p. 64):

I met several people in the math department [at Harvard] who were quite a bit better than I was at math. It changed my view about going into math. You can persevere in the field of math and make incredible breakthroughs, but it probably discouraged me. It made the odds much longer that I could do some world-class thing.

For the gifted who, in their formative years, have been identified by others and themselves as "the smartest" and elevated to the top of the intellectual totem, the prospect of living in the shadow of someone with greater gifts is intolerable. It's the scientist's version of the "mirror, mirror, on the wall" syndrome in the *Snow White* fantasy, and it is a theme that pervades the history of mathematics and science. The fierce competition among "the smartest and the best" has spawned many of the great discoveries from the invention of calculus to the discovery of DNA and the decoding of the human genome. Bezos and Gates are two highly gifted individuals who accommodated the challenge to their supremacy by focusing their energies in fields where their gifts could receive their most productive outlet. All of us have been the beneficiaries of their gifts.

The Climb to the Top

BEGINNING AS AN EMPLOYEE

After graduation from Princeton in 1986, Jeff turned down employment offers from prestigious companies such as Bell Labs and Intel to become the eleventh employee at Fitel. This burgeoning young Manhattan company was pioneering the development of a computer-based global network designed to settle international equity transactions. The network operated as a primitive version of today's financial web sites like E*Trade. By 1987, Bezos was developing computer protocols that enabled different computers to share information at higher speeds and lower costs. Managing accounts in London, Tokyo, and Australia meant that Jeff was jet-setting around the world and learning about international markets at the tender age of 23.

In April 1988, Jeff left Fitel and joined Bankers Trust Company. Within the year, Jeff Bezos was made Vice President–the youngest vice president in its history. At Bankers Trust, he was responsible for managing a small programming department that designed a communications network called BTWorld. This network enabled its *Fortune 500* clients to access information on the assets, earnings and transactions of their pension and profit-sharing plans without waiting for hard-copy printouts. However, Jeff was becoming weary of what he referred to as "first-phase" automation–the use of technology merely to increase speed and efficiency. He was eager to pursue his real passion–"second-phase" automation–which he described as follows (Spector, p. 16):

> *[In second-phase automation], you fundamentally change the underlying business process and do things in a completely new way. So it's more of a revolution instead of an evolution.*

IN PURSUIT OF SECOND-PHASE AUTOMATION

In 1990, Bezos was introduced by a headhunter to David Shaw, founder of D. E. Shaw & Company, one of the most progressive computer-based financial trading firms in New York. David had a Ph.D. in computer science from Stanford and subsequently impressed Jeff with his intellect. Bezos would later say of Shaw (Spector, p. 18):

David Shaw is a very smart guy…He's one of the few people I know who has a fully developed left brain and a fully developed right brain.

It was no surprise that Jeff Bezos was hired in December 1990, at the age of 26, as Vice President of D. E. Shaw & Co. Within two years, he became Senior Vice President. In his new capacity, Jeff was responsible for developing and managing a unit of 24 people dedicated to exploring and securing new markets.

Within a few short years, Jeff would implement many of the "people-management" practices that he witnessed at D.E. Shaw, for example, its high selectivity in hiring. Fewer than 1 percent of the mathematics and computer science applicants were hired at Shaw, and then only after successfully navigating a difficult ladder of interviews. Shaw once observed (Leibovich, p. 84):

We don't always recruit for specific positions. We're happy to warehouse a truly gifted individual on the assumption that they may someday make us money.

The kinds of questions asked in the interviews reflect the climate of creative lateral thinking that D. E. Shaw valued and encouraged. Typically they involved what mathematicians referred to as Fermi questions (named in honor of the Nobel laureate physicist Enrico Fermi, who was famous for his order-of-magnitude problems. For example, the classic Fermi problem –how many piano tuners are there in Chicago?–requires some reasonable assumptions and order-of-magnitude estimates.) A similar culture had developed at Microsoft where prospective candidates were asked questions like, "Why are manholes and manhole covers round?" (Answer: If the cross section were a polygonal shape such as a square, rectangle or octagon, the cover could be dropped into the hole. The reader may wish to test this by cutting such shapes out of a piece of cardboard and then attempting to pass the cut-out through the hole that remains.)

THE SEARCH FOR A MATE

Jeffrey Preston Bezos applied creative lateral thinking to all aspects of his life including his search for a significant other. In Manhattan, he adopted a system of screening potential partners called "women flow"–perusing a sufficient quantity of women, he would increase the probabilities that he would meet one with whom he could have a meaningful relationship. He articulated this intent in a manner that would be most readily understood by a fellow "mathie" (Spector, p. 19):

> *The number one criterion was that I wanted a woman who could get me out of a Third World Prison...Life's too short to hang out with people who are not resourceful.*

Ironically, his "women flow" system turned up a woman who worked right under his nose at D. E. Shaw. Mackenzie Tuttle was an attractive, svelte brunette who was a researcher in Jeff's unit. She was also a graduate of Princeton from the class of '92. It didn't take long for the physical chemistry of love to play out its natural laws, and Jeff and Mackenzie were married in 1993.

THE INTERNET COMES OF AGE

In an ironic twist, 1993 was the same year that the World Wide Web came on line. It had evolved from the response, in 1959, of the Defense Agency Research Projects Administration (DARPA) to the launching of the Soviet *Sputnik*. DARPA created a communications network designed to connect all levels of the military and government in the event of a nuclear attack. Curiously, one of its key employees was Preston Gise, the grandfather who served as mentor to Jeff Bezos. By 1969, this network had evolved into ARPAnet and by the 1970s it had become NSFnet, a network connecting universities and funded by the National Science Foundation. In 1990, the National Science Foundation established an "acceptable-use policy" that provided guidelines for the commercial use of the network. This enabled the creation of Internet service providers (ISPs) such as NETCOM, BBN and MCI to set up their own transmission lines and provide access to businesses and individuals. The Internet was born.

Then Tim Berners-Lee, a researcher at the European Center for Nuclear Research (acronym CERN) in Geneva, Switzerland, then created some computer protocols that enabled users to browse the Internet with simple point-and-click commands. By clicking on highlighted sights, called *hyperlinks*, the user could navigate through the network of different sites distributed throughout the world. The World Wide Web was born. The final piece of the Internet mosaic was put in place in October 1993 when Marc Andreesen and some of his students at the University of Illinois introduced a Web browser called Mosaic. It was specifically designed to retrieve information from the Web using graphics. The commercial potential of the Internet was beginning to emerge.

THE BEZOS VISION

Jeff Bezos is an astute observer of market opportunities. When his boss at D. E. Shaw asked him to research the web as a potential investment opportunity, he was consumed by the possibilities. He took a more incisive look at the potential for e-retailing relative to product potential, price points, margins, pervasiveness and cutting edge plus target markets and demand. He intuitively felt that products like PCs, computer software, music, apparel, books, and office supplies would be best. Then he narrowed the search down to music and books. There were three million books in print and they were conducive to on-line research and display. Bezos discovered that the market sector in 1994 consisted of the *early adopters*, i.e., the types who dominated Internet sites and were also the book buyers. However, this sector constituted only 16 percent of the general population. Today only 16 percent of Americans–the sector consisting of the *laggards*–are not on-line.

In the Bezos analysis, books emerged as the top choice for Internet marketing. Books showed the greatest potential for sales and were easiest and least costly to warehouse and ship. Experience has supported his analysis. However, at this point, Jeff did what most entrepreneurs do when they make such a discovery–he told his boss. Predictably, his boss told him to go back to work where he was effective and to stop chasing fantasy rainbows. Not easily dissuaded, Jeff persisted in analyzing the potential for mass distribution of books through some new "second-phase" automation. His unrelenting research revealed that just six firms controlled the music industry and no firm dominated the book business. Random House was the largest publisher, although with less than a 10 percent market share. The two dominant book retailers were Barnes & Noble and Borders, but each held less than a 25 percent share of the $30-billion market. In 1994 over 51 million books were sold in the United States. Furthermore, Jeff's research revealed that Web usage was growing at the rate of 2300 percent per year. He understood the concept of exponential growth and its implications. He stated with characteristic enthusiasm (Spector, p. 25):

> *You have to keep in mind that human beings aren't good at understanding exponential growth...It's just not something we see in our everyday life. But things don't grow this fast outside of petri dishes. It just doesn't happen. [Something that is growing 2300 percent a year] is invisible today and ubiquitous tomorrow.*

Jeff Bezos envisioned tapping into all the books in print and offering them all on-line direct. No one else could do that in 1994. Such an edge would be dramatic and real-time. It had staggering implications.

Shortly after Jeff's idea to sell books on-line was rejected, he approached David Shaw to say that he was going to resign in order to pursue his dream in setting up a huge on-line bookstore. Shaw told him that on-line bookselling was a great idea, but for someone else who did not already have a great job with a seven-figure income. David Shaw was reluctant to lose Jeff and attempted to persuade him to stay. However, Jeff decided to be guided in his decision by what he termed his "regret-minimization framework." He explained this guiding principle in his own words (Spector, p. 31):

> *I knew that when I was eighty there was no chance that I would regret having walked away from my 1994 Wall Street bonus in the middle of the year...But I did think there was a chance that I might regret significantly not participating in this thing called the Internet, that I believed passionately in. I also knew that if I had tried and failed, I wouldn't regret that. So, once I thought about it that way, it became incredibly easy to make that decision.*

So, Jeff Bezos quit his job that paid about $1 million per year in mid-1994. He told his new wife Mackenzie that they were moving west but didn't know where. He then called Moishe's Moving Company and told them to take the furniture, drive west on I-80 and before they reached Dallas he would call them and tell them where to take their furniture. Bizarre? Perhaps. Such behavior was consistent with the Bezos analytical style. He had analyzed, by state, the sales tax on books and discerned that the best places for such a venture relative to taxes, shipping and a host of other variables were New Mexico, Colorado, Nevada, Oregon or Washington. He worked on his business plan while his new wife drove and he ultimately decided on Seattle because his friend, Nick Hanauer, had told Jeff that Seattle was the center of the universe and also that he wanted to invest in Jeff's new Internet business.

SLEEPLESS IN SEATTLE

While en route west, Jeff and Mackenzie agreed that Seattle would be their new home. Jeff gave Moishe's moving van directions to Nick Hanauer's house where the furniture was to be delivered. There was no time to waste, so Jeff stayed on his cell phone during the journey and set up the logistics for creating this new second-phase automation company that he believed would revolutionize bookselling. By July 5, 1994, this new company was incorporated in the state of Washington as Cadabra Inc.–as in Abracadabra. Within a week after arriving at Nick's house, Jeff and Mackenzie rented a modest home in Bellevue. It had a garage that would serve as Cadabra's first office and warehouse.

Jeff provided the start-up finances for Cadabra out of money he had saved from his employment at D. E. Shaw & Company. In his capacity as founder, chairman of the board and CEO of this one-man corporation, Jeff purchased 10,200,000 shares of common stock for $10,000 and contributed a $15,000 interest-free loan to the company. (This total infusion of $25,000 was subsequently increased by an additional loan of $29,000 in November, 1994.)

In the weeks that followed, Jeff went on a frenetic search for brilliant employees who would help him turn his dream into a reality. Following the principle of hiring only the best–a lesson well learned from D.E. Shaw & Company–Jeff began building networks from contacts he had established at D.E. Shaw, at Princeton, and in other centers that attracted talented people. By November of 1994, Jeff's rigorous hiring techniques and his remarkable skills of persuasion resulted in a nucleus of three gifted individuals who would fuel and grow the company: Shel Kaphan, Paul Barton-Davis, and himself. Mackenzie Bezos improvised as accountant, secretary and office manager.

Between November 1994 and February 1995, Bezos worked relentlessly, sleeping very little and scrambling to create software that would facilitate the ordering of books by e-mail or the Internet. Cadabra was not the first company to sell books on line. Computer Literacy Bookshops in the Silicon Valley had been selling books by e-mail to its customers as early as 1991 and other companies, such as WordsWorth in Cambridge, Massachusetts, had launched a similar initiative. Jeff realized it would not be long before the giants like Barnes & Noble would enter the market and undercut all its competitors with the advantage of large-volume discounts. If Cadabra was to beat the competition, it would have to get big fast–very big and very fast!

The Amazon River is the biggest river in the world. What excited Jeff Bezos was that it was "10 times larger [by volume] than the next biggest river." Jeff wanted his company to be Amazonian, i.e., 10 times the size of the next largest competitor. On February 9, 1995, he registered Cadabra as a corporation in the state of Delaware and named it *Amazon.com* Inc. This name not only signaled Jeff's intention to grow exponentially, but it also possessed that advantage that it started with the letter A, which would place it at the top of lists that were posted alphabetically. While "Abracadabra" and "Aardvark" would have had even greater lexicographical advantage, neither moniker would capture the gargantuan proportions of Jeff's dream.

FUNDING TO GET BIG FAST

Amazon.com's initial seed monies of $54,000 came out of Bezos' pocket. However, that money was quickly consumed in start-up personal survival expenses. After Amazon.com was incorporated, there was an urgent need for another injection of liquidity. The sale to Jeff's father of 582,528 shares of common stock @ $0.1717 per share brought approximately $100,000 into the coffers of Amazon.com and guaranteed its survival for at least another six months.

After this infusion of capital, Amazon.com was able to continue in its quest to get big fast. To do this, it worked feverishly to build the world's largest database of books by tapping into Bowker's *Books in Print* CD, and the book lists from Baker & Taylor and Ingram distributors. Thousands of hours were spent on the development and beta-testing of their web site, its user interface, and order tracking mechanisms. Finally, on July 16, 1995, the Amazon.com web site was launched. This web page was modest by current standards because elaborate visuals took too long to load and the page was designed for function more than form. The philosophy at Amazon.com was: keep the shopping process fast and simple–an approach now described as *frictionless shopping*.

For the first few days following the posting of the web site, orders from friends and relatives trickled in. In an attempt to build morale at Amazon.com, the order-taking software was modified so that the computer would sound a beep each time a new order was received. At first, this device was a pleasant novelty, but as the orders began to arrive fast and furiously, the incessant beeps had to be silenced by a re-jigging of the software. Three days after the web site was launched, Yahoo included the Amazon.com web site on their browser. The resulting explosion in sales was described as similar to "taking a sip through a fire hose."

The downside of this phenomenal growth was the inevitable crisis in liquidity. Servicing orders immediately requires large inventories, which implies a huge capital investment. Eric Dillon, a stock broker for Smith Barney in Seattle, observed (Spector, p 84):

> *Jeff was "dead broke" in that summer of 1995...He was out of his personal funds, he was out of his family's ability [to fund the company], and he was [going to be] out of money in 45 days.*

That was when Jeff Bezos put together a PPM prospectus and began looking for "angel" money (i.e., small amounts of venture capital invested in small start-up companies with potential). By the end of 1995, he had raised $981,000 from an assorted collection of twenty or so venture capitalists. With net sales of $511,000 in that first half-year, Amazon actually sustained a loss of $303,000.

Silicon Valley, which spawned the Internet, is the Mecca of money for start-ups. It is a go-go type of environment where even conservative investors get caught up in the mania of potential opportunities outside the mainstream. Amazon was in Seattle but decided to go to the Valley to find venture capital. Jeff ignored the courting of Seattle and East Coast firms and concentrated his efforts in Silicon Valley. In Jeff's opinion, the war of the web would be understood there better than anywhere. Furthermore, Bezos was obsessive in his commitment to deal only with the best in any enterprise. His first choice was Kleiner, Perkins, Caulfield & Byers, headed by web avatar John Doerr. This firm had successfully launched industry stalwarts Netscape, Intuit, Sun Microsystems, and Compaq.

In the spring of 1996, Kleiner, Perkins *et al.* agreed to a $60-million valuation of Amazon.com, purchasing 3,401,376 shares @ 2.35 per share for a total cash investment of $8 million. This gave Kleiner ownership of 13 percent of the company. It also provided enough seed monies to take Amazon to the next level. Marc Andreesen, co-founder of Netscape, became interested and he and Bezos got to know each other. The two entrepreneurs had a similar view of profitability and both supported the Bezos thesis of growth now and profitability later. Andreesen said (Spector, p. 96):

> *One of the fundamental lessons is that market share now equals revenue later, and if you don't have market share now, you are not going to have revenue later.*

In May 1996, the *Wall Street Journal* featured Amazon.com on its front page. Not only did this promote the Amazon web site, but it alerted the competition, Barnes & Noble. Subsequently it began its own on-line web site, *barnesandnoble.com*. Through 1996 and 1997, although Amazon's sales growth was exponential, investors were skeptical about its ability to compete with the giant Barnes & Noble. Investment bankers were able to raise another $20 million in venture capital for Amazon.com, but not without many months of cajoling. In 1996, Amazon's first full year of business, its net sales had increased to $15.7 million–a staggering 30 times the previous half-year–but it had lost $5.8 million!

On May 15, 1997, Amazon issued an IPO with an opening share price of $18. This meant that Jeff's ownership of 9.88 million shares gave him a personal net worth (at age 33) of $177.8 million–in less than three years after incorporation! Through the IPO, Amazon raised another $35 million, and within a year was selling for $100 a share. With money limitations no longer a barrier, Amazon.com began promoting its web site and sales went through the roof. Managing the growth replaced chasing money as the primary focus of the Amazon management team.

After Jeff had all but conquered the world of books, he was incapable of resting on his laurels or his sailboat. Entrepreneurs like Jeff seldom stop chasing their dreams, which is why they are often called "serial-entrepreneurs." Unlike Alexander the Great, Jeff still had worlds to conquer–the world of books was only stage 1 in his grand plan. In June of 1997 he launched a music site to sell CDs and DVDs. By October of that year, Amazon was the largest seller of CDs with 130,000 titles. In 1998 the restless visionary began selling toys, games, software, and gifts. He had also expanded Amazon.com into Europe with Amazon.co.uk (Great Britain) and Amazon.co.de (Germany). The share price of the stock closed at $259 on December 1998–up over 1400 percent in 18 months! By 1999 he had expanded into consumer electronics, sporting goods, jewelry and leather goods.

THE NEW ECONOMY

Even though Amazon.com was continuing to hemorrhage money, the investors continued to drive up its share price, believing that the economy was undergoing a paradigm shift in which old systems of valuation were becoming obsolete. Many financial pundits were suggesting that the infrastructures created by the dot-com companies would eventually bear fruit in the form of generous profits. The adage was: grow fast now and profits will eventually accrue. As the millennium came to a close, price:earnings ratios were no longer considered viable measures of a dot-com company as a prospective investment. By the end of 1998, Amazon had net sales of $610 million on its books alone, but it lost $124 million from the bottom line. When the stock market turned bearish in early 2000, the share values of Internet stocks plummeted. The bear market deepened throughout 2001 and 2002 and share prices continued their sharp declines. By May 2001, the price of Amazon.com shares had declined to only 15 percent of their high in December 1999.

In its first six years, Amazon had lost over a billion dollars. Financial conservatives painted Bezos as more pariah than creative genius. He had lost $1 billion on over $2 billion in sales. Wall Street deemed this an insidious waste. Amazon was presented in the news as the darling of the new economy that had gone wild and then gone bust. The financial gurus saw him as either the world's greatest salesman and visionary or a hopeless optimist. Bezos had told everyone who would listen that profits would not come quickly. He told his mother, "You will lose your money so consider it gone." He told Wall Street, "*USA Today* took eleven years to become profitable." From half a million in sales in 1995, Amazon.com was on track for sales revenues of $6 billion in 2002 and set the horizons for $10 billion in a few years. By mid 2003, Amazon had achieved profit margins comparable to those of Wal-Mart and Jeff was flying high with his investment in *Blue Origin*, a company dedicated to designing a spacecraft to carry passengers in orbit around the earth.

Bezos' Decade-by-Decade Climb

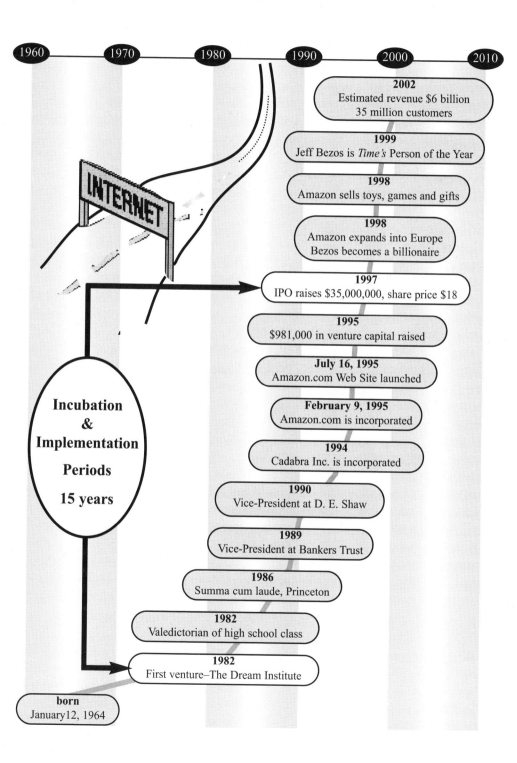

A Personality Profile

COMMUNICATION STYLE: PLAYFUL COLLEGE NERD

Most of us communicate with words; Jeff Bezos communicates with a laugh. It's an infectious laugh that identifies Jeff as precisely as his fingerprint or his DNA. Biographer Robert Spector's description of the Bezos laugh captures its essence as well as anything short of an actual audio rendition (Spector, pp. 183):

> ...That laugh; that now-legendary laugh. "Explosive," said Business Week; "an infectious, gulp-from-the-throat laugh," wrote Fortune; "a long extended bray, startling the uninitiated," waxed Wired; "It's a Tourett-like AHHHH ha ha ha ha bray," wrote Newsweek; "A rapid honk that sounds like a flock of Canadian geese on nitrous oxide," trumpeted Time. "His laugh is a whole-body noise that his mother says 'starts at his little toe and works its way up,'" said the Seattle Times. "In fact, he laughs so frequently it seems trained more to his internal sense of rhythm than to the conversation at hand."

This laugh is an integral part of the nerdy college-kid persona that Jeff conveys in his communication with people. He is affable, playful, fun-loving, brilliant–and yet intensely focused on his vision of e-commerce.

The Bezos powers of persuasion are formidable and derive from the openness, passion and electric energy that he communicates. He used these persuasive powers to recruit Shel Kaphan and Paul Barton-Davis, two first-rate computer people, to abandon high-paying secure positions to help him build Amazon.com. He also used his charm to lure Joy Covey from the Silicon Valley to Seattle where she helped put the financial affairs of Amazon.com in order. The persuasive nature of Jeff's personality has been a major factor in the success and the survival of Amazon.com.

When the Amazon.com web site was launched in July 1995, the web page claimed that this fledgling company was the "Earth's Biggest Bookstore." This brazen assertion belied the fact that the firm wasn't even a bookstore and was never intended to be. A single Barnes & Noble bookstore had more books on its shelves than Amazon had in its warehouse. Grandiose claims and what Trump would call "innocent hyperbole" defined the Bezos approach to promotion. To Jeff it was important that Amazon was perceived as larger-than-life and all promotions were aimed at creating the illusion of magnitude. Appearance was critical to his future so he had to look like a major player long before he was one. The promotions took advantage of consumer ignorance. Most book buyers weren't aware that by 1997, they could order any book in print on-line through barnesandnoble.com. By the end of the millennium, Jeff Bezos and Amazon.com had become inextricably identified with shopping in cyberspace.

INTUITIONAL STYLE: READY, FIRE, STEER

When Jeff Bezos quit his job in 1994 to follow his dream, most observers would have predicted a quick demise. His early business plans were intuitive and quantitatively imprecise. His financial plans could best be described as seat-of-the-pants-with-a-high-probability-of-losing-his-shirt. Practicing a highly frugal approach to expenditure, Amazon.com moved from garage to garage and then from warehouse to warehouse as the need for storage space increased.

The Amazon web site was developed in a similar by-gosh-by-golly fashion, characterized by a succession of trials and errors. This was an inevitable consequence of the fact that Amazon was sailing into uncharted waters with limited financial and human resources. Between 1995 and 1998, Amazon.com was in a predominantly reactive mode, responding to crises by redesigning software, rejigging processes, and compensating customers when systems failed. This style of business planning became known as "ready, fire, steer," compared with the traditional "ready, aim, fire." Jeff argued that getting too involved with "aiming" would ultimately stunt innovation. In the rush to get big fast, there was neither the time nor the resources to invest in detailed planning. What Jeff had was an idea and an instinct that would guide him through the turbulent, uncharted waters, and this became the style at Amazon.

The financial establishment would later express incredulity at his indifference to money. When the financial press tore him apart for losing money, he ignored their criticism. Finally he told the *U.S. News & World Report* (Feb. 2000) "It would be a terrible management mistake to be profitable now." His logic was lost on the masses and the self-serving classes, but Jeff Bezos continued to follow his instincts, with great success, into the new millennium.

CREATIVITY: OBSTACLES ARE OPPORTUNITIES

On occasion, the affable, ebullient boy wonder, Jeff Bezos, would display a Machiavellian bent. In the beta testing of their new web site, it was necessary to emulate a real-world situation in which a customer logs on, buys, pays for, and has delivered a chosen product. Jeff didn't have the available funds to engage an outside company to conduct a standard beta-testing research project. Therefore, he decided to test the system by using friends and family. The purchase of a single book presented a problem because the two giant distributors Ingram and Baker & Taylor adamantly refused to sell him just one book. As wholesalers, they insisted on a minimum shipping order of ten books. Undaunted, Bezos discovered that both distributors had an obscure book on lichens in their catalog, but it was out of print. So Jeff ordered the book he wanted plus nine copies of the book on lichens. The single book he wanted was shipped and the nine copies were placed on backorder and then subsequently dropped. Thus, Amazon.com found a creative solution to its beta-testing problem.

Using "innocent hyperbole," the Amazon.com web site claimed Amazon.com was "Earth's Biggest Bookstore." In response to this claim, Barnes & Noble launched a lawsuit claiming false representation on the basis that Amazon.com was not really a bookstore. Amazon.com countersued on the basis that by failing to charge sales taxes on books sold through barnesandnoble.com they were gaining unlawful advantage over Amazon.com. Both lawsuits were subsequently settled out of court. Bezos had found a weakness and it saved him. When asked about the lawsuit, Bezos said, "Frankly, I'm more concerned about two guys in a garage [than competition from the giants]." As grandpa Gise had taught him, there are no obstacles–if you are creative.

RISK-TAKING PROPENSITY: SWING FOR THE FENCES

Risk-takers are comfortable with ambiguity. They are special in that they get an "adrenaline rush," rather than a rush to the exit, when the going gets tough. When *Success* asked Bezos about his high-wire act in e-commerce, he responded, "High wire has never seemed impossible to me." Testimony to this was his ability to abandon a stable seven-figure income and pursue an entrepreneurial dream that threatened poverty from the outset. Few people have the temperament to get married and then quit their job a month later for some mysterious opportunity in a cyber-netherland. However, entrepreneurs are so inclined; the other 90 percent of the population are not. How did Bezos personally deal with the decision? He first looked deep within his soul and asked himself if this life was to be his destiny. In typical Bezos fashion, he formulated the dilemma as a strategic opportunity with both an upside and a downside and weighed the two using a process he labeled "regret-minimization framework." The strategic life opportunity as expressed in Bezos' words was, "If you feel you will one day regret not taking a chance, then take that chance." He took the chance, but with much reflection on what he would think when he was eighty-five.

What Bezos did was look at the risk of his move. The answer turned out that in his mind the greater risk–to his psyche–was in not doing it. That is the mindset of most great entrepreneurs. The risk seen by others is not perceived to them as a risk. They operate outside conventional sensitivity for risk-taking. The propensity for risk-taking is perhaps the key defining difference between leaders and followers.

Once Bezos was on the precipice of entrepreneurship, where risk and reward scenarios are played out daily, he knew he had to find people with a similar penchant for risk-taking. A potential executive who wasn't willing to live on the edge wasn't hired. Jeff told everyone, "We are swinging for the fences at Amazon. You should expect mistakes." No one was swinging for the fences more than he, since he had bet his marriage, savings, job and lifestyle on his dream in a strange new city and in a brand new industry.

INTENSITY: MANIACALLY FOCUSED

Though "hurry, hurry, hurry," is a theme common to the entrepreneurs profiled in this book and elsewhere, nowhere is the issue of time more critical than in the realm of cyberspace applications. Jeff Bezos had a vision of what he wanted to achieve, and that vision came with an intense urgency that he himself articulated to *Success* magazine (July 1998):

> *In high-growth arenas, speed is essential and a sense of urgency becomes your most valuable asset.*

Business Week described Bezos as "hyperkinetic." Virtually every great entrepreneur is in a perpetual hurry. Speed is their master and in Michael Dell's words, "There are only the quick and the dead." The Bezos mantra was: "Work hard, have fun, and make history. Wake up petrified and afraid every morning. I know we can lose it all. It's not a fear. It's a fact." Bezos is fiercely competitive and never takes the moderate route in any endeavor. During the early years, he wore every hat in the organization and seldom left the office. Dana Brown, head of ordering, often worked through the night ordering books. When the orders were finally transmitted at 4:30 in the morning, no one else was there except Jeff. She admitted to working 15 to 18 hours a day and told the media, "Jeff was always there. I never saw him go home."

Nick Hanauer said of Jeff (Spector, p. 230):

[He is] the most single-mindedly focused person I've ever met–to his detriment; it's all he cares about. He lives, eats, breathes Amazon.com. It occupies virtually his every waking moment. He is maniacally focused. I worry about his health. I worry about what he's going to be like when he's 50.

One worker at Amazon.com observed, "The attitude is, you can work long, hard, and well. At Amazon two out of three won't work." It seems that Jeff Bezos' maniacal focus had permeated the entire work environment at his brainchild company.

Self-Image: Strong Belief in Himself

One ex-Amazon employee told the media, "Jeff Bezos believes that the prospect of failure is incomprehensible." His willingness to stake everything on his dream shows the magnitude of his self-confidence. When Seattle attorney Tom Alberg was asked to consider investing in Amazon.com, he refused, but was so impressed with Jeff he took a seat on the Board of Directors. Bezos' infectious and optimistic persona was what drew Alberg to be part of the team. However, Alberg didn't invest because he believed that Amazon didn't stand a chance against the giant Barnes & Noble. He had said, "When they launch their web site they will crush Amazon." However, the ever-confident Bezos was not dissuaded and continued his onslaught until Alberg had to capitulate or leave. He stayed and invested. Jeff's strong belief in himself and his abilities to solve problems as they arise manifests as a self-confidence that inspires confidence in others. This inner confidence is an important dimension of his magically persuasive personality.

Eccentricities and Personal Paradoxes

The *New York Times Magazine* described Bezos as a "brilliant, charming, hyper and misleadingly goofy mastermind." As "poster child for internet commerce," as he is widely described, Jeff Bezos has cultivated the persona of an eccentric nerd whose brilliance is manifest in his weird laugh; his good-natured, self-deprecating affability; and his trappings of middle class impecuniosity.

There is a legion of stories about Jeff's frugality and his absent-minded professorial approach to business that belie his billionaire status and portray him as a middle-class cult figure. Among these is the story of Jeff's admonition, "We have a strong focus to spend money on things that matter to customers and not spend money on us." To this end, he constructed his own desk out of an 80-pound particle board door to which he attached four makeshift legs. The other office furniture was obtained from auctions or garage sales. He even suggested that small stickers be placed on such furniture to indicate how much was saved in its purchase. Bezos used his door-desk as a symbol of the frugality that Amazon.com practiced to preserve its focus on customer service.

Like Sam Walton, he flaunted his "everyman" image by driving a modest vehicle–for Walton, it was a truck; for Bezos it was a Honda Accord. There is an apparent contradiction between the external persona of Jeff as the child-like, goofy nerd who seems oblivious to the trappings of wealth, and the reality of the intensely-driven entrepreneur who strives with unrelenting focus to dominate all aspects of e-commerce in colossal Amazonian fashion. Leibovich observed (p. 91):

> *Bezos said he wanted Amazon to be an "intense" and "friendly" company, but he'd much sooner give up "friendly" than "intense."*

Perhaps one of the clearest insights into the multi-dimensional nature of the Bezos personality is captured by Mark Leibovich's description of a lunch he had with Jeff Bezos in June of 2001 in an Indian restaurant in Manhattan (Leibovich, pp. 102–3):

> *[After we finished our meal,] the waiter came over with a tray of hot washcloths. Bezos grabbed one, unwrapped it, and worked it furiously over his hands and face. And he couldn't stop. He ran the washcloth up and over his forehead, into his hair, down the back of his neck. He placed it under the front of his shirt...massaged the top of his chest, then his left armpit. He grunted slightly. People from other tables stared, but Bezos was oblivious....His eyes were closed and his head bobbed up and down. He discarded the washcloth onto the table with a satisfied flip. He left it with no regrets, sapped dry, as he rushed outside to a limousine that was waiting for him.*

ACHIEVEMENTS & HONORS

MAGNITUDE OF SUCCESS

When Bezos launched Amazon.com in July 1995, few expected him to survive, let alone become the dominant bookseller in the world. As a young man of 30, he gave up a seven-figure income on Wall Street and then put up $300,000 of family money to back his vision. Never one to sweat the small stuff, he went aggressively after Barnes & Noble and Borders. Few people of sane mind would have put up such money in a battle with giant booksellers.

By late 2001, Amazon had grown from zero customers in 1994 to over 35 million. Many were repeat customers, proving that the services were valued enough to guarantee future sales. Though sales for books and CDs have flattened in 2002, Amazon.com has branched into so many product arenas that it has become the largest on-line retailer in the world by far, with 40 to 50 million customers. It has approximately 15 million site visits per month compared with 6 million at the chief competitor, Barnes & Noble. With sales revenues approaching $6 billion, Amazon is exceeding its growth and revenue targets and is finally generating the long-awaited profits for its shareholders. The following table shows its remarkable exponential growth from its inception to the end of the millennium.

Year	Revenue	Loss
1995	$511,000	$303,000
1996	$15,700,000	$5,800,000
1997	$147,800,000	$35,500,000
1998	$610,000,000	$124,500,000
1999	$1,640,000,000	$350,000,000

The media has not let Jeff Bezos forget that the stock market made him a billionaire long before he has returned a profit to his investors. But the billions he is worth are as tentative as the fluctuating market. Investor pessimism can stifle growth and liquidity, thereby threatening the survival of his company. Through it all, Jeff Bezos has stayed focused on the long term. He implores impatient investors to remember that Amazon.com is in its infancy and that "it's not yet a teen-ager." His mantra has been, "Avoid instant gratification: it is short-term expediency."

Sam Walton, one of the greatest entrepreneurs of the 20th century, revolutionized the bricks-and-mortar marketing of goods. He did this by improving the efficiency of distribution and offering lower prices–what Jeff would call "first-phase automation." However, Jeff Bezos revolutionized the entire world of marketing by transforming it from the concrete world of bricks and mortar to the ethereal realm of cyberspace–a true example of "second-phase automation." In less than a decade, Amazon.com has ushered in a new era of marketing that has changed irrevocably how consumers will shop, order and pay for items that they use.

HONORS

Selected by *Time* magazine as Person of the Year in 1999, Bezos was featured on its cover. In that article, he was described as "the king of cybercommerce." At the time, Jeff was just 35 and the fourth youngest person to be so honored. Those who were younger were no less than Charles Lindbergh, Queen Elizabeth, and Martin Luther King.

Paul Saffo, director of Silicon Valley's Institute for the Future, described Jeff Bezos as "an extraordinarily thoughtful strategist," and commented (Leibovich, p. 93):

> *Jeff is launching this giant cruise missile in a general direction, but he doesn't know where it is going. He's inaugurated a business model of "Ready, Fire, Steer," not "Ready, Aim, Fire."*

His first employer, Graciela Chichilnisky, a Columbia University professor and fellow high-tech entrepreneur, told the media "I bet on Jeff Bezos' brain." In view of what Jeffrey Preston Bezos has been able to do in his first few decades of his life, it certainly seems to be a promising bet.

LESSONS LEARNED FROM JEFF BEZOS

Jeff Bezos is too young and too busy to have written his autobiography in which he presents the secrets of his success. However, many observers have studied his methods, interviewed his employees, and marveled at his revolutionary approaches to e-commerce that have defined the way companies will operate in this new cybernetic medium. A few brief but powerful lessons gleaned from these observations are presented below.

BUILD A CONSUMER-CENTRIC COMPANY

The old adage says, "give 'em what they want and they'll give you what you want." In Amazon's case Bezos gave customers a wide selection, a low price and the ability to buy conveniently with a fast turnaround. He began as a "customer-obsessed" boss and built a "consumer-centric" operation. Programmers were aghast when he insisted that the customer was always right even if they were wrong. That was what built Amazon. When you set out to make the customers' shopping unique and easier, it will ultimately show in sales.

His "customer-obsession" demanded that he hire people who were tolerant of obstreperous and obnoxious customers. The culture at Amazon was carefully built around the Amazon.com shopper. The organization's core competencies had to match those of boss Bezos. If personnel didn't match the mission, they were not hired. At Amazon, the customer was king and the employees were pawns who existed to serve the king's needs. Jeff's awareness of the special importance of customer satisfaction in the Internet medium came from his observation that a dissatisfied customer in a traditional store will tell five friends, while a dissatisfied customer shopping on the Internet may tell 5,000 or even 50,000 friends!

SACRIFICE NOW AND DOMINATE LATER

One of the tragedies of instant-gratification thinking is American's sad loss of the consumer electronic industry to the Japanese. The U.S. had pioneered the industry. Virtually every new product idea and patent was born in America. Televisions evolved out of the RCA patents and labs, stereos were pioneered at Ampex, transistor radios came out of Bell Labs, calculators evolved from work at Texas Instruments, and laser printers, PCs, the mouse, and other computer hardware were products of Parc Labs (Xerox) and others. Why did America lose what they had worked so hard to create? Because of short-term myopia! When Akio Morita came to America, he paid $25,000 on behalf of his company, Sony, for the transistor licensing rights for Japan. MITI and the Bell engineers who invented the transistor told him emphatically that he would be unable to build a transistor radio. He didn't listen and went on to destroy the American radio industry.

Later when Akio Morita was interviewed by the *Wall Street Journal,* he boldly told them, "If I were made dictator of America tomorrow, my first act would be to eliminate the quarterly report." What motivated such a strong statement? He had seen American executives making self-serving decisions like refusing to invest now for the future because it would hurt their bonuses. Morita wrote in *Made in Japan* (p. 197):

> *Management must be willing to take risks. I think Americans listen too much to the securities analysts.*

He personally witnessed the Japanese juggernaut that obliterated industry after industry merely by thinking long-term and without self-serving decisions by executives. In 1960, America was building about 90 percent of the world's consumer electronic products. In 1990, they built less than 5 percent. It had nothing to do with labor rates and all to do with strategic thinking.

Visionaries like Jeff Bezos are always willing to forfeit a little for a lot – the safe present for the opportunistic future. He continues to remind investors, "We are still in day one of the web world opportunities." He is prepared to sustain losses in the imminent future to gain market dominance and then use that advantage to yield substantial profits. Though many regard it as a somewhat risky and unstable business model, Bezos might argue that the short-term thinking of the past has taken a heavy toll on American business.

RECRUIT AND HIRE THE BRIGHTEST AND THE BEST

Bezos had learned at D. E. Shaw & Company the importance of hiring the brightest and best employees. As noted above, Amazon.com used highly rigorous hiring strategies to recruit the most intelligent and driven people who could be counted upon in turn to hire only first-rate employees. He once observed (Leibovich, p. 65):

> *If you start out with A's, [i.e., first-rate people] you get to keep A's. If you start hiring B's, B's hire B's.*

By exercising his greatest powers of persuasion, Bezos was able to recruit and hire a cadré of outstanding people whose A status guaranteed that a generous supply of A's would be hired as the company expanded. In 2003, when Bezos invested in spacecraft builder Blue Origin, the company published a Web site on which it advertised for employees, cautioning aspiring applicants with a note:

> *Our hiring bar is unabashedly extreme...each person occupying a spot must be among the most technically gifted in his or her field.*

The recruitment of the "super-talented" has been applied at Microsoft, where Bill Gates, acutely aware of the importance of hiring intellectual talent, stated (Wallace & Erikson, pp. 259–60):

> *Microsoft's favorite recruiting grounds were Harvard, Yale, MIT, Carnegie Mellon, and a little college near Toronto named the University of Waterloo, which specialized in mathematics ...Microsoft recruiters made personal visits to each of these schools in search of brilliant students, diligent and driven, who were cut from a cloth different from their peers. In short, Microsoft hired clones of its leader, over and over again.*

The productivity of Microsoft and Amazon.com attest to the wisdom of investing substantial time and money into recruitment and hiring.

PRESENT A CHARISMATIC PUBLIC FACE TO ENGENDER LOYALTY

Everyone who knows Bezos describes him as energy incarnate. He set out to make Amazon the dominant force in Internet marketing and became the poster child of Internet commerce. Spector opined (p. 179):

> *The Amazon.com story is a convergence of vision, intelligence, technology, money, and timing, but none of those elements would have mattered without Jeff Bezos' engaging personality, which was sold to the public and the investment community through one of the greatest and cleverest public relations campaigns in modern business history.*

The hard-driving intensity, the jocular eccentricity, the outrageous laugh, and most of all, the visionary passion conspire to create the persona of Jeff Bezos and present the public face of Amazon.com–a face that has done much to endear him to the public and engender customer loyalty.

Michael S. Dell

Avoid Convention and Traditional Dogmas

b. Houston, TX   February 23, 1965

"If you want people to think big, you need to act big."

SELF-DESCRIPTION

"I don't really think of running Dell as working"

"I'm guilty of doing too much, and not seeing mistakes coming"

MOTTOS

"Under-promise and over-deliver."

"Complexity kills and proximity pays."

"Sell direct–disdain inventory–customer is king."

INNOVATION	Selling PCs direct with high-quality customization Number one in the world in 2001 with $34 billion in sales
UNIQUE QUALITY	Ignoring conventional wisdom
OBJECTIVE	"I always knew I wanted to run a business someday."
NET WORTH	$20 billion (*Forbes*, 2001), billionaire at 31
HONORS	2001 Chief Executive of the Year (*Chief Executive Magazine*); Man of the Year (*PC Magazine* 2001) Entrepreneur of the Year (*INC* 2001) Top 25 Managers of the Year (*Business Week* 2001) Youngest CEO of *Fortune* 500 firm at 27
BIRTH ORDER	Middle child of orthopedic dentist (father) and stockbroker (mother)
EDUCATION	University of Texas in Pre-Med, completed one year while building a multi-million-dollar PC Business
PERSONALITY	Overachiever who prefers to be different
HOBBIES	Hunting and fishing
POLITICS	Apolitical
RELIGION	Agnostic
FAMILY	Wife: Susan, Children: four

12

Michael Dell

Avoid Convention and Traditional Dogmas

"Experts are self-serving and highly steeped
in maintaining the status quo."

"Think unconventionally and do exactly what the
competition tends to believe cannot be done."

Overview

In 1984, when Michael Dell was a freshman at the University of Texas, the personal computer industry was in its infancy. The computer giants–IBM, Compaq and Apple–were battling for supremacy in this fledgling market. Meanwhile, the 19-year-old Michael Dell was a teenager with a dream: to build a corporation that would challenge IBM!

In less than two decades, this aggressive teenager not only challenged the giants, but created the Dell Computer Corporation, a $30-billion company that had become the second largest manufacturer of computers in the world. In the process, he achieved a personal net worth of $20 billion and revolutionized the marketing of computer technology. How this young man with a vision rose to the top of the computer world and challenged the giants, using a start-up capital of $1000, is one of the greatest stories in the annals of business enterprise. In its magnitude, it outstrips the Horatio Alger tradition and in its reality, it attests to the efficacy of the free-enterprise system.

Defying conventional wisdom and daring to go where industry leaders would not was the underlying secret of Michael Dell's success. He realized, early in his ascent, that his core competency was not in building computers but in distributing them. He adamantly refused to manufacture anything except those components that he could not buy. This gave him an edge over those who were more bent on protecting their manufacturing plants than optimizing their talents. IBM had refused to change and it cost them dearly. Originally, they saw their core competency as the ability to build computers, but by early 2002, they finally capitulated and stopped making PCs. At that time they had revenues of $3 billion and were losing millions.

When asked by the media about his approach, Dell was candid:

> *We are in the server, notebook and workstation business. We are not in the motherboard or chassis business.*

While motherboards and chassis were key elements in building PCs, offshore firms could make them better and cheaper. It is never savvy to do anything someone else can do better. Dell understood this simple axiom.

IBM, Compaq and Apple vigorously denied the viability of bypassing their distributors and selling PCs direct. However, Michael Dell forced them to sit up and take notice when his direct marketing model enabled him to undercut their prices with computers of higher performance. By the mid-1990's, the Dell Computer Corporation was pioneering direct sales through the Internet and by the end of the millennium, their Internet sales exceeded $50 million per day!

In his 1999 book, *Direct from Dell*, Michael Dell reveals many of the marketing and organizational strategies to which he attributes the success of his corporation. While the essence of these is presented at the end of this chapter, the overarching theme that underpins Michael Dell's strategies is his reliance on research rather than opinion. When Dell decided to design a computer, he did not ask the experts what features it should contain. Instead, he asked the customers what they wanted. By focusing on empirical data gathered from prospective customers and reducing reliance on expert opinion, Michael Dell stayed closely in touch with the reality of the marketplace and increased his chances of success. The magnitude of his success offers undeniable validation of his approach.

The Formative Years

EARLY IMPRESSIONS

Michael Dell was born in Houston, Texas on February 23, 1965, the middle child of an upper-middle-class family. His parents programmed him to follow his older brother into the University of Texas School of Medicine. Michael's father was a practicing orthodontist, his mother, a successful stockbroker. Michael said that the evening meals of his youth were family gatherings that were replete with discussions of world affairs and their implications for stock markets and investment opportunities. His parents would often cite the most and least promising stocks in terms of the buying and selling opportunities they presented. These experiences helped Michael Dell understand at any early age many of the nuances of the business world.

With such a stimulating home environment, it is not surprising that the precocious Michael was in a hurry from a young age. Intuition taught him that the quickest and cheapest path to any goal was a straight line. While still in elementary school, he had discovered this principle and decided to apply it to his formal education. He wrote (*Direct from Dell*, p. xvi):

> When I was in the third grade, I sent away for a high school diploma. I had seen the advertisement in the back of a magazine: "Earn your high school diploma by passing one simple test," it said. It's not that I had anything against school; I liked third grade...but at that age, I was both impatient and curious. If there was a way to get something done more quickly and easily, I wanted to try it. And trading nine years of school for "one simple test" seemed like a pretty good idea to me.

When a salesperson showed up at the door of the Dell residence and asked to see Michael, she was shocked to find a precocious eight-year-old looking for a quick path out of high school. This need to get to the answer and move on in life was innate. It would spawn his later success in the world of personal computers.

The first entrepreneurial venture for young Michael Dell came when he was twelve. He discovered stamp collecting. To fund his entry into this venture, he took a job bussing dishes at a Chinese restaurant. Once he had the money to buy stamps, he began looking within the business of stamp collecting to find a way to make a profit. When he discovered a stamp catalog, allowing him to buy direct from other collectors, it occurred to him to bypass them and create his own auction. The enterprising youth talked his friends into giving him their stamps on consignment. Then he displayed them in a mail-order flyer that he sent off to stamp collectors. The Dell mail-order catalog was even advertised in *Linn's Stamp Journal*. In essence, at age twelve he had created his own direct-response catalog operation to sell a product without a middleman. He earned $2000 at a time when most kids were cutting grass for ice-cream money.

By age sixteen the young wunderkind was off on another innovation, only this time it was in delivering newspapers. Once again he took a non-traditional approach and by-passed conventional distribution methods. Prior to launching his newspaper venture, he spent weeks researching the best and easiest method of getting new customers. Selling newspapers wasn't important to him; selling the *most* was his dream. A small paper route was for other kids. He wanted to become an operator, not a delivery boy. Discovering that newly weds and new homebuyers were the most promising candidates for new subscriptions, he conceived a method by which he could maximize time and money. To obtain the names and addresses of newly-weds in the Houston area, he hired his friends to canvas the courthouses and land registry offices of the communities in and around Houston and record this information from public documents. It worked. In his senior year of high school (1982), Dell earned $18,000 from the sale of subscriptions to *The Houston Post*!

When his high school economics teacher assigned a project requiring the students to complete their tax returns on a real or fictional business, Michael declared his income from these subscriptions on his return. The teacher at first thought he had misplaced a decimal in reporting his earnings, but was dismayed to learn that not only was his income valid, it was more than she was earning as a full-time employee of the Texas school system.

FORMAL EDUCATION

Michael's junior high math teacher, Mrs. Darby, installed a computer terminal through which students could enter equations or programs. Michael was thereafter hooked on computers. After a long period of nagging and cajoling his parents, he was finally rewarded on his fifteenth birthday with his first computer–an Apple II. He immediately rushed to his room with his new computer and began to disassemble it to discover how it worked. On observing their expensive gift reduced to a chaotic array of components, his parents were infuriated. However, Michael was able to reassemble it and, in the process, learn its circuitry. When the IBM PC was introduced in 1981, he bought one, took it apart and reassembled it, once more increasing his understanding of the functions of the component parts.

Gradually, the aspiring entrepreneur became more interested in delving into computers than into schoolbooks. In 1982, at the age of 17, Michael skipped school for a whole week to attend the National Computer Conference, held that year in the Houston Astrodome. This proved to be the epiphany that transformed him from a future medical doctor into the preeminent entrepreneur that he is today.

When he walked into the conference, he was awe-stricken by the new technology. Michael soon discovered that he could buy the same parts as the large corporations like IBM could. Vendors like Intel and Seagate made the chips and hard drives that they would sell to anyone. He recognized the enormous potential of the personal computer market and saw that the demand was exceeding the supply. Unable to anticipate sales volumes, dealers would often overstock PCs. These surplus inventories of PCs, offered at substantial discounts, constituted what was called the "IBM gray market." Michael discovered that he could buy a stripped-down IBM PC from the gray market and upgrade it with components from distributors like Intel for a total cost of about $700. Furthermore, he knew that many people wanted computers that had more memory and more processing power than the standard IBM PCs that were selling in the $3000 range. This provided a margin that enabled him to upgrade and customize the basic PC to meet his schoolmates' needs and at the same time realize a tidy profit.

Michael spoke to resellers and retailers and soon discovered he knew more about what they were selling than they did. He realized that this presented an extraordinary business opportunity. How could others not see this vast opportunity? Anyone could buy parts. Those selling the PCs didn't know how to service them and were getting a ridiculous commission to sell a product they didn't understand. Why not make computers and sell them directly to those who wanted them? The computer shops bought a PC for $2000 and sold it for $3000. To a teenager, such profits seemed enormous.

In 1993, Michael Dell graduated from high school in Houston and entered the University of Texas. As he drove off to Austin, Texas, to take his pre-med classes, he was armed with three PCs in the back of his BMW. Experiencing mixed emotions about school and the world of entrepreneurship, he wrote, "I walked around campus with a book in one hand and a bunch of RAM chips in the other."

In November of his freshman year, Michael's parents paid him a surprise visit. They had correctly surmised that his grades were falling victim to his entrepreneurial activities. In his biography, Michael recreates the classic conflict between the goals of parents and their offspring (*Direct from Dell,* p. 10):

> *My Dad started. "You've got to stop with this computer stuff and concentrate on school," he said. "Get your priorities straight. What do you want to do with your life?"*
> *"I want to compete with IBM!" I said.*
> *He wasn't amused.*

Michael tried to rededicate himself to his studies, but his passion for following his dream drove him deeper into the computer world. After testing his instincts about the marketing advantage of selling direct, he completed his freshman year and then dropped out of school.

The Climb to the Top

LAUNCHED WITH PASSION

Michael's climb to the top had begun during his formative years, but his crossing of the Rubicon, the ultimate decision of his life, came in May of 1984 when he registered the Dell Computer Corporation (doing business as PCs Limited) just one week prior to completing his freshman year and leaving school and a medical career behind.

While a university student, Michael Dell had been earning gross revenues of between $50,000 and $80,000 a month from selling PCs that he upgraded by adding special components. By selling direct instead of through distributors, Michael was able to cut out the middleman and sell his computers cheaper than his competitors. This experience gave him a sense of the potential magnitude of the exploding market for the personal computer, although at that time he did not imagine just how large the market would become. He knew only that if he dedicated himself full-time to the enterprise, the potential rewards were virtually limitless.

With an initial investment of $1000, he founded the corporation and rented a 1000-square-foot office. He hired a few people to take telephone orders, a few to fulfill them, and others to build the upgraded PCs. In his own words (*Direct from Dell,* p. 13):

> *Manufacturing consisted of three guys with screwdrivers sitting at six-foot tables upgrading machines.*

Business was so strong that, within a year, the Dell Computer Corp-oration had graduated from the original 1000-square-foot office in a succession of moves to a 30,000-square-foot building. This rapid growth required Michael to hire staff at an accelerated rate. From early on, he recognized the importance of seeking talented individuals to whom he could delegate the hiring of other first-rate people.

One of his most insightful strategies was to require that his sales people set up their own computers. This helped them identify with the kinds of problems that their customers would experience and to better respond to their needs. Dell noted that this launched the corporation's reputation for excellent service–a reputation that Dell Computer has strived to maintain as its hallmark.

Through the mid-1980s, competition for PC market share intensified. PC companies sprang up like mushrooms and merely assembling components to produce upgraded machines was no longer sufficient to guarantee a share of the market. Components from different suppliers were often incompatible and quality control became more difficult. Also, the market was screaming for faster processing speeds. Michael Dell decided that if he could produce an IBM-compatible machine that was faster than the IBM PC, he would secure a distinct market advantage. IBM had 70 percent of the PC market with their 6-megahertz 286 PC that sold for $3,995, so Michael developed a 12-megahertz compatible machine that sold for $1,995!

When 21-year-old Michael Dell unveiled his new 12-mHz PC at the 1986 Comdex Show, it was the fastest PC on the market. The upstart had beaten IBM to the market with an innovative product. Suddenly the media took notice and *PC Week* put the new Dell machine on its cover.

From that experience Michael learned the importance of leading the pack and the value of promotion to growth. Being first to the market became a key Dell strategy. Michael wrote (*Dell*, p. 117 and p. 136):

> *I believe it is better to be first at the risk of being wrong than it is to be 100 percent perfect two years late...There's no risk in preserving the status quo–but there's no profit either.*

TIME TO REGROUP

The remarkable success of the new 12-mHz PC catapulted Dell into the forefront as a PC manufacturer by the end of 1986. Its sales in that year reached $60 million. However, in spite of this, Michael realized that the short-term planning that defined their operations to date would no longer guarantee the survival of Dell Corporation in the rapidly changing high-tech world of innovation and unpredictable markets.

To establish long-term goals and build a strategic action plan, Michael convened a brainstorming meeting in the fall of 1986. From that meeting emerged a plan that included a sales target of $1 billion to be reached in 1992. To achieve this goal, Dell Computer Corporation resolved to target the large companies by offering the best service in the computer industry. Typically, customers with computer problems were forced to take their computer to a PC dealer or the factory for diagnosis and repairs. However, Dell promised to send a representative to fix the computer on-site within twenty-four hours.

Another initiative to emerge from that brainstorming session was Dell's commitment to expand into the United Kingdom. The same compatibility and service problems that had plagued the PC computer market in the US in the early 1980s were still evident in the United Kingdom, so Michael saw a remarkable market opportunity. However, when Dell U.K. opened for business in June 1987, all but one of the 22 journalists at the press conference assured Michael Dell that his company would fail because direct marketing, in their opinion, was not viable in the British culture. However, Dell U.K. was profitable from its inception, becoming the dominant computer company in the U.K. by 1999 with annual sales of about $2 billion!

A CASH AND CRASH CRUNCH

The plan to target large corporations brought with it the need to fund large receivables and raise significant capital. To achieve this, the Dell

Computer Corporation sought to raise $20 million with a private offering to a small cadré of investors. On October 19, 1987, two days before the private placement would close, the New York Stock Market dropped over 500 points–a virtual crash! In spite of this, Dell's strong reputation and financial potential prevailed with the investors and the private placement added $21 million to Dell's coffers. Michael Dell retained 75% ownership in his firm.

Michael later noted (*Direct from Dell*, p. 33):

> *When we were completing our private stock placement in 1987, a noted industry analyst said we would never grow beyond $150 million in revenue. He was only off by a few zeros.*
>
> *It's fun to do things that people don't think are possible or likely. It's also exciting to achieve the unexpected. Our competitors didn't consider us a threat for a long time, providing us with an even greater opportunity to surprise them with our success.*

Such experiences led to Dell's motto: "ignore conventional wisdom."

At the time of the private offering, Dell Computers was still a fledgling operation. But this cash infusion jump-started its operation and Michael was able to begin implementing his plans. In June 1988, Dell Computer Corporation went public. This raised $30 million and brought the market value of the company to about $85 million.

MORE GROWING PAINS

Through the 1980s, the PC market had been a cottage industry with a large number of small computer companies competing for a slice. As the 1990s approached, Michael Dell realized that a consolidation phase was inevitable, in which the smaller companies would either disappear or be swallowed by larger companies. Though Dell Computer had already reached its annual sales target of $1 billion *before* 1992, this volume was not yet large enough to reduce the per unit cost of developing new innovative products. To survive the imminent global consolidation, Michael decided that the Dell Computer Corporation should grow its sales at an unprecedented rate, despite expert opinion to the contrary.

To achieve the desired growth, Michael priced his products aggressively and sought other methods of marketing. Abandoning Dell's unwavering commitment to direct selling, he embarked on indirect sales through the

Soft Warehouse and discount stores such as the Price Club and Sam's. The plan worked. In 1992, annual sales grew 127% to more than $2 billion. However, Michael realized that this exponential growth in sales had left the manufacturing and the processing functions of the company behind in their capacity to meet the exploding demands. Furthermore the expansion of the product line began to drain the cash reserves and undermine the company's profitability. For the first time in its history, Dell Computer Corporation sustained a quarterly loss. Its share price declined to $30.08, making a public offering an undesirable option for raising capital. The inevitable liquidity crunch followed in 1993 and it quickly became apparent that Dell Computer had to rethink its approach.

John Medica was hired in April 1993 to assess all the notebook products and decide which should be retained and which should be terminated. The result was the decision to cancel *all* the notebooks except the *Latitude XP*, and focus on that single product. The *Latitude XP* was equipped with a new lithium-ion battery that enabled the notebook to run for about four hours without recharging–double the life of the competing notebooks that had nickel-hydride batteries. The breakthrough technology of the lithium battery powered the *Latitude XP* to the top of the laptop world, boosting astronomically the profitability of that department in 1994.

Amidst its restructuring and the release of its *Latitude XP*, Dell Computer followed its expansion into Japan in 1993 with a further expansion into the Pacific Rim. By 1995, Dell had offices in fourteen countries in Europe, and was the second-largest computer company in the UK.

OPERATING ONLINE

The explosion of the personal computer market paved the way for the revolutionary development that we now know as the Internet. The ARPANET project, which had been funded by the US government in the 1960s to provide a communications link for computer science and engineering projects, had evolved through the 1970s and '80s into a commercial network used predominantly by university academics for email transactions. The development of the World Wide Web by Berners-Lee at the European Center for Nuclear Research in 1989 and the Mosaic browser by Marc Andreesen and his colleagues at the University of Illinois in 1993 created an "electronic superhighway" that enabled any user to communicate with any other user throughout the world. By the end of the 1990s, the Internet would become a communication network available to the entire global population.

Michael Dell realized the tremendous potential that the Internet offered in implementing the direct marketing strategies he had always espoused. He foresaw that customers would be able to go online, access information on products, and place orders directly without going through a middleman. Anticipating the new revolution in marketing now known as e-commerce, Dell Computer Corporation launched their web site, www.dell.com, in June 1994.

By 1996, slightly two years after their website launch, www.dell.com was generating about $1 million per day. By 1998, website sales had climbed to about $6 million per day and this figure is reported to have quintupled to $30 million in July 1999. By the year 2000, a mere six years after the website had been established, it was generating a staggering $50 million per day in sales.

Dell's Decade-by-Decade Climb

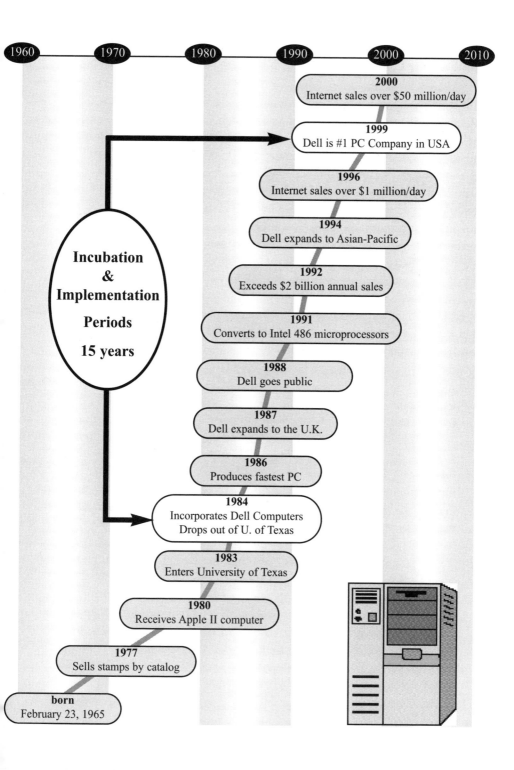

A *Personality Profile*

COMMUNICATION STYLE: DIRECT

Like his method of marketing, Michael Dell's style of communication is direct. He is frank about his failures, unabashed about his successes, and open about his beliefs, intentions and goals. He preaches, "In leadership, it's important to be intuitive, but not at the expense of facts."

The Dell operation is little more than the embodiment of the philosophy and principles of Michael Dell. He learned early that selling direct was a vital strategy in eliminating wasteful margins. Even more important, selling direct causes a more personal relationship between supplier and customer that is not possible in a two-step distribution system. These ideas permeate the firm from top to bottom.

Dell's adamant refusal to allow bureaucracy to become ingrained at Dell helped him more than any other strategy. Bigness is antithetic to growth because it involves committees in key decisions. In his own words (Dell, p. 133):

> *In fact, I believe that much of the confusion that occurs in corporations today stems from stymied communication and complex hierarchies. We're allergic to hierarchy. Hierarchical structure to me fundamentally implies a loss of speed. It implies that there is congestion in the flow of information...That's inconsistent with the speed with which we all need to make decisions, both as leaders and as a company, in this fast-paced marketplace.*

In emphasizing the importance of communications with suppliers, Michael Dell issues this admonition (Dell, p. 197):

> *Communicate directly with decision-makers: Talking candidly–and directly–with your suppliers is as crucial to the health and wealth of your business as communicating with your people and your customers.*

His style of communication reflects his style of operation and his style of marketing–both are direct.

Intuitional Style: Promethean

Great entrepreneurs are highly intuitive but tend to implement their dreams in rational terms. In other words, they are intuitive-thinkers on the Myers-Briggs personality scale and are metaphorical Prometheans. Such people are often capable of flip-flopping between their fantasies and their rational natures. They marry left-brain logic with right-brain vision. This unique ability to adapt to the situation makes them special. Entrepreneurs have a qualitative view with a quantitative rationality.

Writing for *Challenge*, Randy Ford said, "In the general population at least 80 percent favor the use of the left hemisphere of the brain." In the left side of the brain, detail and structure dominate decisions; in the right, the imagination is permitted to run rampant. The right side is the playground of the creative visionary and the zone that gives the entrepreneur a decided edge. In *The Psychology of Consciousness* (1986), Robert Ornstein wrote, "The artist, dancer, and mystic have learned to develop the non-verbal portion of intelligence and therefore have become creative."

It is apparent that Michael Dell operates with a right-brain overview. He sees the big picture in most things and uses his quantitative skills to structure his holistic view. In the PC downturn of 2001, Dell went where he had to go. He began selling PCs in kiosks in Texas malls, promoting them at $599 to the home market in a radical new ad campaign on the QVC TV shopping network. His renegade ad became a classic with an engaging generation X-er touting the benefits of Dell. QVC subsequently broke their one-day sales record for any product with sales of $80 million. That is the nature of entrepreneurial geniuses; they are driven toward opportunity and away from convention.

Risk-Taking Propensity

The Texas wunderkind was not a wild untrammeled risk-taker in the likeness of Ted Turner, Rupert Murdoch or Larry Ellison. Nor was he a classic high-roller like Richard Branson. However, his decision to abandon medical school to embark on a quest to challenge IBM was a significant risk-taking venture, especially in view of his parents' objections to his decision. Taking manageable risks is what Michael Dell has been willing to do, and he has also encouraged his executives to take risks so long as the risks are well-reasoned. Like Sam Walton, he understands the importance of allowing his executives to err without fear of retribution. As he observed (Dell, p. 127):

To encourage people to innovate more, you have to make it safe for them to fail...We have deliberately shaped our culture to accept continual "course corrections" on the learning curve because in order to thrive, we need an environment in which people feel it's okay to experiment.

He told *Fortune* magazine:

What sets Dell apart is its ability to do exactly what the competition tends to believe cannot be done...We are always willing to take the risk since we are a high-risk venture at Dell and we only hire people with a sense of adventure.

INTENSITY: AN OBSESSION WITH SPEED

Ever since childhood, Michael Dell has been on a mission of going further, being better and making a difference. Some call this an excessive drive, others passionate overachieving. No incident better depicts this characteristic than the occasion in the third grade when the audacious youth sent away for a test that would grant him a high school diploma. His desire to "trade in nine years of school for one simple test" reflects an uncommon sense of urgency at a remarkably early age.

The same intensity came to the fore when he launched the Dell Computer Corporation (doing business as PCs Limited) on January 2, 1984. Only 19, he was already selling PCs at the rate of $80,000 a month. Having outgrown his dorm room he had to stop or grow further. He opted for the brass ring. Then he surreptitiously rented a condo off-campus, not daring to tell his parents. One week prior to taking his freshman final exams in May 1984, he was on his way and formally incorporated Dell Computer Corporation. The wannabe entrepreneur wrote (Dell, p. 13):

Convincing my parents to allow me to leave school would have been impossible. So I just went ahead and did it, whatever the consequences. I finished my freshman year and left.

Dell's internal operating strategy has been one of "velocity." Velocity means speed: speed to answer the customers' needs and wants, speed of inventory turnover, speed with vendors, speed with new product introductions, speed to market and speed of gaining dominance in the highly competitive world of computers. No other industry is so wrapped up in speed, and no other firm has made speed so important to their future.

"In our industry," Dell explains, "if you can get people to think about velocity then you can create real value." At meetings he says, "You're either quick or you're dead in managing inventory." Why? Because inventory in the high tech world is like ripe fruit, it will never be worth more than it is today. Treat it like a ripe banana and get it out of the building or it has a tendency to spoil.

Dell elaborates on his rationale for his focus on speed when he says:

> *Component costs decline in value an average of one-half to one percent per week.*

This causes the management at Dell to be more "real-time" than "just in time." He observes (Dell, p. 198), "A little too late is just too late in most businesses today." This attention to velocity has worked well as Dell was able to reduce his inventory to a remarkable level of six days–this in a billion-dollar capital equipment firm.

SELF-IMAGE: A STRONG SELF-CONFIDENCE

To be successful you must believe in your dream. When you believe, you can do more than is otherwise possible. Your thinking becomes contagious and pervades those around you. As a freshman at the University of Texas in 1983, Michael Dell believed he could beat IBM. When his concerned parents visited him in his dorm to find PC parts instead of textbooks, he told a disbelieving dad, "I want to compete with IBM and build better computers than they can." Most people would chalk up such a statement as pure ignorance or the ramblings of a braggart. But the 18-year-old saw the giant's weakness while other more astute participants in the industry never did.

Dell never once questioned his ability to achieve his goals. His optimism became a self-fulfilling mental state. What did a teenager know about running a multi-million dollar enterprise? Nothing! But when one is confident, the natural errors become learning instruments, especially when one is not too proud to ask for help. Armed with a powerful sense of self, Dell refused to back off his direct sales strategy even when the experts kept saying that he was just a flash in the pan and would not last. Most executives in their early 20s would have capitulated to such assaults. Dell never did.

This was never more poignant than in 1997 when industry kingpin Larry Ellison of Oracle predicted the demise of the personal computer. He alarmed Wall Street and even industry pundits with his claim that his dumb terminal NC (Network Computer) would utilize the Internet to download all software, making the PC obsolete. Michael was unperturbed and never spent the millions that his competitors did in building their own NC product. Michael had grown up using and developing personal computers and believed the market wasn't about to abandon word processing and other personalized functions that were hard-wired into the personal computer. Only someone with a very high self-esteem could have taken a contrarian view against one of the richest and most prestigious figures in the hi-tech world.

CRITICAL THINKING: A CONTRARIAN

When he contemplated expansion into Europe and Asia in the 1980s, people warned Michael that the direct model of selling would not work in those regions because such marketing was contrary to their cultures. The maverick Texan went ahead in spite of this advice and succeeded beyond his wildest dreams. He expressed the lesson gleaned from this experience as a personal maxim (Dell, p. 29):

> *The lesson is: Believe in what you're doing. If you've got an idea that's really powerful, you've just got to ignore the people who tell you it won't work, and hire people who embrace your vision.*

In his book, Dell explains in precise detail how to run a corporation that encourages participation from all employees toward a shared corporate goal. He cautioned that "Functions build fiefdoms"–a prescient insight for one so young. He eschewed empire building and segregated authority and responsibility. His reasoning was, "We're a bunch of entrepreneurs who work as a team." He felt that the flat-line organization offered less opportunity for the evils of bureaucracy. Dell proudly points out, "Our employees are owners and to be an owner you have to think like one." He told *Fortune*, "The thing that sets Dell apart is its ability to think unconventionally."

ECCENTRICITIES AND PERSONAL PARADOXES

When Michael Dell set out on his quest to challenge IBM, his dream was to build an enterprise. Though accumulating wealth was a goal, it was not his ultimate goal, for long after he had more money than he could ever spend, he continued to strive to build and expand his corporation. Michael Dell's passion was to create a successful enterprise; the money was a pleasant by-product of this passion and a way of measuring its success. In this way, Dell was typical of the many great entrepreneurs who pursued their passions rather than focusing on making money. The money came and when it came it was a deluge. Ironically, it is often observed that the direct pursuit of money itself usually fails to succeed. This counter-intuitive phenomenon has been studied by the psychiatrist Viktor Frankl who coined the term *paradoxical intention*.

Frankl studied impotent men in Germany. His work led to a new school of therapy he labeled *Logotherapy*, which has an underlying theme based on the principle of paradoxical intention. He discovered that the harder the men tried, the harder it was for them to perform. Only when they stopped trying could they perform. He wrote (Frankl, p. 147):

> *Logotherapy bases its technique called "paradoxical intention" on the twofold fact that fear brings about that which one is afraid of, and that hyper-intention makes impossible what one wishes.*

Not only psychiatrists but also sports psychologists have found that the harder you try the worse you do. Any golf professional will tell you that swinging a golf club harder doesn't make the ball go farther. The same is true of getting a date, writing a novel, inventing a product, coping with stress, or even coping with impotence. Optimum success occurs in any venue when one sets a goal, forgets it and then focuses on the mission at hand. Michael Dell set out to build a company that would challenge IBM and ended up with a mountain of money as a by-product of this passion.

ACHIEVEMENTS & HONORS

MAGNITUDE OF SUCCESS

At age 27, Michael Dell became the youngest CEO of a Fortune 500 company–the very company he founded eight years earlier with an investment of $1000! Even more incredible is the fact that he achieved this in an industry famous for devouring neophyte start-ups. In 1996, Michael Dell became a billionaire. In July 2001, *Forbes* listed him as one of the top ten richest people in America with a net worth of $20 billion. He is frequently referred to as "the richest man in Texas."

Because Dell never knew too much to know he couldn't, he was never afraid of the IBM computer giant, deferentially nicknamed "Big Blue." Once the established computer titan saw Dell's shadow, it was too late.

By 1999, Dell Computer Corporation was the number one PC company in the United States and by 2000, its sales on the Internet exceeded $50 million per day. By 2001 *Fortune* ranked Dell as the 78th largest firm in the United States and #210 worldwide. Speed and quality of customer service distinguished Dell from the traditional firms.

Editorial director of *Chief Executive Magazine* John Brandt wrote:

> *Dell changed the nature of the PC industry he's in. He made a virtual company into a reality.*

Michael himself once bragged (busfans.com2002), "We beat Sun, we beat IBM, we beat Compaq, we beat 'em all."

By his mid-thirties, Dell was heading the most successful personal computer company in the world. When queried about his future, he responded that he was not about to retire to play with his four children.

How did a young Texan with little formal education, no formal computer training, no money and no backing, beat out the likes of Apple, IBM and Compaq? First, he never questioned his ability and learned early not to follow traditional forms of marketing when the market suggested alternative possibilities. When the so-called "experts" told him not to try something radically different, he ignored their advice and followed his instincts.

Michael Dell, like Thomas Edison and Andrew Carnegie long ago, started out by telling everyone exactly what he planned to do. But his ambitions were discounted as those of an impetuous young entrepreneur who would soon learn the penalties of challenging the status quo. Edison had told everyone, "Come right into my lab and see my experiments. I have no secrets." Andrew Carnegie had a similar predilection. "Let them take my factories and my ideas, but let me keep my mind and I'll be back in a few years."

Dell told everyone that he planned to pass on the 25–40 percent retail margins to the consumer by going around the middleman and selling direct. "Eliminate the middleman" was his mantra. For years the big boys ignored him. But in 1997 when IBM, Compaq and Apple heard the footsteps and announced they would begin selling direct, he was finally recognized as an entrepreneurial genius and a tough adversary.

HONORS

In 1991, J. D. Power & Associates ranked Dell Computer Corporation #1 in customer satisfaction. In 2001 Dell was named Chief Executive of the Year by *Chief Executive Magazine*. In the same year he was named Entrepreneur of the Year by *Inc.* magazine. He has been named Man of the Year by *PC Magazine* and was included as one of the Top 25 Managers of the Year by *Business Week*.

LESSONS LEARNED FROM MICHAEL DELL

In his book *Direct from Dell*, Michael presents the following "golden rules" that he offers as maxims to aspiring entrepreneurs.

DELL'S GOLDEN RULE #1: SELL DIRECT

Dell Computer was launched on the principle of taking advantage of an inefficient distribution system for computers. Had one of the industry leaders seen what Michael Dell saw, there might never have been a future for Dell Computer Corporation. Their oversight became his advantage.

Apple, IBM and Compaq were married to long-term distribution arrangements and were reticent to destroy such valued relationships. Dell never had any such allegiances and saw the inefficiency of existing channels as his opportunity to go direct. In his own words (*Direct from Dell*, p. 23):

> *There's a real productivity advantage in the direct model because of the way the sales cycle works. In the indirect model, there are two sales forces: sales from the manufacturer to the dealer, and sales from the dealer to the customer. In the direct model, we have just one sales force, and it's totally focused on the customer.*

From the beginning Dell knew he was going to be different and sell direct. There was no way he would be able to compete with the support functions to the resellers and retailers like his adversaries so he wasn't about to try. His edge was that he had enough margins saved by going direct to provide support needed for his direct customer base.

DELL'S GOLDEN RULE #2: DISDAIN INVENTORY

Selling direct obviates the need to maintain large inventories of product, enabling a company to manufacture on an "as-needed" basis. There are no dealers who require inventory and therefore no need to stockpile huge quantities of product. This frees up capital that would otherwise be tied up in storage facilities. Furthermore, the shelf lives of items in the computer industry is remarkably short and maintaining large inventories can be financially disastrous. Dell Computer Corporation learned this fact the hard way in 1989, when they bulk-purchased more 256K computer chips than needed for the short term. When the 1 Mb chips hit the market, demand for the 256K chips plunged and with it their prices. Dell Corporation was left with a large inventory of chips that it subsequently had to resell at a loss. This hurt their profitability and forced them to raise their prices to compensate for these losses. After that lesson, Dell embraced the golden rule, "disdain inventory," and focused on improving inventory flow as a key business strategy.

DELL'S GOLDEN RULE #3: ALWAYS LISTEN TO THE CUSTOMER

Michael Dell's success derived from selling direct and making sure the customer's satisfaction was paramount in every transaction. In this regard, he often emulated two successful firms–FedEx and Nordstrom–both known for having mastered the customer experience.

Dell labeled his strategic business platform *virtual integration*–a methodology of real-time information feedback from valued customers to ensure that his innovations were congruent with customer needs. He observed (Dell, p. 221):

> *Virtual integration is essential to the process of delivering the optimal customer experience, as it requires a truly integrated effort among all the companies with which you work.*

At Dell, virtual integration means involving all personnel in the system with their counterparts above and below, including vendors and the customer. That is the firm's core mission. In this way, Michael has identified the customer as the focal point of all decisions. The success of the Dell approach reminds business that pleasing the customer is ultimately the critical factor in determining if a company will survive and thrive.

Dell's Business Model

In explaining the rationale for the three golden Dell rules, Michael Dell observed (Dell, p. 22):

> *While other companies had to guess which products their customers wanted, because they built them in advance of taking the order, we knew–because our customers told us before we built the product...Because we didn't have the extra cost of the dealer or the associated inventory, we were able to offer great value to our customers and expand rapidly. And with every new customer, we gathered more information about their product and service requirements. It was the perfect closed loop.*

Dell's "closed loop" is displayed in the flow chart below.

Dell's domination of the personal computer world offers credence to this simplified business model that eliminates all the needless layers between the maker and the consumer. Dell makes it simple to communicate with them, to order, to install and to get support. That is the essence of selling. Make it easy for your customers to buy from you and they will make it easy for you to sell to them.

The ultimate Dell legacy may be: Refuse to listen to experts. By doing so, Michael Dell has changed the way computers are marketed and sold. He achieved this by being innovative, fast, focused and responsive to the customer. In a feature article celebrating Michael Dell's success at the end of the millennium, *Time* magazine observed:

> *Dell is to the computer industry what Dominoes is to pizza delivery: fast, dependable, and ubiquitous.*

Fortune magazine mused:

> *It's scary to think where Michael Dell is going to be in ten years. He's going to be a powerhouse in the computer industry after Lou Gerstner's successor's successor retires.*

13

The Psychology of Entrepreneurship

"An entrepreneur is someone who works sixteen hours a day for himself
[herself] to avoid working eight hours a day for someone else."
–Anonymous

As the world enters the information age and the era of the global
economy, it is becoming increasingly more evident that economic national survival in a competitive world depends heavily
on the entrepreneur. Countries that grow and nurture the entrepreneurial
spirit will continue to flourish, providing employment, an increased standard of living and ultimately individual wealth. This recognition of the
importance of entrepreneurship has brought to the fore a variety of questions centered around the psychological factors that generate and nurture
entrepreneurship. Many disciplines, particularly business and management studies, study questions such as:

- Are entrepreneurs born or bred?
- If entrepreneurs are bred, what are the psychological factors
  that generate and nurture their entrepreneurial growth?
- How do entrepreneurial geniuses evolve?
- In what ways, if any, do the personalities of entrepreneurs differ
  from the rest of the population?

This chapter summarizes some of the research pertaining to these
questions and uses the profiles of the entrepreneurial geniuses featured in
this book to clarify and support the conclusions presented.

Are Entrepreneurs Born or Bred?

IS ENTREPRENEURIAL TALENT CORRELATED WITH IQ?

The use of IQ as a measure of intelligence has recently been at the center of widespread controversy among psychologists and other scholars. When first conceptualized by Alfred Binet and formalized as a quotient by Stern in 1912, IQ was intended as a device for identifying those children in the French schools who required remedial instruction. Since it is readily observed that some people can learn and grasp concepts more quickly and deeply than others, it would seem that there is, in fact, a general innate propensity to learn that differs from one individual to the next–a "general intelligence." Psychologists referred to this general intelligence as the *g factor**. If such an innate quality exists to varying degrees in individuals, then it would seem reasonable that it could be measured and represented quantitatively. Hence, throughout the 20th century, IQ was used to assess individual intelligence for a variety of purposes.

In 1994, two Harvard psychologists, Herrnstein and Murray, published a tome titled *The Bell Curve: The Reshaping of American Life by Difference in Intelligence*. In asserting that IQ is essentially heritable and in characterizing races by IQ, this treatise touched off a maelstrom of controversy that challenged the notion of IQ itself as a useful measure of intelligence. Among the criticisms lodged against the concept of IQ was the challenge to the assumption that human intelligence can be represented on a linear scale, allowing any two people to be compared relative to their IQ's. Questions such as "Who was smarter, Einstein or Mozart?" would seem to be determinable by merely administering an IQ test. However, one school of psychologists argued that proclivities for scientific investigation and musical creation represent different kinds of talents or "intelligences." Howard Gardner, Professor of Education at Harvard University, and others proposed the existence of "multiple intelligences," i.e., that intelligence is a multi-dimensional quality having at least seven different components. This would mean that entrepreneurial talent could be distinct from cognitive talent and may have little correlation to it. From his research, Gardner reported:

> *Highly creative people are more likely to stand out in terms of personality rather than sheer intellectual power. They differ from their peers in ambition, self-confidence, and passion about their work.*

---

*g was taken to stand for the first letter in the word "general."

Andrew Hacker, Professor of Political Science at Queen's College, opined:

On the whole, most such persons [with high IQ scores] will peak during their academic years, or perhaps during an initial job they receive on the strength of test results. However, after that they will soon be surpassed by individuals who possess more applied forms of intelligence that are not revealed by tests that are taken while sitting at desks. People like George Patten, Lee Iacocca, and Newt Gingrich come to mind.

Further support for the concept of multiple intelligences comes from American psychologist Paul Torrance (*Redbook,* March 1987):

Above 115 or 120, IQ scores have little or no bearing on creativity. Creative giftedness may be found anywhere along the scale, except possibly at the bottom.

In *The Ingenuity Gap* (p. 219), Homer-Dixon says that only 10 percent of success is attributable to IQ. In *Intelligence Framed* (1998), Howard Gardner wrote, "The right set of genes hardly suffices to yield a creator." In a University of California study, Frank Barron researched the influence of variables like intelligence on innovative success. He asserted,

For certain intrinsically creative activities, a specific minimum IQ is necessary to engage in the activity at all, but beyond that minimum, which is surprisingly low, creativity has little correlation with scores on IQ tests.

There is no doubt that Getty, Fuller, Stewart and Trump were above average in intelligence, perhaps not in the class of an Einstein in terms of IQ, but talented, and that IQ had relatively little to do with their later success. Only Buckminster Fuller used predominantly high-level cognitive ability in his work. His innovations in engineering, manifest in the geodesic dome and his Dymaxion Car, were products of a creative intellect*.

There seems to be consensus among scholars that there is a positive correlation between IQ and entrepreneurial talent for IQs up to 115 (i.e., within one standard deviation of the mean) but the correlation is weak for IQs above 120. This suggests that entrepreneurial genius is only weakly correlated with IQ.

---

*It is ironic that he is the one who was demeaned most by the intellectuals who never forgave him for daring to contribute to a field in which he had no formal pedigree.

While most will concede that IQ is partially attributable to inheritance, fewer would attribute entrepreneurial talent to genetic factors. Even longevity, long believed to be attributable to genetic factors, has been shown to be 30 percent attributable to genetics and 70 percent attributable to lifestyle and behavior. This author is convinced that entrepreneurial genius is even more skewed towards lifestyle and behavior with as much as 90 percent derived from experience and only a 10 percent contribution from some predisposition such as IQ or innate talent.

Do Entrepreneurs Spawn Entrepreneurial Offspring?

A great deal of data pertains to the influence of a self-employed parent on an aspiring entrepreneur. A 30-year longitudinal study at the Institute for Personality Assessment & Research at the University of California at Berkeley of a database of architects found that those who had acquired high levels of self-reliance at an early age were typically raised in an environment with one or more parents who were self-employed. Other studies have shown that such individuals are more likely to be independent, self-sufficient, and able to cope with ambiguity. Young people steeped in such environments grow up to be more self-reliant, confident, resilient and competent to make their own way in life. Conversely, when the income-earning parent or parents work in the employ of others, the offspring are more likely to seek employment rather than pursue entrepreneurial ventures.

Almost all of the twelve entrepreneurs profiled in this book had self-employed fathers who instilled the ethic of self-sufficiency. At an impressionable age they looked to their primary role model and saw someone who was not dependent on someone else for their livelihood. Though it could be argued that the greater tendency for entrepreneurs to issue from entrepreneurial parents is evidence that a propensity for entrepreneurship is heritable, the conclusion that environmental factors play a greater role seems more plausible.

What Factors Generate Entrepreneurship?

EARLY IMPRINTS

Early imprinting experiences in the formative years played crucially important roles in the later achievements of the twelve entrepreneurs profiled in this book. These experiences came in many forms, including doting parental influence, laissez-faire environments that provided freedom to explore, and a myriad of other factors such as birth order, early trauma, transiency and exposure to fictional heroes. Every subject in this study turned out to be a higher achiever than their parents; in fact their success dwarfed that of their parents.

The consequences of success imprints found in the entrepreneurial genius–those qualities that make such individuals unique and different–are drive, ego, charisma, temerity, tenacity and intuition. The perfectionism that made Hefner, Trump and Stewart successful was not significantly different from the inner passions that drove Edison, Ford and Walton, and not far from the eccentricities that made Coco, Getty and Branson rich and famous. Such personality characteristics are imprinted early, for example, when an eight-year-old is told by an authority figure she is "a super worker" or when an aunt tells a young child, "You are sure competitive." Our prisons are full of individuals whose parents have told them "You're bad." The majority of children grow up to fulfill an internal self-image programmed early by the simplest comments on an impressionable psyche.

Recall that Henry Ford at age 12 was inspired by the horseless carriage near his Michigan farm. He jumped down off his father's horse-drawn wagon and was mesmerized by the sight of a self-propelled vehicle. Fifty years later he would write that, from that moment, he was hooked on the concept of a motor car and his life was transformed.

Ross Perot experienced a different success imprint. At age seven his father tutored him on the art of breaking horses, with the caveat that he would break them or they would break him. It was in this environment that he developed the belief that one must master one's fears or be mastered by them. After some physical trauma and several fractures, he emerged a leader instead of a follower. Those experiences instilled a "can-do" attitude in Perot that never waned.

Michael Dell learned the art of selling direct and violating the norm at age 12 when he formed his own direct-response stamp catalog. He discovered that he could by-pass traditional sales distribution channels and be successful. Twenty years later he would write, "I first experienced the power and rewards of being direct when I was twelve years old" (Dell, p. 3). No wonder he was able to go to battle with giant IBM at 19.

Richard Branson was molded into a risk-taking maverick by an iconoclastic mother. Eve Branson worked diligently to ensure that her son would be prepared to tackle life's challenges head on. When Richard was eight, Eve drove him across London where she deposited him in a park and told him to find his way back home. Eve knew she was flirting with disaster, but felt the learning superceded the risk. When Richard was 10 years old, Eve drove him 50 miles from home and left him with a sandwich and a bicycle to navigate his way back. Eve's conditioning of Richard worked. When you survive such challenges early in life, the ability to start your own magazine at eighteen is already developed. True to the programming, Branson grew up as a fearless entrepreneur willing to undertake any new venture. Ever since those early experiences Richard has never been lost, even when he didn't know where he was–either in a balloon or in business.

One of Sam Walton's imprints came in high school. As a quarterback, he learned to win and never expected to lose, even when the competition was tough. Walton wrote in his memoirs. "I never played in a losing football game in high school. I think that had an important effect on me. It taught me to expect to win." Just as Walton was programmed for winning, Martha Stewart was programmed for perfection. J. Paul Getty's father made a lasting impression on his twelve-year-old son by giving him shares of oil stock and saying, "You are now my boss." Getty grew up with a need to own lots of oil stocks so he could be in control of his destiny.

A different kind of programming–mythical hero-mentoring–exerted its influence on Coco Chanel. When living in an orphanage, Coco escaped into Claudine novels, about a poor country girl who comes to Paris to find fame and fortune. Coco wrote, "I became Claudine." All these case studies reveal that formative imprinting experiences play a key role in developing life-long goals and behaviors. They are the first sparks that ignite the passion that fuels a lifetime of achievement.

GENDER INFLUENCE

The greatest imprinting influence came, most often, from the parent of opposite gender. Groomed by a fearless mother, Richard Branson grew into an untamed business icon. Eve Branson, a flight attendant when flying was more for thrill than transportation, spent many hours grooming her first born to live on the edge. He rose to meet her challenges and succeeded beyond her wildest expectations as a flamboyant risk-taking entrepreneur.

Martha Stewart dedicated her first book to her father. He was her mentor, friend, confidante and role model for perfection. His influence, both positive and negative, molded the Daytime Diva into an overachiever. Henry Ford attributed all of his success to his mother and named his most famous plant for her homeland. As a teenager Sam Walton ran a business with his mother. Michael Dell's mother, who was also a stockbroker, gave him the incentive to pursue business instead of medicine.

Among those influenced by a parent of the same gender, Ross Perot learned the art of salesmanship from his cotton-broker father and J. Paul Getty learned the nuances of the oil business from his attorney father. Donald Trump learned the real estate business under the tutelage of his father. Jeff Bezos, however, was most influenced by his maternal grandfather while spending summers on the elder's Texas ranch. These experiences nurtured the self-reliance that served him as he resisted pressure from Wall Street to declare profits.

In the stories of almost all the entrepreneurs profiled, we see the presence of a strong parent, usually of the opposite gender, mentoring or providing formative experiences. This influence nurtures personality traits and inculcates values that the child internalizes and are manifest decades later in the adult entrepreneur.

SOCIO-ECONOMIC INFLUENCE

In exploring the origins of personality, evidence leans more heavily toward nurture rather than nature. For many reasons, experience emerges as the more critical factor in learning anything from hitting a ball to hitting the boardroom. Being born with a silver spoon is not only unimportant, it can be a detriment to becoming an entrepreneur since it inhibits the learning of the vital survival skills. Virtually all the entrepreneurs profiled in this book came from the middle class and several came from the lower middle class. Coco Chanel, in particular, grew up in an orphanage and spent her entire life compensating for early impecuniosity by spending recklessly. Since the French placed such a high value on prestigious titles and social class, Coco's climb to the top of the imperious world of haute couture was even more remarkable. Coco paid off her siblings to keep her impoverished past a mystery and enable her to maintain a romantic mystical aura. Her adolescent fantasies, spawned by the Colette novels, ultimately became her reality. Rather than an impediment to her success, Coco's lack of economic status in her formative years served as a catalyst, fueling her need to penetrate high society and alter the pompous and affected styles so prevalent in turn-of-the-century Paris.

Others reared without money were Sam Walton, Ross Perot, and Martha Stewart. All worked diligently to build wealth, molding themselves into workaholic overachievers in their quest to overcome a haunting fear of failure. As a teen, Stewart promised that she would grow up to have servants in her household. She succeeded. All the Americans profiled were raised in the vast middle class. Getty, Fuller, Trump and Dell were from the upper middle class and benefited from bigger houses, boarding schools, and nicer vacations. However none were immersed in the country-club mentality. Only Getty and Trump made their mark, albeit a much larger one, in the same profession as their fathers.

MARRIAGE AND CHILDREN

The twelve entrepreneurs in our study tended to marry at roughly the same age as the general population; the median age was 24 (national median 25). Only Martha Stewart married in her teens. Of the others, Donald Trump was the oldest at 31 followed closely by Jeff Bezos at age 30. The entrepreneurs were below average in number of marriages with only four having more than one spouse. J. Paul Getty was a rake with the statistical distinction of having five wives (three of whom were teenagers when he married them) and as many as five mistresses simultaneously during his 60s and 70s. Coco Chanel never married. Chanel had no children but the other eleven had 33, averaging three each. Getty and Perot led with five children. Dell, Trump and Walton had four. Almost all of these entrepreneurial geniuses were highly libidinous, possessing sex drives that either derived from or contributed to their productivity.

FORMAL EDUCATION

Three of these highly successful entrepreneurs never made it through high school. Most were bright, but not brilliant. The parents of Coco

Chanel, Sam Walton and Martha Stewart were gross underachievers. The fathers of Getty, Trump and Dell were successful, but not to the extent of their famous offspring. All of these entrepreneurial geniuses took 8 to 10 years to learn a discipline. A similar time elapsed before they were able to master and apply it. However, in virtually all cases the learning took place outside formal institutions and in the arena of real experience.

The relationship factors that generate entrepreneurial genius are summarized in the table below.

RELATIONSHIP FACTORS OF ENTREPRENEURIAL GENIUS

Subjects	Father's Profession	Socio-Economic Status	Number of Marriages	Age: First Marriage	Total Number of Children
Jeff Bezos	Exxon executive	Middle class	1	30	1
Richard Branson	Lawyer	Middle class	2	22	2
Coco Chanel	Itinerant gypsy	Lower class	0	N.A.	0
Michael Dell	Dentist	Upper-middle class	1	24	4
Henry Ford	Farmer	Lower-middle class	1	22	1
Bucky Fuller	Merchant	Upper-middle class	1	24	2
J. Paul Getty	Lawyer	Upper-middle class	5	29	5
Hugh Hefner	Accountant	Middle class	2	23	4
Ross Perot	Auctioneer cotton broker	Middle class	1	26	5
Martha Stewart	Sales	Lower-middle class	1	19	1
Donald Trump	Developer	Upper-middle class	2	31	4
Sam Walton	Farming	Middle class	1	23	4
Averages (medians)	Self-Employed 83%		1	24	3

How Do Entrepreneurial Geniuses Evolve?

FROM INCUBATION TO IMPLEMENTATION AND THEN EMINENCE

The concept of "instant success" is a myth. First one must learn a craft and then take the time to master it. For this reason, it pays to start early. If you do, your chances of success are significantly enhanced. There is an incubation period in the climb to success that educators call a *learning curve*. While traveling along the learning curve, the learner acquires skills and knowledge that eventually ripen into a mastery that serves as a reservoir or database that will be tapped throughout the learner's life. Harvard's Howard Gardner studied great creative geniuses like Albert Einstein, Martha Graham and Pablo Picasso and found the incubation period to be about ten years. The entrepreneurs profiled in this book similarly took approximately ten years (median time interval) to go from their first learning experiences to the launch of their major enterprise.

On average, these entrepreneurs began the first business ventures, in their ultimate field of specialization, at a median age of 20.5 years, allowing them to implement their learning at a median age of 28.5 years and to make an innovative contribution at 37.5 years of age. (See the table on the facing page.)

Though most people begin to traverse the learning curve in business after graduating from college, the opposite is the case for the entrepreneurial genius. Though the table shows the age at which they began ventures in their chosen area, most of them got a head start on their peers as precocious teens. They catapulted like sprinters off the starting blocks and were well on their way by their mid-twenties.

You may recall that at the tender age of 12, Michael Dell started his first entrepreneurial venture–he launched a stamp catalog after convincing his school chums to consign their stamps so that he had a large selection from which to choose. At 12, Richard Branson had a Christmas tree farm and by 16 he had launched his own publishing company–*Student*–a magazine aimed at the era's dissident students. As a teenager, Henry Ford assembled and sold watches and clocks, nurturing his need to make things for the masses. Martha Stewart embarked on a modeling career at thirteen to earn enough money for college, and Jeff Bezos formed an educational training business while a senior in a Miami high school.

The table below displays the approximate age for each entrepreneur at which the incubation began in their ultimate area of specialization. However, learning is a continuous process and it is difficult to identify an "exact" age. Though the numbers in the table are estimates, they are sufficiently accurate to provide trends when averaging is applied.

INCUBATION & IMPLEMENTATION PERIOD OF ENTREPRENEURIAL GENIUS

Subjects	Age: Incubation Begins	Age: Implementation Begins	Age: Creative Innovation	Total Time for Incubation & Implementation
Jeff Bezos Internet retailing	18 Dream Institute	30 Cadabra Inc.	33 Amazon IPO	15
Richard Branson Virgin opportunities	16 *Student* magazine	22 Virgin Records	36 Virgin Group	20
Coco Chanel Couture & design	15 Learns to sew	27 Opens millinery	37 *flapper* look	22
Michael Dell Personal computers	19 Dell Computer Inc.	23 Dell IPO	34 Dell is #1 in PCs	15
Henry Ford Automobiles	33 Quadricycle	40 Ford Motor Co.	50 Moving Assembly	17
Bucky Fuller Innovations	27 Modular housing	38 Dymaxion Car	53 Geodesic dome	26
J. Paul Getty Oil production	22 Nancy Taylor Oil Lease	39 Accumulating Tide Water Oil	62 Builds first supertankers	40
Hugh Hefner Publishing	16 Writes comic autobiography	27 *Playboy* magazine	34 First Playboy Club	18
Ross Perot System automation	27 Joins IBM	32 Founds EDS	38 EDS has IPO	11
Martha Stewart Lifestyle media	33 Uncatered Affair	46 Contract with Kmart	56 Martha Stewart Omnimedia	23
Donald Trump Real Estate	12 Apprenticeship with father	21 Swifton Village	28 Options on Penn Central Properties	16
Sam Walton Discount retail	22 Joins J. C. Penny	27 Ben Franklin franchise	44 Opens first Wal-Mart store	22
Median (Average)	20.5 years	28.5 years	37.5 years	19 years

This trend to an early start is also apparent in the lives of the many great entrepreneurs who were not profiled in this book. Bill Gates skipped classes in his senior year in high school to program for the giant defense contractor, TRW. It is no accident that Gates was such a phenomenon so early in life. He was ranked the richest man in the world at an earlier age than anyone in history. By age 15, he was operating a venture he had started called *Traf-O-Data*. The small operation generated $20,000 in revenues. He was ready to launch Microsoft at 19. When his Harvard classmates were chasing girls Bill was chasing binary bits and by 30 Gates was wealthy beyond his wildest dreams.

Another early starter, the entrepreneurial whiz kid and founder of Federal Express, Fred Smith, was also well on his way by the time he reached his teen years. At age 15, Fred earned a pilot's license and did crop spraying as a business. Then at 16 he founded a recording company–Ardent Records–that had hits *Big Satin Mama* and *Rock House*. After serving in Vietnam, Smith was ready to launch Federal Express.

The early start allows the aspiring entrepreneur to learn essential skills like negotiating, selling, handling cash and managing inventory as a teenager while others learn in their 20s or later, if at all. A similar period of incubation is evident in sports. Tiger Woods played golf in tournaments at ages five and six. Is it any wonder that he won the U.S. Amateur Championships at 15 or became the best in the world at 25?

Many other examples of early starts can be found in the table shown on the facing page. Notice that the median age at which these entrepreneurs reached millionaire status was 34, for an elapsed time of 18 years between entering the learning curve and reaching eminence. By age 50, most were billionaires. A few, namely Ford, Fuller, and Stewart, were not successful until later in life, since they started their ventures later.

Often precocious, entrepreneurs tend to associate with older people. They are usually mature beyond their years and find comfort in kibitzing and haggling people the age of their parents. They play real games while their peers are still playing kids' games. Perot was breaking horses at age seven and by age 14 had negotiated a special newspaper delivery deal with the head of the local newspaper. Sam Walton began delivering papers at age seven and joined with his mother in a small venture at age thirteen. By 17, he was earning an unheard-of $4000 a year in the middle of the Great Depression when many adults were walking soup lines. Early success groomed him for a life of entrepreneurship.

TIME TO ATTAIN MILLIONAIRE AND BILLIONAIRE STATUS

Subjects	Age: 1st Venture	Age: Became Millionaire	Age: Became Billionaire	Net Worth
Jeff Bezos Internet retailing	18 Dream Institue	33 Amazon IPO	35	$8B–1999 $2B–2001
Richard Branson Virgin opportunities	12/trees 16/*Student*	30	40	$3.3B 2001
Coco Chanel Couture & design	26 Hat salon	35	60	$1B (Est)
Michael Dell Personal computers	12 Sells stamps	23 IPO 1988	33	$20B–2001
Henry Ford Automobiles	18 Repairs watches	45 Model T	60	$2B
Bucky Fuller Innovations	27 Modular housing	Never	Never	$200K
J. Paul Getty Oil production	17 Wildcatting	23	50	$10B
Hugh Hefner Publishing	16 Comic autobiography	35 *Playboy* circulation 1M	Never	$200M
Ross Perot System automation	13 Paper route contract	38 IPO	40	$3B–2001
Martha Stewart Lifestyle media	16 Modeling	41 First book	58 IPO	$1B–2001
Donald Trump Real Estate	21 Swifton Village	28	35	$1.7B–2001
Sam Walton Discount retail	7/ Papers 12/ Milk	32	54 IPO	$93B–2001
Median (Average)	16.5 years	34 years	52 years	$2.5B

SUCCESS AND EMINENCE

By age 31, Michael Dell was a billionaire. He has been noted as the youngest self-made billionaire in American history and the youngest CEO in America by *Fortune* and *Forbes*. Walton made more money than anyone. The *Forbes* rankings list the Walton family with more than $100 billion, far exceeding that of the richest individual, Bill Gates. The least wealthy in this work was Bucky Fuller. The second poorest was Hefner with about $200 million–though second poorest, he still has enough to console himself with a bevy of playmates.

PERSONAL VS. PROFESSIONAL LIFE AND SACRIFICES FOR SUCCESS

The profiles in this book have described the accomplishments, honors and wealth attained by the entrepreneurial geniuses. However, there is a price to be paid for high achievement. This price derives from the reality that one cannot serve two masters in any endeavor. Those who try find only a modicum of success in either, and both are destined to suffer. When striving to reach the pinnacle in any discipline it is important to focus all one's energies to that end, leaving little or no time for a family life. Those who played the game sensed this and played accordingly. Getty, Fuller, Trump, Hefner and Branson were dilettantes with a woman in virtually every port of call. Others like Chanel and Stewart have acknowledged that business came first and lovers second (if at all).

Alexander the Great, Leonardo da Vinci, Joan of Arc, Frank Lloyd Wright, Pablo Picasso, Ernest Hemingway, Margaret Thatcher, Ted Turner and Rupert Murdoch are classic examples of people who sacrificed the personal for the professional. Start-ups demand Herculean effort. Aspiring entrepreneurs are totally absorbed in reaching for the brass ring and are usually working when others are playing. That is the nature of the climb to success where little distinction is made between holidays, weekends or workdays. Intensity and focus are their gods and the family comes in a distant second. Walton's wife and children got used to his not being home. So did Perot's. Stewart's daughter never did–her family suffered while Stewart built her empire. Biographer Oppenheimer described her marriage as a disaster. Hefner never even saw his children when they were young and he paid the price. His daughter Christie finally came back into his life after college, but his oldest son has been estranged for many years. Such is the price of living and working in the fast lane.

How Different is the Entrepreneur?

A study of over 100 entrepreneurs, has shown that the entrepreneurial personality is significantly different from the norm–entrepreneurs are members of the "make-things-happen" group. Although there are personality differences among the great entrepreneurs, there are some respects in which they are all the same. Those who watch golf know that every professional has a unique swing, but there are some fundamentals of the swing that are common to virtually all of them. These fundamentals are intrinsic to the physics of the golf swing and are necessary conditions for successful execution of the shot. In a similar way, a fundamental set of personality attributes seem to pervade the personalities of virtually all the entrepreneurial geniuses, albeit in varying degrees. This suggests that these qualities are necessary (but not sufficient) to ensure entrepreneurial success. In the paragraphs that follow, I present those very qualities which I have gleaned from an analysis of not only the entrepreneurs in this book, but other entrepreneurs who have achieved eminence.

The overarching psychological trait common to all the entrepreneurial geniuses was the passion that drove them forward. From an analysis of these individuals we can construct a profile of the psychological traits that are shared by all entrepreneurial geniuses. The prototype of the entrepreneurial genius exudes the following personality traits:

- strong self-image and the confidence to be different
- intuitive: relies on a powerful intuition
- iconoclastic: innovates through creative destruction
- high risk-taking propensity
- high intensity of purpose and excessive optimism

Though each of the entrepreneurial geniuses profiled possessed all of these traits, the degrees varied from individual to individual. For example, Dell may have been more innovative than some but less charismatic than others. Areas where each individual differs from this prototype have been described in some detail in each chapter under the heading *Eccentricities and Personal Paradoxes*.

Strong Self-Image and the Confidence to be Different

Self-efficacy or internal confidence is prerequisite to membership in the "make-things-happen" group. Until most of us know or understand something well, we are unwilling to initiate significant changes. The fear of being wrong or being ridiculed for an aberrant view has a paralytic effect on us and encourages us to seek the security of conventional practice. This fear impels us to conform to societal norms and confines us to the "care-taker" group, stifling our potential. As Ralph Waldo Emerson reflected in his *Essays: First Series:*

> *Society everywhere is in conspiracy against the manhood [and womanhood] of every one of its members...The virtue in most request is conformity. Self-reliance is its aversion. [Society] loves not realities and creators, but names and customs.*

Conversely, the ability to overcome the fear of being different is one of the defining characteristics of those who challenge traditional practice. The confidence to go out on a limb, to pursue what is not safe and secure, and to go where "angels fear to tread" is at the root of entrepreneurial genius.

What is it that endows certain people with the confidence to be different? As noted earlier, research into the lives and personalities of the great scientists, artists and entrepreneurs suggests that inner strength and self-reliance are usually developed in the formative years, though sometimes not manifested as self-confidence until much later. The factor that forms the bridge from self-reliance to self-confidence seems to be the acquisition of knowledge or expertise in a particular area. Once a person who possesses strong self-reliance acquires a high degree of mastery of a body of knowledge or skill, they develop the confidence to modify or innovate.

Darwin presented his Theory of Evolution that challenged religious doctrine and shed light on the role of natural selection in the development of animal species, only after a prolonged study of birds in the Galapagos. Einstein published his Special Theory of Relativity after a period of intense study and prodigious productivity that brought him to the top of his field in theoretical physics. His theories, though discredited at first, eventually changed our concept of space and time and created a new model of the universe. Henry Ford was ridiculed and fired (as you may recall from Chapter 1) when he proposed a car "for the masses not the classes."

Paradoxically, a strong self-image is most powerful when it is salted with a dose of insecurity. Though insecurity can undermine the success of new ventures, in small doses it can prove highly motivational. It is only counterproductive when it is debilitating, prompting one to abandon a quest. When a fear of failure translates into a motivation to perform, insecurity is productive. Sports psychologists have long known that fear of failure dominates the behavior of many world-class athletes. It does the same for many world-class entrepreneurs. Psychotherapist Alfred Adler found "The more intense the inferiority, the more violent the superiority." Fear of failure was found to pervade the personalities of Bucky Fuller, Hugh Hefner, Donald Trump and Martha Stewart, leading them to become fanatical perfectionists. Their inner self-doubts caused them to try harder and often drove them to strive relentlessly to achieve. It drove Stewart to become an impossible taskmaster. It drove Trump into obsessive-compulsive behaviors as it did for the father of *Playboy.*

Insecurity seethed beneath the arrogant façade of Ted Turner whose father believed that insecurity bred greatness. The same thing occurred in the life of Oracle CEO Larry Ellison. Both men were driven to win at any cost to prove their fathers wrong. They had to show they were worthy and no obstacle was too great to make that happen. In an October 1991 interview, Ted Turner told David Frost "You will hardly ever find a super-achiever anywhere who isn't motivated by a sense of insecurity." Larry Ellison told the media, "If fire doesn't destroy you, you're tempered by it. Thanks dad for influencing me."

David Weeks wrote, "High levels of creativity, extreme competence, and manic work ethic are by-products of anxiety" (*USA Today*, Aug. 18, 1997). Martin Luther King offered confirmation in his aphorism, "The children of darkness are frequently more delusional and zealous than the children of light." After Albert Camus won the Nobel Prize for Literature he wrote, "I don't believe in anything. My only riches are my self-doubts." Months later, he wrote, "I'm pessimistic, ignorant and don't know how to write" (Landrum, 2000, p. 301). Dr. Seuss, after writing *A Cat in the Hat*, announced, "I can't write." Famous author James Michener wrote in his memoirs (Rosellini, 1991):

> *For forty years I've awakened at 4 a.m. in a state of dread, nobody will want to read this. It won't work. I'll never fool em.*

Entrepreneurial geniuses oscillate between an excessive optimism and an overwhelming fear of failure. The two opposing factors seem to coexist in a dynamic equilibrium.

INTUITIVE: RELIES ON A POWERFUL INTUITION

Entrepreneurs tend to leap before they look. But the leap is often a leap of faith where prudence isn't practical. That doesn't mean that entrepreneurs make radical decisions or aren't rational; it just means there isn't much they won't do to achieve their goals. As any world-class athlete will tell you, those who are uncertain, when embroiled in the heat of battle, end up as casualties. Success is a function of belief and "muscle memory" must prevail when the mind starts to question action. When past experience and traditional practice no longer light the path ahead, it's time for the entrepreneur to rely on intuition. Harvard researcher Burton Klein wrote in *Dynamic Economics*:

> *If the entrepreneur wants to give himself the best chance of putting the law of large numbers on his side he will use his intuition to leap to new hypotheses. His riches are his hints, but if his hints are not to be squandered, he must trust his intuition.*

The power of intuitive thinking is often underestimated because much of its mechanism is buried in the subconscious and is, therefore, invisible to the conscious mind. The daily observations and data that we collect as we progress through each day are internalized in a subconscious sense that is often manifested as inspiration. What is commonly described as "gut feeling" is really an intuitive knowledge acquired through experience but not easily quantifiable or explained. However, it is one of the most powerful methods of thought and one used frequently by entrepreneurial geniuses. Its power is directly correlated to the quality of the information stored in the unconscious data base.

Instinct is golden. Einstein relied heavily on his instincts and pressed his mathematical technique into service only after his intuition had hinted at a model of the universe. He asserted, "Intuition is the gift of the gods, but logic is its faithful servant." He once scribbled on his blackboard at Princeton, "Everything that counts, can't be counted, and everything that can be counted, doesn't count." For this physicist, numbers were mere vehicles to a higher order of understanding–the essence or qualitative. Logic's most powerful role lies in its capacity to validate an intuitively perceived truth.

To be a catalyst for change, it is imperative that entrepreneurs think in systems, never pieces. They must integrate the holistic (whole) with the micro (parts) if they are to make their mark in the world. And the vision doesn't have to be profound or esoteric. Hugh Hefner discovered this by tapping into his raging libido and coming out with *Playboy* magazine–a book designed to sate the voyeuristic tendencies of a generation of young males. His gestalt vision of an upscale magazine for males that would serve their fantasies in a respectable forum met a highly receptive market that launched his empire. Similarly Martha Stewart, two decades later, launched the magazine, *Martha Stewart Living*, that tapped into the fantasies of a generation of women. She had an intuitive sense of what women wanted and offered it to them in a variety of venues. J. Paul Getty informed his search for oil in the Middle East by gathering all the data that geologists could offer, and then gambled the last of his fortune on his intuitive belief that there was oil beneath the desert sand; his gamble paid handsomely.

We are trained in school to rationalize, analyze, hypothesize and mechanize. But without the context of a prescient dream, such work is for naught. Intuition is where the true geniuses find their niche in life. But intuition cannot function in a void. It must have a database with a deep reservoir of information from which to draw. Insights incubate and then emerge from within, after the conscious analytical processes of the mind are turned down and the mind yields free rein to the imagination. (This is why the brainstorming process is undertaken without structure.) For the entrepreneurial genius, the mind summons information from the unconscious to deal with problems. If there is a dearth of information in the data base, the intuition is weak. For those with a vast array of information lying dormant in the subconscious, the intuitive thoughts can generate truly magnificent resolutions to deep problems.

Most epiphanies are innate responses to inner knowing. They emerge from a brain that has absorbed a great deal of information and then proceeds relentlessly in a subconscious search for pattern. The results of this search suddenly explode in an instantaneous revelation or a creative vision. Among the most popular legends about the discovery process is the story of the ancient Greek mathematician, Archimedes (287–212 B.C.), who was taking a bath after prolonged contemplation of the relationship between mass and buoyancy. Suddenly a relationship now, known as the Principle of Hydrostatics, came to him in a flash. He was so excited that he jumped out of the bath and ran naked down the street yelling *Eureka!* (I have found it!)

Many great people have attributed their greatness to their intuition. Bertrand Russell wrote, "The sense of certainty and revelation comes before any definite belief." Jonas Salk, the scientist who developed the Polio vaccine, wrote:

> *It is always with excitement that I wake up in the morning wondering what my intuition will toss up to me, like gifts from the sea. I work with it and rely on it. It's my partner.*

In describing the process that led to his creation of the world's first skyscraper, architect Louis Sullivan suggested, "When a design fails to materialize, get away from the drawing board. Leave the office. Take a walk. Allow your mind to roam free. It was on such a stroll that the design for the first skyscraper came to me in a flash."

A similar experience led the great twentieth-century mathematician, Henri Poincaré, to propose the existence of a subconscious mind that solved problems without conscious effort. Poincaré suggested that after a period of intense work or information gathering, the subconscious mind begins scanning the information for patterns and logical connections (as a computer might scan a forensic database for matching finger prints). He describes this stage of mental processing as the *incubation* stage, when ideas percolate in the subconscious. When a match or logical connection is made, the alarm bells sound and a "eureka moment" or period of illumination results. Poincaré explains (Hadamard, 1945, p. 13–14):

> *Disgusted with my failure [to solve the problem I was working on] I went to spend a few days at the seaside and thought of something else. One morning, walking on the bluff, the idea came to me, with just the same characteristics of brevity, suddenness and immediate certainty [as in my previous discoveries]...Most striking at first is this appearance of sudden illumination, a manifest sign of long, unconscious prior work. The role of this unconscious work in mathematical invention appears to me incontestable.*

This quote of Poincaré pertained to his discovery of a class of so-called fuchsian functions that inspired Benoit Mandelbrot, less than a century later (1978), to discover fractal geometry and the mathematics of chaos! Additional examples of the role of the subconscious in the creative process are afforded by the epiphanies of Leonardo da Vinci, Charles Darwin, Albert Einstein, Nikola Tesla, Sigmund Freud and Bucky Fuller. Fuller formulated a concept he labeled *teleology* whereby "Intuitive conversions by the brain could transform experience into generalized principles" (Hatch, p. 263).

An old adage says that if you line up a hundred economists, they will point in a hundred different directions. This statement acknowledges that different economists working from the same or different econometric models will usually forecast dramatically different outcomes. Our society has become so enamored with sophisticated quantitative models that the role of intuition, a subconscious process, is often overlooked. The profiles in this book reveal the dominant role that intuition played in the entrepreneurial climb to success. While quantitative techniques are invaluable for certain things, they have limited use in the generation and incubation of new ideas. Highly creative ideas and the investigation of "what might be" are still the purview of intuitive thought.

The world is shades of gray rather than black and white–it is analog, not digital. The world of the brilliant entrepreneur emanates from intuitive inspiration and not budgets, financial forecasts or market analyses. If we use music as a metaphor, we observe that the eminent jazz musicians seldom play original tunes by the music. They play what they feel from the heart and soul. In this world, the greats like Louis Armstrong improvised while their teachers were reading sheet music. The same will be found to be true in virtually every discipline. Maria Callas' creative performances were the result of myopia–she couldn't see the conductor –and her brilliance evolved out of innovative improvisation, not any prescient rigor. In a similar manner Maria Montessori was able to revolutionize childhood education, recognizing it as "social engineering" rather than "structural indoctrination." Intuition was also the agent driving Picasso's cubism, Edison's incandescent lamp and Einstein's Theories of Relativity. As Fuller observed, "Truth is an approximation."

ICONOCLASTIC: INNOVATES THROUGH CREATIVE DESTRUCTION

The innovative developments described above violated, or in many cases destroyed, existing beliefs or practices. Thomas Kuhn first developed the concept of paradigm shifts in his classic book, *The Structure of Scientific Revolutions* (Kuhn, p. 66):

> All [the groundbreaking] scientific discoveries were causes of or contributors to paradigm change. Furthermore, the changes in which these discoveries were implicated were all destructive as well as constructive. After the discovery, scientists were able to account for a wider range of natural phenomena...but that gain was achieved only by discarding some previously standard beliefs or procedures.

Kuhn's description of the nature of paradigm shifts in scientific revolutions was observed to apply also to paradigm shifts in business. Joseph Schumpeter defined *innovation* in a business environment as *creative destruction*. The great scientists, artists and entrepreneurs first destroy some previous beliefs, which are tacitly assumed, before they can re-invent or innovate.

Altering a paradigm demands a mastery of a field or a depth of understanding beyond the level of others working in the same domain. This makes knowledge of any discipline vital to the process of creative destruction. That is why it takes years–normally eight to ten years–to learn a domain and another ten to master it. Those who succeeded at a young age usually had an early start in knowledge acquisition and rose quickly to a high level of mastery in their domain. It was this level of mastery combined with an internal self-reliance that gave them the confidence to challenge the existing paradigms and embark on the path of creative destruction–*innovation*.

We may recall from our profiles that all the entrepreneurial geniuses were iconoclastic in their innovations. Ford replaced the static assembly line with the moving assembly line, dramatically increasing productivity. Chanel's creation of the boyish "flapper look" replaced the frilly feminine look and set a new trend in women's fashions. Fuller revolutionized architecture with his introduction of the geodesic dome that enabled the enclosure of large areas without pillars and vertical support beams. Bezos' idea of a bookstore in cyberspace revolutionized the traditional methods of merchandising and effectively launched Internet retail. The further any idea extends beyond the bounds of tradition, the greater its chance for abnormal success. The reason for this is that normal success emanates from the normal and abnormal success from the abnormal, just as traditional ideas are spawned in the establishment and radical ideas on the fringe.

An example of innovation by creative destruction in athletics is manifest in the story of Howard Head, a businessman who revolutionized two sports on account of his refusal to believe he was inept. Head blamed his inability to ski on the limitations of wooden skis. Though perhaps an irrational response, blaming the equipment encouraged him to alter the ski equipment, and this made him rich. When a New England ski instructor told him he would never learn to Alpine ski, he retreated to his shop and came out with the first metal ski–the Head Cheater. On his new skis, Head was suddenly able to navigate the difficult slopes that had defeated him before. This Harvard engineer had been fired from his first two jobs for incompetence but that never deterred him. After selling his Head Ski Company to AMF, he retired to the tennis court in his backyard.

Lightning struck twice for Head. After losing to his friends repeatedly in tennis, he followed his usual strategy and blamed the racket for his poor performance. Head retreated to his shop to forge a racket twice the size of existing rackets, featuring a sweet spot with double the area of conventional rackets. This improved his game dramatically and he was soon defeating his most formidable competition. When he checked with the United States Tennis Association, he found there were no size restrictions for tennis rackets, so he rushed down to the U.S. patent office to register his innovation. Thus was born the first oversized tennis racket–the Prince. His second attack against conventional equipment brought him $75 million when he sold out four years later. Howard Head shows us that belief can be powerful fuel for entrepreneurial success. In his words, "You have to believe in the impossible."

Visionary entrepreneurs are typically accused of chasing foolish dreams and unattainable goals. In order to withstand these attacks, the entrepreneur must have a strong internal locus of control, an indomitable self-esteem, and resilience. All creative ventures are the result of an iconoclast chasing a dream against the resistance of an army of traditionalists. The self-confidence that comes from a strong knowledge base and an internal self-reliance requires a critically important personality trait to transform the innovative vision into a reality–a propensity for risk-taking.

RISK-TAKING PROPENSITY

In worldwide polls, Americans repeatedly test highest on independence and risk-taking. In 2001, twenty-seven nations voted America the best place for entrepreneurs. Americans as a group tend to be more goal-oriented than those in most other nations. Albert Einstein wrote:

The American lives even more for his goals for the future than Europeans. Life for him is always becoming, never being.

A review of America's beginnings offers insight into the entrepreneurial personality that is reminiscent of the spirit of the early pioneers who settled the nation. Early settlers were people with a spirit kindred to the entrepreneur. They dared what others feared, went where others would not, and sought new ways to live and work. The former president of the American Psychological Association, Frank Farley, wrote extensively on the "Big T" (high testosterone) personality that founded America. He spoke of Big T people as those thrill-seeking, testosterone-charged personalities who forged ahead of lesser spirits to found the nation. Farley told _USA Today_ (Jan. 10, 2001):

> _Big T's value variety, novelty and change; they like challenges, have high energy levels, tend to be self-confident and feel that fate is in their own hands._

He went on to speak of their proclivity for confronting fear–a common finding in the great entrepreneurs. Farley argued that men who sacrificed the present for an unknown future in America were Big T's.

Like the American pioneer, the entrepreneur is a thrill-seeking intrepid warrior creating superior products or hoping for a better way to earn a living. And like those stalwart 16th-century Europeans who sailed to America, the entrepreneur is a Big T who is high in thrill-seeking, aggression, and creative ideas. Both are in a frenetic search for freedom. America is a melting pot of such individuals seeking freedom and independence. The pioneers were Europeans seeking religious freedom, Asians looking for opportunity, Middle-Easterners searching for hope, Cubans escaping political repression, Latin Americans seeking life's possibilities, and Australians desirous of a larger venue in which to compete. The whole was made better by the sum of its diverse parts.

Entrepreneurs take control of their destiny. Behavioral psychologists describe such self-directed individuals as having an inner locus of control. The entrepreneurial geniuses believe that they, rather than some external force, control their destiny. They lead, set higher goals, have indomitable wills, have less anxiety, and are less likely to conform to authority figures. They tend to be optimists with a penchant for living on the edge. To them, change is exhilarating and the status quo mundane. The entrepreneur prefers the chance to win even if means failing and, like the pioneer, opts for the thrill of chasing possibilities. This eagerness to embrace novelty and to be driven by one's own goals, instead of the safety of following the norm, is manifest as a propensity for risk-taking. A high proclivity for risk is a conspicuous characteristic of entrepreneurial genius–one you probably observed as a recurring theme as you read the profiles in this book.

Living life on the edge is the prime pathway to life in the penthouse. Just as cowardice can lead to courage, so calculated risk usually leads to rewards. Once one gets past the fear, one is groomed for life at the top in any venue. Why? Because fear and vulnerability lead to courage just as surely as taking risks grooms one to take more risks. Soon the individual thrives on what was once feared.

Most entrepreneurs are invigorated by risk and experience a sensation or rush when on the edge of what more safety-oriented people deem risky. What is scary for the more timid is exciting for the adventurous entrepreneur. A very fine line separates the fearful from the fearless. The twelve entrepreneurial geniuses profiled in this book offer insight into the early experiences in the formative years that fostered the development of strong risk-taking propensities. For each of these entrepreneurs, boldness and fearlessness were molded when they were young, in some cases by frequent moving. In other cases, they were nurtured in an environment that provided the freedom to err, fail and not pay severe consequences. When Trump's father allowed him to run a multi-million-dollar enterprise in Cincinnati while in college, he was, in essence, saying, "Go ahead. Sink or swim on your own. The experience will make you or break you." It made him. Ross Perot's father let Ross repeatedly suffer a broken nose trying to break wild horses at age seven. Ross has said the experience groomed him to win as well as lose.

Those who are excessively fearful of losing their money are ill-suited to run their own business. For the entrepreneur, the potential loss stimulates the heart rate and activates the adrenaline. When you are altering systems or changing paradigms, you are out in front of the pack with few support systems to keep you safe. If that causes anxiety, then you are in for a long tortuous journey.

HIGH INTENSITY OF PURPOSE AND EXCESSIVE OPTIMISM

Entrepreneurs typically have a surplus of latent energy, labeled *psychic energy* by Freud. Others call this energy "field drive" or "libidinal energy." This book is full of such hyper-energized people. *Fortune* called Jeff Bezos "hyperkinetic." Martha Stewart is a human dynamo who admits to sleeping only four hours a night. She told Larry King that when necessary she can live on less. Bucky Fuller had a similar predilection. Believing sleep to be a waste of time, he practiced dymaxion sleep–alternately working six hours and going into a trance for thirty minutes–for weeks at a time. It was Fuller's way of optimizing his output, in a process he called *ephemeralization*–achieving more and more with less and less. Sam Walton wrote, "I have been over-blessed with drive and ambition. I have always pursued everything with a true passion–some would call an obsession" (Walton, p. 15). Richard Branson said "I have always thrived on havoc and adrenaline." When Disneyland opened, Walt Disney never left the park for three months. Thomas Edison was famous for sleeping on his workbench and not leaving his workplace for days or weeks at a time. He didn't want to leave his lab for fear he would miss out on some great mystery while asleep. At age 65, he averaged 122 hours a week in his workplace.

World-class athletes intuitively know the importance of high energy and positively charged thinking. Sports psychologists describe *positive thinking* as getting past the point of uncertainty to succeed. It's not just believing, but rather it is the degree to which you can overcome the fear of failing. In *Competitive Anxiety in Sport*, Martens says (p. 222):

> *Uncertainty about winning or losing in competition can be determined by the person's perceived probability of success or probability of failure...uncertainty increases to a point at which there is an equal chance of the outcome being positive or negative.*

This means that until you believe more than 50 percent that you can, you can't. Examples in sports abound, especially with men like Mohammed Ali and Michael Jordan who believed beyond what might seem justifiable, yet their belief took them to unimagined heights. In other words, success is inextricably tied to believing it is possible. Even failing is helpful as long as it is perceived as just another step to success. The only differences among the top ten tennis players, golfers, or ballplayers is in their mindset. This is also true in business. Marginal talent with excess optimism can achieve at a very high level.

Entrepreneurial geniuses are so energized that they don't have time for the sicknesses that beset more ordinary individuals. They are so driven that they seem to live longer, more productive lives than the rest of humanity. Examples in history are rampant. Picasso, Frank Lloyd Wright and Helena Rubinstein lived life on the edge, but were productive well into their senior years. Such people seem to get on the treadmill and don't get off until the machine is turned off. When they do get ill, they are bedridden–yet when they hit the wall, they tend to recover quickly. Plato (428–348 B.C.) is a classic example of a man of exceptional longevity, arguably attributable to his passionate commitment to his dream. As one of the world's first great entrepreneurs, Plato opened The Academy–the very first university. He had been expelled from Athens and didn't return until he was forty. That was beyond the life expectancy in that era, making him old when he opened his university where he taught Aristotle. He operated the school until the day he died at eighty years of age. He had exceeded the normal life expectancy by over forty years!

There are many people who have the requisite confidence, knowledge, intuitive capacity and risk-taking propensity to become successful entrepreneurs, but they lack the engine that would drive them to that success. That engine is an intensity of purpose and passion is its fuel. Why are entrepreneurs so passionate? Because they are chasing their own dreams, not someone else's. Consequently, the job is pleasure, not work. Joseph Campbell described this as a state of "bliss," and implored people to stop chasing the dreams of others and focus on their own.

One manifestation of passion is the so-called *polyphasic* behavior that accompanies an intensity of purpose. This is the multi-tasking kind of behavior, displayed by someone attempting to do several things at once, like reading while watching television to wring double the productivity out of each moment. Polyphasic behavior is a consequence of setting personal goals that are unrealistically optimistic. In the quest to achieve these goals, the polyphasic person attempts to juggle several tasks at once. Frank Lloyd Wright had a myriad of projects in the works simultaneously, just as Picasso had five pictures in progress at the same time. Ted Turner, Berry Gordy and Rupert Murdoch were entrepreneurs with a similar polyphasic pattern of behavior, as were politicians John F. Kennedy and Margaret Thatcher.

The Nature of Entrepreneurial Genius

Our study of entrepreneurial genius shows that it pays to be the first-born, but that isn't critical to success. The first born is usually more prone to lead, on account of their leadership position relative to the other siblings. However, being first born does not ensure leadership potential, it merely offers an advantage in the unconscious programming acquired in those early years as leader of one's siblings.

Far more important than birth order is having a parent who is self-employed. This tends to build an inner sense of self for coping, self-reliance and independence. Only two of these subjects had parents who worked in traditional 9-to-5 jobs. Formal education is important in certain disciplines, however, it isn't _how_ the education occurs but that it _does_ occur. Just seven of these twelve subjects had the benefit of a college degree. But it was their other qualities that contributed most to their success, not their pedigree. Fuller was the only entrepreneur working in a scholarly field, but he was kicked out of Harvard twice and never earned a degree. Trump attended Wharton to enhance his move into business, but it was more of a career move than an educational device. Richard Branson, Henry Ford and Coco Chanel never finished high school but all made billions.

To succeed in the world of entrepreneurship it is far more important to be a Type A personality than a college graduate with an A standing. It is also good to be an iconoclast–to be able to ignore conventional wisdom. Of the entrepreneurial geniuses studied, 92 percent were Type A personalities. A psychological term for such personalities is _hypomanic_, meaning a euphoric and manic behavior that, in excess, becomes a bipolar condition. An excessive sense of urgency is prevalent in the Type A personality. Type A's misconstrue self-worth with achievement, so they feel they must achieve or pay the consequences. Coco Chanel was the only one studied who was not classified a Type A since she was more prone to enjoy the fruits of her success, though she was fiercely competitive and a difficult boss.

Most of the entrepreneurs studied were _Big T_ personalities. That is, they lived on the edge in most things and were prone to risk it all to achieve their dreams. Such a high-energy disposition was associated with enhanced creativity, aggressiveness and sex drive. Such can be seen in the likes of Getty, Fuller, Trump, Hefner and Branson. Risk-taking was very important in their success as it is for all entrepreneurs who must gamble all to win all. No other factor seems as important as pushing the limits in all things. Nine of the dozen entrepreneurs actually operated with a death-wish kind of mentality. In this respect, Branson's behavior was the most flagrant, but he was followed closely by Getty and Trump. Leverage was their vehicle and an exaggerated sense of urgency drove them relentlessly. Understandably, most of the great entrepreneurs were Machiavellian–they believed that the ends justify the means. This prompted them to manipulate the world to fit their needs and their vision. They were also control freaks who were demanding, yet strangely, quite charismatic. Eight had a cult-like magnetism that helped them achieve beyond the norm. The great entrepreneurs were all abnormal–but, as noted above, they all tended to exhibit the same abnormalities. These qualities are summarized in the table on the opposite page.

BEHAVIORAL DATA OF ENTREPRENEURIAL GENIUS
2 FEMALES, 10 MALES

Subjects	Birth Order	Parents Self-Employ	Formal Educat	Icono-clast	Type A/B	Big T	Hypo-mania	Charm/hype	High Machs
Males									
Jeff Bezos	1st	NO	MA	I++	A+++	T++	M+++	C++	NO
Richard Branson	1st	YES	Gr. 10	I+++	A+++	T+++	M++	C+++	MACH
Michael Dell	middle	YES	Gr. 13	I++	A+++	T++	M+	C+	MACH
Henry Ford	1st	YES	Gr. 8	I+++	A++	T+++	M	C+	MACH
Bucky Fuller	2nd	YES	Gr. 12	I+++	A+++	T+++	M+++	C+++	NO
Jean Paul Getty	2nd	YES	BA	I+++	A+	T+++	NO	C+++	MACH
Hugh Hefner	1st	NO	BA	I+++	A+	T+++	M+	C+++	NO
Ross Perot	1st	YES	BS	I+	A+++	T+++	M+++	C+++	MACH
Donald Trump	2nd	YES	MBA	I+++	A+++	T+++	M+++	C+++	MACH
Sam Walton	1st	YES	BA	I+++	A+	T+++	NO	C+++	NO
Males (10)	1st 70%	Yes 80%	College 60%	Icono 100%	Type A 100%	Big T 100%	HypoM 80%	Charm 100%	Mach 60%
Females									
Coco Chanel	2nd	YES	Gr. 8	I+++	B	T+++	M+	C+++	MACH
Martha Stewart	2nd	YES	BA	I++	A+++	T	M+++	C++	MACH
Females (2)	1st 0%	Yes 100%	College 50%	Icono 100%	Type A 50%	Big T 100%	HypoM 100%	Charm 100%	Mach 100%
Grand Totals (12)	58%	83%	58%	100%	92%	100%	83%	100%	67%

Iconoclasts:	I+++ Independent to a fault and refuse to conform to conventional traditions
Type A:	A+++ Confuse self-worth with achievement and time is all-important
Big T:	High testosterone/thrill-seeking (high creativity, risk-taking, aggression and sex drive)
Hypomania:	Manic behavior–extremes of euphoria and depression or bipolar behaviors– 4 hrs sleep
Charisma:	C+++ Charming, enthusiastic, and a magnetic persona: cult-like attraction.
MACH:	Machiavellian proclivity–the end justifies the means

When the study described above was expanded to a more comprehensive study involving 50 entrepreneurial geniuses, the patterns displayed in the table once again emerged. These findings are presented in the bar graph on the following page. The entrepreneurial group included 12 females and 38 males. Seven personality traits are displayed along the horizontal axis. Each bar shows the percentage of the 50 entrepreneurs possessing each of these traits. Since these are personality anomalies, each trait represents a deviation from "normal behavior." The graph shows that each of these abnormal personality characteristics is an attribute of more than 80 percent of the entrepreneurs surveyed. In these personality traits, we have found a characterization of the entrepreneurial personality.

Personality Traits of 50 Entrepreneurial Geniuses

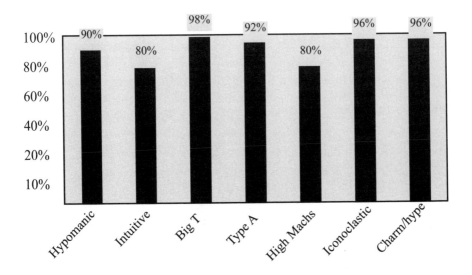

In the next chapter, I invite you to investigate your own personality traits and your predisposition to an entrepreneurial venture. If you are embued with the entrepreneurial spirit, then you might choose to get started on a project that you've always wanted to attempt but were reluctant to try (recall Jeff Bezos' regret minimalization principle). I will share with you the most powerful lessons learned from a selection of the world's greatest entrepreneurs. The most important ingredient that you will need to add to the mix is your passion.

14

How Entrepreneurial Are You?

"The man who produces an idea in any rational endeavor–the man who discovers new technology–is the permanent benefactor of humanity…in proportion to the mental energy he spent, the man who creates a new invention receives but a small percentage of his value in terms of material payment, no matter what fortune he makes, no matter what millions he earns."

–Ayn Rand, *The Objectivist Newsletters*

During the past three decades, my speaking tours and lectures have brought me face to face with thousands of aspiring entrepreneurs. From them I have learned how many talented people, imbued with energy and entrepreneurial spirit, have failed to pursue their dreams simply because they are afraid to take that first bold step. My intent in writing this chapter is two-fold. First, I want to provide you with the opportunity to assess your own proclivity for entrepreneurship. To this purpose, I have included an assessment instrument and scoring device at the end of this chapter. My second intent is to help those who aspire to entrepreneurial activities to discover their own potential and bring it to fruition. To this end, I present in this chapter the twelve principles of entrepreneurial success that I unabashedly refer to as *Landrum's Laws of Entrepreneurial Genius*. These are the winning attitudes and behaviors that I have gleaned from the entrepreneurs profiled in this book. They represent what researchers call a "best practices" analysis of what generates entrepreneurial success. You may have noticed that each of these laws is the name of a chapter in this book and that law is associated with the entrepreneurial genius who is profiled as its most exemplary practitioner.

If you are intent on developing your entrepreneurial skills and talents, you may first have to overcome some of the impediments of earlier teachings or beliefs that have inhibited you from taking the challenge in the past. Changes in beliefs and attitudes must precede changes in behavior, so I will first present some preliminary ideas that may seem trite but are absolutely vital to the entrepreneurial mindset. Without the "right" attitudes toward failure, luck, risk and convention, we cannot work in harmony with our goals and our likelihood of success is much diminished.

OUR GREATEST LIMITATIONS ARE SELF-IMPOSED

How often have you heard someone denigrate the success of another with comments, such as, "She slept her way to the top" or "He just happened to be in the right place at the right time"? These are typical assertions of those troubled by their own lack of success. It is often comforting to believe that those who succeeded did so because they had extraordinary advantages such as inherited wealth, special talents, help from friends or merely "dumb luck." In this way, we can avoid the pain of acknowledging our own squandered opportunities. From the profiles in this book and the analyses in the preceding chapters we know that passion, hard work, intuition and tenacity all played a key role in the great entrepreneurial successes. Rarely was inherited wealth, high IQ or patronage a major factor in the ultimate success of an entrepreneur.

In spite of this information, the great multitude shrink from the challenge to follow their dreams because they have deep-seated feelings of inferiority and believe they are incapable of greatness. If you interviewed someone who is locked in a job they hate and inquired why they don't pursue a career in something that they find exciting, you would eventually run into the "I can't because" syndrome. Deep in the psyche of these people is the belief that they lack the intelligence, contacts, education or talents to achieve greatness in anything. These beliefs masquerade in responses such as "I can't because I have a family to support," or "I can't because I don't have the proper education or training." The "I can't because" syndrome is a symptom of an inner acceptance of the status quo. The "I can't" becomes a self-fulfilling prophecy that signals acceptance and denies "I can."

A study reported in the *Journal for Research in Mathematics Education* indicated that a large majority of Black and Hispanic students in a comprehensive survey admitted that they regarded mathematics as the domain of white males. It is little wonder that these groups did not perform as well as the white males in the national mathematics testing. When a race, gender or individual believes they have limitations, they inadvertently impose these limitations on themselves. Achieving success in anything begins with shedding our self-imposed limitations and taking control.

HOW DO WE SEIZE CONTROL OF OUR LIVES?

The accuracy of the old adage that we become as we think is evident when we look at the people around us. Most people live life marching to someone else's tune. How many of the people around you are wage slaves, commuting to work early in the morning and returning in the evening, exhausted and looking forward to the weekend for some respite? In their day-to-day struggle to survive, they play out the old coal-miner's lyric, "[I shovel] sixteen tons and what do I get, another day older and deeper in debt." They have been programmed early to seek what someone else felt was important. Then one day they awaken and realize that they have become a member of the "watch-things-happen," or worse, the "wonder-what-happened" group. Most of us are indoctrinated with the values of our parents, mentors, teachers or preachers, not realizing that we are allowed to have our own distinct sets of values. Our programmed inner tapes lead us down roads well traveled but not always where we would have chosen had we known that the option was ours. Few stories are sadder than those of individuals who detest what they do, where they work, who they associate with–all because they never realized that there is an option to clinging to a lifestyle they hate. What a waste!

If you find yourself in this position, you can take control of your life. Go within yourself and find what makes you feel good. What gives you goosebumps? That is where you must spend your time. The true entrepreneurial genius does just that. Michael Dell was misunderstood by his well-meaning parents when he spent his textbook monies on computer parts instead of pre-med textbooks. Jeff Bezos' boss couldn't understand how someone could walk away from a $1-million-a-year job to do his own thing. Only you know what is the driving force within. To throw off the shackles of your imprisonment, find your passion and pursue it–no matter the consequences.

DESTINY AND SUCCESS IMPRINTS

Everyone is primed for a different race. For some, the need to help and nurture drives them to the ministry or nursing. Others have a need to be around people and are drawn to sales or politics. Michener had to write, Picasso had to paint, Martin Luther King was meant to lead, and Henry Ford was meant to be an entrepreneur. Their internal tapes were imprinted early. Some of us prefer peanut butter, brunettes, ocean waves, sonnets, Madonna or James Bond. That is why we have horse racing and NASCAR–individual preferences vary greatly.

The big question is: To what extent can our tapes be re-programmed? Can an aspiring extrovert transform herself from an introvert? Absolutely! But the longer you have played at one, the longer it takes to change. The more experiential inputs–imprints on your tape, if you will–have been played, the longer and more arduous the change process, but it can be done. We know that superlearning–behavior modification–takes place in trauma and people can be shocked into change. We have learned this from war and other traumatic events. For example, Bucky Fuller was transformed one night as he stood by Lake Michigan contemplating suicide. Then, in an instantaneous epiphany, he turned 180 degrees and decided to spend his life pursuing his inner dreams. Walt Disney experienced a similar transformation when he was fired as a cartoonist and had to file for bankruptcy. After being fired at age 32, Martha Stewart metamorphosed from a housewife, mother and stockbroker into the queen of catering.

BEHAVIOR MODIFICATION AND REPROGRAMMING

The human system can be compared to a personal computer in that it comes equipped with ROM (read-only memory) that is unalterable and with RAM (random-access memory) that can be adapted by the user to solve problems. Altering the personal computer and your own path is tantamount to loading different operating systems and application software programs that will take you to different venues. The basic core of potentialities or competencies may be enhanced but they must first be reprogrammed with new codes that alter the drivers and potential functions. Until we reprogram ourselves, it is improbable that we will optimize our outputs.

ISN'T LUCK A LARGE PART OF SUCCESS?

Some may argue that many people possessing all the personality traits consistent with entrepreneurial success have found only failure because the right opportunities never appeared. They would further assert that this book profiles only those who have succeeded and ignores a multitude of people who possess the right behaviors but have failed in spite of their efforts. It is certainly true that success is never 100% guaranteed by any particular approach and that "bad luck" can sometimes destroy an entrepreneurial venture. Indeed, the psychological traits and behaviors observed in the profiles and distilled later in this chapter are "necessary" rather than "sufficient." That is, there is little or no chance of success without a large measure of the "winning behaviors", yet such behaviors do not guarantee immediate success. The important point, however, is that the probability of success increases with the passion, intuition, tenacity and intensity of the aspiring entrepreneur. A plethora of research on business management has revealed that high achievers perceive the attainment of their goals to be within their locus of control, while the underachievers tend to believe that success is rooted in external factors such as luck. This difference in perception is the difference that stacks the odds for success strongly in favor of the person with the winning behaviors. When someone told humorist Will Rogers that his success was pure luck, he responded with the now famous line, "Sure, but the harder I works, the luckier I gets!"

To put to rest the idea that success is mostly attributable to luck, we need only recall the old cliché that the successful bronco buster is one who has climbed on a horse just one more time than he has fallen off. The successful entrepreneur is one who follows a string of failures with a success. The story of Henry Ford's climb to the top illustrates how Henry used his failures to learn how to succeed. Few people succeed on their first attempt at anything. Ford's biography gives validity to the old business adage, *Success is what happens when readiness meets opportunity*. Opportunities come in great numbers; it's the readiness of the aspiring entrepreneurs that enables them to recognize and exploit the opportunities as they emerge.

HOW DO WE GET READY?

Readiness means preparation. Being ready for success implies the long-term development and honing of a knowledge or skill that positions a person to recognize and pounce on an opportunity when it appears. It is during this period of intense learning, called *incubation*, that an unconscious knowledge evolves. This unconscious knowledge manifests as intuition. Once developed, this intuition serves the entrepreneur as a "sixth sense" or instinct guiding all business decisions. Being invisible, intuition and its contribution to success are often undervalued today in favor of more formal computer-generated quantitative modeling techniques.

As we saw in Chapter 13, analysis of the great entrepreneurial geniuses reveals that it takes approximately ten years to master a craft or an enterprise and then another ten to creatively alter it. Instantaneous success in any discipline is a myth. The rich and famous get there through many years of arduous work and in the process acquire the skills, knowledge and intuition needed to scale the ladder to success.

If it takes about 20 years to reach the creative innovation stage, then how do we account for the early success of people like professional golfer Tiger Woods? A close look at Tiger's life reveals that he was engaged in his first golf competition at age five, won the U.S. Amateur title at age 15, and became the #1 golfer in the world by age 25–two decades from his first entry! Henry Ford didn't start building cars until his thirties and consequently wasn't a huge success until his fifties. Michael Dell launched his first direct selling model at age twelve when he earned $2000 selling stamps in a mail order catalog. It isn't a coincidence that he launched Dell Computers at 19 and was a billionaire by age 33. Recall the table in Chapter 13 showing the incubation and implementation periods on the learning curves for the dozen entrepreneurs profiled in this book. This verifies the approximate 20-year period from beginning to creative innovation and suggests that the earlier you begin, the earlier you succeed. This may seem simplistic, but it is true whether you're chasing golf balls or chasing business. Howard Gardner observed (Gardner, 1998, p. 119):

> It takes about a decade to master a domain and up to an additional decade to fashion work that is creative enough to alter that domain.

With this in mind, we need to discover our passion and get started as soon as possible. However, before we begin, we suggest you take the test *Are You an Entrepreneur?* found at the end of this chapter.

Winning Behaviors of Entrepreneurial Genius

Most entrepreneurs began their ventures merely to earn money. They had not yet discovered their passion, though their early imprints may have initiated an interest in a particular area. In Coco Chanel's case, it was sewing hats and dresses, for Sam Walton it was running a variety store, and for Michael Dell it was assembling computers from components and selling them. However, as they passed through the incubation stage, learning and enhancing their expertise, they began to see opportunities that fired their imagination and their passion. The original pursuit of money metamorphosed into a passion to innovate, expand and enhance their enterprise. Money became only a barometer to measure their success. Getty, Walton and Ford all tried to retire, but their passion for pursuing what gave them goosebumps drove them back into their enterprises.

In the paragraphs that follow, we expand on each of these winning behaviors by quoting some of the research and recalling incidents from the profiles of these entrepreneurial geniuses. There is no particular hierarchy to these behaviors since they are all equally important and none is a prerequisite for another. Hence they are presented in the same order as they appear in the chapter sequence.

TO LEARN HOW TO SUCCEED, FAIL

Many people take failure personally and are defeated by its negative imprint on the psyche. The successful entrepreneur sees failure as a temporary roadblock necessitating a detour, while traditionalists see failure as something to avoid at all cost. Consequently, failure for many is highly debilitating. However, it isn't what *happens* to us that is important, but rather how we deal with it. That is the fundamental difference between entrepreneurs who alter paradigms and traditionalists who bask in the security of a corner office. Henry Ford failed often, but saw those failures as learning experiences on the way to building an automobile dynasty. He and Thomas Edison became close friends when they discovered that they both viewed the world through a similar filter. Both men built empires through a process known by the formal term "heuristic learning," i.e., trial and error. They were both experimenters, having acquired a tolerance for failed trials. Had they taken their failures personally, it would have debilitated them. Neither would have had such an impact on the world.

You may recall that Ford failed miserably as a farmer, employee and engineer, and as the head of his own firm. He experienced two bankruptcies prior to his great success and suffered the ultimate indignity of being fired from his own firm after only four months on the job—yet he forged onward. He knew where he was going, and bided his time using the failures to learn. Such temerity takes an indomitable will and a strong sense of self. Thomas Edison was of a similar ilk. He too regarded all failure as a step to success. When a reporter asked why he had failed after thousands of experiments on the incandescent light bulb, the intractable Edison responded:

> *I didn't fail. What I did was successfully eliminate 3000 fallacious theories. Yet in only two cases did my experiments prove the truth of my theory, the rest were unacceptable for my needs.*

Others have found a similar path to the top. Renowned composer Igor Stravinsky wrote, "I have learned as a composer chiefly through my mistakes and pursuits of false assumptions, not by my exposure to founts of wisdom and knowledge."

Both Bucky Fuller and Martha Stewart developed their breakthrough ideas shortly after they had been fired. They used misfortune to grow and become more than they had been. Fuller decided to end it all after being fired from a Chicago firm but changed his mind and would later write, "I'm the world's most successful failure." Stewart went through a similar trauma. She failed as a stockbroker and subsequently created her catering empire. In each of her moves to the top she experienced failure–her marriage, friends, and more recently the ImClone stock debacle. In no case did she allow the failures to deter her from moving ahead. In a similar way, Coco Chanel lost her business when the Nazis occupied Paris, only to return after the war to become bigger and better than ever.

SYNTHESIZE TO SUCCESS BY ATTACKING WEAKNESS

Entrepreneurial geniuses adapt. They attack their weaknesses and give free rein to their strengths. By doing so they become more than they would otherwise be. This is somewhat paradoxical–jump right into your worst nightmare and it serves you well! Why does this work? For the simple reason that once you have faced your biggest adversaries, especially those residing within you, nothing else can defeat you. You will own your destiny. In other words, if you hate the dark, take a dark ride and it will no longer be a threat. If you are afraid of the water, take scuba lessons. If afraid of flying, take flying lessons. If too shy, join Toastmasters. If you fear numbers, get a degree in mathematics–not to master its intricacies, but to show yourself that numbers are your forte, not your nemesis. Once armed with a pedigree in your weakness, no one, including yourself, will ever again question your ability in that arena. The Wizard of Oz didn't give out hearts and brains; he dispensed pedigrees of hope. When you confront your greatest weaknesses, you will emerge much stronger and with more psychological tools to confront a much wider range of problems. In short, *move towards the danger!*

A baseball player who hits right-handed might apply this principle of confronting one's weakness by developing his ability to hit left-handed. As a switch-hitter, the player can adapt his swing to the pitcher he faces. The idea of moving toward your weaknesses can be extended to include developing the weaker parts of your personality. For example, if you are too aggressive, try being more sensitive. If too nurturing, practice being more detached. Males need to develop the feminine side of their nature and conversely, females need to develop their masculine side. It's analogous to developing an "ambidextrous personality." *Fortune* magazine wrote (Aug. 8, 1994), "Women entrepreneurs are more like men entrepreneurs than they are like other women." University of Chicago psychologist Mihaly Csikszentmihalyi studied 91 creative geniuses for his book *Creativity* (1996) and concluded:

> *Creative people escape rigid gender stereotyping. They have a tendency towards androgyny. They not only have the strengths of their own gender but those of the other.*

Psychologist Nathaniel Brandon, expressing the same idea, wrote, "Creative individuals are those who can integrate both male and female aspects of personality."

This author's research uncovered a similar propensity in great leaders. The Russians dubbed Margaret Thatcher the "Iron Lady" for her truculent ways and indomitable style. For them she was far too aggressive for a woman. Had Margaret been more submissive and less competitive, the Russians might have treated her more kindly on a personal level, but history would have been less kind. Thatcher was a great leader precisely because she was able to adapt to the needs of the moment. Her aggressiveness in a patriarchal society is what made her effective. It led her friend President Reagan to say, "Thatcher is the best man in England."

Coco Chanel is a prime example of someone who had developed both the male and female dimensions of her personality. Her personal friend and confidante, poet Jean Cocteau, described her as a woman whose sexual appetites were virile. "She sets out to conquer like a man" (Madsen, p. 120). Androgyny pervaded her very being and everything she designed or wore. The Coco approach to couture was a genderless style, yet a casually elegant fashion for women of taste. In the process, Chanel destroyed the frilly femininity that dominated turn-of-the-century fashion. One journalist wrote, "She invented expensive clothes ideal for the tomboy." Biographer Madsen said (p. 78):

> *She cut her hair to the length of young boys' and always dressed in defiance with a masculine edge.*

Confirming a need for opposition, she admitted, "I've been in business without being a businesswoman." *Vogue* opined (Madsen, p. 116):

> *[Chanel is]...a revolutionist, non-conformist, a lone rebel who let women out of the prison of tight corsets; women no longer exist, only the boys created by Chanel.*

Had Joan of Arc dressed as a girl and not cut her hair, it is unlikely the men of the time would have followed her into battle. Virginia Woolf wrote, "I have the feelings of a woman but only the words of a man." Martha Stewart, like Coco, is able to play both feminine and masculine roles when the situation demands. During her marriage to lawyer Andy Stewart she was the dominant personality. One reporter described Stewart as trying to make herself into a combination of "Betty Crocker, Julia Child, Emily Post, Miss Manners and Rupert Murdoch." Close friends in Westport, Connecticut described her as more the brassy powerbroker than the domestic diva portrayed on TV. Coincidentally, both she and Murdoch rule with a similar style–both are control freaks who take few prisoners.

"S" is the place that Carl Jung described as the conjunction of the male and female in the unconscious–the *syzygy*. It is that point of synthesis where logic meets vision, the practical meets the emotional, and the global comes together with the local. It is the integration of passion and passivity, the surreal and the real, and the micro and macro. The "S" spot is where the entrepreneurial genius can make ephemeral visions fit a rational world. It is where rationality harmonizes with emotion.

The entrepreneur operates with a credo that is both surreal and pragmatic. To describe the successful integration of the conception of what might be with the pragmatic consideration of what can be done, we use the expression, *synthesizing to success*. This is where the philosophic humanitarianism of Ford came to fruition with his need to "democratize the automobile" and make it "the people's car." It is the philosophical mantra of Bezos making the web easy for all who care to do business there. It is where Bucky Fuller conceived of a geodesic dome that would cover New York City and protect it from inclement weather. That same place allowed Bill Gates to give free rein to his visionary dreams of a "PC on every desk" through pervasive software programs. It is where the entrepreneur can dream impossible dreams but quantify them for the masses. The diagram on the opposite page attempts to illustrate the balance between the surreal and the practical that constitutes synthesizing to success.

SYNTHESIZING TO SUCCESS
BE WHAT YOU ARE AND WHAT YOU ARE NOT

S is that point–syzygy or synergy–where the micro and macro cross, where weakness is offset by strength, the masculine meets the feminine, the global is also local, and the real meets the surreal.

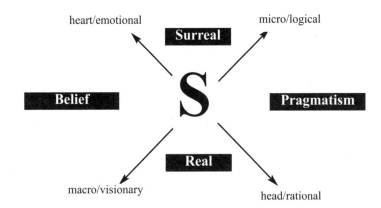

If all this seems "flaky" or simplistic to you, remember that all great ideas were once considered eccentric, outrageous or vague when first expressed. The essential idea here is that we must constantly challenge our old beliefs and our traditional ways of doing things. An important way to do this is to become receptive to those aspects of our nature that are dormant or undeveloped and ensure that they are given the opportunity to take us to new levels of awareness and understanding. This process might be described as the mental equivalent of a body builder changing his routine and working sets of muscles that were hitherto undeveloped.

TEST THE LIMITS: BIG WINS DEMAND BIG RISKS

Leverage is one type of risk-taking. With it one can grow exponentially or fall even faster. The poster boy for leverage in this work is J. Paul Getty, although Walton, Trump and Branson were not far behind. All were willing to bet existing assets on future opportunities and use them as collateral to grow. Getty used existing oil holdings to buy new ones and the multiplying effect made him a billionaire. His more conservative mother, trustee of his father's funds, was not thrilled, but leverage made him rich beyond his wildest dreams. Biographers characterized Getty as a miser. It is true that he watched every nickel, but frugality and a propensity for risk-taking are uncorrelated. Getty had a gambler's flare that catapulted him to the top of the list of the world's richest people.

For Getty, money equaled power. His power and strong libidinal drives led to a virtual harem of women who constituted his entourage for many years. Flamboyant daring is also sexy and Getty used his on-the-edge nature to make money and seduce women. In Getty's own words, "The meek shall inherit the earth but not the mineral rights." But the telling remarks about his feelings on risk came from his memoirs, "I buy when everyone else is selling and hold on until everyone is buying." As with most entrepreneurs, Getty had little regard for the security-driven corporate types whom he saw as incapable of adding to American's wealth. He wrote, "There are one hundred men seeking security to one man willing to risk his fortune."

Others in this book had a penchant similar to Getty's. Few men tested fate with the abandon of Richard Branson. The founder of the Virgin Group had numerous near-death adventures in the air. His adventures in business were equally risky. When asked about his daredevil antics he admitted, "I want to push myself to the limits, testing formidable odds." When facing insolvency, most executives cut back. Not Branson. He expanded and went even deeper into debt. In his memoir *Losing My Virginity* he wrote, "A cash crisis is not time to contract, but to expand" (Branson, p. 110). This temerity caused many less adventurous employees to leave but it also led to unprecedented growth.

Michael Dell had a similar propensity. He told his executives, "To make people successful you must make it safe for them to fail." Trump confirmed the same when he said, "I don't think anything scares me." His fearless approach to investing was evident in his wild leveraging in the late 1980s that nearly destroyed his empire. Trump used leverage like normal people use credit cards. When questioned about his aggressive style, he admitted, "To me business is nothing but a game."

CHASE A VISION, NEVER MONEY

Recall the quotation at the beginning of Chapter 13: "An entrepreneur is someone who works sixteen hours a day for himself [herself] to avoid working eight hours a day for someone else." This sheds some light on both the motivation and the reality of the entrepreneur's choice. Though initially working for money, the entrepreneur is eventually driven more by the passion than by the monetary rewards of the business. While money is usually a consideration, it is rarely the focal point of a mission. That's why all the entrepreneurs profiled in this book pressed on in their ventures long after they had more money than they could ever spend. Money was not the prime focus of any of the wealthiest entrepreneurs, although it was often used as a barometer of success.

Bucky Fuller made a career of developing innovative prototypes, such as the Dymaxion House, the Dymaxion Car and the geodesic dome. Then, when the opportunity for profits was imminent, he would abandon the project and move onto his next venture. Reflecting his disdain for accumulating substantial wealth, he wrote in *Critical Path* (Fuller, p. 276):

You can make money or make sense because the two are mutually exclusive. The drive to make money is inherently entropic for it seeks to monopolize order .

Despite total disregard for money as a prime focus, every one of the visionaries profiled in this book made more than they ever imagined. Money flowed to them because they executed a prescient idea better than their adversaries. British billionaire Richard Branson commented (*Fortune*, March 2001, p. 71):

I can honestly say, I have never gone into business to make money. I make up my mind about a business proposal or new people I meet within 30 seconds...Too much money early on will ensure failure later. If companies don't know that they can run out of money, they won't be thinking of ways not to run out of money.

Biographer Ward Kimball said of Walt Disney, "If you want to know the real secret of Disney's success, it's that he never tried to make money." He quoted Walt as saying (*Investors Business Daily*, Oct. 24, 2000, p. A4):

I've only thought of money in one way and that is to do something with. I plow back everything I make into the company. If I can't have fun with it, I'm not going to take it with me.

Thomas Edison never made one decision based on the money he could make. When he was told no one would take a chance on producing his incandescent light bulb, he vowed, "It is factories or death." Then he put up the money to build the first GE plants. In building Microsoft, Bill Gates' decisions were based on what was needed to expand and grow his company; money was not the prime consideration. For the entrepreneurial genius, money is an important tool and vital to building a business, but it pales relative to the larger issues of people, products, promotion and market penetration.

Chasing the right things is a theme that pervades the annals of successful entrepreneurship. The absence of this orientation in large traditional organizations explains why they notoriously failed at innovation. Such companies rarely lead the pack in breakthrough product innovation. Ted Turner created CNN, not the networks who should have. The innovative Fed Ex–overnight package delivery–was the brainchild of a young Vietnam pilot named Fred Smith, not of the U.S. Postal Service.

Jeff Bezos offered an insightful glimpse into the reason for this irony:

> *As companies get bigger, they have something to lose. When they do, the natural tendency is to get risk-averse. They lose their boldness. They lose the spirit to innovate. They lose their pioneering qualities. I am bound and determined not to let that happen to Amazon.com.*

Passion to realize their vision is what fuels great entrepreneurs. They operate on the precipice of change and enjoy the view. Salaried executives are seldom willing to compete in such an uncertain world. Entrepreneurs are as fiercely competitive as boxers and when faced with catastrophe have the tenacity of a dog defending a bone. Few of these qualities are found in the corporate world where security is valued and risk is an undesirable threat. The entrepreneurial genius is an iconoclast, often labeled as dilettante, flaky, unrealistic, dogmatic, and dictatorial.

Great entrepreneurs rarely allow money to interfere with their climb to success. They prefer chasing ideas to chasing money. In the world of capitalism, we use money to keep score. However, if you have a prescient insight and execute your vision well, the money will be delivered in trucks. You will make more money than you ever dreamed. But if you try to make money as a goal, it will probably elude you. (The reason for this irony is explained more fully near the end of this chapter in the section titled, *Paradoxical Intention: Trying Too Hard is Counter-Productive*.) Strangely, those people who chase money seldom get much. Those who pursue their vision with a passion end up with billions.

IF IT AIN'T BROKE, BREAK IT!

Sam Walton has instructed us, "if it ain't broke, break it!" This is merely another way of saying one must creatively destroy in order to innovate. Those unwilling or incapable of destroying existing paradigms or prod-ucts will never succeed. They are programmed to follow traditional paths that impede their creativity. The price of abandoning your creative ideas is evident in the old business adage: *if you don't do it, someone else will.* Coco Chanel defied the world of couture by making black dresses acceptable for occasions other than mourning. Prior to Ross Perot, computers were bought or leased, never bought and leased. When his employer IBM refused to buy into his radical idea, he went ahead and did it himself. Henry Ford was equally radical when he dared alter conventional factory methods by bringing the assembly line to the workers instead of having the workers move to the line. Hugh Hefner defied the moral majority by daring to flagrantly launch a classy magazine with full nudity. Michael Dell defied the experts by selling PCs direct, bypassing traditional distribution channels. What is this message? Unless you are willing to break with tradition you will not be able to alter the world. The contemplation of radical change is often frustrated by fear: the fear of rejection, the fear of being wrong, the fear of losing money, the fear of losing respect, the fear of being an outcast among peers!

In *Spirit of Enterprise* (1984), George Gilder wrote:

> *Entrepreneurship entails breaking the looking glass of established ideas and stepping into the often greasy and fetid bins of creation.*

Eric Winslow and George Solomon wrote a treatise on the subject concluding, "Entrepreneurs are more than mildly non-conformist, they are mildly sociopathic. They are analogous to the dropouts of the sixties." Philosopher Frederick Nietzsche offered further validation in *Thus Spake Zarathustra*:

> *Whoever wants to be the creator of good and evil must first be an annihilator and break values. Thus, the greatest evil belongs to the greatest goodness; but that is being creative.*

START WITH THE ANSWER–REAL OR FANTASY

Leonardo da Vinci wrote, "Consider first the end." This was his prescient advice for those desirous of pursuing a life in science, art and building. The entrepreneurial genius does the same–begins with a goal and works backwards to the present. Only in that way does the entrepreneur see the steps along the journey that lead to that destination. Then the entrepreneur forgets the original goal and works diligently on the fundamental pieces that lead to that goal. Philosophical novelist Ayn Rand described her approach to her novels in commenting, "I think in reverse." By this, she meant that she conceived how her novel would end and worked backward through the steps that would lead to that end, then dedicated all her writing passion to developing each of the steps.

Believe and the World Will Follow You–Anywhere

Self-confidence is key to all success. In fact, until you believe, not much is possible. Most entrepreneurs have a high internal locus of control, believing themselves responsible for their own destiny and able to achieve whatever task is at hand. At the extreme end of this spectrum is arrogance. An optimism that exceeds one's ability to achieve manifests itself as false bravado or arrogance. The peril inherent in arrogance is captured in the adage, "Pride goeth before a fall." Frank Lloyd Wright had such a reputation and so has Donald Trump. Some characterize Trump as an egomaniac. This epithet doesn't seem to bother him because he knows that he must believe in his dreams or he would never have achieved what he has.

Ross Perot has a similar penchant for egomania. When Perot sold EDS to General Motors he was asked to take a seat on the Board of Directors. It was more honorary than functional, but not to the Texas Tycoon. The directors at GM didn't expect him to show up, let alone come in and tell them how to run their automobile empire. But that was the style of the Texas gunslinger. Despite having no knowledge of the highly complex auto industry, Perot not only showed up at the board meetings, but also had the audacity to challenge Chairman Roger Smith on virtually every item on the agenda. Soon *persona non grata*, he was asked to leave. That same haughty sense of self led to his running for the U.S. Presidency not once, but twice–1992 and 1996. An army of faithful followers loved his folksy down-home style when he brashly announced he was going to Washington to show those city slickers how to run the country. Such a Napoleonic complex and "can do" attitude led him to the top as an entrepreneur, though such arrogance was less effective in the political arena.

Passionate Perfection Is the Path to Power

The mother of modern dance, Isadora Duncan, wrote, "I was so into my work I would go into a state of static ecstasy." Such passion breaks down almost any barrier and in so doing becomes the pathway to productivity and peace. Why? Because when one becomes so excited, so dedicated, so intensely involved in one's dream that all else takes second place, the ultimate result is success. Passion overcomes most adversity and permits the entrepreneur to function well outside the more grounded mainstream without fear. Martha Stewart is this book's poster girl for passion. She is passion incarnate, working most of the twenty hours a day she is awake.

The road behind Martha is strewn with many corpses, a negative conse-quence of excessive passion. Biographer Christopher Byron wrote in *Martha, Inc.* (2002) an insightful analysis of her charm and flipside cru-elty. He said, "She was sacrificing every personal relationship in order to expand her sphere of influence." Passion and perfection were her mantra throughout her journey to the top.

Zealots like Martha are passionate to a fault. The pure freneticism and raw energy that fuels the success of the passionate entrepreneur is often also the catalyst for their failures. The pure cathartic energy exuded by such people earns them characterizations as weird or eccentric. The pas-sionate get more done in a shorter time–maniacs on a mission–but the price they pay can be high indeed. In *Paradoxes of Creativity* (1990) Jacques Barzun wrote:

> *Passionate madness is the reason why psychopathic personalities are often creators and why their productions are perfectly sane.*

Napoleon Hill reported similar findings in *Think & Grow Rich*, his research on America's great industrialists. Hill wrote, "Sex energy [passion] is the creative energy of all geniuses."

To Be Big, Think Big–Real Big

Trump often said in his memoirs about making deals, "To be big you must think big." It is no accident that Trump owns the largest penthouse in Manhattan and one of the most elegant and stately mansions in Palm Beach, Mar-a-Lago. He was not content with owning a couple of huge casinos in Atlantic City, he had to own the largest–The Taj Mahal. If it wasn't big, Trump wasn't interested. He displayed unabashed pride in his achievements when he challenged the New York media, "Who has done more for New York City than I have?" Such a strong sense of self is key to what he has achieved. "I like to think big and it gives me a big advantage." He is right.

Those who change the world are the people who dream big, think big and execute in grand style. Ford dreamed of superhighways when horses were still the primary mode of transportation, Bucky Fuller dreamed of encapsulating cities within large geodesic domes and Bezos is now dreaming of commercial space travel. Thinking big is allowing yourself to enter the "S" spot or seeking the syzygy, where the imagination is encouraged to run amok–unfettered by what is and in pursuit of what might be. It is this ability that turns an entrepreneur into a visionary.

IMAGE IS EVERYTHING IN BRANDING

In *Charismatic Leadership* (1989), Canadian educator Jay Conger spoke of charisma as a necessary characteristic of success. It is also a critical component of entrepreneurial genius. Conger says, "Charismatic leaders have always personified the forces of change: unconventionality, vision and entrepreneurial spirit." These words describe Richard Branson, this book's poster boy for charismatic power. The founder of Virgin has left little doubt that image is everything in his world of products and services. By dressing in drag to launch Virgin Brides and driving a tank into Times Square in New York City to launch Virgin Cola, Branson has proven that flamboyance can get press coverage that generates brand equity for commercial products. You may recall from his profile (Chapter 10) how he avoided potential lawsuits from false claims that Virgin Cola was an aphrodisiac–he merely stated that there was no scientific evidence supporting [the widely held belief] that Virgin Cola was an aphrodisiac. That was pure promotional genius!

Few businessmen in history have had the nerve or verve to attempt the wild promotional schemes seen at Virgin Airlines. Brand equity was vital to sales and Branson knew he didn't have the cash to compete with British Airways. However, he was able to do what they couldn't, i.e., take off on international balloon rides in a brazen but life-threatening scheme to set a world record and gain media attention. How many business men would risk their lives to build brand recognition? Market studies have found that Branson established an image equal in magnitude to that of James Bond. The British press has coined the adjective *bransonesque* to describe such flamboyant promotional behavior. When Branson calls a press conference, few dare miss it. What reporter would want to miss his arrival, hanging precariously from a helicopter, at his 1989 wedding to long-time love Joan Templeman. The greatest product in the world will not sell without brand recognition. That has never been a problem for Virgin Enterprises where the boss understands that press coverage is godly.

Effective communication is the key to entrepreneurial success. Coco Chanel personified such talent for communication. At the House of Chanel she insisted on having the best address and the most elegant showroom. She inevitably appeared impeccably attired at all events. Style was her business and she oozed it. She was one of the first to show that form can exceed function. The girl reared in an orphanage went out of her way to show that splendor was not costly, but absolutely necessary for the elite. Before she was able to afford her rent, she would arrive at her showroom in a Rolls-Royce from her abode at the fashionable Ritz Hotel. Fashion, grace and elegance were her forte, attracting the aristocracy to her shop in downtown Paris. Part of this whole role-playing, so critical to her success, was articulated in a philosophy that said, "aloofness equates with mystique." Coco made herself into the Mistress of Mystique, writing "A client seen is a client lost." For Coco, building a mystique–a mysterious image–was vital to success. When courted by the richest man in Europe, she saw fit to remind him, "There are a lot of duchesses but only one Coco Chanel."

AVOID INSTANT GRATIFICATION

Entrepreneurial geniuses worship at the altar of risk and tend to sacrifice the present for the future. In contrast, corporate executives are inclined to sacrifice the future for the present, while worshiping at the altar of security. Instant gratification is the bane of innovation. That is why most entrepreneurs are at odds with politicians. To someone in a job that must demonstrate immediate results, "now" is infinitely more important than "tomorrow." Entrepreneurs cannot afford to be so inclined. Bezos was berated by Wall Street mavens for not buying into the quarterly-profit mania that permeates the psyche of traditional executives. But Jeff was never motivated by the need to keep his job and therefore refused to trade off long-term market share for near-term stock prices. The corporate slogan is "make the quarterly profits and keep Wall Street happy." That is contrary to the entrepreneurial culture that says "optimize long-term market share and product viability, and profits will eventually come, but do not sacrifice the future for an early win." Entrepreneurs seldom fall prey to the quarterly profit syndrome.

Jeff Bezos got it right when he said, "The landscape of people who do new things and expect to be profitable quickly is littered with corpses" (Spector, p. 85). Wall Street never bought into this philosophy. From a far more self-serving perspective, it denigrated him for his penchant for placing market share and growth above profits. Had profits been the prime motivator for him, he would never have quit a million-dollar-a-year job to launch Amazon in the first place. Jeff went for two years at Amazon without a paycheck. The street has also denigrated him for the *get-big-fast* strategy. But Bezos knew, better than they, that if he didn't create a strong base to compete effectively with Barnes & Noble, he wouldn't be around. He knew from day one that selling over the web demands a critical mass of customers. Wall Street is only interested in short-run profits it can tout to sell stock. The visionary entrepreneur and traditional executives see the world from entirely different perspectives. The former lives in the long term and the latter in the short. Amazon.com stock prices, and to a lesser extent Jeff's personal fortune, paid a price for his long-term view up to 2002. Frustrated analysts were incensed that he made a billion dollars before Amazon.com made a profit. Bezos added insult to injury with his statement, "In December 1995 we were profitable for about one hour. It was probably a big mistake." However, by mid-2003, Amazon was declaring significant profits.

For Henry Ford, long-term goals were the only goals worth setting. It got him fired from two different ventures, but in the long run it made him a billionaire. In those first ventures, the power elite wanted the quick profits associated with high-priced cars for the affluent markets. Ford knew the big gains lay with the masses, not the classes, and in the end he had his way with the launch of the Model T. What initially got him fired eventually made him rich and famous. That is true for many.

AVOID CONVENTION AND TRADITIONAL DOGMAS

Four centuries ago, the brilliant scientist and philosopher, Francis Bacon, observed, "Authority is worthless." Why would a philosopher express such a negative view of the establishment? As a man of insight, victimized by those in power, he observed how they were grounded in the status quo and inclined to demean anything new and original. He observed that they were so steeped in *what is* that they had a difficult time accepting *what might be*. This *expert* syndrome pervades all established venues: the more established the expert, the more virulent the disease.

In business, experts tend to protect their own values or markets. When Bell Labs sold the rights to the transistor to fledgling start-up Sony of Japan, they were acting within their legal rights. However, this sale helped destroy the American radio industry. Bell Labs were protecting their own dominant market position in vacuum tube production. Fear of losing market share often interferes with innovative product introductions. The great entrepreneurs are seldom steeped in fear, because they are too busy trying to change the world to worry about others who might destroy them. Realizing that there is only so much energy in every human spirit, they use it positively. Edison admonished his adversaries, "Nothing here is private. Everyone is at liberty to see all he can and Edison will tell them all the rest" (Josephson 1959). For Edison there were no secrets. That was his strength, and he refused to allow a fear of losing market share to dissipate his energy.

Ironically, like most experts, Edison himself eventually fell victim to the expert syndrome. The Wizard of Menlo Park went to his grave denying the viability of alternating current–the electrical grid that now lights our cities and powers our factories. Why? Because he had operated with direct current. It seems that the need to protect the psyche is even greater than the need to protect assets. The reason for this is that people, even great people like Einstein who denied the viability of quantum physics, have such a psychological investment in *what is* that they are unable to see *what might be*. Thomas Kuhn described this predilection, pointing out that until the reigning experts die off, new paradigms and scientific revolutions will never be accepted.

Aspiring entrepreneurs should be willing to dismiss expert opinion when it runs contrary to their own instincts. Freud liked to say that when too many people agreed with his ideas he might be in trouble. Walt Disney came to use adversarial opinion as a motivating force. When he was working on the first ever full-length animated film, *Snow White*, everyone of note in Hollywood demeaned it, including his brother Roy. No less a titan than Louis B. Mayer labeled the animated film "Disney's Folly."

Those who fall into the category of "expert" know so much that they are aware of the magnitude of what they don't know. This awareness of their own limitations often prompts them to seek the advice and support of other experts to mitigate risk. However, by definition, entrepreneurship *is* risk; mitigating it is contrary to the process. Both Estée Lauder and Mary Kay Ash were told by their legal counsels not to go forward with their entrepreneurial ventures. Fortunately, neither of them listened! Such advice is not only misleading from the perspective of a business strategy, but can also prove disastrous by thwarting potentially innovative breakthrough ideas.

Without risk there are no potential rewards. Risk and reward are positively correlated, i.e., for every risk removed, a potential bit of reward will be removed. In 1996, Michael Dell told *Fortune* magazine, "The thing that sets Dell apart [and generates significant rewards] is its ability to do exactly what the competition tends to believe cannot be done." The quest for absolute rigor in sales projections and market analysis has been aptly described as *rigor mortis.*

When just starting out, the young Michael Dell was told he would fail because he was not doing what the experts were doing. But Dell was too young and too naïve to listen. After many such forays into adversarial waters he said (Dell, p. 12):

Sometimes it's better not to ask or listen when people tell you something can't be done. I didn't ask for permission or approval. I just went ahead and did it.

In *Direct from Dell*, he advised entrepreneurs to "think unconventionally." He modeled this approach when he launched Dell Computer Corporation in England. No fewer than 22 journalists showed up at his British press conference; virtually every one of them wrote of his early demise. Ignoring their chilling predictions, he proceeded and within three years was number one in Britain, reaching $2 billion in revenues. It was a good thing he ignored those pompous "experts."

Similarly, Ross Perot was told he was on the wrong track with EDS. His bosses at IBM told him he was crazy. Sam Walton experienced much the same. When he told his franchisor, the Butler Brothers in Chicago, of his idea for retailing, they told him to go back to Arkansas and do what he knows. The nay-sayers told him he would never be able to compete with the likes of Kmart and Target. What if he had listened? The world of retail would have been different.

Most people fear the ambiguities, contradictions and paradoxes of life that create a *cognitive dissonance*–a confusion about how they should proceed. Entrepreneurs rarely get lost, even when they don't know where they are. What they find exhilarating, the rest of the world finds debilitating. The twelve entrepreneurs profiled in this book violated traditional thinking and conventional practice to create new products and processes. In so doing, they displayed a tolerance for the cognitive dissonance that comes with swimming against the current. They did what they were not supposed to do and that is precisely what made them great. Few people have such temerity. Chanel No. 5 became the best-selling perfume in history despite the fact that Coco violated every principle of the industry. In a similar manner, Michael Dell challenged the traditional distribution systems of the computer industry. Hefner did the same in publishing, as did Walton in retailing. It is what made them great. Had they not been highly adept at confronting and embracing cognitive dissonance, they would not have attained such high levels of achievement.

With all their eccentricities, compulsions and what some might refer to as personality disorders, the great entrepreneurs all shared some fundamental winning behaviors that brought them extraordinary measures of success. These are summarized on the opposite page as *Landrum's Laws of Entrepreneurial Genius.*

LANDRUM'S LAWS OF ENTREPRENEURIAL GENIUS

1. **TO LEARN HOW TO SUCCEED, FAIL**
   Breakdown leads to breakthrough & crises to creativity.

2. **SYNTHESIZE TO SUCCESS BY ATTACKING WEAKNESS**
   To be the best you can be, be what you're not.

3. **TEST THE LIMITS: BIG WINS DEMAND BIG RISKS**
   Fear is the mortal enemy of the entrepreneur.

4. **CHASE A VISION, NEVER MONEY**
   Execute elegantly and money will be delivered in trucks.

5. **IF IT AIN'T BROKE, BREAK IT**
   Creative destruction—the secret of creative genius.

6. **START WITH THE ANSWER–REAL OR FANTASY**
   Intuitive insight is magic.

7. **BELIEVE AND THE WORLD WILL FOLLOW YOU–ANYWHERE**
   Identify a market void, whether real or imagined, and fill it.

8. **PASSIONATE PERFECTION IS THE PATH TO POWER**
   Energy emanates from a driven person on a mission.

9. **TO BE BIG, THINK BIG–REAL BIG**
   To be big, dream big and in full color using the full spectrum.

10. **IMAGE IS EVERYTHING IN BRANDING**
    Charisma & hype are catalysts for building brand equity.

11. **AVOID INSTANT GRATIFICATION**
    Sacrifice the present for the future and you'll own the future.

12. **AVOID CONVENTION AND TRADITIONAL DOGMAS**
    They are self-serving and too steeped in mediocrity.

Entrepreneurial Eminence Transcends Operating Expertise

Landrum's Laws of Entrepreneurial Genius are not intended as a blueprint on how to proceed to become a great entrepreneur. There is no simple algorithm or recipe that can serve as a step-by-step program for success. The idea is to reach within yourself to tap into your own resources, passions and intuition. While reading the profiles in this book, you have probably realized that great entrepreneurs operate in a world of their own making that is more metaphysical than physical, more unconscious than conscious and more surreal than real. At some point they have risen above convention and entered an ethereal zone that transcends the perspective of all but a few visionaries. Philosophy is more important in their decisions than function and the long term far more important than the short. This makes them abnormal and their abnormality is what makes them great.

My intent in this book is to inspire you to get in touch with your own potential and to let you know that it's okay to be different. In fact, you cannot be exceptional without being exceptionally different. Though not a profound concept, it is one that is truly understood by only a small fraction of the world's population, and these are the people who constitute the make-things-happen group.

Paradoxical Intention: Trying Too Hard Is Counterproductive

Sometimes my students interpret the driven intensity and "workaholic" tendencies of the entrepreneurial geniuses as an admonition to work harder. They believe that doubling their efforts will double their results. A half-century ago, German psychiatrist Viktor Frankl stumbled upon the principle of *paradoxical intention* while working with impotent men. He found that the harder they tried to perform, the less chance they had. Success came only when they stopped trying. Because the concept of achieving success by trying less is counterintuitive, Frankl used the adjective "paradoxical" in describing the syndrome. In his classic treatise, *Man's Search for Meaning*, he writes (Frankl, p. 16–7):

> *Don't aim at success–the more you aim at it and make it a target, the more you are going to miss it. For success, like happiness, cannot be pursued, it must ensue, and it only does so as the unintended side effect of one's personal dedication to a cause greater than oneself.*

The principle of paradoxical intention applies to the great entrepreneurs who did not focus on money but rather on their passion, allowing the money to come as a by-product. Modern business captures this idea in the adage, "Don't work harder, work smarter."

WHEN IS THE RIGHT TIME TO LAUNCH AN ENTREPRENEURIAL VENTURE?

Many entrepreneurs acquired their skills while employed by someone else. Ford was employed as an engineer, Hefner as promotional copywriter, Perot as a salesman for IBM and Bezos as Vice-President of a financial trading firm. During this employment, they were in their incubation phase, acquiring skills and knowledge that would serve them later when they embarked on their own entrepreneurial ventures. Some of these entrepreneurial geniuses, such as Ford and Perot, pursued their first entrepreneurial ventures on the side while they were fully employed. Others, like Bezos, quit their day jobs before embarking on their venture. The preferable approach depends on a variety of factors, including one's family situation, financial resources and field of endeavor.

Once you feel you have acquired the skills and knowledge to embark on an entrepreneurial venture, you should proceed undaunted by the prevailing economic conditions or predictions of future gloom. In fact, it has been found that most great breakthroughs have occurred during periods of breakdown, giving credence to the assertion that crisis is the mother of creativity. Soichiro Honda only started building Honda motorcycles after his parts factory was bombed in Tokyo. Henry Ford, Walt Disney and Bucky Fuller only started ventures after they were fired. Martha Stewart started catering after the 1970s Wall Street debacle. Hewlett-Packard emerged in 1938 during the Great Depression when Bill Hewlett and David Packard were hard pressed to find employment. Other examples of great ventures that were born in periods of crisis:

- Henry Ford launched his firm during the 1902–1904 recession.
- Walt Disney started his cartoon company in a Hollywood garage during the 1923–24 recession.
- Bill Gates dropped out of Harvard to start Microsoft during the depths of the 1975 recession.

How you proceed should depend on your own risk-taking propensity. If you take risks beyond your comfort level, your effectiveness will be undermined by your short-term financial concerns. Of course, lower risks usually yield lower rewards, but that is preferable to total failure. If you are not setting out to become a billionaire, then it is not necessary to take huge risks. It is most important that you build your knowledge and skills until you find your passion and your vision. Then pursue your vision with an intensity that balances the rewards you seek with the risks you are prepared to take. But remember to think big–real big. I wish you well and know you will enjoy the ride.

Are You an Entrepreneur?

DIRECTIONS: For each of the 40 statements below, assign scores between 1 and 5 to indicate the accuracy of each statement as it applies to you. A score of 1 means that the statement does *not* accurately describe you, while a score of 5 means it describes you accurately. Record the subtotal in each box.

A. COMMUNICATIONS STYLE (CHARISMA)   1-2-3-4-5
1. You have a rich and fluent vocabulary. _____
2. You are excellent at self-expression. _____
3. Others are attracted to you and follow your lead. _____
4. You fantasize about your dreams to anyone who will listen. _____
5. Your confidence overcomes the negativity of others. _____

   Total .... ☐

B. VIEW OF THE WORLD (INTUITIVENESS)   1-2-3-4-5
6. You see the big picture in most things. _____
7. You are more interested in the qualitative than the quantitative. _____
8. You see the importance of "possibilities" in your life. _____
9. You are often referred to as a flake or renegade. _____
10. Long-term concepts are more appealing than short-term. _____

   Total .... ☐

C. CREATIVITY (INNOVATION)   1-2-3-4-5
11. Fantasy is more important to you than reality. _____
12. You are inquisitive to a fault. _____
13. You have a strong need to know–seeker of new knowledge. _____
14. You prefer math to accounting, the abstract to the routine. _____
15. You are intolerant of useless conformity. _____

   Total... ☐

D. LIFESTYLE (RISK-TAKING PROPENSITY)   1-2-3-4-5
16. You thrive on tackling new adventures. _____
17. You are willing to get lost to experience something new. _____
18. You prefer a challenge to a known routine. _____
19. You prefer new opportunities to safe and secure havens. _____
20. You never do anything just for money. _____

   Total .... ☐

E. INTENSITY (DRIVE)   1-2-3-4-5

21. You are impatient and intolerant of others.

22. You prefer to work independently.

23. You are easily bored with routine tasks.

24. You enjoy juggling many tasks vs. one assignment.

25. You eat, talk, walk and think faster than most.

Total ....

F. SELF-IMAGE (SELF-CONFIDENCE)   1-2-3-4-5

26. You believe you can accomplish something never attempted.

27. You are more optimistic than pessimistic.

28. You need little direction once given a task.

29. Others often regard you as arrogant.

30. You give candid responses to controversial questions.

Total ....

G. CRITICAL THINKING STYLE (ICONOCLASTIC)   1-2-3-4-5

31. You would rather be different than perfect.

32. You ask many questions in lectures.

33. You have a compulsion to simplify the complex.

34. You seek the similarities and differences in things and people.

35. You are flexible and ingenious.

Total ....

H. SELF-SUFFICIENCY (INDEPENDENCE)   1-2-3-4-5

36. You need few support systems to perform tasks.

37. Achievement is very important to you.

38. You prefer variety to structure.

39. You grasp new concepts quickly.

40. You get things done without being told.

Total ....

See next page for the results of your self-assessment.

ARE YOU AN ENTREPRENEUR?

SCORING DEVICE

This assessment instrument was based on my research on 50 eminent entrepreneurs and 50 visionary leaders, artists and scientists. Propensity for entrepreneurship, as in most things, is a matter of degree and your assessment of this degree is, of course, subjective. For these reasons, the results of this assessment should be regarded as a first step in determining whether you're cut out to be an entrepreneur. If you score high in entrepreneurial propensity, it does not guarantee that you will be a successful entrepreneur, and a low score should not discourage you from pursuing your passion in an entrepreneurial direction. However, the power of this instrument is that it provides a mechanism for you to assess the likelihood that you have the personality that is consistent with entrepreneurial success. Some people are better suited to work for themselves, while others are more content with a job; a few (3–6%) should spend their lives creating new paradigms or changing the world.

To determine your overall entrepreneurial propensity, total the numbers in the eight boxes from A through H to obtain a grand total. Then find where your total fits in the table below to determine your preferred career path.

For each of the eight personality characteristics (A through H), a score between 18 and 25 indicates a strong presence of that trait in your personality.

Charisma is critical to selling your ideas, raising money, and motivating a work force.
Intuition is important in identifying market needs and creating products to meet them.
Strong self-image is necessary to sustain you against the resistance of nay-sayers.
Risk-taking propensity is a prerequisite to charting new unknown territory.
Iconoclastic thinking is also a prerequisite to the creative destruction necessary.
Passion is highly correlated with success; get excited or get a job.

Score	Entrepreneurial Propensity	Preferred Career Path
175–200	Excellent	Work on state-of-the-art ventures/products.
140–174	Good chance	Be a professional or operate your own business.
100–139	Fair chance	Pursue marketing ventures or create a small business.
75–100	Some chance	Work in a corporate environment.
<75	Little chance	Word for a bureaucracy, e.g., government

ENTREPRENEURSHIP

Baumeister, Roy & Smart, Laura. (1996) "The Dark Side of High Self-Esteem." *American Psychological Association Psychological Review,* Vol. 103.

Bygrave, William. (1997) *The Portable MBA in Entrepreneurship.* New York: John Wiley & Sons.

Collins, James & Porras, Jerry. (1997) *Built to Last.* New York: Harper.

Drucker, Peter. (1985) *Innovation and Entrepreneurship.* New York: Harper & Row.

Farley, Frank. (May 1986) "Type T Personality." *Psychology Today.* pp. 46–52.

Franzini, Louis & John Grossberg. (1995) *Eccentric & Bizarre Behaviors.* New York: John Wiley & Sons.

Garber, Michael. (1995) *The E-Myth.* New York: Harper Business.

Gardner, Howard (1983) *Frames of Mind: The Theory of Multiple Intelligences.* New York: Basic Books.

Gilder, George. (1984) *The Spirit of Enterprise.* New York: Simon & Schuster.

Hill, Napoleon. (1960) *Think and Grow Rich.* New York: Fawcett Crest.

Homer-Dixon, Thomas. (2000) *The Ingenuity Gap.* New York: Knopf.

Hutchison, Michael. (1990) *The Anatomy of Sex and Power.* New York: Morrow.

Jamison, Kay. (1994) *Touched with Fire.* New York: The Free Press.

Martens, Rainer, Robin Vealey, & Damon Burton. (1990) *Competitive Anxiety in Sport.* Champaigne, IL.: Human Kinetics Books.

Peterson, Karen S. (Sept 14, 1998) "Power, Sex, Risk." *USA Today.* p. D6.

Pickover, Clifford. (1998) *Strange Brains and Genius.* New York: William Morrow.

Saxon, A.H. (1989) *P. T. Barnum: The Legend and the Man.* New York: Columbia University Press.

Sciabarra, Chris Mathew. (1995) *Ayn Rand: The Russian Radical.* Penn State University Press.

Storr, Anthony. (1996) *Feet of Clay: Saints, Sinners & Madmen–A Study of Gurus.* New York: Free Press.

Time – Collector's Edition. (July 2001) "American Legends"–Builders & Titans Section.

Zubov, V. P. (1968) *Leonardo da Vinci.* New York: Barnes & Noble.

GENERAL REFERENCES

Adler, Alfred. (1979) *Superiority and Social Interest*. 3rd rev. ed. New York: Norton & Co.

Boorstin, Daniel. (1992) *The Creators*. New York: Random House.

Branden, Nathaniel. (1994) *Six Pillars of Self-Esteem*. New York: Bantam.

Buckingham, Marcus & Coffman, Curt. (1999) *First, Break All the Rules*. New York: Simon & Schuster.

Collins, James & Jerry Porras. (1997) *Built to Last*. New York: Harper Business.

Clark, Barbara. (1988) *Growing Up Gifted*. 3rd ed. Columbus, OH: Merrill.

Conger, Jay. (1989) *The Charismatic Leader*. San Francisco, CA: Jossey-Bass.

Csikszentmihalyi, Mihaly. (1996) *Creativity: Flow and the Psychology of Discovery and Invention*. New York: Harper Collins.

Frankl, Viktor. (1959) *Man's Search for Meaning*. New York: Pocket Books.

Gardner, Howard. (1997) *Extraordinary Minds*. New York: Basic Books.

_____ (1993) *Creating Minds*. New York: Basic Books.

_____ (1983) *Frames of Mind: The Theory of Multiple Intelligences*. New York: Basic Books.

Ghiselin, Brewster. (1952) *The Creative Process*. Berkeley CA: Berkeley Press.

Gilder, George. (1984) *The Spirit of Enterprise*. New York: Simon & Schuster.

Goleman, Daniel. (1995) *Emotional Intelligence*. New York: Bantam.

Hadamard, Jacques. (1945) *An Essay on the Psychology of Invention in the Mathematical Field*. Princeton: Princeton University Press.

Heatherton, Todd F. & Joel Weinberger. (1993) *Can Personality Change?*. Washington D.C.: American Psychological Association.

Hershman, D. & Lieb, J. (1988) *The Key to Genius: Manic Depression and the Creative Life*. Buffalo, N.Y.: Prometheus.

Hirsh, Sandra & Kummerow, Jean. (1989) *Life Types*. New York: Time Warner.

Hopkins, Jim. (2001) "Bad Times Spawn Great Start-ups: Entrepreneurs Flourish when Recession Strikes." *USA Today*. Dec 18, p. B-1.

Jung, Carl & Joseph Campbell. Ed. (1971) *The Portable Jung*. New York: Penguin Books.

Keirsey, David. (1987) *Portraits of Temperament*. Del Mar, CA.:Prometheus Books.

Keirsey, D. & Bates, M. (1984) *Please Understand Me*. Del Mar, Ca.: Prometheus Books.

Klein, Burton. (1977) *Dynamic Economics*. Cambridge, MA: Harvard University Press.

GENERAL REFERENCES

Kuhn, T. S. (1962) *The Structure of Scientific Revolutions.* Chicago: University of Chicago Press.

Landrum, Gene. (2001) *Sybaritic Genius.* Naples, FL: Genie-Vision Books.

_____ (1999) *Eight Keys to Greatness.* Buffalo, N.Y.: Prometheus Books.

_____ (1997) *Profiles of Black Success.* Buffalo, N.Y.: Prometheus Books.

_____ (1996) *Profiles of Power & Success.* Buffalo, N.Y.: Prometheus Books.

_____ (1994) *Profiles of Female Genius.* Buffalo, N.Y.: Prometheus Books.

_____ (1993) *Profiles of Genius.* Buffalo, N.Y.: Prometheus Books.

Leman, Kevin. (1985) *The Birth Order Book.* New York: Dell Publishing.

Ludwig, Arnold. (1995) *The Price of Greatness.* New York: Guilford Press.

Ornstein, Robert. (1972) *The Psychology of Consciousness.* New York: Penguin.

Ouchi, William. (1981) *Theory Z.* New York: Avon.

Prigogine, Ilya & Isabelle Stengers. (1984) *Order Out of Chaos.* New York: Bantam Books.

Silver, A. David. (1985) *Entrepreneurial Megabucks.* New York: Wiley.

Simonton, Dean Keith. (1994) *Greatness.* New York: Guilford Press.

Sternberg, Robert. (1996) *Successful Intelligence.* New York: Simon & Schuster.

Storr, Anthony. (1996) *Feet of Clay: Saints, Sinners & Madmen–A Study of Gurus.* New York: Free Press.

_____ (1993) *The Dynamics of Creation.* New York: Ballantine.

Sulloway, Frank. (1996) *Born to Rebel: Birth Order, Family Dynamics, and Creative Lives.* New York: Pantheon Books.

Tobach, E., L. R. Aronson & E. Shaw. Eds. (1971) *The Biopsychology of Development.* New York: Academic Press.

Walker, Evan Harris. (2000) *The Physics of Consciousness.* New York: Perseus Books.

Weeks, David & Jamie James. (1995) *Eccentrics: A Study of Sanity and Strangeness.* New York: Villard.

Wilson, Robert Anton. (1990) *Quantum Psychology.* Phoenix, AZ.: Falcon Press.

Wolinsky, Stephen. (1994) *The Tao of Chaos.* Norfolk, CT: Bramble Books

SUBJECT REFERENCES

HENRY FORD

Bennett, Harry & Paul Marcus (1951) *Ford: We Never Called Him Henry*, New York: Tor.

Collier, Peter, & David Horowitz. (1987) *The Fords: An American Epic*. New York: Summitt Books.

Collins, James & Porras, Jerry. (1997) *Built to Last*. New York: Harper Business.

Gilder, George. (1984) *The Spirit of Enterprise*. New York: Simon & Schuster.

Herndon, Booton. (1970) *Ford*. New York: Avon.

Lacey, Robert. (1986) *Ford, The Men and the Machine*. New York: Ballantine Books.

Time–Collector's Edition. (July 2001) "American Legends"–Builders & Titans, p. 58.

COCO CHANEL

Berman, Phyllis. (April 3, 1989) "The Billionaire Behind Chanel." *Forbes*, p. 104.

Madsen, Axel. (1990) *Chanel*. New York: Henry Holt.

McColl, Patricia. (Sept 13, 1999) "Coco Chanel Interview" *WWD,* p. S-20.

Sischy, Ingrid. (Jan. 25, 1971) "The Designer Coco Chanel." *Time 100: Artists & Entertainers:* Web site: www.web1.infotrac.Galegroup.com.

Thomas, Dana. (Aug. 20, 2000) "Fashions." *New York Times,* p. 123.

Time. (June 8, 1998) "Coco Chanel." v151, p 98.

Wallach, Janet. (1998) *Chanel: Her Style & Her Life*. New York: Doubleday.

J. PAUL GETTY

Getty, J. Paul. (1983) *How to Be Rich*. New York: The Berkley Publishing Group.

Lenzner, Robert. (1986) *The Great Getty*. New York: Crown.

Miller, Russell. (1985) *The House of Getty*. New York: Henry Holt.

Perkins, Jack. (2000) "The Gettys." *A&E Biography*.

BUCKMINSTER FULLER

Baldwin, J. (1996) *BuckyWorks: Buckminster Fuller's Ideas Today*. New York: John Wiley & Sons.

BFI Institute. (World Wide website: www.bfi.org). "Who is Buckminster Fuller?"

Fuller, R. Buckminster. (1981) *Critical Path*. New York: St. Martin's Press.

Hatch, Alden. (1974) *Buckminster Fuller*. New York: Crown.

SAM WALTON

Collins, James & Porras, Jerry. (1997) *Built to Last*. New York: Harper Business.

Hisrich, Robert & Michael Peters. (2002) "Sam Walton." *Entrepreneurship*. 5th edition. Boston: McGraw-Hill. p. 559.

Jain, Subhash. (2001) "Wal-Mart vs K-Mart." *Market Planning & Strategy Casebook*. Cincinnatti, OH.: South-Western College Publishing. p. 328.

Neuborne, Ellen. (Apr 6, 2001) "Pioneer Changed Face of Retailing." *USA Today,* p.B-1.

Peter, J. Paul & James H. Donnelly. (2001) *Marketing Management: Case Studies*. New York: McGraw-Hill.

Shah, Amit & Tyra Phipps. (2001) "Wal-Mart Stores Inc." *Strategic Management: Concepts and Cases*, ed. Fred David. New Jersey: Prentice-Hall. p. 41.

Time–Collector's Edition. (July 2001) "American Legends"–Builders & Titans Section. p. 80.

Trimble, Vance. (1991) *Sam Walton: The Inside Story of America's Richest Man*. New York: Dutton.

Walton, Sam. (1992) *Sam Walton: Made in America*. New York: Bantam Books.

HUGH HEFNER

A&E Biography Special (Feb 2002) "Hefner's Lifestyle at the Mansion."

David, Fred. (2001) "Playboy Enterprises, Inc." *Strategic Management*. New Jersey: Prentice-Hall. p. 382.

Jain, Subhash. (2001) "Playboy Enterprises." *Market Planning & Strategy Casebook,* Cincinnatti, OH: South-Western College Publishing. p. 358.

Lawrimore, Kay. (2001) "Playboy Enterprises Inc." in *Strategic Management: Concepts and Cases,* ed Fred David. New Jersey: Prentice-Hall. p. 481.

Miller, Russell. (1984) *Bunny*. New York: Signet Books.

Talese, Gay. (1980) *Thy Neighbor's Wife*. New York: Dell.

ROSS PEROT

Fineman, Howard. (June 29, 1992) "Perot's Second Act." *Newsweek,* p. 18.

Follett, Ken. (1984) *On Wings of Eagles*. New York: Signet.

Hartman, Curtis. (Jan. 1989) "Cowboy Capitalist–Ross Perot." *Inc.,* vol. 11, p. 54.

Perkins, Jack. (1999) "Ross Perot." *A&E Biography*.

Posner, Gerald. (1996) *Citizen Perot*. New York: Random House.

Stewart, Thomas. (June 15, 1992) "What America Thinks of Perot." *Fortune,* p. 62.

MARTHA STEWART

Byron, Christopher. (2002) *Martha, Inc.:The Incredible Story of Martha Stewart Living Omnimedia.* New York: Wiley.

Didion, Joan. (Feb. 2000) "Everywoman.com." *New Yorker.*

Forbes. (March 20, 2000) "The Celebrity 100."

Hisrich, Robert & Michael Peters. (2002) "Martha Stewart." *Entrepreneurship.* 5th edition. Martha Stewart. Boston: McGraw-Hill. p. 221.

McMurdy, Deidre. (Dec. 4, 2000) "A Brand Called Martha." *Maclean's*, Vol. 113, p. 49.

Oppenheimer, Jerry. (1997) *Martha Stewart-Just Desserts*, New York: Avon Books.

Smith, Harry. (Nov. 20, 2001) *A&E Martha Stewart TV Special*

Talbot, Margaret. (May 16, 1966) "Les Tres Riches Heures de Martha Stewart." *The New Republic.*

Tyrnauer, Matt. (Sept. 2001) "Inside the Martha Stewart Dream Factory–Empire by Martha." *Vanity Fair,* p. 364.

DONALD TRUMP

Blair, G. A. (2000) *The Trumps.* New York: Simon & Schuster.

Blair, Gwenda. (Dec. 2001) "How I Did a Great Job–Donald Trump." *Forbes*, p. 23.

Forbes (Oct. 2000) "Wealthiest in the World Listing"

Trump, Donald & Charles Leerhsen. (1999) *Trump: Surviving at the Top.* New York: Random House.

Trump, Donald & Bonher, Kate. (1997) *Trump: The Art of the Comeback.* New York: Random House.

O'Donnell, John R. (1991) *Trumped! The Inside Story of the Real Donald Trump-his Cunning Rise and his Spectacular Fall.* New York: Simon & Schuster.

Time (Jan. 16, 1989) "Flashy Symbol of the Acquisitive Age." p. 48.

Trump, Donald & Schwartz, Tony. (1987) *Trump: The Art of the Deal.* New York: Warner Books.

RICHARD BRANSON

Angelo, Bonnie. (June 24, 1996) "Many Times a Virgin." *Time,* vol. 147, p. 26.

Branson, Richard. (1998) *Losing My Virginity.* New York: Random House.

Brown, Mick. (1988) *Richard Branson.* London: Michael Joseph.

Carnoy, David. (April 1998) "Richard Branson." *Success,* p. 62.

Cooper, Cord. (Sept. 28, 1999) "The Sky's the Limit." *Investors Business Daily,* p. A-4.

Ferry, Jeffrey. (Nov. 1989) "Branson's Misunderstood Midas Touch." *Business,* p. 99.

Lieberman, David. (April 8, 1996) "Music Strikes Chord with Virgin's Branson." *USA Today,* p. B-3.

Moore, Martha. (July 5, 1995) "Rash, Brash, Branson has Virgin Soaring." *USA Today,* p. B-4.

Shepler, J. E. (May 23, 2001). from World Wide Web site: www.com/articles/Branson

Wells, Melanie. (July 3, 2000) "Red Baron Branson." *Forbes*, p. 151.

JEFF BEZOS

Brooker, Katrina. (2000) "Beautiful Dreamer." *Fortune*, Dec 18, vol. 142, p. 234.

Forbes Magazine. (Oct. 2000) "Wealthiest in the World Listing."

Goodson, Margie (2001) "Amazon.com, Inc." in *Strategic Management: Concepts and Cases,* ed. Fred David. New Jersey: Prentice-Hall. p. 21.

Hazelton, Lesley. (July 1998) "Jeff Bezos: How He Built His Billion-dollar Net Worth Before His Company Turned a Profit." *Success.*

Price, Christopher. (Feb. 2, 2000) *The Financial Times,* p. 15.

Spector, Robert. (2000) *Amazon.com: Get Big Fast.* New York: Harper Business.

MICHAEL DELL

Dell, Michael. (1999) *Direct From Dell.* New York: Harper Business.

Forbes (June 10, 1991) "Dell Computers". vol. 147, p.10.

Forbes (Oct. 2000) "Wealthiest in the World Listing."

Hisrich, Robert & Michael Peters. (2002) "Michael Dell." *Entrepreneurship.* 5th edition. Boston: McGraw-Hill. p. 253.

Jain, Subhash. (2001) "The Dell Corporation." *Market Planning & Strategy Casebook.* Cincinnatti, OH: South-Western College Publishing. pp. 16-34.

McWilliams, Gary. (June 8, 2001) "Lean Machine–How Dell Fine Tunes Its PC Pricing to Gain Edge in Slow Market," *WSJ,* p. A-1.

Sales & Marketing Management (Sept. 2001) "SM&M's Best e-Business Strategy" [Michael Dell Grand e-plan] p. 28.

Seminario, Nicole. (2001) "Dell Computer Corporation." *Strategic Management: Concepts and Cases,* ed. Fred David. New Jersey: Prentice-Hall. p. 330.

Stewart, Thomas. (Aug. 2, 1999) "Does Michael Dell Need Stock Options?" *Fortune.* vol. 140, p. 240.

Ward, Leah Beth. (Oct. 21, 1991) "The Kid Who Turned Computers into Commodities." *Forbes.* vol. 148, p. 318.